Managerial Economics:
Applications, Strategy, and Tactics

Ninth Edition

James R. McGuigan

JRM Investments

R. Charles Moyer

Babcock Graduate School of Management

Wake Forest University

Frederick H. deB. Harris

Babcock Graduate School of Management

Wake Forest University

Prepared by

Richard D. Marcus

University of Wisconsin – Milwaukee

SOUTH-WESTERN
THOMSON LEARNING

Australia · Canada · Mexico · Singapore · Spain · United Kingdom · United States

Study Guide to accompany *Managerial Economics: Applications, Strategy, and Tactics, Ninth Edition* by McGuigan, Moyer, and Harris.

Acquisitions Editor: Michael W. Worls
Senior Developmental Editor: Susanna C. Smart
Senior Marketing Manager: Lisa L. Lysne
Media Technology Editor: Vicky True
Media Development Editor: Peggy Buskey
Media Production Editor: John Barans
Production Editor: Amy S. Gabriel
Manufacturing Coordinator: Charlene Taylor & Sandee Milewski
Printer: Webcom

Printed in Canada
  2 3 4 5 03

For more information contact South-Western, 5101 Madison Road, Cincinnati, Ohio, 45227 or find us on the Internet at http://www.swcollege.com

For permission to use material from this text or product, contact us by
• **telephone: 1-800-730-2214**
• **fax: 1-800-730-2215**
• **web: http://www.thomsonrights.com**

Library of Congress Cataloging-in-Publication Data
0-324-05882-9

Contents

		Page Number

PART I - INTRODUCTION

Chapter 1   Introduction and Goals of the Firm 5

Chapter 2   Fundamental Economic Concepts 18

PART II - DEMAND AND FORECASTING

Chapter 3   Demand Analysis 39

Appendix 3A   Indifference Curve Analysis of Demand 55

Chapter 4   Estimation of Demand 62

Appendix 4A   Nonlinear Regression Models 84

Chapter 5   Business and Economic Forecasting 91

Chapter 6   Exchange Rates and International Trade: Managing Exports 109

PART III - PRODUCTION AND COST

Chapter 7   Production Economics 120

Appendix 7A   Maximization of Production Output
Subject to a Cost Constraint 137

Appendix 7B   Production and Linear Programming 140

Chapter 8   Cost Analysis 147

Appendix 8A   The Cobb-Douglas Production Function
and the Long-Run Cost Function 157

Chapter 9   Applications of Cost Theory 165

Appendix 9A   The Learning Curve 178

PART IV - PRICING AND OUTPUT DECISIONS: STATEGY AND TACTICS

Chapter 10   Prices, Output, and Strategy:
                   Pure and Monopolistic Competition 183

Chapter 11   Competitive Markets under Asymmetric Information 198

Chapter 12   Price and Output Determination: Monopoly and Dominant
                   Firms.. 208

Chapter 13   Price and Output Determination: Oligopoly 223

Chapter 14   Game-Theoretic Rivalry: Best-Practice Tactics 240

Appendix 14A   Capacity Planning and Pricing Against a Low-Cost Competitor:
                   A Case Study of Piedmont Airlines and People Express 251

Chapter 15   Organizational Form, Governance, and Mechanism Design 255

Chapter 16   Pricing Techniques and Analysis... 264

Appendix 16A   Revenue Management.. 283

Chapter 17   Government Regulation... 290

Appendix 17A   Economic Externalities and Market Failure 303

PART V - LONG-TERM INVESTMENT DECISIONS AND RISK MANAGEMENT

Chapter 18   Long-Term Investment Analysis 312

APPENDICES

Web Chapter A   Optimization Techniques... 324

Web A Appendix   Constrained Optimization and Lagrangian Multiplier
                   Techniques 337

Web Chapter B   Linear-Programming Applications 346

Appendix A   The Time Value of Money 356

Appendix B   Tables 362

PREFACE

This *Study Guide*, to accompany the ninth edition of *Managerial Economics: Applications, Strategy, and Tactics* by McGugian, Moyer and Harris, provides a self-study of the fundamental issues of demand analysis and forecasting, production and cost, and pricing and output decisions that face managers. Increased emphasis is placed on international economic issues.

Each chapter is outlined, with key formulas and concepts emphasized. The outline is followed by true/false and multiple choice questions. These questions provide you a basic check that you understand the material. Answers are given in the chapter after each set of questions for quick reference. Solved problems are presented in "story problem" format, so that you are challenged first to set up the problem, and then to solve it. The worked problems are aimed at solving problems that managers actually face. To this end, names of actual firms are often used, but the problems facing them are fictionalized.

Throughout the study guide, examples of "computer output" of regression analysis appear. The emphasis is on reading the output, and applying economic theory and economic meaning to interpreting their content. Internet addresses are included to give additional sources of data or information, in a section called "Net Sources" at the end of each chapter.

The best way to learn managerial economics is to be challenged with problems and to solve them. It is my hope that this Study Guide offers interesting and challenging problems for you to solve. This training of the mind to think critically and to find the key elements of business problems, will be valuable in many careers.

I wish to thank Mr. Tom Elwell for careful work on improving the clarity of the questions and the accuracy of the answers.

Richard D. Marcus, Ph.D.
marcus@uwm.edu

PART I - INTRODUCTION

Chapter 1

Introduction and Goals of the Firm

This chapter shows that managerial economics is that part of economics applied to the decisions that managers must make. When managers make decisions that maximize firm profits, they simultaneously maximize shareholder wealth and promote efficient allocation of resources. Sometimes managers aim at objectives other than profit, such as their own security. To avoid non-profit maximizing behavior, a growing number of firms are structuring compensation plans for managers that promote long-term profitability.

A. Shareholder Wealth Maximization

    1. To align the interests of the shareholders of Salomon Brothers with the interests of its chairman, Deryck Maughn, most of the chairman's compensation is based on the *performance* of the company relative to its five major competitors.

    2. Executive compensation is based on Salomon Brothers' return on equity and return on equity of their competitors. The bonus can be as large as $24 million.

B. Managerial Economics and Economic Theory

    1. Managerial Economics extracts the parts of economics, particularly microeconomics, useful for making decisions faced by managers: pricing, production, cost analysis, market structure, and strategy.

    2. *Microeconomics*--deals with economics of micro units: individuals, households, firms or industries.

    3. *Macroeconomics*--studies market aggregates, such as whole countries, the market for all labor, inflation, business cycles, and unemployment.

    4. The traditional definition of economics: "The science of allocating scarce resources among competing ends." For-profit firms as well as not-for-profit (NFP) organizations face a variety of trade-offs.

    5. Steps in decision making include: Establish and identify objectives, define the problem, find possible alternative solutions, select the best solution, and implement that choice.

C. The Role of Profits

1. *Economic cost* (or opportunity cost) is the highest valued benefit that must be sacrificed as a result of choosing an alternative.

2. *Economic profit* is the difference between revenues and total economic cost (including the economic or opportunity cost of owner supplied resources such as time and capital).

3. Theories of why profit varies across industries:

   a. RISK-BEARING THEORY. A compensation for investing in riskier endeavors. Example: investing in the stock of Circus Circus.

   b. DYNAMIC EQUILIBRIUM (OR FRICTIONAL) THEORY OF PROFIT. Industries earning above normal profits (economic profits) will eventually find more competition. Added competition will bring profits back to normal (zero economic profits) over time. Competition directs resources to industries with the greatest profit.

   c. MONOPOLY THEORY OF PROFIT. Barriers, such as governmental regulations, are the source of higher than normal profits.

   d. INNOVATION THEORY OF PROFIT. There is a reward for developing new ideas, new construction technologies, and for finding new markets.

   e. MANAGERIAL EFFICIENCY THEORY OF PROFIT. Exceptional managerial skills can produce superior profits.

4. Circus Circus, a Las Vegas casino and hotel, earned exceptionally high returns in 1994, but a similar firm, Bally's, earned rather low returns. High average returns tend to occur in industries with high risk.

D. Objective of the Firm

1. *Profit maximization* as a goal implies that decisions that raise revenues more than costs or lower costs more than reduce revenues should be selected. This is a short term objective.

2. *Shareholder wealth maximization* as a goal implies that decisions that increase the present value of expected *future* profits should be selected. Even decisions that reduce today's profits, yet substantially raise future profits, may be appropriate decisions. This is a long-term business goal.

3. The price of a share of stock can be thought of as the present value of expected future cash flows per share. Cash flows are discounted at the shareholders required rate of return, k_e.

4. The value of the firm, VALUE, is the price per share, V_0, times the number of shares outstanding.

$$\text{VALUE} = V_0 \bullet \text{Shares Outstanding} = \left\{ \sum_{t=1}^{\infty} \pi_t /(1+k_e)^{\,t} \right\} \bullet \text{Shares Outstanding}$$

5. *Profit*, π, is total revenue minus total cost (TR - TC). *Total revenue* for a single product firm is price times quantity, $P \cdot Q$. *Total cost* (TC) is total variable cost plus fixed cost, F. *Total variable cost* is the variable cost per unit, V, times the number of units, Q. Hence, $\pi = P \cdot Q - V \cdot Q - F$. When profit is divided by the number of shares, this provides an approximate measure of *cash flow per share*.

6. Through substitution for profit per share as cash flow per share gives the *determinants of firm value*:

$$V_0 \bullet \text{Shares Outstanding} = \sum_{t=1}^{\infty} [\, P_t \cdot Q_t - V_t \cdot Q_t - F_t \,]/(1+k_e)^{\,t} \bullet \text{Shares Outstanding}$$

7. Business decisions affect the amount and timing of revenues, costs, and the discount rate used by investors. For example, selecting a capital-intensive technology may raise fixed costs, F, but lower variable costs per unit, V.

8. The value formula in (6) above helps organize our thinking about economic decisions that managers must make. If firm is perceived as less risky, then a reduction in required rate of return, k_e, raises the value of the firm.

9. Expected future profits are not the same as accounting profits. Accounting profits do not consider the opportunity cost of capital invested by owners or actual cash flows collected or paid by the company. In practice, managers who base their decisions on ways to maximize the present value of *cash flows*, will make decisions that maximize the wealth of shareholders.

10. Profit maximization is the primary goal of William Buffett, CEO of **Berkshire Hathaway**, who has produced higher profits and higher share values than market averages over time.

E. Managerial Actions to Influence Shareholder Wealth

1. Some determinants of profits are outside the direct control of managers. *Economic Environment Factors* include the level of economic activity (recession or boom), tax rates, competition, governmental regulations, unionization, and international

economic exposure. Also *Conditions in Financial Markets* such as interest rates, investor sentiment, and anticipated inflation affect profitability.

2. Other determinants of profits are within the direct control of managers. *Major Policy Decisions* include product mix, production technology, marketing network, investment strategies, employment policies and compensation, form of organization, capital structure (use of debt versus equity), working capital management, and dividend policies.

F. Agency Problems and Alternative Objectives for the Firm

1. Modern corporations allow the managers to have no, or limited, ownership participation in the profitability of the firm. Shareholders may want profits, but managers may wish to relax. The shareholders are *principals*, whereas the managers are *agents*. Conflicting motivations between these groups are called *agency problems*.

2. Solutions to agency problems involve compensation that is based on the performance of agents. Some firms are experimenting with compensation plans by extending to all workers stock options, bonuses, and grants of stock, so that employees have added incentives to increase their company's value.

G. Implications of Shareholder Wealth Maximization

1. Critics claim that aligning compensation with shareholder interests leads to short run objectives.

2. *Maximization* of the present value of expected cash flows works well if the following conditions are met:

    a. COMPLETE MARKETS -- there are liquid markets to buy and sell the firm's inputs, contaminants (including polluting by-products), and common property resources.

    b. NO SIGNIFICANT ASYMMETRIC INFORMATION -- buyers and sellers all know the same things.

    c. KNOWN RECONTRACTING COSTS -- future input costs are part of the present value of expected cash flows. The existence of future and forward markets in inputs can help lock-in future input costs.

3. The Saturn Corporation offers an example of an initially successful new car company that faced meager profits over time. Its low price provided low profit margins for Saturn. Low returns lead to less reinvestment into new models. Middle-aged Saturn buyers traded up to larger Japanese imports.

H. Goals in the Public Sector and the Not-For-Profit (NFP) Enterprise

1. NFP organizations such as performing arts groups, most hospitals, universities, and volunteer organizations receive a substantial portion of their financial support from contributions, and some support from "clients" who use their services.

2. Instead of profit, NFP organizations may have as their goals:
   a. Maximization of the quantity of output, subject to a breakeven constraint.
   b. Maximization of the utility (happiness) of NFP administrators.
   c. Maximization of cash flows.
   d. Maximization of the utility of contributors to the NFP organization.

3. Which goal that the NFP manager selects affects the types of decisions made. A manager of a food shelter may decide to maximize the utility of contributors or donors by selecting only "healthy foods" to give to clients; or may decide that the objective is to give out the greatest volume of food possible (not necessarily the most nutritious).

4. Public sector managers are frequently *monitored* with regard to how they perform their jobs. If reducing the cost per bed over a year rewards a VA hospital administrator, then the administrator may become quite efficient with respect to costs. However, the "friendliness" of the hospital staff is harder to measure, so friendliness will tend not be a high priority of the public sector manager.

5. In contrast, in the for-profit hotel business, perceptions about the friendliness of the hotel staff have a direct effect on repeat business and profits.

I. Managing a Globally Competitive Economy

1. Managerial innovations, such as "just-in-time" inventory methods, efficient transfer pricing, and total quality management concepts can be learned by observing successful competitors in the U.S. or abroad. Global managers need to be up-to-date with the tools of managerial economics to compete and win in the world marketplace.

True and False Questions

Agree or disagree with the following statements, and correct the part that is erroneous.

1. The goal of shareholder wealth maximization implies that managerial decisions maximize only the current quarter's expected profits of the firm.

2. Macroeconomics deals with large firms, big business deals, and huge deficits.

3. An example of an *agency problem* is a store manager, who avoids taking a risk, so that he cannot be 'blamed' for making a bad decision.

4. If you owned and worked in your own card shop, and if you did not pay yourself a wage, then you have ignored an economic cost of running your business.

5. Decisions that do not affect the amount of revenues and costs, but change the timing of receipts and disbursement will not affect the value of the firm.

6. The amount of profits is entirely under the control of the manager.

7. Not-for-profit organizations can't earn profits, so they have no goals.

8. In the long run, all firms earn the same rate of return.

Answers
1. Disagree. Expected long run profits of the firm affects firm value. A loss in the current quarter that leads to profits later may be an appropriate strategy.
2. Disagree. Macroeconomics deals with market aggregates, such as whole countries, the market for all labor, inflation, business cycles, and unemployment.
3. True.
4. True.
5. Disagree. Timing affects the present value of the firm. Monies received sooner are more valuable than the same amount received later.
6. Disagree. *Economic Environment Factors* and *Conditions in Financial Markets* are outside the control of managers, and do affect profitability.
7. Disagree. The goals of NFP may vary, such as maximizing number of clients served or maximizing the happiness of the organization's management. But they do have goals.
8. Disagree. Barriers to free trade, as in some kinds of governmental regulations, can create monopoly. There may be differences in risk, degrees of innovation, and there may be changes in technology and tastes that create above normal, and below normal, profit rates in different industries even over long periods of time.

Multiple Choice Questions

1. Which of the following are likely to increase the value of the firm, based on the shareholders wealth-maximization model of the firm?
   a. The rate of inflation increases substantially.
   b. A previously nonunion workforce votes to unionize.
   c. A technological breakthrough allows the firm to reduce its cost of production.
   d. the government implements strict pollution control requirements.

2. The Russian Republic has continued its sale of formerly state-run enterprises. When a steel factory is sold, the value should be based:
   a. mostly on the past output levels assigned it by central planners.
   b. primarily on the future earning potential in a competitive economy.
   c. on the cost of the buildings, adjusted by appropriate depreciation measures.
   d. in comparing the facilities with equivalent facilities in the United States.

3. The Agency Problem shows up in many different situations within a firm. Which is NOT a good example of this problem?
   a. Firm managers sometime want to relax on the job.
   b. Diversified stockholders are more eager to accept risks than are firm managers.
   c. Firm managers receive cash bonuses based on the performance of the firm.
   d. Employees sometime take items from the store in which they work.

4. Executive compensation should:
   a. be an increasing function of the firm's expenses.
   b. be an increasing function of the sales revenue received by the firm.
   c. create incentives so that managers act like owners of the firm.
   d. avoid making the executives own shares in the company.

5. Which of the following may be an example of an *agency problem*?
   a. time not spent on actual business by an employee on an out-of-state business trip.
   b. output of a piece rate garment worker.
   c. the job performance of a parking lot attendant.
   d. work performance of a manager of a card shop, who also owns the card shop.

6. To reduce *agency costs*, firms incur costs in all these areas EXCEPT:
   a. compensation inducements to executives to take actions that shareholders want.
   b. payment of payroll taxes.
   c. expenditures to monitor the actions of managers, including internal audits.
   d. bonding expenditures to protect the owners from managerial dishonesty.

7. Economics is traditionally defined as the science that:
   a. shows people how to get rich using the stock market.
   b. tries to prove how humans differ from other species.
   c. deals with the allocation of scarce resources among competing ends.
   d. provides a guide to the successful management of a personal business.

8. In the shareholder wealth maximization model, the value of a firm's stock is equal to the present value of all expected future _____ discounted at the stockholders' required rate of return.
   a. cash flows
   b. revenues
   c. outlays
   d. costs

9. The branch of economics that deals with the analysis of the whole economy is called:
   a. shareholder wealth maximization.
   b. macroeconomics.
   c. gestalt economics.
   d. microeconomics.

10. Which of the following will improve shareholder wealth, which is implicit in the formula:

$$VALUE = \sum_{t=1}^{\infty} [\, P_t \cdot Q_t - V_t \cdot Q_t - F_t \,]/(1+k_e)^t \cdot \text{Shares Outstanding}$$

   a. larger quantity of sales, Q_t, assuming price is greater than average variable cost.
   b. higher discount rate on equity, k_e.
   c. higher fixed costs per period, F_t.
   d. all of the above.

11. Agency problems between managers and shareholders can be reduced by:
   a. paying managers based on the profitability of the firm.
   b. requiring managers to own shares of the company.
   c. paying managers stock options, which improve in value as the stock price rises.
   d. all of the above.

12. If shareholders do not mind their firm being taken over by merger or acquisition when the price is high, but managers prefer to fight takeovers, what can shareholders do?
   a. offer a Christmas bonus of $500 every year to management.
   b. offer free life insurance policies to all employees.
   c. offer a golden parachute contract (a very large severance package) if management loses their position in a takeover.
   d. offer an extra week of paid vacation to employees who have worked at this company for over five years.

13. One important difference between socialist and market economies is:
   a. private incentives are rewarded highly in socialist countries.
   b. all citizens are always wealthier in market economies than in socialist economies.
   c. decision making on what to produce is decentralized in socialist economies.
   d. decision making on what to produce is decentralized in market economies.

14. The saying "there is no such thing as a free lunch" really means that:
   a. the food stamp program costs taxpayers a lot of money.
   b. because resources are scarce, all services and goods have an economic cost or opportunity cost associated with them.
   c. because of inflation, products are becoming free.
   d. because of cutbacks by the Department of Health and Human Services, free school lunches are no longer available.

15. Which of the following "theories of profit" best reflects the rapid increase in profits earned by oil companies after the invasion of Kuwait by Iraq?
    a. dynamic equilibrium (frictional) theory of profit
    b. innovation theory of profit
    c. monopoly profit theory of profit
    d. managerial efficiency theory of profit

16. The drug industry earned 26.5% returns, whereas other Value Line firms earned 15%. What theory of profit best reflects the performance of the drug industry?
    a. the risk-bearing theory of profit
    b. the dynamic equilibrium (frictional) theory of profit
    c. the over-investment hypothesis theory of profit
    d. the managerial efficiency theory of profit

Answers

1. c	8. a	15. a
2. b	9. b	16. a
3. c	10. a	
4. c	11. d	
5. a	12. c	
6. b	13. d	
7. c	14. b	

Problems or Short Essays

1. With approximately 100 new satellites launched each year, who is responsible for the "space junk" that accumulates each year? How can the space-junk problem be solved?

2. Managers of publicly owned enterprises must face shareholders at annual meetings. They must report the quarterly and annual earnings for the year. If they take on projects that do not have a quick payback, they are afraid that shareholders will become angry, call their directors, and seek new management. How can shareholders reward managers who take a long-run view to profitability to avoid this agency problem?

3. The value of a firm can be represented by the present value of the stream of profits:

$$VALUE = \sum_{t=1}^{\infty} [P_t \cdot Q_t - V_t \cdot Q_t - F_t]/(1+k_e)^t \cdot \text{Shares Outstanding}$$

   a. If managerial decisions increase the perceived *risk* of the firm, what variables above increase?

      b. What variables are changed in the value function above if management attempts to improve the perceived *quality* of their products through more precise quality control?

4. What is the value today of a single $200 cash flow in two years, if one's perceived rate of return is 15%?

Answers

1. The problem of space junk is due to "common property resources." As no one owns orbital space, no one seems responsible for keeping the space free of costly debris. This is the same problem for air and water pollution. The solution typically requires the creation of property rights. For example, the United Nations, or other international groups, could be given orbital paths "rights". These rights could be auctioned off, with the winner having a 99-year lease. This privatizes orbital space. Firms will be more careful not to damage their own space.

2. Tying current profitability performance to current management compensation tends to emphasize the short run.

    Shareholders may wish their directors to devise compensation that pays bonuses in the future for good long-term performance. For example, stock options or warrants that expire in the distant future become more valuable as the value of the firm improves. Managers may wish to explain to shareholders that they are investing for the long run, and that current earnings are low because of the investment. If this is a true explanation of lower current earnings, most shareholders would approve.

    Furthermore, when managers own shares directly, this creates incentives for management to improve shareholder wealth.

3a.   Increases in the perceived risk will not change expected cash flows but it will increase the discount rate, k_e. For example, if investment decisions increase the correlation of the firm's returns with returns in the market in general, the perceived riskiness of the firm may increase.

3b.   The price and quantity of the improved quality product may raise both P and Q. However, the cost per unit (V) will likely rise due to more effort at quality control. There may be additional fixed cost (F) as well.

4.   It is the present value of $200 in two years, which is $200/(1.15)^2 = 151.23

Worked Problems

1. **Menlo Boulevard Construction, Inc.** expects to build seventeen garages this year and eighteen garages next year. Each garage sells for $8,900 this year and $9,100 next year. Expenses (materials and labor) are anticipated to be $3,600 per garage this year and $3,750 next year, with fixed costs of $44,200 per year for the noncancellable rental contract on trucks and equipment in both years. Assume that taxes are zero and that all revenues and expenses are received or paid at the end of each respective year. What is the present value of Menlo's expected profits at a 10% required rate of return for discounting?

   Answer: Expected profits this year is: $\pi_0 = (8{,}900 \cdot 17 - 3{,}600 \cdot 17) - 44{,}200 = \$45{,}900$. Expected profits next year is: $\pi_1 = (9{,}100 \cdot 18 - 3{,}750 \cdot 18) - 44{,}200 = \$52{,}100$. Hence, the present value of Menlo's stream of profits over the two years is:
   $$V = \frac{\$45{,}900}{(1.10)} + \frac{\$52{,}100}{(1.10)^2} = \$84{,}785.12.$$

2. **American Appraisal, Inc.** sends you to the Russian Republic to evaluate the selling prices for formerly state-run enterprises. You arrive at a building 35 kilometers from Moscow, knowing little Russian language and no Russian or Soviet accounting methods. Through translators, you find that the building had been used to make green glass bottles for mineral water. You can count the number of 1950-vintage bottle-making machines in the building, the inventory of completed glass bottles, but there exists little information as to how many bottles could be made per day, how many workers had previously worked there, or any other record. No other bottle firms have been privatized.

   a. There are three primary appraisal techniques: (1) evaluate the sale price of equivalent "businesses" or so-called *comparables*; (2) evaluate the replacement cost of the machinery; or (3) the discounted present value of the expected future cash flows. Which of these three appraisal techniques would you use in this situation?

      Answer: We would likely select number 3.

      Unlike real estate appraisal, where there are many similar properties being sold, there may be few equivalent bottle businesses that have been sold in Eastern Europe or the former Soviet Union. So technique (1) would be difficult.

      It is also hard to imagine why one would wish to "replace" out-dated machinery, although one could find out how many bottles each machine could process per hour, and determine how many old machines are equivalent to a new machine. So technique (2) would have limited usefulness in this situation.

      Therefore, the only reasonably useful approach is to use a measure of the discounted present value of expected future cash flows, as in technique (3). We could find out the selling prices of new bottles, the quantity of bottles that this factory would make, and find local wage rates. This assumes that the factory continues to operate as a bottle-making operation. The value of the property could be greater or lower, if there are other uses for the building and land. In addition, we will need to check for environmental hazards left on the property, and find out the cost for a clean up.

b. A French firm that is considering selling wine in green glass bottles will use the appraisal. The French firm would invest in the purchase. What issues does this introduce when considering the appropriate discount rate to use when deciding whether to buy this bottle factory.

Answer: The discount rate reflects the cost of borrowing and compensates for the riskiness of the investment. Since the Russian political situation is not stable, there is a risk that should the French firm buy the factory; some new government that could appear in a few years may possibly confiscate it. Foreign owned properties have historically been expropriated after political revolutions. Hence, the discount rate would be higher to purchase this factory than a similar factory in France or the U.S.

Net Sources

1. Profits vary across industrial groups. Economic theory suggests reasons for variation in profitability include differences in competition and risk. For information on profitability by industry groups look at:

   Market Guide Industries, a service of Yahoo Finance. It presents firm data grouped by industries on profit margins, return on assets, and other financial accounting data at: *biz.yahoo.com/p/industries.html*

   Bureau of Labor Statistics (BLS) - the principal fact-finding agency for the Federal Government in the broad field of labor economics and statistics at: *stats.bls.gov/*

   Statistical Abstract of the United States provides data divided by industries as well as states. It is available in the reference section of libraries or more conveniently at: *www.census.gov/statab/www/*

2. **Standard Industrial Classifications** (SIC) are numbers assigned to industry groups. The site gives 2-digit and 4-digit SIC codes for industries. Examples include:
   - 31 LEATHER AND LEATHER PRODUCTS
   - 32 STONE, CLAY, AND GLASS PRODUCTS
   - 33 PRIMARY METAL INDUSTRIES
   - 34 FABRICATED METAL PRODUCTS

To find 4-digit classifications of industries, look at:
www.wave.net/upg/immigration/sic_index.html Or for the newer six-digit North
American Industry Classification system, NAICS, look at: *http://www.naics.com/*

3.   **PROJECT:** Compare the average ROA (return on assets) of two distinctly
       different industries from: *biz.yahoo.com/p/industries.html*. Select three firms from
       each industry to find the average ROA for the industry. Use average ROAs in both
       industries. Do the differences appear consistent with differences in risk, friction,
       monopoly power, innovation, or managerial efficiency (which are the five reasons
       for differences in profits across industries)?

Chapter 2

Fundamental Economic Concepts

Economic problems involve tradeoffs. An economic problem can be illustrated in the pricing decisions by Delta Airlines whether or not to reallocate unsold first class seats to the discount status, if it is unsure whether the first class seats will ever be sold. This chapter provides some of the basic tools of managerial economics. These include concepts of marginal analysis, net present value, the tradeoff between risk and return, and the different meanings and uses of the term risk.

A. Marginal Analysis

    1. *Marginal return (or benefit)* is the change in total benefits from doing an activity. *Marginal cost* is the change in total cost from doing an activity.

    2. If the marginal benefits exceed the marginal costs of a proposed action, then the action should be taken.

    3. For example, insulation is measured in R-values. The higher the R-value of the insulation, the lower is the cost of heating and air conditioning (the marginal benefit). However, the higher the R-value of the insulation, the higher the total costs of the insulation project.

B. Total, Marginal, and Average Relationships

    1. Tables, graphs, and/or algebraic expressions can show the relationships among total profit, average profit, and marginal profit. Similar relations occur for output (total, average, and marginal product) and cost (total, average, and marginal cost).

    2. TABLES: For each output, denoted as Q, list the profit associated with it, $\pi(Q)$. *Average profit*, $\pi_A(Q) = \pi(Q)/Q$, which is total profit divided by quantity. *Marginal profit*, $\Delta\pi(Q) = \pi(Q) - \pi(Q - 1)$, which is the profit attributable to the last unit.

    3. Total profit is maximized, when marginal profit is zero.

18

Handwritten annotations:

Price

MC

MR

Q

MR-MC

MR-MC=0

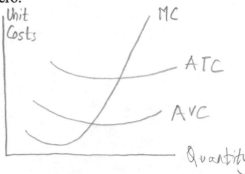

4. GRAPHS: Total profit rises up to a maximum. Marginal profit is the slope of the total profit curve. The slope of the total profit is zero at its maximum, because the slope of the horizontal line is zero. Hence, marginal profit is zero at maximum profit.

5. Profit is total revenue minus total economic cost. Marginal profit is marginal revenue (MR) minus marginal cost (MC). A *decision rule* for maximizing profits is to find the output where MR = MC, because we know at that point marginal profits must be zero.

C. The Net Present Value Concept

1. To find managerial decision rules that maximize shareholder wealth over a long period of time, we must consider the present value of the costs as well as the present value of the benefits. The *net present value* is the sum of the present values of all the costs and benefits.

2. Present value recognizes that a dollar received in the future is worth less than a dollar in hand today, because a dollar today could be invested to earn a return. To compare monies in the future with today, the future dollars must be discounted by a *present value interest factor*, $PVIF = 1/(1+i)$, where i is the interest compensation for postponing receiving cash one period.

3. For dollars received in *n* periods, the discount factor is $PVIF_n = [\, 1/(1+i)\,]^n$.

4. *Net Present Value* (NPV) = Present value of future returns minus Initial outlay.

5. *NPV Rule:* Do all projects that have positive net present values. By doing this, the manager maximizes shareholder wealth.

6. Some investments may increase NPV, but at the same time, they may increase risk. Whether the extra risk is acceptable, depends on what is the acceptable rate of return for that risk.

D. The Meaning and Measurement of Risk

1. An investment decision is *risk free* only when the dollar returns and initial investment are certain. But most managerial decisions involve huge uncertainties. There is almost always a possibility that cash flows will be less than expected, and sometimes the possibility that the cash flows will be negative (a loss).

2. Variability in the outcomes can be described using *probability distributions*. Variability is one common meaning of the idea of risk. The more variable are the possible outcomes, the riskier is the project.

3. The sum of the probabilities, p_j, must equal one: $\sum_{j=1}^{n} p_j = 1$. This assures that all possible outcomes, r_j, have been exhausted, and each outcome is *discrete*. Probabilities can be thought of as the percentage likelihood that each outcome, or state of nature, occurs.

4. *Expected Value*, is the weighted average of the possible outcomes:

$$r^{\hat{}} = \sum_{j=1}^{n} p_j \cdot r_j = 1.$$

5. *Standard Deviation* (σ) measures the dispersion of outcomes around its expected value.

$$\sigma = \sqrt{\sum_{j=1}^{n} (r_j - r^{\hat{}})^2 \cdot p_j}.$$

6. The expected values and standard deviations of two projects, with differing cash flows and differing probability distributions, can be compared.

7. If two projects have the same expected value, we may wish to select the one with the lower standard deviation. Or if two projects have the same standard deviations, we wish to select the one with the higher expected value. If one project has a higher expected value and a higher standard deviation, then the choice depends on a tradeoff between risk and return.

8. *Continuous probability distributions* can be drawn as a curve. The area under the whole curve (which represents probabilities) must equal one. *Normal probability distributions* are bell-like and symmetrical, so the *mode* (or most frequent value) equals the expected value.

9. If distributions are approximately normal, we can say that an outcome between plus and minus one standard deviation from expected value occurs 68 percent of the time; plus and minus two standard deviations 95 percent of the time; plus and minus three standard deviations 99 percent of the time.

10. To find how many standard deviations a particular outcome (r_j) is away from the expected value ($r^{\hat{}}$), we calculate $z = (r_j - r^{\hat{}})/\sigma$. If the outcome, r_j, is 9, and if $\sigma = 3$ and the expected $r^{\hat{}} = 3$, then $z = 2$. We know that 9 is 2σ from 3. Since $\pm 2\sigma$ occurs about 95 percent of the time, and because the normal distribution is symmetric, there is only about a 2.5% chance of finding an outcome of 9 or larger.

E. Practical Business Use of Risk Measurement

1. The assignment of probabilities to conditions in the world (major Middle East ground war, stock market boom, Presidential assassination, *etc.*) is very subjective. Therefore, both expected values and standard deviations are based on educated guesses.

2. Nevertheless, firms do have notions of what the most pessimistic and most optimistic outcomes would be. Assuming a normal distribution, we can generate a probability distribution.

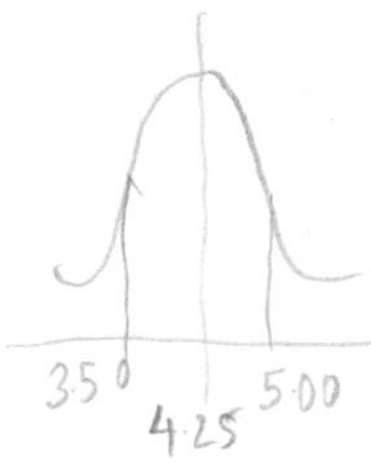

3. EXAMPLE: The most optimistic pricing of a new product, say not exceeded 5% of the time, is \$5, whereas the most pessimistic is \$3.50. Assuming normality, the mean would be \$4.25. The z-value that leaves 5% in the tail above \$5.00 is 1.645 [See Table 1 at the end of the textbook]. Hence, the standard deviation must be \$.46. {This is the solution to: $z = 1.645 = (\$5 - \$4.25)/\sigma$}.

4. Large projects obviously tend to have larger standard deviations than smaller projects. To compare projects of unequal sizes or scales, we use the coefficient of variation. The *coefficient of variation* is $v = \sigma / \hat{r}$, which is a relative measure of risk.

5. Suppose $\sigma = 50$ and $\hat{r} = 10$, then $v = 5$. If we did the same project twice, the expected value would double, and the standard deviation doubles, but the coefficient of variation remains at 5.

F. The Relation of Risk and Return

1. Investors in risk free Treasury bills realize that higher returns are available elsewhere, but they are willing to forgo those returns to have less risk. Other investors select more risky securities to increase their expected returns.

2. We can decompose the required return into two parts, the risk-free return plus a risk premium.

   Required Return = Risk-free Return + Risk Premium.

   The greater the risk, the greater must be the risk premium as a reward for accepting that risk.

3. Two mutually exclusive projects with different risks can be compared using the NPV rule. We can discount the riskier project with a higher required return (because of its higher risk premium). The different discount rates *adjust* for risk. The project with higher risk-adjusted NPV should be selected.

G. Risk and Decision Analysis

1. THE LANGUAGE OF A DECISION PROBLEM: A *decision-maker* is a person who has to choose between at least two alternative choices where there is a reasonable doubt as to which of the alternatives will best achieve the objective. The *uncertain environment* consists of factors that influence the outcome but cannot be controlled by the decision-maker.

2. *Certainty* exists if each action is known to lead to a specific outcome.

3. *Risk* exists when the possible outcomes and their probabilities are known.

4. *Uncertainty* exists when the probabilities are unknown or not even meaningful; we think of this as the risk of 'unknowingness'.

H. Expected Marginal Utility Approach

1. *The St. Petersburg Paradox* is a gamble of tossing a fair coin, where the payoff doubles for every consecutive head that appears. The *expected monetary value* of this gamble is: $\$2 \cdot (.5) + \$4 \cdot (.25) + \$8 \cdot (.125) + \$16 \cdot (.0625) + ... = 1 + 1 + 1 + ... = \infty$.

   - But no one would be willing to wager all he or she owns to get into this bet. It must be that people make decisions by criteria other than maximizing expected monetary payoff.

   - Expected monetary payoff is: $\sum_{i=1}^{n} P_i \cdot R_i$, where P's are probabilities and R's are outcomes.

2. If each monetary outcome, R_i , were assigned a *utility* (or happiness) value, $U_i = U(R_i)$, then an alternative objective is *expected utility maximization*. Expected utility, $E(U)$, is:

$$E(U) = \sum_{i=1}^{n} P_i \cdot U_i$$

3. EXAMPLE OF DECISISON USING EXPECTED UTILITY: Should you move your firm to Mexico? If successful, the payoff is $10 million with a 68% chance of success. If unsuccessful, the payoff is a loss of $8.8 million. The utility of success and failure, respectively, is: +2000 and -4800.

   SOLUTION: *Expected value* of the Mexican move is .68(10 million) + .32(-8.8 million) = +$3.984 million. But the *expected utility* of the move is .68(2000) + .32(-4800) = - 176. According to expected utility maximization the firm, should not and will not make the move because it leads to a negative expected utility.

I. Risk Aversion and Diminishing Marginal Utility

1. There may be a biological advantage for humans to be risk averse, but economists suggest that the people have utility functions that rise at diminishing rates in wealth and money. The utility of your first $10,000 in income is greater than the utility of the next $10,000, *etc.* MARGINAL UTILITY is positive, but gets smaller as income rises.

2. If people do have *DIMINISHING MARGINAL UTILITY IN WEALTH*, then a certain level of wealth is preferred to an equivalent fair gamble; that is, $100 for certain is preferred to a 50:50 gamble of $0 and $200

3. People with diminishing marginal utility in wealth would be willing to pay someone to reduce their risk, as we do with fire, life, health, and auto insurance. Those who prefer a certain wealth to a fair gamble of equivalent value are called *risk averse*.

4. If utility rises at a constant rate in wealth or income, then *marginal utility is constant*. People would be *risk neutral* in this situation.

5. If utility rises at an increasing rate as wealth rises, people would act like *risk lovers*. *Risk lovers* have increasing marginal utility in wealth or income.

J. Decision Tree Approach

1. One way to analyze the different payoffs is to diagram the sequence of events, their payoffs, and their probabilities.

2. A decision choice is made, creating two or more branches. Different *states of the world* (*e.g.*, economic boom, recession, *etc.*) affect the payoffs in each branch.

3. Sometimes, the decision tree diagram is extended out further as more time periods are considered. This allows varying probabilities over time, since in real business situations, if success occurs in the first period, success is even more likely in future periods.

K. Risk Adjusted Discount Rates

1. Rather than using a firm's cost of capital, a firm could use a higher discount rate to analyze investments that have substantial risks. Using *net present value* (NPV), we use a risk-adjusted discount rate (k^*) to discount the stream of expected net cash flows, NCF_t. NINV is the net investment in the initial period. The risk adjusted net present value is:

$$NPV = \sum_{t=1}^{n} NCF_t / (1 + k^*)^t - NINV$$

2. The *risk premium* is the difference between the risk-adjusted rate and the firm's cost of capital ($k^* - k$).

3. The magnitude of k^*, the risk-adjusted discount rate, depends on the project. Sometimes information on costs of capital in industries similar to this project can be used.

4. For totally new product lines; however, the selection of the appropriate risk-adjusted discount rate is subjective. Analysts should be aware that those who advocate the project would want a low discount rate, whereas those who are opposed will feel that a higher rate is warranted.

L. Simulation Approach

1. Net cash flows, are typically the after-tax revenues less expenses incurred by the firm. NCF_t = [revenues - expenses - depreciation](1- marginal tax rate) + depreciation. Depreciation is not a cash expense, so we add it back. Since revenues are the number of units sold times the price (n·p) and expenses are the number of units sold times the unit production and selling costs, n·(s+c), we could write it as:

$$NCF_t = [\, n{\cdot}p - n(s+c) - D \,](1{-}t) + D$$

2. Simulation allows assignments of probability distributions to the number of units sold, prices, costs, and even tax rates. *Expected NCF's* can be generated by simulation.

M. Managing Risk and Uncertainty

1. In risky situations, managers tend to ask for more information. In part, this is a stall for time. But this may mean trying to "test market" the project to learn more. It may mean hiring the expert opinion of others. Firms hire outside lawyers, accountants, banking experts, etc. Credit rating services, such as Moody's, sell information to manage risk.

2. *Diversification* is investing in a *portfolio* of securities with different risk-return characteristics. When some of the securities have negative returns, others may have positive returns.

   a. *Portfolio risk* (σ_p) depends on the weights (W_A and W_B), standard deviations of the securities in the portfolio (σ_A and σ_B), and on the *correlation coefficients* (ρ_{AB}) between securities. The risk of a two-security portfolio is:

   $$\sigma_p = \sqrt{ W_A{}^2{\cdot}\sigma_A{}^2 + W_B{}^2{\cdot}\sigma_B{}^2 + 2{\cdot}W_A{\cdot}W_B{\cdot}\rho_{AB}{\cdot}\sigma_A{\cdot}\sigma_B }$$

b. If the correlation coefficient, ρ_{AB}, equals one, no risk reduction is achieved. When $\rho_{AB} < 1$, then $\sigma_p < w_A \cdot \sigma_A + w_B \cdot \sigma_B$. Hence, portfolio risk is less than the weighted average of the standard deviations in the portfolio.

3. *Hedging* limits risk by making an offsetting investment. Investing in securities that are negatively correlated provides some hedging benefits.

4. *Insurance* offers a directly observable expense (called the premium) to reduce specific kinds of risks. This shifts the pure risks of fire, floods, political upheaval, and lawsuits to insurance syndicates that hold a large portfolio of these risks.

4. Some risks can be managed by gaining control over the environment. Firms often seek ways to differentiate their product from others. By creating some market power, they can insulate their firm's operations somewhat from the vagaries of the competitive marketplace.

5. *Limited Use of Firm-Specific Assets.* Assets that are general can be redeployed or sold more readily than assets that are only valuable to this particular firm.

True and False Questions

Agree or disagree with the following statements, and correct the part that is erroneous.

1. Risk analysis in decision making in a firm is a purely objective calculation of expected value, standard deviation, and coefficient of variation.

2. If the marginal cost of an action exceeds its marginal benefit, then we should not do it.

3. It is impossible for marginal profits to decline, when average profits are positive.

4. When MR is zero, total profits are at a maximum.

5. When MR > MC, a small increase in output would create positive marginal profit.

6. If the required rate of return is 10%, and the cash flow next period is $100, we should do the project if the initial outlay is $90.

7. The mode of a normal distribution is its standard deviation.

8. If the *z*-value of an outcome is 1, then that means the outcome is 1 standard deviation from the expected value.

9. If the initial investment is $1,000, and the present value of expected future cash flows is $880, then we *should* undertake the investment.

10. Do only those projects with zero NPV.

11. Investing in a widely diversified portfolio of stocks does not eliminate the risk that the whole market rises and falls.

12. Building a new McDonald's franchise represents *uncertainty*, whereas trying to develop brand new inebriating flavors for breath mints (cognac-spiked mints) has *risk*.

13. All upward rising utility functions demonstrate risk aversion.

14. Expected utility maximizers might decide not to invest in a project with an infinite expected value, such as the St. Petersburg Paradox.

15. If the utility of success is 600, and the utility of failure is -200, then we "ought" to undertake this gamble.

16. If two mutually exclusive capital projects are being compared, the project with the greater risk should be assigned a higher risk-adjusted discount rate, and the risk-adjusted net present values will tell you which is the better choice.

17. Portfolio risk depends entirely on the weights of the assets in the portfolio and the standard deviations (or variances) of the assets in the portfolio.

Answers
1. Disagree. Probabilities and outcomes are often subjective, based upon rough estimates.
2. True.
3. Disagree. Marginal profits tend to decline rapidly, hitting zero when profits are at a maximum. But average profits tend to be positive over wide ranges of output. When marginal profit equals average profit, we are at a point of maximum average profit.
4. Disagree. When marginal profits are zero, then total profits are at a maximum.
5. True.
6. True, the NPV is .9090, which is positive.
7. Disagree. The mode of a normal distribution is its expected value.
8. True.
9. Disagree. The Net Present Value is -$220 [1,000 - 880 = -220]. We should do only those projects with positive NPV.
10. Disagree. Do all projects with positive NPV. A zero NPV project does not increase wealth of shareholders.
11. True.
12. Disagree. The McDonald's franchise has risk, the new breath mint has risk and uncertainty. We may have little knowledge about how a new product will be received.
13. Disagree. A straight line rising utility function in wealth would have constant marginal utility.

14. True.
15. Disagree. The expected utility of the gamble depends on the probabilities of success and failure. If the probability of success is 10% and the probability of failure is 90%, then expected utility is: .10·(600) + .90·(-200) = 60 -180 = -120. We "ought" not to undertake this gamble.
16. True.
17. Disagree. Portfolio variance also depends on the correlation coefficients between assets

Multiple Choice Questions

1. Net Cash Flows (NCFs) from *Investment A* will be 100, 100, and 100 for the first three years. NCFs from *Investment B* ,will be 80, 100, and 120 for the first three years. The present values will be:
   a. the same, regardless of the discount rate used.
   b. greater for Investment B if the discount rate is positive.
   c. greater for Investment A if the discount rate is positive.
   d. greater, if the NCFs were lower.

2. A change in the level of an economic activity is desirable and should be undertaken as long as the marginal benefits exceed the _____.
   a. marginal returns
   b. total costs
   c. marginal costs
   d. average costs

3. The level of an economic activity should be increased to the point where the _____ is zero.
   a. marginal cost
   b. average cost
   c. total cost
   d. marginal profit

For questions 4 and 5 use the following symmetrical continuous probability distributions:

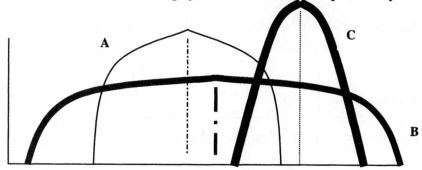

4. Which of the preceding distributions has the greatest standard deviation?
    a. A
    b. B
    c. C
    d. cannot be determined.

5. Which of these distributions has the greatest expected value?
    a. A
    b. B
    c. C
    d. cannot be determined.

6. The primary difference between the standard deviation and the coefficients of variation as measures of risk are:
    a. the standard deviation is a measure of relative risk whereas the coefficient of variation is a measure of absolute risk
    b. the coefficient of variation is a measure of relative risk whereas the standard deviation is a measure of absolute risk
    c. the standard deviation will always equal the coefficient of variation
    d. none of the above.

7. If the variance of outcomes for a project were 100, and the expected value of the project were 10 then the coefficient of variation would be: (Hint: first find the standard deviation to find the coefficient of variation, v)
    a. 100
    b. 25
    c. 5
    d. 1
    e. none of the above

8. A project to reduce breakage of products has the following probability distribution with related value of each outcome:

Description	Probability	Outcome
Failure	.20	-10
Success	.80	5

Calculate the expected value of the project. The answer is:
    a. 0
    b. 1
    c. 2
    d. 3
    e. 5

9. The <u>standard deviation</u> of the breakage reduction project in question #8 is:
   a. 40
   b. 36
   c. 6
   d. 4
   e. none of the above

10. Suppose a project to increase worker morale requires an initial $1,000 outlay expense. In one year, the project is likely to provide added production of $2,680. By the second year, however, additional costs of $510 are incurred. The project's net cash flow are:
    $$-1,000; +2,680; -510$$
    Suppose the required rate of return is 25%. Calculate the risk adjusted present value of this project. It is:
    a. 106.00
    b. 560.00
    c. 817.60
    d. 1560.60
    e. none of these

11. The larger is the coefficient of variation of an investment project:
    a. the higher is the slope of the profit curve.
    b. the more the model is explained.
    c. the lower is the risk of a project.
    d. the higher is the risk of a project.

12. If two projects have identical coefficients of variation, then:
    a. both projects must have identical standard deviations.
    b. both project must have identical expected values.
    c. none of the above.

13. As a manager you must decide whether or not to make a risky acquisition. The outcomes are:

	Acquisition	No Acquisition
Recession	-150 million	-50 million
Boom	800 million	250 million

    Let the probability of recession be 50% and the probability of boom be 50%. What is the expected value of an acquisition?
    a. 610 million
    b. 220 million
    c. 190 million
    d. 325 million

14. We expect that the annual after-tax cash flows of Cyber-Tronix will be $200,000 per year for the next 15 years. If the discount factor is 12 percent,
    a. we could calculate the present value of this stream of 15 cash flows.
    b. we know that the cash flow stream is worth exactly $200,000 today.
    c. we suspect that the value of Cyber-Tronix will RISE if the discount rate went up to 13 percent.
    d. we would suspect that the value of Cyber-Tronix will FALL if the number of years went up from 15 to 30.

15. The number of defective products in a sample of 1000 has an expected value of $\hat{r}=5$. The standard deviation, σ, is 3 defective products.
    a. The z-value for $r_j = 11$ defective products is 1.
    b. The z-value for $r_j = 8$ defective products is 1.
    c. The z-value for $r_j = 5$ defective products is 1.
    d. The z-value for $r_j = 0$ defective products is 0.

16. Suppose my utility function in wealth is: $U = 100 \cdot W - W^2$. I am offered a gamble that will pay me either $10 or $40, with equal probabilities. The gamble costs me $15 to try. Should I gamble in this case if I am an *expected utility maximizer*?
    a. no one gambles who uses expected utility maximization.
    b. The certain utility is greater than the expected utility of the gamble so I should not gamble.
    c. The expected utility of the gamble is greater than the certain utility, so I should gamble.
    d. The expected utility of the gamble equals the certain utility, so I am indifferent.

17. Which of the following actions would NOT provide risk-reducing benefits:
    a. If you owned a portfolio of bonds, and you decided to sell Treasury bond futures.
    b. If you owned some stock in Hershey's, and you decided to sell call options in Hershey stock.
    c. If you owned stock in auto companies, so you decided to buy more stock in automobile companies to diversify.
    d. If you owned corn growing in your fields, so you decided to sell corn futures.

18. What is the portfolio risk (σ_{HF}) of an equally weighted portfolio of Hershey's and Ford Motor stock, if $\sigma_H = 10$, $\sigma_F = 30$, and the correlation coefficient (ρ) is .60.
    a. $\sigma_{HF} = 18.44$
    b. we cannot solve it because we are not told the portfolio weights.
    c. $\sigma_{HF} = 20$
    d. since there is positive correlation, it must be higher than 30.

19. In a survey, it is found that Gloria King is indifferent between winning $100 for sure, or entering a gamble in which 50% of the time she wins $200 and 50% of the time she wins nothing. Then we know:
    a. that Ms. King is a risk lover.
    b. that Ms. King is risk neutral.
    c. that Ms. King is risk averse.

20. Given the following information, which project is relatively more risky?
    (HINT: Think about the *coefficient of variation* = standard deviation/expected value.)

    Project A: variance = 100   Project B: variance = 144
    expected value = 10   expected value = 24

    a. Project A is riskier.
    b. Project B is riskier.
    c. Project A and B has the same risk.

21. Which of the following is not considered an appropriate way for managers to deal with risk?
    a. When making investments in assets, attempt to purchase assets that are general purpose rather than firm specific.
    b. Where reasonable, purchase insurance on outcomes that would be disastrous such as the death of key personnel.
    c. Gains control over some of the environmental variables or gather more information.
    d. All of the above are approaches to managing risks.

22. A farmer in Iowa is growing corn, and wishes to *hedge* against adverse price movements in corn. To hedge, the Iowan should:
    a. buy corn in the cash market.
    b. sell commodity futures contracts on corn at the Chicago Board of Trade.
    c. sell financial futures contracts on Treasury securities at the Chicago Board of Trade.
    d. buy commodity futures contracts on corn at the Chicago Board of Trade.

23. A treasurer should *hedge* borrowing costs on money to be borrowed in 3-months:
    a. by borrowing the money today, rather than waiting.
    b. by waiting until 3-months, and then borrow.
    c. by selling 3-month Eurodollar Time Deposit futures contracts on the Chicago Mercantile Exchange.
    d. by buying 3-month Eurodollar Time Deposit futures contracts on the Chicago Mercantile Exchange.

Answers
1. c
2. c
3. d

4. b

5. c

6. b

7. d (The standard deviation is 10, when the variance is 100, so the coefficient of variation is 1.)

8. c

9. c

10. c

11. d

12. c (Two projects may have different standard deviations, but if their expected values differ proportionally, they will have the same coefficient of variation.)

13. d

14. a

15. b

16. c (Certain utility = 1275; Expected utility of the gamble = 1650).

17. c (Buying non-automobile firms would be a better method to diversify).

18. a (Remember that $\sigma_p^2 = W_A^2 \cdot \sigma_A^2 + W_B^2 \cdot \sigma_B^2 + 2 \cdot W_A \cdot W_B \cdot \rho_{AB} \cdot \sigma_A \cdot \sigma_B = .25 \cdot 100 + .25 \cdot 300 + 2 \cdot .5 \cdot .5 \cdot 10 \cdot 30 \cdot .6 = 340$. The square root is 18.44).

19. b

20. a

21. d

22. b (By waiting to sell corn at harvest, the farmer is betting that corn prices will rise. If corn prices rise, then corn futures will also rise. To hedge, the farmer must sell corn futures (an investment that gains value if corn prices fall).

23. c (By waiting to borrow, the treasurer is betting that interest rates will decline and the value of Eurodollar Time Deposit futures contracts will rise. To hedge, the treasurer must do the *opposite*; that is, the treasure should sell Eurodollar Time Deposits to bet that interest rates will rise.)

Problems or Short Essays

1. Under what circumstances would you not find a Risk Premium for investments with different levels of risk?

2. Do shareholders want managers to avoid most risks?

3. a. Find the *coefficients of variation* for an acquisition and no acquisition in multiple choice problem #13.

   b. Explain how it is possible that it could be riskier not to do the acquisition than to go through with the acquisition project.

4. a. Building one new Subway sandwich shop has an expected net cash flow of either 10 or 20, which are equally likely. Find the expected net cash flow and its coefficient of variation.

   b. Building <u>two</u> new Subway sandwich shops provides equally likely net cash flows of either 20 or 40. Find the expected net cash flow for doubling the investment, and it coefficient of variation.

5. From the following data, determine the number of units that maximizes average profit and maximizes marginal profit

Output (Q)	0	1	2	3	4	5	6	7
Total Profit (π)	-100	50	116	180	220	250	270	280

Answers

1. If most people were *risk neutral*, that is, risk did not bother them, there would be no reward for accepting risk.

2. Shareholders seek maximization of shareholder wealth. If avoiding risks reduces profit potential, then shareholders will not be achieving maximum profit. Since shareholders are frequently diversified across many different investments, shareholders would be able to assume the level of risk with which they are comfortable. Therefore, shareholders want managers who accept reasonable risks with positive NPVs.

3a. Acquisition: 475 million/325 million = 1.4615
    No Acquisition: 150 million/100 million = 1.5000

3b. The "No Acquisition" decision was *more* risky in this case, adjusted for the fact that the scale of the two choices was different. It may be that the acquisition was in a different industry, which provided some natural diversification across different economic climates.

4a. The expected net cash flow is 15, with standard deviation of 5 and coefficient of variation of .333.

4b. The expected net cash flow doubles to 30, with standard deviation of 10. The coefficient of variation remains unchanged at .333. Note that in reality, it is impossible to exactly duplicate the investment. Two sandwich shops would likely offer a greater range of outcomes, as one shop might do well, whereas the second one might flop due to differences in their location.

5. Average Profit is π/Q. It is maximized at the third unit of output. Marginal Profit is $\Delta\pi/\Delta Q$. Marginal Profit is maximized at the first unit of output.

Output (Q)	**0**	**1**	**2**	**3**	**4**	**5**	**6**	**7**
Total Profit (π)	-100	50	116	180	220	250	270	280
Average Profit	--	50	58	60	55	50	45	40
Marginal Profit	--	150	66	64	40	30	20	10

Worked Problems

1. The manager of Research and Development for **Centipede Complex, Inc.**, must give her approval to one of two projects. Project Mordor would explore the creation of dark smoke to shield invasion forces. Project Gandalf would explore electrical interruption devices to confuse the enemy. She has developed the following probabilities and outcomes for the Mordor and Gandalf projects for different states of the world.

R&D Projects	States of the World	Probabilities	Outcomes
Project	major cuts in defense spending	.30	-100
Mordor's	competitors develop Mordor first	.10	-300
Prob. & Payout	Centipede develops Mordor first	.60	6000
Project	major cuts in defense spending	.30	-200
Gandalf's	competitors develop Gandalf first	.25	-400
Prob. & Payout	Centipede develops Gandalf first	.45	9000

a. What is the expected value of the Mordor and Gandalf projects?

> *Answer:* Mordor's expected value is:
> $\hat{r} = .30 \cdot (-100) + .10 \cdot (-300) + .6 \cdot 6000 = 3,540$.
> Gandalf's expected value is: $R_g = .30 \cdot (-200) + .25 \cdot (-400) + .45 \cdot 9000 = 3,890$.

b. What is the variance and standard deviations of the Mordor and Gandalf projects?

> *Answer:* Mordor's variance is:
> $\sigma^2_m = .30 \cdot (-100 - 3540)^2 + .10 \cdot (-300 - 3540)^2 + .60 \cdot (6000 - 3540)^2 = 9,080,400$.
> Mordor's standard deviation, σ_m is 3,013.37, which is the square root of the variance.
>
> Gandalf's variance is:
> $\sigma^2_g = .30 \cdot (-200 - 3890)^2 + .25 \cdot (-400 - 3890)^2 + .45 \cdot (9000 - 3890)^2 = 21,369,900$.
> Gandalf's standard deviation, σ_g is 4,622.76, which is the square root of the variance.

c. What are the coefficient of variations of the Mordor and Gandalf projects?

Answer: Mordor's coefficient of variation is: $v_m = \sigma_m/\hat{r}_m = 3013.37/3540 = .8512$. Gandalf's coefficient of variation is: $v_g = \sigma_g/\hat{r}_g = 4622.76/3890 = 1.1884$.

d. Assuming that the initial outlay is about the same for both projects, and that only one project can be funded, which project should the R&D manager of Centipede select, and why?

Answer: Project Gandalf has a higher expected return, but a higher risk both relatively (in the coefficient of variation) and absolutely (in the variance and standard deviation).

Which project the manager *should* select depends on one's point of view. As a stockholder of Centipede Complex, I want her to pick Gandalf because of its higher expected value. I want her to ignore risk. If the R&D manager is *risk neutral*, she should select Gandalf.

But if she is *risk averse*, sensing that a bad outcome might get her fired, she may have Centipede Complex look at Project Mordor, since the expected values of the two projects are fairly close.

2. **Hershey Corporation** did extensive product testing on chocolate that doesn't melt in the heat of the dessert (some of the testing was successful in Desert Storm). The hope is that this new chocolate bar will catch on for picnics, lunch boxes, and camping.

However, the chocolate bar market is mature. The marketing expense of the new product will have to be extensive. Using spreadsheets, Hershey has estimated the future revenues and expenses to be:

	Year 1	Year 2	Year 3	Year 4	Year 5
Revenues	1000	4000	5000	6000	6000
Operating Expenses	2000	1000	1000	1000	1000
Marketing Expenses	3000	3000	1000	0	0

a. Ignoring taxes, estimate the annual cash flows over five years for the Desert Storm bar.

Answer: They are: -4000 in Year 1; 0 in Year 2; 3000 in Year 3; 5000 in Year 4; and 5000 in Year 5.

b. If the initial cost of expanding the Desert Storm bar is 2,000, and the discount rate is 8%, what is the Net Present Value of the Desert Storm bar (ignoring taxes and all years after year 5)? Assume that all cash flows occur at the end of each of the five years and that there is no salvage value, and that sales of Desert Storm do not cannibalize other Hershey chocolate bar sales. Should Hershey's produce this bar?

Answer: The Net Present Value is: $NPV = -2000 + -4000/1.08 + 0/(1.08)^2 + 3000/(1.08)^3 + 5000/(1.08)^4 + 5000/(1.08)^5 = 3,755.85$. Hershey should go ahead and sell this new chocolate bar.

3. **TeleStock**, a new home internet service for investing in stocks via modems and personal computers, offers a free 30-day trial period. Revenues are highly dependent on retaining customers after the trial period is over. The firm has been slowly expanding its market Northward, from its home town in Houston, Texas. In each new state, it advertises in local newspapers, local editions of the *Wall Street Journal* and *Investor's Daily*. As TeleStock enters new markets, it has noticed a steady decline in the customer retention rate (the percent who keeps the service more than 30 days). Should TeleStock stop entering new markets because of this declining average retention rate?

Answer: The average retention is declining, but that does not mean that the new markets are not profitable. The management of TeleStock should determine where the added costs of entering a market are less than the added revenues generated from entering a new market. This is the basis of marginal analysis.

4. Maribeth George intends on investing in **Tyson Chicken** and **Microsoft Computers**. She expects Tyson to return 12% and Microsoft to return 15%. But she anticipates that the standard deviation for Tyson is 8% and the standard deviation for Microsoft is 18%. The correlation coefficient between the stocks is 0.20.

a. Find the expected return on the portfolio, if Ms. George puts 40% of her investment funds in Tyson and the rest in Microsoft.

Answer: The expected return is: $.40 \cdot (.12) + .6 \cdot (.15) = .048 + .09 = $ **.138**.

b. Find the *portfolio risk*, that is, the standard deviation of the portfolio using 40% and 60% as portfolio weights as in part (a) above.

Answer: Portfolio risk is: $\sigma_p = \sqrt{W_A^2 \cdot \sigma_A^2 + W_B^2 \cdot \sigma_B^2 + 2 \cdot W_A \cdot W_B \cdot \rho_{AB} \cdot \sigma_A \cdot \sigma_B}$. By substituting the relevant numbers:

$$\sigma_p = \sqrt{.40 \cdot (.08)^2 + .60 \cdot (.18)^2 + 2 \cdot (.40) \cdot (.6) \cdot (.20) \cdot (.08) \cdot (.18)} = \sqrt{.0233824}.$$ This equals .1529. The standard deviation of the portfolio is 15.29 percent.

Net Sources

1. Mutual fund families have websites that address assessing one's risk tolerance.

   T. Rowe Price Investing Tutorial   *www.troweprice.com/mutual/step1.html*
   A tutorial on investing in mutual funds, identifying one's objectives, and risk tolerance.

   Strong Funds: *www.eStrong.com/*
   To take a risk tolerance quiz enter the *Learning Center.* Then go to *Investing Concepts*, then to *Principles & Theories*, and finally to *The Main Types of Investment Risk.* Click on the *Risk Tolerance Quiz.*

   Fidelity Funds: *www.fidelity.com/*
   Go to search to search for "tools". The asset allocation planner involves a questionnaire to plan your own risk profile and asset mix. Or go directly *personal100.fidelity.com:80/global/search/content/toolbox.shtml.tvsr*

2. Larger banks provide economic analysis and investor information.

   M&I Bank*: www.mitrust.com/* Enter "Market Review." Good economic outlook information as well as a stock market is presented.

   Wells Fargo: *http://www.wellsfargo.com* provides an *Investment Basics* area in their *Resource Center* to learn more about risk.

   Citibank: *http://www.citibank.com/* provides market watch, financial news, and international news.

3. **Certified Financial Planner (CFP)**   *www.cfp-board.org/*

   CFP's Board of Standard. This site offers information on becoming licensed as a CFP. Certified Financial Planners work with clients to arrange appropriate investment strategies to achieve the client's objectives.

4. **Chartered Financial Analyst (CFA)**   *www.aimr.com/*

   Association for Investment Management and Research runs the CFA exams. Managers of pools of money in insurance, mutual funds, and bank trust services tend to desire achieving the CFA designation in three exam levels over a three-year period.

5. PROJECT 1: The power of compounding is be explored at:

http://www.estrong.com/strongweb/strong/jsp/planning/tools/compound.jsp At a 14% rate of return, how much would you have, if you invested $200 per month out of every paycheck for the next 30 years?

6. PROJECT 2:   *http://www.gilt.co.uk/index.htm*

Bonds issued by the British government are called Gilts. This is the "Everything you need to understand Gilts" site. Read about deflation and gilts. Deflation is a problem in Japan. Also the Japanese stock market has made no progress in the 1990's. Explain how bonds behave during times of deflation.

PART II - DEMAND AND FORECASTING

Chapter 3

Demand Analysis

Because the demand for a firm's goods and services plays such a central role in determining the cash flows that the firm will be able to generate, and thus the value of the firm, it is important to have a solid understanding of demand concepts. This understanding permits managers to react to changes in demand in a manner that maximizes profits and shareholders' wealth. The essential tools for predicting changes in the demand function are the *price, income, and cross price elasticities.*

A. Demand Analysis

1. An important contributor to firm risk arises from sudden shifts in demand for the product or service. Demand analysis serves two managerial objectives: (1) it provides the insights necessary for effective management of demand, and (2) it aids in forecasting sales and revenues.

2. *The Demand Schedule or Curve* depicts the greatest quantity of a good or service that a consumer or group of consumers is willing to buy at each price, holding everything else constant. Income, prices of related products, and other influences on demand are held constant in a manner much like a scientific experiment would attempt to control all factors except the one being tested.

3. The most prominent feature of the demand curve is its downward slope. Price and quantity are negatively related. Economic reasons for the downward slope include:

   a. *income effect*--as the price of a good declines, the consumer can purchase more of all goods since his or her *real income* increased.

   b. *substitution effect*--as the price declines, the good becomes relatively cheaper.

4. A *rational consumer* is someone who seeks to maximize satisfaction. Rational consumers will reorganize consumption until the marginal utility in each good per dollar is equal:

$$\text{Optimality Condition is } MU_A/P_A = MU_B/P_B = MU_C/P_C = \ldots$$

If MU per dollar in A and B differ, the consumer can improve *utility* by purchasing more of the one with higher MU per dollar, and less of the other.

5. Demand curves may be linear or nonlinear. If nonlinear, their slope changes at different prices.

B. The Demand Function

1. The Demand Curve only considered the relationship of price and quantity, holding "other factors" constant. The *Demand Function* includes all of the factors which significantly influence the quantity demanded.

$$Q_D = f(P, P^s, P^c, Y, P^e, A, A^c, T^A, T/S)$$

The price of the good, P, is negatively related to Q_D. The higher is the price of substitute goods, P^s, the greater is the quantity demanded of one's own goods. The higher is the price of complementary goods, P^c, the smaller is the quantity demanded.

2. The effect of income, Y, may be either positive or negative. The expected future price, P^e, of a product can be a great stimulus for sales. If a rumor spreads that toilet paper is likely to become expensive in the next month, customers will immediately hoard it.

3. Advertising, A, and advertising expenditures by competitors, A^c also affect the quantity demanded. Adjustment time period, T^A, permits a greater quantity demanded over a longer time period. T/S is taxes or subsidies -- the impact of taxes is negative whereas the impact of subsidies is positive.

4. Other factors affecting the quantity demanded:

   a. *Tastes*--fads, lifestyles change over time.

   b. *Durable goods*--more volatile since purchases usually can be postponed.

   c. *Time*--the quantity demanded over the next two minutes *vs.* the next year differs.

   d. *Derived demand*--the demand for a *producer's good* ultimately depends on the demand for the final good.

C. Price Elasticity of Demand

1. The slope of the demand curve gives some indication of how sensitive quantity demanded is to price. But slopes are quite different using different units of measure.

Economists developed the concept of an *elasticity* that is completely independent of the units of measurement.

2. A *price elasticity*, E_D, is the percentage change in quantity divided by the percentage change in its price, other things equal (*ceteris paribus*).

$$E_D = \frac{\%\Delta Q}{\%\Delta P}$$

3. *Arc Price Elasticity*--is used to calculate a price elasticity between two prices. Since we do not want the calculation to be altered by the *direction* of the price movement, we use the "average" quantity (Q_{AVE}) and the "average" price (P_{AVE}).

$$E_D = \frac{\%\Delta Q}{\%\Delta P} = \frac{\Delta Q / Q_{AVE}}{\Delta P / P_{AVE}} = \frac{(Q2 - Q1)/(Q1+Q2)/2}{(P2 - P1)/(P1+P2)/2} = \frac{(Q2 - Q1)/(Q1+Q2)}{(P2 - P1)/(P1+P2)}$$

4. EXAMPLE: Suppose we sold 900 hair curlers at $10 a piece over three months. We then offered a "sale" price at $8 and found we sold 1100 over the next three months. Assuming that other demand factors did not change appreciably, we estimate the *arc price elasticity* is -.9, which is the ratio (+200/1000)/(-2/9).

5. *Point Price Elasticity*--when the demand curve is known, the price elasticity at each point on the curve is called the <u>point price elasticity</u>. The point price elasticity is:

$$E_D = (\partial Q/\partial P)\cdot(P/Q).$$

$(\partial Q/\partial P)$ as the partial derivative of the demand function Q, with respect to price. It is the slope of the demand function at a point.

6. EXAMPLE: Assume we have estimated the following demand curve: $Q_D = 150 - 10P$ What is the *point price elasticity* when P = $5 and $Q_D = 100$? $(\partial Q/\partial P) = -10$, so $E_D = (-10)(5/100) = -.5$. The price elasticity is -.5.

7. ANOTHER EXAMPLE: If a 10% price increase leads to a 12% decline in quantity demanded, the price elasticity is -1.2; which is -(12%)/(10%).

D. <u>Elastic, Inelastic, and Unit Elastic</u>

1. If the **absolute value** of $E_D = 1$, the demand is *unit elastic*.

2. If the **absolute value** of $E_D < 1$, the demand is *inelastic*.
3. If the **absolute value** of $E_D > 1$, the demand is *elastic*.

4. *Perfectly elastic* demand curves are flat or horizontal, $E_D = -\infty$.

5. A vertical demand curve is *perfectly inelastic*, $E_D = 0$.

E. Relationship of Total Revenue, Marginal Revenue, and Price Elasticity

1. The estimated arc or point price elasticity is an essential tool in predicting the impact of price changes on total revenue.

2. Total revenue is $TR = P \cdot Q$, so $\%\Delta TR = \%\Delta P + \%\Delta Q$. If demand is *inelastic*, a price increase will increase TR. If demand is *elastic*, a price increase will reduce TR. If demand is *unit elastic*, then a price increase (or decrease) will not change TR.

3. If a manager wishes to increase TR, he or she should raise the price of the product if demand is inelastic, and should cut price if demand is *elastic*.

4. Marginal revenue, MR, is a function of the price elasticity:

$$MR = P(\, 1 + 1/E_D)$$

Note that when demand is perfectly elastic, $E_D = -\infty$, then MR = P.

F. Factors Affecting Price Elasticities

1. *Availability and Closeness of Substitutes*--the greater the number of substitute goods available to the consumer, the more price elastic is the good.

2. *Percentage of Budget*--the demand for high priced goods tends to be more elastic than the demand for inexpensive items, as they typically are a larger portion of one's budget.

3. *Durable Goods*--the demand for durable goods tends to be more price elastic than the demand for non-durable goods.

4. *Time Frame*--the demand for many products tends to become more elastic over longer time periods. Right now, if you were offered for only $30 a round-trip plane ticket to Paris leaving tomorrow, a few economics students would immediately start packing to go! But if that offer said that you could leave anytime within the next six months, the offer becomes nearly irresistible.

5. *Luxury Goods vs. Necessities*--luxury items tend to be more elastic than necessity items.

6. Note that opening up to free <u>international trade</u> tends to increase the number of close substitutes for the domestic products. This has the effect of reducing the power of domestic monopolies by increasing the effective amount of competition.

G. Income Elasticity of Demand

1. The *income elasticity* (E_Y) is the percentage change in quantity demanded divided by the percentage change in income.

2. *Arc Income Elasticity*, where Y is income:

$$E_Y = \frac{\%\Delta Q}{\%\Delta Y} = \frac{\Delta Q/Q_{AVE}}{\Delta Y/Y_{AVE}} = \frac{(Q2 - Q1)/(Q1+Q2)/2}{(Y2 - Y1)/(Y1+Y2)/2} = \frac{(Q2 - Q1)/(Q1+Q2)}{(Y2 - Y1)/(Y1+Y2)}$$

3. EXAMPLE: Associated with an increase in disposable personal income from $100 million to $110 million, suppose there was an increase in boat sales from 50,000 to 60,000 units. We can readily estimate the income elasticity over this range:

$$E_Y = \frac{(60000 - 50000)/(55000)}{(110 - 100)/(105)} = \frac{10/55}{10/105} = 1.91$$

4. A 10 percent increase in income would be expected to result in a 19.1 percent increase in boat sales, other things equal.

5. *Point Income Elasticity*--provides a measure of this responsiveness of quantity to income at a specific point on a demand function, where $\partial Q/\partial I$ = the partial derivative of quantity with respect to income.

$$E_Y = (\partial Q/\partial Y)\cdot(Y/Q).$$

6. EXAMPLE: Suppose that a demand function for new single-family housing construction has been estimated as: $Q_D = 600 - 20 P + 300 Y$, where P, Y, and Q are measured in thousands. If the average price were $100,000, and average per capita income were $10,000, we predict that there will be 1,600,000 new single-family homes built. That is, $600 - 20(100) + 300(10) = 1600$ thousand homes. $(\partial Q/\partial Y)$ equals 300. The income elasticity at the point where (P=100 and Y=10) is: $E_D = (300)(10/1600) = 1.875$. A 1 percent increase in income increases the quantity demanded of single-family new home construction by 1.875 percent.

7. If $E_Y \geq 0$, it is a *normal good*. If $E_Y < 0$, then the product is an *inferior good*.

8. When the income elasticity is **high** as one or greater ($E_Y \geq 1$), the product is often called a *luxury*. If the income elasticities are **low**, as in between zero and one ($0 \leq E_Y < 1$), these are called *necessities*.

H. Cross Price Elasticities

1. The *cross price elasticity* of demand (E_x), is the percentage change in the quantity demanded of one good divided by the percentage change in the price of a different good.

2. *Arc Cross Price Elasticity* is:

$$E_x = \frac{(Q_{A2} - Q_{A1})/(Q_{A1}+Q_{A2})}{(P_{B2} - P_{B1})/(P_{B1}+P_{B2})}$$

3. *Point cross price elasticity* is: $E_x = (\partial Q_A/\partial P_B) \cdot (P_B/Q_A)$

4. If the cross price elasticity is positive, the goods are called *substitutes*. If the cross price elasticity is negative, the goods are called *complements*.

I. Other Elasticities

1. The *Advertising Elasticity* (E_A) is the percentage change in quantity demanded divided by the percentage change in advertising expenditures.

2. The *Supply Price Elasticity* is the percentage change in quantity supplied divided by the percentage change in price. If supply is vertical, then the supply elasticity will be zero. If supply is horizontal, then the supply elasticity is infinite.

True and False Questions

Agree or disagree with the following statements, and correct the part that is erroneous.

1. If income rises and if the product is a normal good, then the demand curve shifts out and to the right.

2. If income falls and if the product is a luxury good, then the demand curve shifts out and to the right.

3. If the price elasticity of automobiles were -2.1, a price increase will raise total revenue.
4. We would expect the cross price elasticity between propane gas and fuel oil used for home heating to be negative.

5. When airline fares were deregulated in 1979, ticket prices fell substantially yet airline total revenue increased! Air travel must be unit elastic.

6. The business cycle raises and lowers income levels. Companies that manufacture durable goods typically find that the income elasticity of their products is high. Companies which sell consumer non-durable products find that the income elasticity of their products is low. Therefore, investing in firms which sell durable goods would be less risky than investing in firms which sell non-durable products over the business cycle. Which one?

Answers
1. True.
2. Disagree. The demand curve shifts in and to the left when income falls for luxury goods as well as all normal goods.
3. Disagree. When demand is elastic, a price increase will reduce total revenue.
4. Disagree. The cross price elasticity for substitutes is positive.
5. Disagree. Air travel must have been elastic. The price decrease led to higher total revenue for the airlines.
6. Disagree. Durable products would tend to make the company riskier, as the income elasticity is likely to be much higher.

Multiple Choice Questions

1. If the cross price elasticity measured between the quantity of compact discs sold and the price of hit movies sold on VCR tapes is positive, then two products are referred to as:
   a. complements.
   b. inferior goods.
   c. substitutes.
   d. normal goods.
   e. luxuries.

2. If demand is elastic, a price cut:
   a. lowers total revenue, but increases quantity sold.
   b. lowers total revenue, and lowers the quantity sold.
   c. raises total revenue, but lowers the quantity sold.
   d. raises total revenue, and raises the quantity sold.

3. Suppose we estimate that the demand elasticity for Coach purses is -.8 at their current high prices. Then we know:
   a. a 1% increase in price raises quantity 1.8%.
   b. that marginal revenue is positive at current prices.
   c. that marginal revenue is negative at current prices.
   d. that Coach purses are highly elastic.

4. Over the past year Lo-Cal Liquors has had an average sale of 1000 bottles of Diet Bourbon per month. In the months when Lo-Cal Liquors ran sales on its Lo-Cal Scotch, cutting its price from $7 to $5 per bottle, sales of Diet Bourbon declined to 600 bottles per month. The *arc cross price elasticity* of demand between Diet Bourbon and Lo-Cal Scotch is?
   a. -1.5
   b. -1.4
   c. +1.4
   d. +1.5

5. Given the following demand function for spring break trips to beach, compute the *point price elasticity* (E_D) when P=$399 and Y=$6000.

$$Q = -55650 - 8 \cdot P + 12 \cdot Y$$

   a. $0.00 > E_D > -0.20$
   b. $E_D = -.24259$
   c. $E_D = -.38991$
   d. $-1.50 > E_D > -2.00$
   e. none of the above

6. Which of the following changes would NOT be expected to *shift* the demand curve for vacation travel in the United States?
   a. an increase in the price of vacation travel.
   b. an increase in consumers' incomes.
   c. an increase in the price of substitute goods, such as entertainment.
   d. an increase in the expected future price for vacation travel.

7. An automobile would be an example of:
   a. a consumer non-durable good.
   b. a durable good.
   c. an inferior good.
   d. a producer good.

8. If the income elasticity was positive, then this indicates that the products are:
   a. complements   b. substitutes.
   c. normal goods.   d. inferior goods.

9. If income rises 10% and quantity of video recorders sold rises 13.5%, then the income elasticity is:
   a. negative
   b. .667
   c. 1.0
   d. 1.35

10. If the income elasticity for compact discs is 3, and if income rises 5%, what do you forecast for sales of compact discs?
    a. a rise of 5%
    b. a rise of 10%
    c. a rise of 15%
    d. a rise of 20%
    e. none of these.

11. If a decrease in income leads to an increase in the quantity of liver demanded, we can conclude that liver is a:
    a. normal good.
    b. inferior good.
    c. complementary good.
    d. substitute good.

12. The price elasticity facing the Internet is -.5, the income elasticity is +7.4. Suppose that income is expected to increase 4% this year, and that the price of access to the Internet is anticipated to rise 2%, what is the percentage increase expected from this information for users of the Internet?
    a. $-.5 + 3\% = 2.5\%$
    b. $(-.5 \cdot 2\%) + (7.4 \cdot 4\%) = 28.6\%$
    c. $(-.5 \cdot 4\%) + (7.4 \cdot 2\%) = 12.8\%$
    d. insufficient information to answer.

13. A price increase:
    a. raises total revenue, if demand is inelastic.
    b. lowers total revenue, if demand is elastic.
    c. neither raises nor lowers revenue, if demand is unit elastic.
    d. all of the above.

14. Which of the following is more likely to be an inferior good.
    a. A Ford Taurus Wagon with 120,000 miles.
    b. Automobiles made by Ford, Mercury, or Lincoln.
    c. Any automobile.
    d. Any form of transportation, air, sea, or land.

15. The demand elasticity facing a firm is perfectly elastic. In that case,
    a. MR equals Price
    b. MR is below the demand curve.
    c. MR rises
    d. MR is negative.

16. Letters, Inc. has estimated the following demand curve for its FAX machine: Q = 3,000 - 1.5•P. Calculate the point elasticity of demand when P = $600.
    a. $E_D = -1.50$
    b. $E_D = -0.43$
    c. $E_D = -0.20$
    d. $E_D = -5.25$

17. Assume that Coca-Cola is elastic, then an increase in the price of Coca-Cola does which of the following?
    a. Decreases total revenue for Coke.
    b. Increases total revenue for Coke.
    c. Total revenue remains the same for Coke after the price increase.
    d. Total revenue always rises after a price increase.

18. Income elasticity is defined as:
    a. the change in Q divided by the change in Y (income).
    b. the percentage change in Q divided by the percentage change in Y
    c. the percentage change in Y divided by the percentage change in Q
    d. the change in Y divided by the change in Q

19. If income rises by 4 percent and the quantity sold of a product rises by 6 percent. This evidence suggests that the income elasticity is:
    a. negative.
    b. positive, but less than one.
    c. greater than one.
    d. zero.

20. Select the correct statement regarding the price elasticity of demand (E_D).
    a. The greater the number of substitutes, the greater the E_D.
    b. The greater the time horizon, the less the E_D.
    c. The greater the proportion of income spent on the good, the less the E_D.
    d. All of the above are correct.

21. If demand is <u>elastic</u>, *a price increase*:
    a. lowers total revenue and increases quantity sold.
    b. lowers total revenue and lowers the quantity sold.
    c. raises total revenue and lowers the quantity sold.
    d. raises total revenue and raises the quantity sold.

22. If demand is <u>inelastic</u>, *a price increase*:
    a. lowers total revenue and increases quantity sold.
    b. lowers total revenue and lowers the quantity sold.
    c. raises total revenue and lowers the quantity sold.
    d. raises total revenue and raises the quantity sold.

23. The cross elasticity for goods that are substitutes and goods that are complements is:
    a. Substitutes $E_x < 0$; complements $E_x > 0$
    b. Substitutes $E_x > 1$; complements $0 < E_x < 1$
    c. Substitutes $E_x < -1$; complements $E_x > -1$
    d. Substitutes $E_x > 0$; complements $E_x < 0$

24. Marginal revenue can be expressed in elasticity form as $MR = P(1 + 1/E_P)$. Land's End sells mock turtleneck sweaters for $29. The price elasticity is estimated to be approximately -3.0. According to this information:
    a. MR = $29
    b. MR is greater than $29
    c. MR is $19.33
    d. MR is $9.67

25. The demand for tulips in Holland is estimated to be: $Q_D = 30 + 5\,Y + 15\,P$
    Where Y is income in Euros, Q is the quantity of tulips in units, and P is price in Euros. What is the *point* income elasticity of tulips at P = 6 Euros and Y = 20 Euros.
    a. +.2222
    b. +.4545
    c. +2.200
    d. +5.000

Answers

1. c	6. a	11. b	16. b	21. b
2. d	7. b	12. b	17. a	22. c
3. c	8. c	13. d	18. b	23. d
4. d	9. d	14. a	19. c	24. c
5. b	10. c	15. a	20. a	25. b

Problems or Short Essays

1. The concept of elasticity is very general. Describe what might be meant by the *temperature elasticity* of demand when used in the context of electric utilities or natural gas utilities.

2. If the price of VCRs declines by 20 percent, and the quantity sold rises 40 percent, what is the price elasticity of VCRs, *ceteris paribus*.

3. The cross price elasticity between the demand for Washington State apples relative to Pennsylvania apples is +0.7. What can be said about the perceived differences in quality between the two apple varieties? How would your answer change if the cross price elasticity were only +0.1?

4. Automobile manufacturers have discovered that the price elasticity of demand for autos is much higher for short duration manufacturer rebates (a type of sale) than if the price

were lowered permanently. Therefore, a temporary price cut raises more revenue than a permanent price reduction. What is it about the nature of automobiles that would explain this?

5. Price increases reduce the quantity of the product a manufacturer sells and produces. Less production usually means less total cost. Would it be reasonable for a profit maximizing firm to *raise price* if demand were unit elastic? If demand were inelastic?

6. Would you forecast quantity demanded to rise or fall, if your product were an *inferior good* and we moved into a recession and its resulting lower income?

Answers

1. The *temperature elasticity* could be estimated as the percentage change in megawatts of electricity (or hundred weights of gas) demanded divided by a percentage change in the temperature. It would show the sensitivity of demand for electricity (or gas) to temperature changes.

2. $E_D = (40\%)/(-20\%) = -2$. *Ceteris paribus* means that other variables are held constant.

3. A positive cross price elasticity indicates that they are substitutes, but not perfectly substitutable. If the cross price elasticity becomes zero, the goods are independent.

4. Since cars are durable goods and since they are high priced, many consumers time their purchases to take advantage of rebates, low interest financing, and year-end sales.

5. Yes. If demand is *unit elastic*, higher prices do not reduce revenue, but they would likely reduce some variable costs. If demand is *inelastic*, a price increase both raises revenue and lowers cost. In both cases, profit increases.

6. Rise.

Worked Problems

1. If the advertising budget of **Bultmann Buick** were increased by 10 percent, and the advertising elasticity were +3.2, by what percentage will the quantity demanded of Buicks rise?

   Answer: Buick sales will rise by about 32%. This is readily shown by noting that the advertising elasticity is the percentage change in quantity divided by the percentage change in advertising.

   $E_{QA} = (\%\ \text{Change in Q})/(\%\ \text{Change in A}) = 3.2 = (\%\ \textbf{Change in Q})/10\%$. We solve for the unknown (the % Change in Q). Hence, quantity increases by about 32%.

Note, however, that elasticities are designed for small, incremental changes. A 10% increase in the advertising budget is fairly substantial; nevertheless, 32% is as close as we can estimate with the data available in this question.

2. The price elasticity of demand for personal computers at **FastCalc Computers, International** is estimated to be -2.2. If the price of FastCalc's personal computers declines 20 percent, what will be the expected percentage increase in the quantity of computers sold?

Answer: FastCalc should enjoy an increase of about 44%. To show this, remember that the price elasticity is the percentage change in quantity divided by the percentage change in price.

E_D = (% Change in Q)/(% Change in P) = -2.2 = (**% Change in Q**)/(-20%). Therefore, the (% Change in Q) must be +44%. But the same *caveat* as in the advertising elasticity problem #1 applies for a major price reduction of 20%.

3. The **Fruity Frozen Yogurt Factory** has reduced the price of its popular I.M. Good Sundae from $2.25 to $1.75. As a result, the firm's daily sales of these sundaes have increased from 1,500 per day to 1,800 per day. Compute the arc price elasticity. Have you any price recommendation to offer, if you were a stockholder in the Fruity Frozen Yogurt Factory.

Answer: Using the *arc price elasticity formula*, the elasticity is:

E_D = [(Q2 - Q1)/(Q1+Q2)]/(P2 - P1)/(P1+P2) = (300/3300)/(-.50/4.00) = -.7272. We find that I.M. Good Sundaes are **inelastic**.

As a stockholder, I recommend raising (rather than lowering) price. When demand is inelastic, a higher price raises total revenue and reduces the quantity sold (which may lower costs a little). When revenues rise and costs decline, it must be that profits are increasing.

4. The bus fare in Fayetteville, Arkansas has just been increased from 50 cents to a dollar. As a result, the bus ridership has declined from 100,000 to 70,000 riders per month.

a. Compute the *arc price elasticity*. Was demand for bus rides elastic or inelastic?

Answer: One way to write the arc price elasticity is:
E_D = [(Q2 - Q1)/(Q1+Q2)/2]/[(P2 - P1)/(P1+P2)/2] = (% Change in Q) / (% Change in P) =

[(100,000 - 70,000)/(100,000 + 70,000)/2] /[(1.00 - .50)/(1.00+.50)/2] =

[-30,000/85,000]/[.50/.75].

-.3529/.6667 = -.5294. Bus ridership appears to be **inelastic**.

b. If the bus fare were subsequently reduced back to 50 cents, do you think ridership would return to 100,000 riders per month? Why?

Answer: We would suppose that answer would be "less than 100,000 riders per month" because some previously discouraged bus riders might have found alternative modes of transportation, moved closer to work or stores, or ceased commuting altogether. This reminds us that pricing *experiments* may have long-term deleterious effects, since the experiment may change the future behavior of the clients.

5. A number of empirical studies of automobile demand have found that the price elasticity is approximately -1.3 and the income elasticity is +3.0. If sales are currently 9 million units, and if prices rise 6 percent, and income rises 4 percent, how many cars will be sold next year?

Answer: The percentage change in the quantity of cars sold depends on both the effect of the price change (E_D) and the effect of the income change (E_Y). We note that the percentage change in car sales can be written:

(% Change in Q) = E_D·(% Change in P) + E_Y·(% Change in Y) =

(-1.3)·6% + 3·4% = +4.2%. So an increase of 4.2% overall would increase the total number of cars sold to: (1.042)·9 million = **9.378 million cars**.

6. The demand function for bicycles in Missouri has been estimated to be:

$$Q = 50 + 15·Y - .5·P$$

where Y is income in **thousands** of dollars, Q is quantity demanded in units, and P is the price per unit. Calculate the *point price elasticity* of demand when P = $150 and income is $15,000. At this price, are these bikes elastic or inelastic?

Answer: At a price of $150 and income Y=15, the total number of bicycles demanded would be 200, since 50 + 15·15 - .5·150 equals 200.

The point price elasticity for bicycle demand, $E_D = (\partial Q/\partial P)·(P/Q) =$

-.5·(150/200) = -.375, which is **inelastic**.

[Note that I=15 because income is measured in thousands of dollars.]

7. Two goods have a cross price elasticity of +1.2. If the price of one of the goods increases by 5 percent, what will happen to the quantity demanded for the other product, holding constant all other factors?

> *Answer:* The quantity demanded of the other good will increase by about 6%, because it will appear cheaper.
>
> To show this, remember that (% Change in Q1)/(% Change in P2) = 1.2. Plugging in the 5% price increase for good 2, we find (**% Change in Q1**)/5% = 1.2, the numerator must be +6%.

8. In an attempt to increase revenues, the **Wonder Wigs** firm is considering a 4 percent increase in price of their wigs and an 11 percent increase in advertising of their location and selection.

   a. If the price elasticity of wig demand is -1.5 and the advertising elasticity of demand is +0.6, will <u>total revenue</u> increase or decrease?

   > *Answer:* Total revenue is influenced by the change in price and the change in quantity. First, as in Worked Problem #5, the percentage change in quantity = (-1.5)·4% + (.6)·(11%) = +.6%. Second, the price rises 4%. With both price and quantity rising, total revenue will increase about 4.6%, since the percentage change in total revenue is the sum of the percentage change in price plus the percentage change in quantity.

   b. Instead of raising price 4 percent and raising advertising expenditures, how else could the Wonder Wig firm increase total revenue?

   > *Answer:* Instead of raising price and advertising, the firm could *cut price* to raise revenue, since demand is elastic.

Net Sources

1. Companies use the Internet to sell products to consumers, but also to expand stockholder interests in the firm. Much like annual reports, firms wish to give a good impression of their industry and products. You will note that firm homepages sometime give their recent stock price.

2. **Annual Reports:** Publicly traded companies report to their shareholders. The economic condition of their industry and the sensitivity of their product to price changes is sometimes discussed. Look at the following firm annual reports. Look for information on whether their products might be elastic or inelastic?

Intel:	*www.intel.com/intel/annual99/index2.htm/*
General Electric:	*www.ge.com/investor/annuals.htm*
Coke:	*annualreport2000.coca-cola.com/*

3. **Trade Associations and Business Organizations:** Firms work with other firms in trade associations. They meet periodically to learn of innovations, socialize, and work to improve the standing of their industry. One common interest is legislation: keeping burdensome regulations at a minimum, or finding ways to restrict entry into the industry from abroad. The following are interesting sites:

American Bankers Association:	*www.aba.com/*
National Cotton Council:	*www.cotton.org/*
American Medical Association:	*www.ama-assn.org/*
US Chamber of Commerce:	*www.uschamber.org/*

4. **PROJECT**: See how the U.S. Chamber of Commerce membership feels about immigration, health care reform, labor law reform, tobacco prohibition, the minimum wage, OSHA, or issues dealing with natural resources and the environment. Click on "Political Advocacy" to see.

Appendix 3A

Indifference Curve Analysis of Demand

Demand theory can be developed from the idea that consumers have choices. Constrained by a budget, consumers select those goods and services that maximize their happiness or utility. Maximization of utility can be used to derive downward sloping demand curves, and is a fundamental tool for economic theory.

A. Preferences and Consumer Choice

1. For the case of two goods, Q_A and Q_B, the consumer has a utility function, U, in equation: $U = U(Q_A, Q_B)$. There are four assumptions about the nature of consumers' choice:

   a. *Consumers can rank preferences.* Consumers can say if one bundle of goods is preferred to another, or if they are indifferent between bundles.

   b. *Consumers prefer more to less.* More of A, or more of B is always a good thing.

   c. *Consumers have transitive preferences.* If bundle of goods X_1 is preferred to bundle X_2, and if X_2 is preferred to X_3, then it follows that the consumer would prefer X_1 to X_3.

   d. *Consumers display diminishing marginal rates of substitution between goods.* Individuals are willing to give up some units of Q_A for one unit of Q_B, but they are willing only to give up smaller amounts of Q_A to get still more Q_B as they continue to substitute Q_B for Q_A.

2. An *indifference curve* is the locus of all bundles of goods that have the same level of utility. An *indifference map* is a collection of indifference curves drawn over various commodity bundles, much like the contour lines on a topographical map.

B. Properties of Indifference Maps

1. Indifference curves higher and to the right are at higher utility levels.

2. The indifference curves between two goods is drawn *convex* to the origin, because this obeys assumption 4 that consumers display diminishing marginal rates of substitution.

3. Indifference curves over two goods slope downward.

4. Indifference curves do not cross.

C. Deriving the Demand Curve Using Indifference Curves

1. The budget constraint is $M = P_A \cdot Q_A + P_B \cdot Q_B$, where P_A and P_B are the prices of the two goods. Rearranging the budget constraint into an equation for a line:
$Q_A = M/P_A - (P_B/P_A) \cdot Q_B$ where M/P_A is the intercept, and $-(P_B/P_A)$ is the slope.

2. The highest indifference curve is tangent to the budget constraint.

D. Optimal Consumption Principle

1. The slope of the indifference curve is the ratio of <u>marginal utilities</u> of the two products ($-MU_B/MU_A$). This can be shown by totally differentiating the utility function.

2. The slope of the budget line ($-P_B/P_A$), which is the ratio of the prices of the two goods, is equal to the slope of the indifference curve.

3. Marginal utility per dollar in A must equal the marginal utility per dollar in B at maximum utility:

Optimal Consumption Principle: $MU_A/P_A = MU_B/P_B$.

4. If $MU_A/P_A > MU_B/P_B$, then the consumer gets more satisfaction per dollar in Q_A than Q_B. By reducing consumption of Q_B and increasing consumption of Q_A, the individual could increase utility. For example, let $MU_A = 10$ and $P_A = \$1$, whereas let $MU_B = 5$ and $P_B = \$5$. By reducing one's purchases of Q_B by one unit, utility falls 5 units. But the \$5 released from purchases of Q_B can be spent on purchases of 5 units of Q_A. This increases utility by 50. The net effect is an increase in utility merely by rearranging consumption.

E. Derivation of Demand from Indifference Curves

1. If P_B becomes cheaper, the consumer will find that his or her budget constraint rotates outward. The consumer is able to buy more Q_B as P_B declines.

2. At lower prices for Q_B, the consumer selects more Q_B. By plotting the price and quantity choices we trace out the demand curve. The demand curve, therefore, was "derived" from the indifference map and shifts in the price of Q_B.

F. Substitution and Income Effects

1. There are two reasons for the downward slope of the derived demand curve:

   a. First, they buy more B because it is relatively cheaper. This is known as the substitution effect.

   b. Second, they buy more B because they are in effect richer when the price of B declines. A lower price of B raises consumers' real income, known as the income effect.

2. Products with low income elasticities will display little income effects.

3. Products with indifference curves, which are nearly straight lines, show that the products are nearly perfect substitutes in consumption. Hence, they will have large substitution effects.

True and False Questions

Agree or disagree with the following statements, and correct the part that is erroneous.

1. If the marginal utility per dollar of food were greater than the marginal utility per dollar in entertainment, then consumers should consume only entertainment to increase utility?

2. The income effect has a greater impact in determining the demand curve for most products than the substitution effect.

3. Suppose that risk is something people disliked; that is, risk is a "bad" rather than a good. Suppose that return is clearly a "good." The indifference map for risk and return would have upward rising curves.

4. As the price declines for a product, the substitution effect leads people to buy *more* of it, and the income effect always leads them to buy *more* of the good.

Answers
1. Disagree. The consumer should purchase *more* entertainment and *less* food, but as the consumer buys more and more entertainment, the marginal utility of entertainment begins to decline. Similarly, as the consumer holds less and less food, the marginal

utility of food increases. Therefore, in general we do not expect the consumer to *specialize* in entertainment alone.

2. Disagree. Price changes may have quite small real income effects, whereas the shoppers are continually looking for low relative prices.

3. True.

4. Disagree. If the product is an inferior good, more real income will lead them to buy *less* of the good.

Multiple Choice Questions

1. To use indifference maps,
   a. you have to be able to measure happiness or utility.
   b. you have to be able to compare preferences between bundles of goods.
   c. you must have no opinion on preferences to be indifferent.
   d. you must use a highway map to read the indifference map.

2. I'd rather take a trip to Maui than a trip to Scotland. If I had to choose between a trip to Paris and Maui, I would prefer Paris. Given a choice between Scotland and Paris, I know that I'd rather go to Paris.
   a. my preferences violate the principle that more is better than less.
   b. my preferences violate transitivity of preferences.
   c. my preferences show that my indifference curves intersect.
   d. my preferences do not violate any rules.

3. If indifference curves were *concave* instead of convex, then:
   a. the indifference curve tangent to the budget line would not be utility maximizing.
   b. consumers would tend to specialize in all of one good or the other.
   c. consumers would display increasing marginal rates of substitution in consumption.
   d. all of the above.

4. Suppose the marginal utility of A is 40 and the marginal utility of B is 80. Suppose also that the price of A is $10 and the price of B is $15.
   a. marginal utility per dollar in all products is equal.
   b. the marginal utility per dollar in A is higher than the marginal utility per dollar in B.
   c. the marginal utility per dollar in B is higher than the marginal utility per dollar in A.
   d. the person should increase the consumption of A and reduce the consumption of B.

5. If indifference curves were nearly straight lines,
   a. a small changes in price would tend to lead to large shifts in the consumption basket of goods selected.
   b. a small changes in price would tend to lead to very little change in the consumption basket of goods selected.
   c. we would say that the two goods were close substitutes.
   d. Both (a) and (c) above

6. A price increase tends to reduce purchases of a good. According to the model of consumer choice, the *primary* reason for this reduction is:
   a. the substitution effect.
   b. inferior goods.
   c. luxury goods.
   d. the income effect.

7. A price cut will tend to:
   a. increase purchases of a good due to the substitution effect, but reduce purchases of the good because of the income effect, assuming the good is a normal good.
   b. decrease purchases of good due to the income effect and also reduce purchases of the good because of the substitution effect.
   c. increase purchases of the good due to the substitution and income effects, assuming the good is a normal good.
   d. increase purchases of the good due to the substitution and income effect, assuming the good is an inferior good.

8. Food (F) and entertainment (E) are both goods. You have been given an allotment of 17 units of food and 4 units of entertainment. Which is NOT TRUE?
   a. A point with F=18 and E=4 is on a higher indifference curve.
   b. A point with F=17 and E=6 is on a higher indifference curve.
   c. A point with F=15 and E=5 could possibly have the same utility as the initial allotment.
   d. A point with F=15 and E=4 is on a higher indifference curve.

Answers
1. b
2. d   (these preferences obey the rules of transitive preferences)
3. d
4. c   (the marginal utility per dollar in A is 4, whereas the marginal utility per dollar in B is 5.33).
5. d
6. a
7. c
8. d

Worked Problems

1. Suppose Travis' utility function for entertainment, which includes CD's (C), and movie tickets (M), is:

$$U = C^{.4} \cdot M^{.2}$$

a. Find Travis' marginal utility for movie tickets. Determine if he has diminishing marginal utility in movie tickets.

   Answer: Marginal utility is the first derivative of Travis' utility function with respect to movie tickets, M. $MU_M = .2C^{.4} \cdot M^{-.8}$.

   MU_M declines in additional movie tickets, since the first derivative of the MU function is negative: $(\partial MU_M / \partial M) = -1.6C^{.4} \cdot M^{-1.8} < 0$.

b. If Travis has a budget of $75 for entertainment, and each CD costs $10, and each movie ticket costs $5, what is his optimal consumption bundle of CDs and tickets? Assume that these are the only entertainment options available to him.

   Answer: Travis' budget constraint is $75 = 10 \cdot C + 5 \cdot M$. This can be solved using Lagrangian Multipliers, as discussed in Appendix 3A.

   $\text{Max } L = C^{.4} \cdot M^{.2} - \lambda(10 \cdot C + 5 \cdot M - 75)$

   (i) $L_C = .4C^{-.6} \cdot M^{.2} - \lambda \cdot 10 = 0$
   (ii) $L_M = .2C^{.4} \cdot M^{-.8} - \lambda \cdot 5 = 0$
   (iii) $L_\lambda = 10 \cdot C + 5 \cdot M - 75 = 0$

   Equations (i) and (ii) can be written as ratios to cancel out lambda. This would be: $.4C^{-.6} \cdot M^{.2} / .2C^{.4} \cdot M^{-.8} = 10/5$.

   This reduces to: $2C/M = 2$, or that $C = M$. Substituting C=M into the budget constraint, we find that **C = 5** and **M = 5**.

c. If you solved the constrained optimization problem using Lagrangians, what is the value of lambda, and what is its economic interpretation?

Answer: To find lambda, substitute the solution in part (b) into either (i) or (ii).

In (i) we find: $.4(5^{-.6}) \cdot (5^{.2}) - \lambda \cdot .5 = 0$.
The solution is **lambda = .0210**, which is the **marginal utility** of relaxing the budget constraint one unit to $76.

2. Jenny Kohler consumes computer game cartridges, G, and all other goods, A. Obviously, most of Jenny's consumption is A, and a small part of her consumption is spent on G. The marginal utility for all other goods is currently 1, and the price of all other goods is $1. Jenny Kohler's utility function for game cartridges, holding all other goods constant, is given by:

$$U = 46 \cdot G - 7.5 \cdot G^2$$

If each game cartridge costs $24, then find the optimal number of cartridges such that the marginal utility of game cartridges per dollar equals the marginal utility per dollar in all other goods.

Answer: The complete utility function for Jenny would include both G and A. But holding all other goods constant, we are looking at the utility function for game cartridges.

Jenny would maximize utility by finding where $MU_G/P_G = MU_A/P_A = 1$.

Since cartridges cost $24, $MU_G/24 = 1/1 = 1$, or $MU_G = .0417$.

The marginal utility of game cartridges is the derivative of her utility.

$MU_G = 46 - 15 \cdot G = .0417$. Hence G = 3.064, or about 3 game cartridges.

Chapter 4

Estimation of Demand

Consumer fads, recessions and booms, price rivalry, and new product introductions are a few sources of risk. To create strategies to profit from these changes, firms need knowledge about demand and how demand is changing. Clues to the future come from experiments and from examining the past. Both market research and statistical techniques are used to describe relationships between past events as a guide to future events. Regression and correlation analyses are basic tools to determine the degree of association of one economic variable to another. *Regression analysis* helps to answer the question: How much will sales decline if our competitor reduces his price? How much will sales increase if the gross domestic product rises 3% this year?

A. Demand Estimation Using Marketing Research Techniques

1. *Consumer Surveys:* ask a sample of consumers about their attitudes toward products, their likelihood to purchase items (especially major durable goods such as automobiles), and whether or not they remember advertising campaigns. Survey results are sensitive to the selection of the sample, the way that questions are worded, and the manner the survey is presented (telephone, in person, through the mail, *etc.*). Surveys are particularly useful for trying to gauge interest in new products.

2. *Consumer Clinics* and *Focus Groups:* experimental groups are designed to emulate a market with money, products to purchase, and negotiation. They are subject to the *Hawthorne Effect* where the participants, knowing that they are being observed, behave better or differently than if they were not involved in an "exciting experiment!"

3. *Market Experiments in Test Stores:* collect demand information by trying different prices, products, or packaging in selected markets or test stores. There are risks of offending customers who find they paid higher prices, or got non-standard designed products. There are often substantial costs for running these experiments, as well.

4. *Historical Data:* what happened in the past can be a guide to the future. Most econometric models require market data over time and/or data across several markets.

B. Statistical Estimation of the Demand Function

1. The *demand function* lists price, price of substitutes and complements, expected future prices, income, and other variables as determinants of market demand.

2. The steps to take may include-- identification of the variables.

    i) Learning about the factors that affect the specific market being examined: Are there stocks of used products available? Is the product seasonal, cyclical, or durable?

    ii) List all of the factors that would seem important. These may be promotional expenditures, disposable income, the selling price, and prices of related products.

3. Collecting the data.

4. Formulate the demand model.

    i) This step considers the *functional form* of model to use (linear, double-log, *etc.*) and the type of statistical techniques to use (regression analysis, descriptive statistics, *etc.*).

    ii) In some cases, both supply and demand functions will be part of the model.

5. Estimate the parameters of the model.

    i) Determine which of the variables were statistically significant and if the signs of the coefficients make sense from an economic point of view.

    ii) Try alternative variables and functional forms.

6. Developing forecasts or estimates from the demand model.

C. Functional Forms Used for Demand Estimation

1. *Linear Model*--is a common form:

$$Q_D = \alpha + \beta_1 \cdot A + \beta_2 \cdot P + \beta_3 \cdot Y + \varepsilon$$

where A is promotional expenditures, Y is disposable income, P is price, and ε is the error term.

THE MODEL IMPLIES:

a. The effect of each variable is independent of the other variables.

b. The effect of each variable is constant.

c. The promotional elasticity is: $\quad E_A = \text{\ss}_1 \cdot A/Q$

c. The price elasticity is: $\quad E_D = \text{\ss}_2 \cdot P/Q$

d. The income elasticity is: $\quad E_Y = \text{\ss}_3 \cdot Y/Q$

2. *Multiplicative Model*--the next most common form:

$$Q_D = \alpha \cdot A^{\text{\ss}1} \cdot P^{\text{\ss}2} \cdot Y^{\text{\ss}3}$$

THE MODEL IMPLIES:

a. The model is double-log or *log linear*:

$$\log Q_D = \log \alpha + \text{\ss}_1 \cdot \log A + \text{\ss}_2 \cdot \log P + \text{\ss}_3 \cdot \log Y + \varepsilon$$

b. The effect of each variable depends on all the other variables.

c. The effect of each variable is nonlinear.

d. The promotional elasticity is: $\quad E_A = \text{\ss}_1$

e. The price elasticity is: $\quad E_D = \text{\ss}_2$

f. The income elasticity is: $\quad E_Y = \text{\ss}_3$

3. Semi-logarithmic transformations, reciprocals, and polynomials (quadratic, cubic, and higher degree polynomials) offer additional choices for functional forms. Generally the one that fits best is the best one to use for forecasting purposes. So the highest R-square or adjusted R-square is the one to select. See Appendix 4A for nonlinear regression models.

D. Simple Linear Regression Model

1. *Correlation* determines the strength of association between variables, whereas *regression analysis* is used to find functional relationships.

2. ASSUMPTIONS: Three assumptions of a simple linear regression: $Y = \alpha + \beta \cdot X + \varepsilon$

   a. Dependent variable, Y, is random

   b. $E(Y \mid X) = \alpha + \beta \cdot X$

   c. The stochastic disturbance, ε, or error term has mean zero and is assumed to be independent.

3. The coefficients, α and β, which minimize the squared error are: $\alpha = Y - \beta \cdot X$ and $\beta = Cov(X,Y)/Var(X)$.

4. Solutions to regression can be found:

   a. manually using a worksheet for expected values, variances, and covariances.

   b. many statistical calculators perform simple linear regressions.

   c. both simple and multiple linear regression can be estimated using statistical packages such as SAS, SPSS, Minitab, TSP, E-view, and ForeProfit.

5. The regression equation estimated can be used for **forecasting**. Suppose the expected future X is X^*, then the forecast for $Y = \alpha + \beta \cdot X^*$.

6. The *standard deviation of the estimate*, s_e, is a measure of the accuracy of estimation. The smaller is the standard deviation for the error terms, the more accurate forecast. An *approximate* 95-prediction interval for Y is $\pm 2 \cdot s_e$.

E. Inferences about the Population Regression Coefficients

1. The observed coefficients, α and β, are sample estimates of population coefficients. The *standard deviation of the coefficient*, s_β, is proportional to a ratio of s_e and the standard deviation of X.

2. The standard approach proposes a null hypothesis $H_0: \beta = \beta_0$ versus an alternative hypothesis $H_a: \beta \neq \beta_0$. Let the observed coefficient be, b. The estimated t-statistic is:

$$t = (b - \beta_0)/s_\beta$$

3. Large t-statistics indicate that the observed coefficient is different from the null hypothesis. If the absolute value of the estimated t-statistic is greater than the critical t-statistic, then we can *reject the null hypothesis.*

4. The *critical t-statistic* depends on sample size. The number of *degrees of freedom* (d.f.) is the number of observations minus the number of independent variables minus one.

    . a. For large samples (n > 30), a critical t-statistic of 2 can be used as a rule of thumb, since $t_{.025,\infty} = 1.96 \approx 2$.

    b. For small samples (n ≤ 30), we use the t-table in the Appendix.

5. The estimated t-statistics that appear in many statistical packages, including ForeProfit, test if the observed coefficient is significantly different from zero. That is the estimated t-statistic used is: $t = (b - 0)/s_\beta \equiv b/s_\beta$.

6. EXAMPLE: Suppose the simple linear regression results in the following:
    $Y = 2.4 + .57 \cdot X$, with a standard error on the slope coefficient of .34. The estimated t-statistic on the hypothesis that the slope is zero would be 1.676. Whether the sample size were small or large, at the conventional .05 significance level, we could not reject the hypothesis that the slope equals zero. Informally we say that X is insignificant.

F. Correlation Coefficient

1. The measure of the degree of association between two variables is the correlation coefficient, *r*. The correlation coefficient between two variables X and Y is the covariance of X and Y divided by the product of the standard deviation of X and the standard deviation of Y. $r = \text{Cov}(X,Y) / \sigma_X \cdot \sigma_Y$.

2. The correlation coefficient ranges from -1 to +1. Zero indicates no correlation, whereas +1 is perfect positive correlation and -1 is perfect negative correlation.

G. Analysis of Variance

1. The regression model can be used to predict the values of the dependent variable.

2. The *coefficient of determination*, or R^2, is the percent of the dependent variable's variation that is explained by the independent variable or variables. An R^2 of .67 implies that 67% of the variation in the dependent variable is "explained" by the model, and of course, 33% of the variation is left unexplained.

3. An *F-test* can be used to test if the estimated regression explains a significant portion of the dependent variable. Using the F-table in the Appendix, if the calculated F ratio is greater than the critical F value, then we can reject the hypothesis that there is no relationship between the dependent variable and the independent variable or variables.

H. Multiple Linear Regression Model

1. Most economic relations depend on several independent variables. The quantity demanded is typically dependent on price, price charged by competitors, and other variables. We can write a general linear function in m-variables as:

$$Y = \alpha + \beta_1 \cdot X_1 + \beta_2 \cdot X_2 + \beta_3 \cdot X_3 + \beta_4 \cdot X_4 + \dots + \beta_m \cdot X_m + \varepsilon$$

2. Additional assumptions for multiple regression are (i) the number of observations must exceed the number of independent variables plus 1; and (ii) no exact linear relationship exists among the independent variables.

3. The independent variables can be numerical (such as age, income) or categorical (gender or marital status). Categorical variables can be transformed into *dummy variables*. Gender (M or F) can be changed into zero-one independent variable, as in D={1 if female, and 0 if male}.

4. Estimating multiple linear regressions involves matrix algebra. Computer software, such as ForeProfit, SAS, SPSS, Excel, Lotus 1-2-3, or Minitab do these computations swiftly.

5. The *standard error of the estimate*, s_e, can be used to construct prediction intervals. An *approximate* 95-prediction interval for Y is $\pm 2 \cdot s_e$, just as it was for simple linear regression.

6. Similarly, *each* coefficient can be subjected to hypothesis testing. The null hypothesis H_o: $b_i = \beta_o$ versus an alternative hypothesis H_a: $b_i \neq \beta_o$.

7. The estimated t-statistic is: $t_i = (b_i - \beta_o)/s_{bi}$. As before, the hypothesis may be whether or not a particular coefficient is different from zero. In that case, the estimated t-statistic is: $t_i = b_i/s_{bi}$.

8. The coefficient of determination, or R^2, is the percent of the variation in the dependent variable explained by all of the independent variables. The coefficient of determination is nondecreasing in the number of variables used. Some software programs, such as ForeProfit, provide an *Adjusted R^2* that may rise or fall as more variables are included into the regression.

9. The *F-ratio* tests if all the coefficients equal zero. A large F-ratio indicates that we can reject the hypothesis that none of the variables matter statistically.

I. Problems in Applying the Regression Model

1. *Autocorrelation* (sometimes called serial correlation) is the violation of the assumption that error terms are independent. If the error terms have a pattern, clearly the best solution is to find the explanatory variable or variables which "explain" the pattern.

   a. THE PROBLEM: Although coefficients are unbiased, t-statistics are unreliable.

   b. THE DIAGNOSIS: Plot the residuals to look for pattern, or more precisely, use the *Durbin-Watson* statistic. Durbin-Watson, d, close to 2 indicates no serious autocorrelation. A quick rule of thumb: d > 2.5 or d < 1.5 indicates the presence of some autocorrelation. For an exact test, the book's appendix contains a Durbin-Watson table for determining critical Durbin-Watson points.

   c. THE CURE: The first best solution is to find the missing explanatory variables. Alternatively, the data can be transformed into first differences that eliminates first order autocorrelation.

2. *Heteroscedasticity* is the violation that error terms have constant variance. If the variance increases or decreases, the standard error of estimate will depend on which range of data is used.

   a. THE PROBLEM: Although the coefficients are unbiased, t-statistics are unreliable.

   b. THE DIAGNOSIS: Plot the residuals to look for violations from *homoscedasticity* (constant variance). Alternatively, a table of the absolute value of residuals and the independent variables may help detect heteroscedasticity.

   c. THE CURE: Transform the data into groups, or transform data by using logarithms.

3. *Specification and Measurement Errors*. Specification error is a violation that one or more significant explanatory variables are omitted from the model. Measurement error is a violation since the data does not represent the true variable.

   a. THE PROBLEM: Coefficients may be biased, as omitted variables or errors may be correlated with independent variables.

b. THE DIAGNOSIS: Try other functional forms and other variables. Determine if the estimates of the coefficients are highly dependent on the group of variables selected, or if the coefficient estimates are relatively insensitive to functional form specified or variables selected.

c. THE CURE: For measurement error, try to use better data especially for independent variables. For specification errors, try a variety of models to find the best fitting model.

4. *Multicollinearity* is the violation that the independent variables are indeed *independent* of each other.

a. THE PROBLEM: Although the coefficients are unbiased, the coefficients are unreliable as slight variations in a sample will lead to large swings in coefficient values, and the t-statistics are unreliable.

b. THE DIAGNOSIS: Regressions with relatively high coefficients of determination, but with mostly insignificant coefficients, according to t-tests, exhibit classic symptoms of multicollinearity.

c. THE CURE: Some suggest dropping a variable from the model if it is highly correlated with other variables. If the purpose of the model is forecasting, and since the coefficients are unbiased, perhaps the multicollinearity can be ignored. Dropping a variable may reduce the explanatory power of a forecasting model.

J. Simultaneous Equations and the Identification Problem

1. When demand does not change, and supply shifts over time, the observed equilibrium points will all be on the demand curve. Agricultural products have fluctuating supply but relatively stable demand functions. A single equation model would correctly estimate the demand function.

2. When supply does not change, and demand shifts around over time, the observed equilibrium points will all be on the supply curve. A single equation model would estimate the supply function.

3. When both demand and supply curves shift over time, the observed equilibrium points will not provide estimates for either the true demand function or the true supply function.

4. The problem is that price appears in BOTH the demand and supply functions. Hence, price is not a true independent variable, but is determined *endogenously* within a system of equations of demand and supply.

5. To avoid the problem of simultaneity, econometric models attempt to explain each endogenous variable as functions of the other variables in the model. These equations are called the *structural equations*. Modeling a system of equations attempts to eliminate the simultaneity problem.

6. Techniques such as *Two Stage Least Squares* are well suited to estimate a system of equations. For such systems to be estimated correctly, generally there must be sufficient numbers of independent or *exogenous* variables in the other equations for the system to be *identified*, which means that the coefficients of the reduced form regressions can be used to find the coefficients in the structural equation.

7. *Simultaneous Equations* typically involve a violation of the assumption that the independent variables are *independent* of other forces.

   a. THE PROBLEM: Coefficients are biased if important simultaneous relationships are ignored in the model.

   b. THE DIAGNOSIS: Economic reasoning can sometimes detect important omissions in modeling. Trying different functional forms and different equational systems can help detect if models using systems of equations provide better forecasts or higher explanatory power.

   c. THE CURE: Demand and supply models suggest simultaneity of price and quantity. Develop the structural equations in the model. Use techniques such as *two stage least squares* to provide unbiased estimates of the coefficients.

K. Applications of Empirical Demand Functions

   1. Leisure activities, such as the per capita membership in the United State Chess Federation (USCF) can be examined using regression analysis.

   2. It is found that price, income, number of TV stations, and other variables can explain a remarkable 96.8% of the variation in USCF membership.

True and False Questions

Agree or disagree with the following statements, and correct the part that is erroneous.

1. Multiple regression implies that variables are multiplied together.

2. The larger is the standard deviation of the estimate, the more precise is the prediction interval for forecasting.

3. The smaller is the standard error of the estimate, the larger will be the t-statistics, other things equal.

4. If historical relationships are used to predict future relationships between variables, we assume that the future will be similar to the past.

5. A linear regression is the most general functional form to use.

6. Adding more variables to an equation cannot reduce the coefficient of determination.

7. Correlation coefficients between two variables, X and Y, show whether causation is from Y to X, or from X to Y.

8. A manager could reasonably expect to use price of inputs, prices of substitutes, and income in a single equation demand model.

9. A linear functional form for demand functions assumes that price elasticities are constant.

10. Multiplicative functional forms for demand functions assume that the marginal effects of each variable depend on the values of all the other variables.

11. When deciding which functional form to select, always select the functional form with the highest price elasticity.

12. If the automobile price elasticity is -.70, the predicted percentage change in automobile of sales after a price increases 6 percent would be -8.5714 percent.

13. A linear regression model: $Q = a + b P + c I$, would likely produce a *demand function* if the product being studied were fresh strawberries.

14. In large samples, a t-statistic of 1 means that the coefficient is significantly different from zero.

15. When two independent variables in a regression are highly correlated with each other, we tend to have the econometric problem called autocorrelation.

Answers
1. Disagree. Multiple regression implies that there are several independent variables in the regression.
2. Disagree. The larger the standard deviation of the estimate, the wider and hence *less* precise will be the range of forecasting.
3. True.
4. True.

5. Disagree. A linear form is quite restrictive. A polynomial of degree n, where n is quite large, is more general in that it allows many different shapes.

6. True; however the adjusted R-square can decline as the number of variables increases in a regression.

7. Disagree. Correlation shows association, not causation.

8. Disagree. Prices of inputs is considered a supply equation variable.

9. Disagree. In linear demand functions, the point price elasticity is the coefficient on price times the price divided by the estimated quantity, $E_D = \beta_1 \cdot P/Q$.

10. True.

11. Disagree. Typically, the best fitting regression would be the best model. The highest R^2 or highest adjusted R-square would help in the selection.

12. Disagree. It would be -4.2 percent.

13. True. Strawberry supply tends to vary a great deal, whereas strawberry demand may tend to be relatively stable.

14. Disagree. Only if the t-statistic were greater than 2, would we tend to say that the coefficient was significantly different from zero.

15. Disagree. When two independent variables are highly correlated, we tend to find the problem of multicollinearity.

Multiple Choice Questions

1. Given a multiplicative demand curve of the form $Q_D = .4 \cdot P^{-.2} \cdot Y^{.3} \cdot A^{1.2}$ where Q = quantity, P = price, Y = income, and A = advertising, the price elasticity is:
   a. -.2
   b. .3
   c. 1.2
   d. 1.7

2. Given a linear demand curve of the form: $Q_d = .4 - .2 \cdot P + .3 \cdot Y + 1.2 \cdot A$, where Q = quantity, P = price, Y = income, and A = advertising, the income elasticity is:
   a. -.2
   b. .3
   c. 1.2
   d. depends on the income and the quantity

3. Given a double log demand curve of the form: $\log Q_d = -.91 - .2 \cdot \log P + .3 \log Y + 1.2 \log A$, where Q = quantity, P = price, Y = income, and A = advertising, the advertising elasticity of demand is:
   a. -.2
   b. .3
   c. 1.2
   d. 1.7
   e. depends on the price and the quantity

In questions 4 to 6 use the following:

A double log demand function was estimated using multiple regression analysis.

$$\log Q_X = a + b \log P_X + c \log Y + d \log P_R$$

With the dependent variable as $\log Q_X$, the results of this estimation were:

Independent Variable(s):	Beta	t-statistic
Constant Included	3.0	6.0
$\log P_X$	-1.6	-8.0
$\log Y$	0.3	3.0
$\log P_R$	-0.6	-2.0

---

4. The price elasticity, in this regression, is best described as:
   a. inelastic.
   b. unit elastic.
   c. elastic.
   d. inferior good.

5. If income rises by 10%, the quantity sold of commodity X will be expected to:
   a. increase by approximately 3%
   b. decrease by approximately 30%
   c. increase by approximately 6%
   d. increase by approximately 16%

6. The related good empirically appears to be a complementary good, as its coefficient is negative. If the price of the related good, P_R, falls by 20%, the quantity sold of commodity X will be expected to:
   a. fall by approximately 12%
   b. rise by approximately 12%
   c. fall by approximately 6%
   d. rise by approximately 6%

7. Error terms have a constant variance around regression line.
   a. multicollinearity
   b. autocorrelation
   c. heteroscedasticity
   d. none of the above

8. Error terms have increasing or decreasing variance around the regression line.

a. multicollinearity	b.	autocorrelation
c. heteroscedasticity	d.	none of the above

9. Linear regression analysis (ordinary least squares) fits a straight line through the data in such a way that:
   a. the errors are minimized.
   b. the sum of the errors is minimized.
   c. the sum of the absolute values of the errors is minimized.
   d. the sum of the squared errors is minimized.

10. Monthly data for sales of Ski Boards (Q) were used to explore the impact of price (P), and per capital national GDP (Y). With the parentheses containing the t-values, the results were:

$$\log Q = 0.4 - 1.6 \cdot \log P + 2.3 \cdot \log Y \qquad R^2 = .356$$
$$\quad\;\; (1.1)\;\; (-2.7) \qquad (0.82)$$

   a. Ski Boards are significantly affected by per capital GDP.
   b. Ski Boards are inelastic.
   c. A 1-% increase in price will reduce the quantity of Ski Boards demanded by 1.6%.
   d. All of the above.

In Questions 11 and 12 consider the estimation of the linear relation: $Y = a + bX$

The OLS regression output for a sample size of 29 observations is presented below:		
Dependent Variable: Y	R-Square: 0.7891	
	F-Ratio: 143.452	
Independent Variable(s):	Beta	Standard Error
Constant Included	22.34	10.789
X	2.33	1.356

11. How many *degrees of freedom* are there?
   a. 30
   b. 29
   c. 28
   d. 27

12. What is the estimated t-statistic for the estimated coefficient on X under the null hypothesis that $b = 0$? [Hint: estimated t-statistic is $t = (b - 0) / s_b$]
   a. 2.331
   b. 1.718
   c. 1.356
   d. .5817

13. Per capita membership in the United States Chess Federation is estimated using annual data and a linear functional form. Some of the results are presented below.

Membership = 146.8 - .263·P + .003·I + 5.036·Fischer -24.2·TV Stations

where P is price, I is per capital disposable income (inflation adjusted), Fischer is a dummy variable which is 1 in those years when Bobby Fischer was World Chess Champion, and TV Stations is the number of stations per 100,000 people.

Which of the following is correct?
a. Chess membership is a normal good.
b. Price increases have no effect on membership.
c. Television increases membership in the USCF.
d. Bobby Fischer was so good at chess that he apparently turned off people to the game.

For problems 14 and 15: Data on Income (in thousands of dollars), Age (years), Education (years), Experience on the job (years) was available for twenty people. Data is shown here:

Income	Age	Ed.	Exper.
5	29	2	9
9.7	36	4	18
28.4	41	8	21
8.8	30	8	12
21	34	8	14
26.6	36	10	16
25.4	61	12	16
23.1	29	12	9
22.5	54	12	18
19.5	30	12	5
21.7	28	12	7
24.8	29	13	9
30.1	35	14	12
28.5	65	15	19
24.8	59	14	17
26	30	15	6
38.9	40	16	17
22.1	23	16	1
33.1	58	17	10
48.3	60	21	17

Multiple regression analysis provided the following information:
The regression equation is:

Income = - 7.06 - 0.211 Age + 2.25 Education + 1.02 Experience

Variable	Coef	Stdev	t-ratio	p
Constant	-7.060	3.368	-2.10	0.052
Age	-0.2115	0.1098	-1.93	0.072
Education	2.2452	0.2534	8.86	0.000
Experience	1.0240	0.2518	4.07	0.001

$s = 3.784$ R-sq = 87.4%   R-sq(adj) = 85.1%

14. According to these regression results on INCOME:
    a. More than 50% of the variation in income is explained.
    b. Education is insignificant.
    c. Experience does not significantly raise income.
    d. A year of education is worth $1,000 additional income.

15. According to the regression results on INCOME:
    a. all the coefficients are significant at the 95% confidence level.
    b. the SIGNS of all of the coefficients make economic sense.
    c. a year of education appears to raise income more than a year of experience.
    d. it is highly unlikely that Age and Experience would lead to the problem of multicollinearity in this regression.

16. Your salary has been tied to sales revenue, where you are the manager of Maxine's Costume Emporium. Running a quick regression on numbers of costumes rented (Q), price (P), gross domestic product (GDP), and a seasonal variable for Mardi Gras, defined as a dummy variable which equals one if it is Mardi Gras season, you find:

    $$\text{Log } Q = .67 - .567 \text{ Log } P + 1.04 \text{ Log } GDP + .689 \text{ D}_{\text{Mardi Gras}}$$

    What would you suggest Maxine's Costume Emporium should do with its pricing policy to improve your own salary?
    a. Suggest lowering the rental prices on costumes.
    b. Suggest raising the rental prices on costumes, since demand is inelastic.
    c. Changing the calendar in the store so that Every Day is Mardi Gras.
    d. Start looking for a new job, since the price elasticity is negative.

17. When there is multicollinearity in an estimated regression equation,
    a. the coefficients are biased.
    b. the t-statistics are likely to be small even if the R-square is large.
    c. the coefficient of determination is likely to be small.
    d. the Durbin-Watson statistic equals 2.

18. The higher is the R^2 of a regression, the
    a. better is the fit.   b. greater is the problem of heteroscedasticity.
    c. coefficients are insignificant. d. greater is the problem of autocorrelation.

Answers

1. a
2. d
3. c
4. c
5. a
6. b (They are complementary goods, so a price reduction by the related good increases the quantity demanded of X. by 12%)
7. c
8. d
9. d
10. c
11. d
12. b
13. a
14. a
15. c
16. b
17. b
18. a

Matching An Econometric Diagnosis with its Name

For each problem in applying the regression model, answer one of the following terms.

   a. autocorrelation
   b. heteroscedasticity
   c. specification and measurement error
   d. multicollinearity
   e. simultaneous equation relationships

1.____ "The regression seemed to have a high R^2, but when I tested the null hypotheses that the coefficients were different from zero, they seemed insignificant."

2.____ "The regression software output said that the Durbin-Watson statistic was a low 1.12."

3.____ "Marla estimated a linear regression equation for demand, based on price, income, and competitor's prices. The thing that bothers me is that she did not seem to consider that supply affects price, too."

4.____ "After finishing the regression, I looked at a plot of the residuals. It seemed they tended to get larger and larger in absolute value over time."

5.____ "The data we get in our industry from the National association is always too high. They seem to think we want to hear good news for refrigerator demand and housing starts, rather than wanting to hear what really is happening."

Answers
1. d
2. a
3. e
4. b
5. c

Worked Problems

1. The product manager for a line of single-servings of **Spaghetti In A Bag** designed for the microwave tried pricing experiments in twelve different cities in the country. She had data for the quantity of monthly sales in cases (Q) and price (P) per serving in each city, per capita income (I) and per capita advertising (A) budgets in each the city. She selected as the best fit a linear form. The regression results were:

$$Q = 230 - 102 \cdot P + .011 \cdot I + 22 \cdot A \qquad R^2 = .78$$

a. If the average price is $1.59, the average I = $10,000, and the average A = $1.2, what is the predicted monthly sales in cases in a typical city?

Answer: Solve this by substituting into the demand equation: $Q = 230 - 102 \cdot P + .011 \cdot I + 22 \cdot A = 230 - 102 \cdot (1.59) + .011 \cdot (10000) + 22 \cdot (1.2) = \mathbf{204.22}$

b. If the price were $1.79 in Cincinnati, Ohio, and sales were 169.5 cases, estimate the price elasticity in the Cincinnati? At that price, is Spaghetti In A Bag elastic or inelastic? Would a still higher price raise or lower revenue in Cincinnati?

Answer: $E_D = (\partial Q/\partial P) \cdot (P/Q) = -102 \cdot (1.79/169.5) = -1.077$, which is elastic. A price increase would **reduce** total revenue in Cincinnati.

c. In Tuscaloosa, Alabama, advertising expenditure was $1.80 per capita. Sales averaged 190 cases per month over the three month experiment. What is the advertising elasticity in Tuscaloosa?

Answer: The advertising elasticity is $E_A = (\partial Q/\partial A) \cdot (A/Q) = 22 \cdot (1.80/190) = .208$. This indicates that a 1% increase in advertising in Tuscaloosa raises the quantity sold by only .208%.

d. If the advertising budget in Tuscaloosa were reduced 10%, what is the expected decline in sales? (Use the advertising elasticity to estimate the decline in monthly sales.)

Answer: If E_A = .208, then we would expect a 2.08 percent decline in sales in Tuscaloosa if advertising were reduced 10%. A 2.08 percent decline from 190 cases, would be down to about 186 cases.

2. A linear demand regression model found the following:

Dependent Variable: QUANTITY

Independent Variable(s):	Beta	t-statistic
Constant Included	10	2.5
PRICE	-2	1.3
INCOME	3	4.0

Summary of `Goodness of fit' statistics:
    Degrees of Freedom = 35
    R-square = .6510
    Adjusted R-Square = .6320
    Estimated F = 7.960
    Durbin-Watson statistic = 0.89

a. Write the demand function as an equation.

Answer: QUANTITY = 10 - 2·PRICE + 3·INCOME

b. Do the signs of the coefficients make economic sense?

Answer: Yes. Price is negatively related to quantity, which is consistent with economic theory, and income is positively related to quantity, which is true of any normal good.

c. If PRICE = 5 and INCOME = 12, what is the predicted QUANTITY sold?

Answer: QUANTITY = 10 - 2·5 + 3·12 = **36**

d. Find the point price elasticity at PRICE = 5 and INCOME = 12.

Answer: The price elasticity is: $E_D = (\partial Q/\partial P) \cdot (P/Q) = (-2) \cdot 5/36 = -10/36 = -.2777$. Demand is inelastic.

. e. Which of the above coefficients are significantly different from zero?

Answer: It appears that INCOME is significant, whereas PRICE is not significant at the .05 significance level.

, f. Test the hypothesis that the coefficient on INCOME is equal to 1. Can you reject this hypothesis?

Answer: Yes. The standard error on INCOME must be .75, so the estimated t-statistic is: $t = (3 - 1)/.75 = 2.667$, which is significantly different from 1.

g. Does there appear to be any econometric problems with the model given above?

Answer: Yes. The Durbin-Watson statistic shows that autocorrelation may be a problem.

3. You have been hired by **Heat Wave Industries** as a business intern to forecast sales of microwaves. The Vice-President of Operations, to whom you report, has asked you to help her with the economics of several of her business problems. In order to keep the numbers small, we will deal with "units" of output. Working together with your market research department, you have come up with three possible equations for forecasting microwave demand:

A. $Q = 4.2 - .4 \cdot I + .6 \cdot M + .2 \cdot U$ R^2 is .926
    (4.4) (2.0) (3.1) (2.0)

B. $Q = 3.8 + 0.2 \cdot I - 0.2 \cdot U + 0.6 \cdot A$ R^2 is .868
    (2.02) (3.02) (1.07) (2.03)

C. $Q = 3.0 - 0.2 \cdot P + 0.1 \cdot I + 0.1 \cdot M$ R^2 is .928
    (4.1) (2.2) (6.4) (3.21)

Where Q is the number of units of microwaves demanded, I is the disposable personal income, M is the number of new marriages, U is the unemployment rate, P is the price of microwaves, and A is the dollar volume of automobile sales. The numbers in the parentheses contain the t-values.

(i) Which forecasting equation do you recommend as the "best fitting?"

Answer: We would select regression (C), as it has the best fitting regression based on the coefficient of determination (R^2).

(ii) Given the following data, use equation B to forecast NEXT year's sales at Heat Wave.

Variable	This Year	Next Year
I	50	60
M	10	20
U	7	6
P	20	25
A	7	8

Answer: By substituting the predicted values into equation B, we find,

$Q = 3.8 + 0.2 \cdot I - 0.2 \cdot U + 0.6 \cdot A = 3.8 + 0.2(60) - 0.2(6) + 0.6(8) = 19.4$ units.

(iii) In equation A, which of the coefficients have the "wrong" sign from economic intuition?

Answer: The negative sign on income is counter-intuitive. We would expect microwaves to be a normal good, so the sign "should" be positive. Similarly, the positive sign on unemployment is odd. We would expect sales of microwaves to rise as the unemployment rate declines.

4. **Household Manufacturing** has collected the following data on quantity sold (Q), price (P), income (I), and advertising (A).

Period	Quantity	Price	Income	Advertising
1	120	8.0	10	3
2	165	4.0	22	7
3	120	7.0	20	5
4	165	3.0	20	8
5	180	4.0	30	8
6	90	10.0	19	6
7	150	4.0	18	10.2
8	190	1.6	25	9.3
9	160	5.0	30	8
10	200	2.0	35	9.5

a. Use the multiple regression package in "ForeProfit" or other regression packages to estimate the <u>linear</u> relationship between quantity as the dependent variable and price, income, and advertising as independent variables with a constant term included. Write the linear <u>equation</u> that you find.

Answer: The regression results are:

Dependent variable: Q

Independent variable(s):	Beta	t-statistic
Constant included	205.86	10.64
P	-12.24	-8.70
I	1.41	3.35
A	-3.34	-1.86

Summary of `Goodness of fit' statistics:

Degrees of freedom = 6

R-square = .973

Adj R-Sqr = .959

Estimated F = 71.67

This can be written as the following linear equation:

$$Q = 205.86 - 12.24 \cdot P + 1.41 \cdot I - 3.34 \cdot A$$

b. Do the signs of the coefficients make economic sense? Which of the coefficients are significant? (alpha = .025, df = 6, critical t-statistic = 2.447)

Answer: The sign on advertising is negative, which means that advertising hurts sales. This does not make economic sense. We cannot reject the hypothesis, however, that the advertising coefficient equals zero. Price and income, have the expected signs and are both significantly different from zero.

Net Sources

Discussion of empirical demand elasticities appears in the popular press, legal cases, and in academic journals.

1. **Economic Journals:** Article abstracts and search tools are available for finding work on particular industries in the following sites:

EconBase: *www.elsevier.com:80/homepage/sae/econbase/menu.sht* (67 Journals and many thousands of articles of economics journals published by Elsevier)

Journal of Agricultural and Applied Economics: *www.agecon.uga.edu/~jaae/jaae.htm* (Explores applied problem in international economics and agriculture)

Rand Review *www.rand.org* (Policy issues analyzed using economics)

2. **Business Periodicals:** Discussion of firm activity, responses to changing demand conditions, pricing, and other issues can be found by reading about firms.

The Economist magazine	*www.economist.com/*
USA Today	*www.usatoday.com/*
Business Week	*www.businessweek.com/*
Money magazine	*www.money.com/money/*
Fortune magazine	*www.fortune.com/*

3. **PROJECT:** In the Fortune magazine site above, enter the *Fortune 500* list. Find the 500th largest firm, and read its page by clicking its stock ticker. For example, if GM is the largest firm, the click GM. As you do this, think about what data you would like to have to estimate the demand curve for that firm's most prominent product or service.

Appendix 4A

Nonlinear Regression Models

Many relationships in economics and business are nonlinear. The growth pattern for many businesses, plants, and animals has a period of fast growth, followed by more moderate growth rates. Some of the many nonlinear models, which may be applied to demand models, are discussed in this appendix. The text of this appendix is available on the Internet. The discussion of this appendix is placed here, next to materials in Chapter 4.

A. Nonlinear Regression Models

1. *Semi-logarithmic transformations.* Relationships between variables may not be linear. Sometimes taking the logarithm of the dependent variable or an independent variable improves the R^2. Examples are:

$$\log Y = \alpha + \beta \cdot X \quad \text{or} \quad Y = \alpha + \beta \cdot \log X$$

The first example is one where Y grows exponentially at rate β in X; that is, β percent growth per period. In the second example in the box, Y doubles each time X increases by the square of X.

2. *Double-Log Transformations.* Multiplicative relationships in demand functions and production functions are quite common. An example is: $Q = A \cdot K^{\alpha} \cdot L^{\beta}$

The log of both sides is: $\log Q = \log A + \alpha \cdot \log K + \beta \cdot \log L$

Least squares regression can be applied to the transformed data. ForeProfit allows transformation of dependent and independent variables to logarithms, squares of variables, and reciprocals.

3. *Reciprocal Transformations.* The relationship between variables may be inversely related. Sometimes taking the reciprocal of a variable improves the fit of the regression as in the example: $Y = \alpha + \beta \cdot (1/X)$

4. *Polynomial Transformations.* Quadratic, cubic, and higher degree polynomial relationships among variables are not uncommon in business and economics. Generally profit and revenue is a cubic function of output. Quadratic functions are U-shaped or arch-shaped. Cubic functions have an S-shape. For example:

$$\pi = \alpha \cdot Q + \beta \cdot Q^2 + \gamma \cdot Q^3 \text{ is a cubic profit function.}$$

If higher order polynomials substantially increase the coefficient of determination, then the added complexity may be worth it. If the adjusted R-square increases with higher polynomial orders, then include these nonlinear variables.

True and False Questions

Agree or disagree with the following statements, and correct the part that is erroneous.

1. The weight of an English Springer Spaniel puppy, W, between the age of 1 week and 50 weeks, has been collected. Using this time series of data, we would expect a linear regression model: $W = a + b \cdot T$ would work well to predict the weight at week 51, where T is time in weeks.

2. If we use a double log transformation, then the regression is linear in the logarithms of the variables.

3. A polynomial transformation of degree three is called quadratic.

4. The price (P) of a zero coupon bond, other things equal, rises closer and closer to its Par Value as time passes. Suppose T represents the number of months left until the zero coupon bond matures. If we had several observations on the price of the bond, and market interest rates (R), we could explore the following reciprocal transformation: $P_T = b \cdot (1/T) + c \cdot R$

In this regression, we would expect **b** to be negative and **c** to be positive.

5. The earnings regression on a sample of 5,250 workers gave the following result: $E = .45 + .043 \cdot \text{Log } T$, where T was the number of years the workers were employed (called tenure on the job). We can conclude that workers in this sample typically received a 4.3 percent increase per year.

Answers:

1. Disagree. Growth of animals is not likely to be linear. We may wish to try alternative transformations. One possibility is a cubic polynomial: $W = a + b \cdot T + c \cdot T^2 + d \cdot T^3$, because growth rates may follow an S-curve, rising rapidly, rising moderately, and finally rising very little.

2. True.
3. Disagree. A polynomial of degree three is cubic. A polynomial of degree two is quadratic. The degree of a polynomial depends on the largest *power* to which a variable is raised. If a variable is squared, it is quadratic. If it is cubed (raised to the power three) it is cubic.
4. Disagree. We would expect **b** to be positive. As T gets closer to zero, (1/T) rises. The price should also rise as (1/T) rises; hence, **b** should be positive. Also, **c** should be negative, because increases in the interest rates R make bonds less valuable.
5. True.

Multiple Choice Questions

1. Consider the nonlinear function: $Y = a \cdot X^b \cdot Z^c$
   If we wanted to estimate this function using the double-log transformation, the estimation we would actually "run" is:
   a. $Y = a + bX + cZ$
   b. $\log Y = (\log a) + b(\log X) + c(\log Z)$
   c. $Y = a + b(\log X) + c(\log Z)$
   d. none of the above.

In questions 2 through 4, use the following quarterly sales forecasting model of the form:

$$S_t = a + b \cdot T + c_1 \cdot D1 + c_2 \cdot D2 + c_3 \cdot D3$$

The dollar volume of sales, S_t, was estimated using quarterly data for the period 1994-I through 2001-IV. The variables D1, D2, and D3 are, respectively, dummy variables for the first, second, and third quarters. (For example, D3 is equal to one if the observation is from the third quarter and is zero otherwise.) T is a time variable which measures in integers the number of quarters, with 1994-I = 1, for 32 quarters. The results of this estimation were:

Dependent Variable: S_t F-Ratio: 85.487
Observations: 32   R-Square: 0.7631

Variable	parameter estimate	standard error
Intercept	150.0	2.0
T	12.0	0.5
D1	-60.0	20.0
D2	-40.0	25.0
D3	-50.0	10.0

Note: Use 2.052 as the critical value of t-statistic at the 95% confidence level.

2. The forecast for the third quarter of 2002 (where T = 35) is:
   a. 570
   b. 520
   c. 112
   d. 484

3. What is the estimated *intercept* of the trend line in the second quarter?
   a. 150
   b. 90
   c. 110
   d. 100

4. The estimates indicate that:
   a. sales in the fourth quarter are significantly greater than sales in any other quarter.
   b. sales in the first quarter are significantly greater than sales in any other quarter.
   c. sales in the second and third quarters are significantly less than sales in the first quarter.
   d. sales in the first and third quarters are significantly less than sales in the fourth quarter.

5. Product life cycles are often thought to have a period of rapid growth, followed by declining growth, and eventual declining sales. If Q is sales measured in quantity sold, and T is time, which of the following functional forms would tend to pick up a product life cycle shape.
   a. $Q = a + b \cdot T + c \cdot T_2$
   b. $\log Q = a + b \cdot \log T$
   c. $\log Q = a + b \cdot T$
   d. $Q = a + b \cdot T + c \cdot T_2 + d \cdot T_3$

6. One functional form used to model the concept of saturation (as after some amount of income, people do not want more) is $Q = \alpha - 1/I$, where I is income and Q is quantity. If we drew this functional form for $\alpha > 0$ and $I > 1$, we find:
   a. This form rises to a peak, and then declines.
   b. This form rises at a slower and slower rate up to the highest point (α).
   c. This form continuously declines toward zero.
   d. This reciprocal form is U-shaped.

7. Consider the following model: $Y = \alpha + \beta_1 X + \beta_2 X^2 + \beta_3 X^3$. This form is called:
   a. linear
   b. cubic
   c. quadratic
   d. reciprocal

8. Not all demand "curves" are straight lines. We expect, for example, that the impact of price increases grows as the price rises. Which of the following demand estimates shows an increasing marginal impact of price on quantity?

a. $Q = 1,000 - 17 P$

b. $Q = 450 - 2 P + .5 P^2$

c. $Q = 2,600 + 5 P - 3 P^2$

d. $Q = 55,000 + .006 P$

Answers:

1. b

2. b ($S_{35} = 150 + 12 \cdot 35 - 60 \cdot 0 - 40 \cdot 0 - 50 \cdot 1 = 520$ for the third quarter of 2002)

3. c (the intercept is $150 - 60 = 90$, where $D2 = 1$)

4. d

5. d (a cubic shape will have two turning points, as it is S-shaped)

6. b (when I is infinite, Q is α).

7. b

8. c

Worked Problems

1. A single equation log linear demand function was estimated for Canadian copper. Data were transformed using natural logarithms. Define Q as tons of copper used annually. Let P be the average real price per pound in Canadian dollars each year. I is per capita real income at the start of each year. A is the average real price per pound of aluminum (a substitute for copper). X is an index of Canadian industrial production. The annual data came from the past fourteen years. (Parentheses contain standard deviations of the coefficients).

$$\log Q = 3.2 - 1.04 \cdot \log P + 2.21 \cdot \log I + .67 \cdot \log A + 1.5 \cdot \log X$$
$$\quad\quad (.3) \quad\quad (.5) \quad\quad\quad (.14) \quad\quad (.12)$$

$R^2 = .834$ 38 observations

a. What are the price, income, and cross-price elasticities for Canadian copper?

Answer: -1.04 is the price elasticity. 2.21 and .67 are the income and cross-price elasticities.

b. Is copper demand elastic or inelastic? Is copper a normal good or an inferior good? Is aluminum a substitute or a complement according to the regression results?

Answer: Copper is elastic. It is a normal good. Aluminum is a substitute.

c. If industrial production grew at 4%, what percentage growth in the Canadian demand for copper do you predict?

Answer: Since the elasticity of industrial production is 1.5, a 4% increase in industrial production would increase copper demand by +6 percent.

d. Test the hypothesis that the price elasticity is zero at conventional statistical levels of significance. Test the hypothesis that the coefficient on log P equals -1.

Answer: We reject the hypothesis that the coefficient on log P is zero (t= -8.5), but we cannot reject the hypothesis that the coefficient on log P is minus one, or unit elastic. The estimated $t = (b - 1)/\sigma = (-1.04 - (-1))/.3 = -.04/.3 = -.133$.

2. Economists have estimated the annual demand for Huffy bicycles in Northern California to be multiplicative:

$$Q_D = .34 \cdot P^{-5.3} \cdot I^{.9} \cdot A^{.24} \cdot P_M^{-.77}$$

where Q_D is the number of Huffy bicycles sold in Northern California, P is the average price of Huffy bicycles, I is disposal income in Northern California, A is the dollar amount of advertising done by Huffy, and P_M is the average price of mopeds.

a. Interpret the exponents of the independent variables.

Answer: The coefficients are elasticities of price, disposable income, advertising, and a cross price elasticity with mopeds.

b. Do the signs of the exponents make economic sense to you? Which does not make sense?

Answer: All make sense except the sign for mopeds. We would think that mopeds would be substitutes for bicycles.

c. If Huffy expands its advertising budget 3%, what percentage increase in Huffy sales in this region is anticipated?

Answer: Because of the estimated advertising elasticity is .24, a 3% increase in advertising will increase the number of Huffy bicycles sold by +.72 percent.

3. A log-linear demand function was estimated of the form, $Q_D = a \cdot P^b \cdot Y^c \cdot P_s^d$

The OLS results of this estimation for the dependent variable log Q were:

Independent Variable(s):	Beta	t-stat.	Std error
Constant Included	2.5	5.0	0.5
log P	-1.7	-8.5	0.2
log Y	0.4	4.0	0.1
log P_s	-0.6	2.0	0.3

Summary of `Goodness of fit' statistics:

Degrees of Freedom = 22
R-square = .9567
Adjusted R-Square = .9389

Note: Variables have their usual meanings for price, income, and price of a substitute good.

a. Is this demand curve elastic or inelastic?

Answer: It is elastic. $E_D = -1.7$, which is the coefficient on the double log regression.

b. If income rises 4 percent, what is the predicted percentage change in the quantity demanded?

Answer: With an income elasticity of .4, a 4% increase in income leads to a 1.6 percent increase in quantity.

c. What is the *critical* t-statistic for the hypothesis that the coefficient on log P equals zero at the .05 significance level? HINT: Look at Table 2 in the appendix of the textbook.

Answer: The critical t-statistic is 2.074 with 22 degrees of freedom.

d. Test the hypothesis that the coefficient on log P equal -1 (is unit elastic).

Answer: The estimate t-statistic is $\{(-1.7 + 1)/.2\} = -3.5$, which (in absolute value) is larger than the critical t-statistic of 2.074. We can reject the hypothesis that demand is unit elastic.

Chapter 5

Business and Economic Forecasting

Public and private enterprises operate under conditions of uncertainty. Management wishes to limit or control this uncertainty by predicting changes in the economic variables of costs, price, sales, and interest rates. Accurate forecasting can assist in the development of strategies to promote profitable trends and to reduce the harm from unprofitable ones. A forecast is merely a prediction concerning the future. Good forecasting will reduce, but not eliminate, the uncertainty that all managers feel.

A. Significance of Forecasting

1. Ford Motor Company was surprised by the shift of interest away from passenger cars to trucks and minivans. Ford began to emphasize its Explorer, a sports utility vehicle. Time will tell if this was good forecasting.

2. Good forecasting reduces uncertainty for managerial decision making.

3. The selection of forecasting techniques depends in part on the level of economic aggregation involved. The *hierarchy of forecasting* is:
    a. national economy, as in GNP.
    b. sectors of the economy, as in agriculture or plant & equipment expenditures.
    c. industry forecasts, as in the automobile industry.
    d. firm forecasts, as in the sales forecast for Ford, Jaguar, or SAAB.

4. The choice of a particular forecasting method depends on several *criteria*:
    a. costs of the forecasting method compared with its gains.
    b. complexity of the relationships among variables.
    c. the time period involved (long term *vs.* short term).
    d. the accuracy needed in the forecast.
    e. the lead-time between receiving information and the decision to be made.

5. The accuracy of a forecasting model is measured by how close the actual variable (Y), ends up to the forecasting variable ($\hat{Y}$). Forecast error is the difference ($\hat{Y}$-Y).

6. The average forecast error, over a series of N forecasts and actual figures, is called the root mean square error, RMSE:

$$RMSE = \sqrt{(1/N)\cdot\Sigma(\hat{Y}_t - Y_t)^2}$$

The smaller is RMSE, the better is the forecasting method.

7. The RMSE depends in part on the size of the variables being forecasted. Theil's U adjusts for size of the forecasted variables in the denominator. When RMSE equals zero in the numerator, then U = 0. The smaller is U, the better the accuracy.

$$\text{Theil's U} = RMSE / [\sqrt{(1/N)\cdot\Sigma(\hat{Y}_t)} + \sqrt{(1/N))\cdot\Sigma(Y_t)}]$$

B. Categories of Alternative Forecasting Techniques

1. Some techniques are qualitative in nature, whereas others are quantitative. *Qualitative techniques* that forecast direction of movements include surveys, opinion polling, and use of comparative statics with supply and demand curves.

2. There are two major branches of *quantitative techniques* which attempt to forecast the precise number for an economic variable.

   a. One branch uses *smoothing techniques* and forms of *time series* analyses such as *naive forecasting techniques* to predict the future from trends and patterns in the past. There need not be any economic rationale for the pattern, but if a pattern is seen, it is used to project the future.

   b. Another branch uses *econometric models* of macroeconomic systems or microeconomic demand and supply functions to predict the future. Economic theory is used to explain the relationships between variables, industries, or people.

3. Most forecasting is a blend of features of qualitative and quantitative techniques. This chapter emphasizes techniques that are often suitable for many kinds of managerial forecasting problems.

C. Time Series Analysis

1. *Time series data* are a series of observations ordered by time, whereas *cross sectional data* are an array of values at the same moment in time. Some data sets have elements of both time series and cross section, as in sales data over time for a dozen cities.

2. *Secular Trends* can be found visually by graphing data. More often, regression analysis is the primary tool for estimating the upward or downward drift in economic variables over time.

3. *Cyclical Variations* occur when there are major expansions and contractions in the economy, or a particular industry.

4. *Seasonal Variations* can be added with methods such as the ratio-to-trend method. Daily, weekly, monthly, or quarterly data provide trends. But if a particular part of the season is above or below the trend, the forecast is adjusted up or down by that percentage.

D. An Elementary Model: Naive Forecasting

1. The simplest model states that the forecast value of a variable for the next period (Y_{t+1}) will be the same as the value for the present period: $\hat{Y}_{t+1} = Y_t$. This model is easy to use and is particularly useful for forecasting over a short time period when the variation in Y is random.

2. Linear trends in the data can be included by adjusting to: $\hat{Y}_{t+1} = Y_t + (Y_t - Y_{t-1})$.

3. *Seasonal adjustments*. The naive model may be that the value for the same quarter in the previous year as the forecast for this quarter, plus an annual adjustment for year to year growth.

E. Secular Trends: Time Series Analysis

1. Many economic time series tend to grow over time. Appropriate forecasting models for secular trend include a linear trend and a constant rate of growth model.

   a. *Linear Trend Regression Model*: $\hat{Y}_t = \alpha + \beta{\cdot}t + \varepsilon_t$. The forecast, $\hat{Y}_t$, for period t is [$\alpha + \beta{\cdot}t$], since the expected error term is zero.

   b. *Constant Rate of Growth Trends:* $\hat{Y}_t = Y_0{\cdot}(1+g)^t$. This is best for variables that are growing a constant percent rate. Taking the natural logarithms of both sides yields:

$$\log \hat{Y}_t = \log Y_0 + [\log(1+g)]{\cdot}t = \alpha + \beta{\cdot}t$$

where $\alpha = \log Y_0$ and $\beta = \log(1+g)$ which is equivalent to a continuously compounded rate of growth. The formula is semi-log, since only the dependent variable remains in logarithms.

c.   *Declining Rate of Growth Trends*: As products saturate the market, it is not uncommon to find sales growth rates decline.

$$\log \hat{Y}_t = B_1 - B_2[1/t]$$

If both B_1 and B_2 are positive, the function rises at a declining pattern with a shape like the following curve.

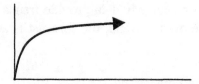

2. Population data are modeled using a constant rate of growth trend, whereas accumulation of inventory may better be modeled using a linear trend. However, the choice between models is an empirical rather than a theoretical issue. Use the one that works the best. The model with the better R-square or the lower root mean square error is the model that should be selected.

F. Seasonal Variations

1. Some time series patterns have predictable variation over the season. The demand for ice cream cones, for example, is greater in the summer than in the winter.

2. A *seasonal adjustment* can be calculated by finding the percentage of forecast error in the past. If sales in the month of August are on average 7% higher than was predicted over the past several years, the seasonally adjusted forecast for August should be 7% higher than would be predicted without the adjustment.

G. Seasonal Patterns and Dummy Variables

1. In the fourth quarter of each year the Christmas buying season hits. One popular technique uses *dummy variables*. A new variable, call it D for dummy, is created. Let D equal 1 if the quarter is a fourth quarter, and zero otherwise. The linear regression equation with the dummy using quarterly data would be:

$$\hat{Y}_t = a_0 + a_1 \cdot t + a_2 \cdot D + \varepsilon_t$$

2. If the coefficient on the dummy equals zero, then there is no unusually high or low values for $\hat{Y}_t$ in the fourth quarter. But if the coefficient on D is positive, this provides a quantitative measure of the impact of fourth quarter above the other quarters.

3. Dummy variables may be used for any data that is categorical, rather than numerical. Since there are four quarters in a year, as many as three dummy variables may be defined. The omitted quarter is the intercept.

H. Smoothing Techniques

1. *Moving Averages*--the forecast for the next period is the average of the last several periods. Moving averages assumes that there is no secular trend. A moving average of the past N periods can be used to predict the next period, as in:

$$Y_{t+1} = [Y_t + Y_{t-1} + Y_{t-2} + ... + Y_{t-N+1}]/N$$

2. The best moving average is the one that minimizes the sum of squared errors. The standard moving average uses an equal-weighted average of past observations. The weighing can be altered in numerous ways, including first-order exponential smoothing.

3. *First-Order Exponential Smoothing* is a weighted average forecast of the naive forecast (the most recent observation, Y_t) and a past forecast, Y_t, where: $0 < w < 1$.

$$\hat{Y}_{t+1} = w \cdot Y_t + (1 - w) \cdot \hat{Y}_t$$

By recursion, it can be shown that the forecast is *geometrically declining weighted forecast* of the past observations, with the greatest weights on the most recent observations and the smallest weights on the most distant observations:

$$\hat{Y}_{t+1} = w \cdot Y_t + (1 - w) \cdot w \cdot Y_{t-1} + (1 - w)^2 \cdot w \cdot Y_{t-2} + (1 - w)^3 \cdot w \cdot Y_{t-3} + ...$$

I. Barometric Techniques

1. *Barometric Forecasting Techniques.* Managers wish to find indicators that will foretell the future of the economy, their industry, or their product. Andrew Carnegie used to count the number of smoke-belching chimneys in Pittsburgh to forecast the level of business activity and consequently the demand for steel.

   a. If these indicators occur before changes in our economic variable of interest, they are called *leading indicators*.

   b. If they occur at the same time, they are *coincident indicators*.

   c. If they occur after changes in our variable of interest, they are *lagging indicators*.

2. Often forecasters have several indicators. To group them into together into a single measure, forecasters form either a:

    a.   *Diffusion index* -- typically the proportion of indicators that are positive.

    b.   *Composite index* -- a weighted average of several indicators.

3. *Survey and Polling Techniques.* Surveying opinion of prospective customers is another qualitative forecasting tool for making near-term predictions. Especially in the case of a new product, there is no past data to use to forecast the future. Attitudes of the prospective users of the product may be the only guide as to its future acceptance or rejection.

4. Some common sources for survey data are:

    a.   *Plant and equipment expenditures.* The <u>Survey of Current Business</u> publishes a quarterly plant and equipment expenditure survey and a capital appropriations survey.

    b.   *Inventory changes and sales expectations.* The National Association of Purchasing Agents conducts a survey of purchasing executives each month.

    c.   *Consumer expenditure plans.* The Survey Research Center at the University of Michigan surveys consumers on the likelihood of making future durable goods purchases and their attitudes to consumer indebtedness.

5. Sales Forecasting often relies on *Expert Opinion.* Polling the subjective opinion of business experts or salespeople is helpful. Those who have had a long association with the industry tend to have extensive knowledge which helps to predict the future direction of industry sales, costs, or prices.

    a.   The average opinion of a group is usually called the *consensus forecast*. Use of the average or median opinion can help to avoid extremes in forecasts.

    b.   *Surveys of consumer intentions* -- repeated surveys of potential customers often shows patterns that are helpful in forecasting. This is particularly true for the automobile industry.

J. Econometric Models

1. Econometric models use statistical techniques and economic theory to *explain* relationships between variables.

2. *Single-Equation Models* use one equation to represent the relationships among variables, as in a single demand function. All variables (whether they are logged, squared, dummy variable, *etc.*) are entered as independent variables to explain variation in the dependent variable. As an example:

$$Y^\wedge_t = a_0 + a_1 \cdot X_t + a_2 \cdot W_t + a_3 \cdot Z_t + a_4 \cdot \log X_t + a_5 \cdot D_t + etc.$$

   where X, W, Z, log X, and a dummy variable D, are all independent variables.

3. Sometimes, time series methods must be used to predict future independent variables, and those forecasts are used to forecast the dependent variable. The accuracy of the forecasted variable, $Y^\wedge_t$, depends on the precision of the regression and the accuracy of the forecasted independent variables, as well.

4. *Multiple-Equation Models* are used in economics. For example, a demand equation and a supply equation can be modeled separately. Other examples come from macroeconomics, with household consumption, business investment, and governmental sectors all modeled separately, but the entire economy is composed of all of these sectors.

True and False Questions

Agree or disagree with the following statements, and correct the part that is erroneous.

1. A manager would always prefer an econometric model for forecasting instead of a naive forecasting model.

2. A hierarchy of forecasting means that aggregation into larger units provides more accurate forecasts.

3. A consensus forecast from a group of experts tends to out perform a single expert over a period of time.

4. A "diffusion index" is the a measure of the amount of confusion among potential customers.

5. Some barometric indicators are leading, some are coincident, and some are lagging indicators.

6. Surveys can be used as a qualitative forecasting technique.

7. Secular trends, cyclical variations, seasonal variations, and random variations in time-series data mean the same thing.

8. A moving average can be a better forecasting technique than a linear trend when the random fluctuations are quite pronounced.

9. A linear trend can only go up, whereas a constant growth rate forecasting model allows growth and decline.

10. There are four years in each political cycle. Some people believe that a business cycle is greatly influenced by this political cycle. Using twenty years of annual data, a dummy variable would take on the values, 1, 2, 3, or 4 depending on the year of the political cycle.

11. Using 5 years of monthly data, we can use at most 11 monthly dummy variables to find a seasonal pattern.

12. It is impossible to forecast then next number from the following short series of numbers: {5, 13, and 15}.

Answers
1. Disagree. If a simple naive model provided more accurate forecasts, he or she would use it instead of a fancy econometric model.
2. Disagree. Macroeconomic models sometimes are more, and sometimes are less accurate. The hierarchy merely refers to different degrees of aggregation in economic modeling.
3. True.
4. Disagree. A "diffusion index" is a way to group several indicators, as in 4 of 10 indicators (40%) predict growth in sales.
5. True.
6. True.
7. Disagree. Secular trend is the long-term growth or decline in a series, whereas cyclical is intermediate movements up and down with the longer trend. Seasonal variations deal with regular calendar cycles. Random variations have no cyclical or trend characteristics.
8. True. A moving average can smooth the random variations.
9. Disagree. Both can grow or decline.

10. Disagree. Dummy variables take on either 0 or 1. You could use three dummy variables for three of the years in the cycle.

11. True.

12. Disagree. Most of us would suggest the number 16 or 17. It looks like the early growth phase is slowing down. Notice that we did not even have to know WHAT it was we were forecasting.

Multiple Choice Questions

1. An example of a *time series* data set is one for which the:
   a. data would be collected for a given firm for several consecutive periods (*e.g.,* months).
   b. data would be collected for several different firms at a single point in time.
   c. regression analysis comes from data randomly taken from different points in time.
   d. use of regression analysis would impossible.

2. To model population trends in San Diego, California, from 1940 to the present, probably the best forecasting model would be:
   a. linear trend regression.
   b. constant rate of growth trend regression.
   c. three-year moving average.
   d. first order exponential smoothing.

3. Surveys of opinion and sentiment:
   a. provide the basic quantitative material for forecasting.
   b. are too subjective to be of any use.
   c. provide qualitative information on attitudes even before trends appear in sales.
   d. are useful only in political issues.

4. Dummy variables are primarily used to:
   a. find the intelligence quotient of the researcher.
   b. measure the trend over time.
   c. measure the effect of a variable that can be only one of two categories.
   d. add a quadratic variable to the regression.

5. We would expect that a constant percentage growth rate regression would be better than a linear trend regression model to predict the future:
   a. board feet of wood using a time series of successive years of tree growth.
   b. time it will take to complete a knitting project, from a time series of the amount of knitting completed at successive hours of work.
   c. both a and b
   d. neither a nor b

6. Suppose that over the past four years, sales revenue (in millions) has been 1.5, 1.8, 2.1, and 2.4. We observe that:
   a. a three-period moving average forecast would be 2.1 million.
   b. the series seems to display a linear trend.
   c. the naive forecast for next period would be 2.4 million.
   d. all of the above.

7. The optimal smoothing constant (w) for using first order exponential smoothing is the value which:
   a. most closely approaches 1.
   b. is closest to zero.
   c. minimizes the sum of the differences between forecasted and actual observations.
   d. minimizes the root mean square error.

8. In a linear trend regression, the forecast for sales, S, is $S_t = 240 + 3 \cdot T$, then:
   a. the 240 is the forecast of sales at time 0.
   b. the 3 is the percentage rate of growth of sales.
   c. the forecast is 247, at time 7.
   d. sales are trending down.

9. In a constant percentage rate of growth forecasting model for the quantity demanded, Q, the regression estimated was: $\text{Log } Q_t = 1.04 + .06 \cdot T$, then:
   a. the quantity is rising at 4% per period.
   b. the forecast for quantity demanded at time $T = 10$ is $Q_t = 1.64$.
   c. the forecast for quantity demanded at time $T = 5$ is $\text{Log } Q_t = 1.34$.
   d. the forecast for quantity is declining modestly.

10. Three leading indicators have been collected regarding growth of the economy. Giving equal weight to the following indicators, report the results using a *diffusion index*.

    Indicator #1 +3%
    Indicator #2 +4%
    Indicator #3 -1%

    a. The index is up an average of 2%.
    b. The index is 2/3 or 67%.
    c. Eliminate the negative outlier and index is up an average of 3.5%.
    d. Eliminate the highest and lowest and the index is up 3%.

11. Using the data in question 10, the *composite index* is:
    a. up 6%
    b. up 2%
    c. up 67%
    d. down 33%

12. Sales data for February through July are:

February	300
March	267
April	321
May	318
June	390
July	324

    a. The two-month moving average is 324.
    b. The three-month moving average is 324.
    c. The four-month moving average is 324.
    d. The five-month moving average is 324.

13. Assume a regression equation of $Y = 5.0 + 3.0 \cdot X$ where X is units of fertilizer and Y are bushels of wheat. Select the correct statement.
    a. A one-unit increase in fertilizer will cause an 8-bushel increase in wheat.
    b. A one-unit increase in fertilizer will cause a 3-bushel increase in wheat.
    c. A one-unit increase in fertilizer will cause a 3% increase in bushels of wheat.
    d. None of the above.

14. Assume a demand equation of. $\log Q = 3.00 \log Y - 0.5 \log P$, where P is price and Y is income. Select the correct statement:
    a. A one-unit increase in P will decrease Q by 0.5 units.
    b. A 0.5 unit increase in P will decrease Q by one unit.
    c. A one percent increase in P will decrease Q by 0.5 percent.
    d. A 0.5 percent increase in P will decrease Q by one percent.

15. Select the incorrect statement: First order exponential smoothing is a forecasting technique which:
    a. is a weighted average of the actual prior period values and the forecasted prior period values.
    b. uses a smoothing constant, w, which is between zero and one.
    c. is used when data observations from several years ago contain more information than recent data observations.
    d. works best when there is no significant trend in the data.

16. The forecasting technique which attempts to forecast short-run changes, and makes use of leading economic indicators, is known as:
    a. barometric forecasting
    b. time-series forecasting
    c. naïve forecasting
    d. moving averages

17. A dummy variable (D=1) is used for seasonally adjusting fourth quarter sales, using data over three years. Let sales be given as: Sales = $300 + 10 \cdot T + 18 \cdot D$. What are forecasted sales for the fourth quarter in fourth year (T = 16 and D = 1)?
    a. 358
    b. 460
    c. 310
    d. 478

18. Over a four-year period, a firm's sales (millions) were $200, $220, $180, and $200. Use exponential smoothing with a smoothing constant (alpha) of .5 to forecast the fifth period's sales. A worksheet is partially completed to aid your calculations.

	Actual	Forecasted
Worksheet:	200	200
	220	200
	180	
	200	
	?	_____

    a. $197.50
    b. $195.00
    c. $200.00
    d. $199.50

19. Economic indicators or barometric forecasting can be used for qualitative forecasting. Which of the following would you expect to be a good leading indicator for refrigerator sales?
    a. the help wanted index in the New York Times
    b. the consumer price index
    c. the diffusion index for the stock market by the eleven elves who appear on Louis Rukeyser's *Wall Street Week* TV show.
    d. the index of new housing starts

20. Using a semi-log regression model on 17 years of data on per capita real personal income in Cologne, Germany. The results given as follows:
    $$\text{Ln Income} = 4 + .013\ T \qquad R^2 = .782 \qquad N = 17$$
    $$(3.14)$$
    The parenthesis contains the t-statistic. These results show:
    a. that the R^2 is too large.
    b. that per capita real income grew at 1.3% per year continuously compounded.
    c. that there was no trend in the data for personal real income per capita in Cologne.
    d. that .013, the coefficient on time, was insignificantly different from zero. [Note: The critical t-value for 15 degrees of freedom is 2.131.]

Answers

1.	a	11.	b
2.	b	12.	d
3.	c	13.	b
4.	c	14.	c
5.	a	15.	c
6.	d	16.	c
7.	d	17.	d
8.	a	18.	a
9.	c	19.	d
10.	b	20.	b

Worked Problems

1. Monthly ice cream sales of the **Prizer Creamery International** is estimated by a regression trend line over the past 14 months to be:$S_t = 30{,}950 + 87.5 \cdot t$. Ice cream sales are measured in gallons. Predict the sales in gallons in month 15.

    Answer: Substitute 15 for T in the equation. The forecast would be:
    $30{,}950 + 87.5(15) = 32{,}262.5$ gallons.

2. Macroeconomic forecasters predict no particular change in general business conditions. The marketing department predicts that the competitors will soon announce a price increase. As a product manager, what is your qualitative forecast for sales of your product?

    Answer: Our demand curve will shift out and to the right. We expect more sales, and we will have room to raise our price somewhat as well. These are comparative static results using familiar supply and demand curves.

3. Profits in the airline industry are inversely related to the price of fuel oil, and lag fuel oil prices by around 6 months. What is the qualitative forecast for airline profitability if fuel oil prices have recently begun to rise?

    Answer: Profits in the airline industry will decline about 6 months after the increase in fuel oil prices. Airline stock prices may react faster than accounting profits, as the expected future profits affect investors' valuation of firms.

4. Five economists have given five different forecasts for interest rates, GNP, and automobile sales. Form a consensus forecast for interest rates, GNP, and automobile

sales from the following, where the consensus is measured both as a median and a mean.

	Interest Rates	GNP	Auto Sales
Prof. Gloom	+ 1 percent	- 1 percent	- 2 percent
Mr. Modest	no change	+ 1 percent	no change
Miss Cheerful	- 1 percent	+ 5 percent	+ 3 percent
Ms. Money	- 1 percent	+ 2 percent	no change
Dr. Boom	- 2 percent	+ 4 percent	+ 1 percent

Answer: The consensus forecast for <u>interest rates</u>: Median is a decline of 1 percent, Mean is a decline of 0.6 percent.

The consensus forecast for <u>GNP</u>: Median is an increase of 2 percent, Mean is an increase of 2.2 percent.

The consensus forecast for <u>Auto Sales</u>: Median is no change; Mean is an increase of 0.4 percent.

5. The survey of potential buyers taken by **New Age Products, Ltd.** of a new adult flavor of gum (Amaretto Spice Gum) found the following. Fifteen percent say they would not try it; 20% say they would be willing to try it, but would not likely chew it in the future; and 65% say they would eagerly try this new product and perhaps continue to use it. The same survey asked how they felt about a different flavor (Horseradish Sour Gum). The results were that 47% said they would not try it; 50% said they would be willing to try it, but would not likely chew it in the future; and 3% said they would eagerly try this new product and perhaps continue to use it. What is the likely forecast for the two different new gum products?

Answer: The survey results at New Age Products, Ltd., not unexpectedly, show a much larger group of potential repeat customers for the Amaretto Spice Gum flavor than the Horseradish Sour Gum flavor. We would expect that survey respondents know their preferences concerning the kinds of flavors they like and dislike, especially in regard to candy snacks. Therefore, we should not proceed any further with the Horseradish Sour Gum. The name is enough for customers overwhelmingly to reject it. The Amaretto Spice Gum may, however, succeed.

6. **The Chicago-Style Hot Dog Co.** estimated a linear time series regression for using data from the past fifteen years.

a. Use their regression to forecast the next three years of sales (t=16, 17, and 18), where Y = sales, t = the time trend (1 to 15).

$$Y_t = 12,000 + 33 \cdot t \qquad R^2 = .87$$

Answer: By substituting t=16, 17, and 18 into the equation we find: 12,528 for t=16; 12,561 for t=17; 12,594 for t=18. These are the forecasts for Chicago-Style Hot Dogs.

b. Suppose the Chicago-Style Hot Dog Co. estimated a semi-log regression using natural logarithms. What do you forecast for sales over the next three years?

$$\log Y_t = 9.3 + .011 \cdot t \qquad R^2 = .90$$

Answer: By substituting t=16 into the semi-log equation, we find that the $\log Y_{16}$ = 9.476. The anti-log of 9.476 is found by taking the exponential of 9.476; that is, $e^{9.476}$ which is Y_{16} = 13,042.91.

By identical procedures we can find that $\log Y_{17}$ = 9.487 which is Y_{17} = 13,187.17; and the $\log Y_{18}$ = 9.498 which is Y_{18} = 13,333.03;

c. Which forecasting equation should you select?

Answer: The better fitting model is the constant growth model which has a higher coefficient of determination (R^2).

7. **Zacks Investment** and **IBES** are two competing services that forecast earnings of companies. You attempt to determine which forecast service has the lowest average forecast error for earnings of Service Merchandise Co. To keep from biasing the results with your own views, you list the two forecasters as H and G, after randomly picking which firm is H or which firm is G. Four years of hypothetical data are provided:

H	*G*	*actual earnings*
.87	.86	.84
1.03	1.01	1.05
1.10	1.11	1.01
1.00	.99	.88

Does H or G have the **lowest** root mean square error? Are there alternative ways to look at which prediction is most accurate?

Answer: The root mean square error (RMSE) for H is:

$$\{(1/4)[(.84 - .87)^2 + (1.05\text{-}1.03)^2 + (1.01\text{-}1.10)^2 + (.88\text{-}1.00)^2]\}^{1/2} = .0771$$

The root mean square error for G is:

$$\{(1/4)[(.84 - .86)^2 + (1.05\text{-}1.01)^2 + (1.01\text{-}1.11)^2 + (.88\text{-}.99)^2]\}^{1/2} = .0776$$

We find that H has slightly lower RMSE for this small sample.

Alternative ways to compare accuracy involve seeing which is the better forecasting technique in each year. We see that G is more accurate in the first and last years, whereas H is more accurate in the two middle years. These kinds of tests are nonparametric, since we are not relying on means or other moments of the distribution.

8. Mary Elizabeth McCartney is forecasting her firm's salary expense using time series methods. She has data for the past eight years, with E for salary expense. She tried three functional forms, with T as the time trend.

Data

E	T	T^2	T^3	l/T
67000	1	1	1	1
72333	2	4	8	0.5
79900	3	9	27	0.333333
99300	4	16	64	0.25
144000	5	25	125	0.2
222000	6	36	216	0.166666
399300	7	49	343	0.142857
389600	8	64	512	0.125

MODEL (i) $E = a + b \cdot T + c \cdot T^2$ *Quadratic*

	Coeff.	Std. Error
Constant	+88394.48	---
T	-30848.90	28904.78
T^2	+9200.19	3135.163

$$R^2 = .939217$$

MODEL (ii) $E = a + b \cdot T^3 + c \cdot (1/T)$ *Cubic with a reciprocal term*

	Coeff.	Std. Error
Constant	68864.58	---
T^3	723.65	116.25
(1/T)	-5645.00	72821.25

$$R^2 = .928071$$

MODEL (iii) $E = a + b \cdot T$ *Linear*

	Coeff.	Std. Error
Constant	-49608.40	---
T	+51952.79	9444.21

$$R^2 = .834533$$

a. Predict salary expense in period 9 using a *3-year moving average*.

Answer: The three-year moving average is found by adding the salary expense in periods 6, 7, and 8, and then dividing by 3. That is, **336,966.67** = [(222,000 + 399,300 + 389,600)/3]

b. Using the simplest *naive forecast*, what will salary expense be in period 9?

Answer: The naive forecast would be **389,600.00**, which is what it was in period 8.

c. Which forecasting *regression model* should Mary select?

Answer: There are different meanings to "should", but if Mary wishes to predict as accurately as possible, she should select the Quadratic model. It is the best fitting regression.

d. What is the forecasted salary expense using the *linear model* for period 9?

Answer: By substituting T=9 into the linear model, we get E = -49608.40 +51952.79·T = **417,966.71**.

e. What is the forecasted salary expense using the *quadratic model* for period 9?

Answer: Similar to d, substitute T=9 and $T^2 = 81$ into:

$$E = +88394.48 - 30848.90 \cdot T + 9200.19 \cdot T^2 = \mathbf{555,969.77}$$

f. Look at your predictions in a, b, d, and e above. Which particular **number** do you think Mary *should* present at next week's budget meeting with the CFO? Why?

>*Answer:* This is a more complex question, which does not really have only one correct answer.

>If Mary thought that salary growth had stopped, then she should predict $389,600, the *naive forecast*.

>If she thinks that there will be some additional salary growth, then perhaps the *linear forecast*, 417,966.71.

>The quadratic model fits the past data the best, but the prediction from the *quadratic model* may seem too high.

>Forecasting often requires judgment. Go back to the table of data, do you think the CFO would believe $555,969 for salary expense given the past eight years of data? Probably not.

Net Sources

1. Leading indicators are readily available on the Internet. Four great sites are:

- The **Conference Board** Business Cycle Indicators at: *www.tcb-indicators.org/*

- **Business Cycle Indicators** *www.cris.com/~Netlink/bci/whatBCI.html* Offers a discussion of economic indicators, divided into 16 categories. Offers 10-year charts and international comparisons of industrial production.

- **The Dismal Scientist** *www.dismal.com/* The Dismal Scientist covers over 65 economic releases from over 15 countries. For more sites, you may wish to visits *www.economy.com* as well.

- **FRED Database**, at: *www.stls.frb.org/fred/* The Federal Reserve of St. Louis includes data on the money supply, interest rates, daily exchange rates since 1971, and extensive regional data.

2. **PROJECT:** Enter the FRED Database from the Federal Reserve Bank of St. Louis. Go to into "Interest Rates." Go to the 3-Month Treasury Bill Rate-Secondary Market. This is monthly time series. Use this series to forecast 3-Month T-bill rates for next month. What is your forecast? You can use trends, moving averages, or naïve forecasting methods.

Chapter 6

Exchange Rates and International Trade:
Managing Exports

Firms increasingly are becoming multinational. Exporting and importing are impacted by changes in international exchange rates. Differences in long run inflation rates (according to the theory of purchasing power parity) help explain long-term exchange rate movements. This chapter also addresses regional trading blocs in Europe, North American, and the Far East, as well as a discussion of trade deficits.

A. Import-Export Sales and Exchange Rates

    1. The relative competitiveness of products around the world is affected by changes in exchange rates. Even if the price of a BMW stays the same in Germany, the cost to foreign purchases changes as the exchange rate changes.

    2. US exporters, such as Cummins Engine, face problems when the dollar strengthens in value. Their replacement engines become more expensive to foreign purchasers, if they keep the dollar price of engines constant when the dollar rises in value.

    3. Types of risks facing firms in global economies include:

        a. *Translation risk exposure* - the value of a company's assets and liabilities fluctuates as exchange rates change. This requires an accounting adjustment on the firm's balance sheet.

        b. *Transaction risk exposure* - occurs when contracts to pay or be paid are denominated in a foreign currency. The values of those contracts change whenever exchange rates change.

        c. *Foreign exchange operating risk exposure* - the competitiveness of a product can be altered by changes in exchange rates. Even selling in one's domestic currency is impacted, as foreign products can become better or worse substitutes.

B. The Market for US Dollars as Foreign Exchange

    1. As the demand and supply of a foreign currency change, the exchange rate changes to balance supply with demand. This is of a flexible exchange rates system. Much like

the shifting price of a share of IBM, the market price of foreign currencies change minute to minute as new information and traders buy and sell currencies.

2. If Americans buy more imported goods (for example, a Mercedes), the Mercedes US dealerships will purchase them in Euros through wire transfers arranged with their banks.

3. Increases in demand for imported goods by US customers raise the demand for foreign currencies. This raises the price of foreign currencies, and lowers the value of the dollar. If we drew demand and supply curves for US dollars, increases in imports imply a rightward shift in the supply of dollars. Dollars fall in value.

4. Increases in demand for US exports raises the demand for US dollars. This raises the value of the dollar, and lowers the price of foreign currencies. If we drew demand and supply curves for US dollars, increases in exports imply a rightward shift in the demand for of dollars. Dollars rise in value.

5. Governments can and do intervene in markets through buying and selling foreign currencies. They have shown the greatest impact in currency markets when governments have *coordinated intervention*, such as the time when the major industrialized countries worked together to reduce the value of the US dollar from 1985-1988.

C. <u>Foreign Exchange Risk Management</u>

1. Changes in foreign currencies present risk. A *hedge* is a risk-reducing strategy of taking offsetting positions in the ownership of an asset. Ownership of French francs presents a risk that they fall in value. A hedge involves selling an asset denominated in French francs.

2. Types of hedges include:

   a. *Internal hedges* – multinational firms buy and sell within the firm denominated in any currency that they select. A receivable to Mercedes in dollars from the US can be used to pay an expense of Mercedes in dollars.

   b. Hedges using *forward contracts* – firms can offset exposure in a foreign currency by buying or selling that amount of currency in a forward contract. A forward contract is arranged with a bank.

   c. Hedges using *currency options* – contracts that permit, but do not require, purchase or sale of currencies at specific exchange rates.

d. Hedges using *future contracts* – firm may offset risk exposure through using a futures contract for that currency. If a firm expects to receive ten million yen, they could sell yen futures contracts of approximately ten million yen.

e. Hedges using *currency swaps* – firms or others may agree to exchange (swap) streams of payments in different currencies, with an agreement as to make adjustments at each settlement date depending on movements in the *spot exchange rate* (the rate of exchange available today).

D. Long-Run Exchange Rate Determinants

1. The direction of trade flows affect exchange rates. Countries tend to have declining value of their currency when they run trade deficits, and tend to have rising currency values when they run trade surpluses.

2. Long-run trends in exchange rates are affected by differences in inflation-adjusted interest rates. High relative interest rates attract investors, tending to raise the value of the currency. High real interest rates increase the demand for US financial assets, increasing the demand for dollars.

3. Inflation differentials play a role in long-run trends in exchange rates. High anticipated inflation in one currency makes future receivables in that currency less attractive. Countries with high inflation tend to have depreciating currencies; countries with low relative inflation tend to have appreciating currencies. This is the basis of PPP, the relative purchasing power parity.

E. Purchasing Power Parity

1. *Purchasing power parity* says that the price of traded goods tends to be equal around the world if exchange rates are flexible and there are no significant costs or barriers to trade. High inflation rates make traded goods in that country unattractive, but depreciation of the currency offsets the higher price. The combined effect makes the price (exchange-rate adjusted) of traded goods equal across the globe – *the law of one price*.

2. Relative PPP

$$\frac{S_1}{S_0} = \frac{1 + (\pi_h)}{(1 + \pi_f)}$$

Where S_1/S_0 is the price relative of the expected change in the direct quote of a currency. The right side of the equation is the ratio of home and foreign inflation rates. If the foreign inflation rises (π_f), then the domestic expected future spot rates S_1 declines.

3. Problems (or qualifications) with relative PPP include:

    a. PPP is sensitive to the starting point, S_0. If the base time period is not in equilibrium, it is unlikely that expected inflation rates will accurately predict changes in exchange rates.

    b. Differences in the traded goods, or cross-cultural differences, may reduce the tendency for the law of one price to equilibrate price differences.

    c. The inflation rate measures may include non-traded goods.

    d. PPP tends to work better in the long run than in short run changes in inflationary expectations.

4. The *Big Mac Index* can be used to test PPP. If Big Macs cost $2 in the US and €2.5 in Europe, this suggests an exchange rate of $.80/€ = ($2/€2.5).

F. Introduction Trade and Trading Blocs

    1. Countries restrict trade through tariffs, quotas, and currency restrictions.

    2. Presently, several regions have reduced trade restrictions across countries within their region, which are viewed as trading blocs. The six regions are MERCOSUR (in South America), NAFTA (in North America), EU (the European Union, or often the European Community), and looser arrangements in Southeast Asia (ASEAN) and APEC throughout the Pacific area including the US, Mexico, and Canada.

    3. *Comparative Advantage* – countries or firms should produce more of those goods for which they have lower relative cost. Even if one country is lower in cost in ALL goods, it still should produce more of the goods that it produces relatively more cheaply than other countries.

    4. In a two-country example, to find which country holds a comparative advantage, determine the tradeoff in terms of goods. The country that has the lower cost in goods foregone has the lower relative cost. If it costs $120 in the US to make a carburetor and $300 to make chips, the "cost" of a carburetor is the .4 chips foregone (take the ratio $120/$300 to find .4 chips).

	Relative Cost in US	Relative Cost in Japan
Automotive carburetors	.4 Chips	1.25 Chips
Computer Chips	2.5 Carburetors	.8 Carburetors

In this example, the US relative cost of carburetors is much lower than that of the Japanese (1.25 Chips), whereas the Japanese relative cost of chips (.8 Carburetors) is much lower than that of the US. Japan should make chips and US should make carburetors.

6. The *European Union* is an example of gains that can occur by improving the ease of trade among the countries in Europe.

7. The *Optimal Currency Area* involves the question of how many different currencies are best. If all of Europe has only one currency, trade is quite easy. But if Italy needs assistance, for example, reducing the value of the Euro for the whole group of countries doesn't target the single ailing region. Hence, it is an open question as to how many currencies Europe should have.

G. Trade Deficits and the Balance of Payments

1. The *current account* reflects goods and service trade flows, receipts and payments US assets abroad and foreign assets in the US, and unilateral governmental and private transfers (such as foreign aid or gifts to foreign family members).

2. The *capital account* reflects capital inflows and outflows of foreign assets. The capital account includes transfers in and out of securities, bonds, and financial claims on other assets and liabilities, as well as official reserves, International Monetary Fund balances and gold.

3. If the current account is in deficit, the needed funds may come from borrowing from abroad (a capital account inflow). The current account (deficit or surplus) comes from a capital account (surplus or deficit) to balance payments. This is the idea behind the accounting identity of the balance of payments.

True and False Questions

Agree or disagree with the following statements, and correct the part that is erroneous.

1. As the dollar gains value, US exporters find it easier to export.

2. U.S. Farm-Raised Catfish Trading Co. of Jackson, Mississippi tells its many Japanese customers that it must be paid in dollars, not yen. According to its glossy annual report, this policy eliminates all its currency risk.

3. Foreign direct investment by Canadians in the US shows up on the US Balance of Payments as a capital account inflow.

4. Exports of Trek Bicycles from the US to Mexico shows up on the US Balance of Payments as a capital account outflow.

5. If a country has an absolute advantage in all goods, it still will have a limited number of goods for which it has a comparative advantage.

6. If the US Federal Reserve wishes to drive up the value of the dollar, it could lower interest rates.

7. MERCOSUR is a customs union to secure free flow of goods and services in parts of South America.

Answers
1. Disagree. As the dollar gains in value, the price of US products appears high to the rest of the world, making it harder to export.
2. Disagree. The catfish firm has no transaction risk, to be sure, but it does experience currency risk. As the $ rises, US catfish looks more expensive to the world market for fish protein, and foreign sources of catfish are cheaper for the US fish processing industry. The firm may experience a drop of in its sales in times of a strong dollar.
3. True.
4. Disagree. Exports of goods are a current account inflow.
5. True.
6. Disagree. As the US Federal Reserve lowers interest rates, fixed-rate investments in the US appear less attractive. There would be less demand for the dollar, and the value of the dollar would likely decline.
7. True.

Multiple Choice Questions

1. If the Japanese raise their interest rates, this will tend to:
   a. lower US demand for yen in the foreign exchange market.
   b. raise the value of the dollar.
   c. raise the value of the yen.
   d. raise the supply of yen in the foreign exchange market.

2. In discussions of international exchange rates, a hedge is:
    a. shrubbery used to divide properties.
    b. a risk-reducing strategy of taking offsetting positions in the ownership of an asset.
    c. any purchase of a forward or futures contract in foreign currencies.
    d. any purchase of foreign currencies at the spot price.

3. Which of the following is NOT likely to increase the value of Euro against other currencies?
    a. An increase in the inflation rate in Europe.
    b. An increase in the real interest rates in Europe.
    c. An increase in the growth rate of European GDP.
    d. A decrease in the European trade deficit.

4. If you fear the dollar will rise against the Brazilian REAL, with a resulting adverse change in the dollar value of your Brazilian automotive subsidiary, you could hedge by:
    a. Reducing liabilities in your Brazilian subsidiary.
    b. Buying REAL forward in the amount of your net asset exposure.
    c. Selling REAL forward in the amount of your net asset exposure.
    d. Expanding your assets in your Brazilian subsidiary.

5   The U.S. dollar to Japanese yen exchange rate was $1 = ¥ 130. During the year, U.S. inflation is expected to be 3%, whereas Japanese inflation will likely be 0%. According to relative purchasing power parity, what price should the yen achieve in one year?
    Hint: $S_1/ S_0 = [1 + (\pi_h)]/ [1 + (\pi_f)]$, where S_1/ S_0 is the ratio of direct quotes for the yen now (0) and expected in future period (1).
    a. $1 = ¥ 130.
    b. $1 = ¥ 136.7.
    c. $1 = ¥ 133.9.
    d. $1 = ¥ 126.2

6. The economics of international trade predicts that countries will tend to specialize. Which of the following theories identifies specialization as a force leading to gains from international trade?
    a. product life cycle theory of international trade
    b. theory of diversification
    c. the theory of comparative advantage
    d. the theory of globalization

7. If a German purchases a U.S. government security
   a. the supply of dollars rises
   b. the federal government deficit declines
   c. the demand for dollars rises
   d. the U.S. money supply rises

8. A slowdown in U.S. economic growth will
   a. boost the value of the dollar because inflation fears will be calmed
   b. boost the value of the dollar because the Federal Reserve will expand the money supply
   c. lower the value of the dollar because the U.S. will be a less attractive place in which to invest.
   d. lower the value of the dollar because interest rates will rise

9. A weak Mexican peso is most likely to cause
   a. less unemployment and less inflation in Mexico
   b. less unemployment but more inflation in Mexico
   c. more unemployment and less inflation in Mexico
   d. more unemployment but less inflation in Mexico

10. As the real value of the dollar rises, the balance on current account is likely to
    a. stay the same
    b. depend on the time of day.
    c. increase
    d. decrease

11. Tourism by German citizens in Florida shows up on the
    a. US official reserves of foreign currencies
    b. US current account as an inflow
    c. German capital account as an outflow
    d. none of the above, since travel is a service

12. If a real value of a nation's freely floating currency increases, and the nation's current account is initially zero, its capital account will most likely be
    a. in deficit
    b. in surplus

13. A nation that is running a savings deficit
    a. must spend less than it produces
    b. will invest domestically more than it saves
    c. must have a net capital outflow
    d. all of the above

14. The most likely way to reduce the Japanese trade surplus is to
    a. relax quotas on imports from Japan
    b. increase Japanese savings
    c. increase Japanese consumption
    d. revalue the Japanese yen

15. If the US dollar continues to depreciate from now through the end of the year, then:
    a. US exporters will tend to lose sales to foreign customers.
    b. The US importer will tend to find that its cost of imported goods falls, helping its bottom line.
    c. The US importer and exporter will be unaffected by the changing values for foreign exchange.
    d. The US exporter will be helped by the depreciating dollar as foreigners will see US goods as being much cheaper.

16. Purchasing power parity (PPP) is the theory that says that that countries with
    a. LOW relative inflation rates will have rising values for their exchange rates.
    b. HIGH inflation rates have rising values for their exchange rates.
    c. HIGH growth will tend to find that they have negative interest rates.
    d. LOW interest rates tend to have HIGH inflation.

17. If the domestic prices for traded goods rises 25 percent in Mexico and 10 percent in the US over the same period, what would happened to the Mexican peso/US dollar exchange rate?
    a. the peso rises in value; that is, the direct quote of the peso rises in the US.
    b. the peso falls in value; that is, the direct quote of the peso falls in the US.

18. Use the idea of purchasing power parity on the *Big Mac Index*. A Big Mac sells for about $2 in the US. The exchange rate with England is $1.50 per pound (£). If purchasing power parity worked perfectly for identical Big Macs, what is the price in pounds for Big Macs in England? Ignore all transaction costs.
    a. £1
    b. £1.33
    c. £2
    d. £3

Answers

1. c	6. c	11. b	16. a
2. b	7. c	12. b	17. b
3 a	8. c	13. b	18. b
4. c	9. b	14. c	
5. d	10. d	15. d	

Worked Problems

1. Microsoft charges 180 DM for its upgrade of Windows 95 in Köln, Germany. It costs Microsoft 40 DM per upgrade to package the upgrade (box, booklet, diskettes, shrink-wrap, *etc.*). This cost is not expected to change; however, the German mark has been depreciating. If it falls from $.55 to $.51, what price will Microsoft have to charge to maintain its dollar profit margin?

   Answer: 190.98 DM. Before the depreciating mark the profit margin was $77.00. We calculate (180 DM - 40 DM)($.55) = $77.00. If the mark goes to $.51, the profit margin would fall to $71.40 if the price remained at 180 DM. To keep the margin constant, the price would have to be 40 DM + $77/.51 = 190.98 DM to cover costs and still maintain its profit margin.

2. The German mark is quoted against the US dollar at $.56, and the French franc is quoted against the German mark at .30 DM. What is the value of the dollar in Paris?

   Answer: This is an example of cross rates. The answer is FF5.95/$. The product of the dollar price of the mark and the mark price of the franc is dollar price of the franc. [$.56/DM]•{.30DM/FF} = ($.168/FF). In Paris, the direct quote for a dollar would be FF5.95/$, which is inverse of $.168/FF.

3. It costs $100 to build a wooden table and $40 to manufacture a pair of men's athletic shoes in the US. If costs 39,000¥ to build a wooden table and 7,800¥ to manufacture a pair of men's athletic shoes in Japan.

   a. If the yen's exchange rate were 130¥ to the dollar, which country has an absolute advantage in both tables and shoes?

      Answer: The US has an absolute advantage in both products. Tables cost $100 in the US and $300 in Japan (39,000¥ / [130¥/$] = $300). Shoes cost $40 to make in the US, whereas they cost $60 to make in Japan (7,800¥ / [130¥/$] = $60).

   b. Which country has a comparative advantage in shoes? Which country has a comparative advantage in tables?

      Answer: The relative cost of a table in the US is 2.5 pairs of shoes [$100/$40]. The relative cost of tables in Japan is 5 pairs of shoes

[39,000¥ / 7,800¥ = 5]. The US has a comparative advantage in wooden tables, since 2.5 is cheaper than 5.

The relative cost of shoes in the US is .4 tables [$40/$100]. The relative cost of shoes in Japan is .2 tables. Japan as a comparative advantage in shoes, since .2 is less than .4.

Net Sources

There are many sites to explore for exchange rate information and trade movements. A few of interest include:

1. **Daily Exchange Rates.** Visit *www.oanda.com/convert/classic/* which computes daily exchange rates conversions for 164 currencies. This makes it possible to determine the cross rates between the Czech Koruna and the Iranian Rial, or any other of the 22,732 possible cross rates among 164 forms of money including gold.

2. **World Stock Prices and Exchange Rates.** Yahoo offers */quote.yahoo.com/m3/* to examine Yahoo Finance for exchange rates. Then enter the clickable site: "Major World Indices" to examine world stock markets.

3. **The World Bank.** Visit *www.worldbank.org/* and enter "Countries and Regions," which offers information by country, maps, short histories, and activities in which the World Bank is a partner.

4. **PROJECT:** Using Yahoo's Finance site at *quote.yahoo.com*, examine first the World markets under the heading features. Note which countries had big one-day increases in stock prices and which countries with big one-day declines in stock prices. Next examine World Currencies. For those stock markets that rose substantially, did their currency also rise in value? For those stock markets that declined, did the currency of those countries generally decline in value? Why would you tend to think that there is a positive correlation between a country's currency and stock markets?

PART III - PRODUCTION AND COST

Chapter 7

Production Economics

Managers must decide not only what to produce for the market, but also how to produce it in the *most efficient* or *least cost* manner. This chapter develops a widely accepted tool for judging whether or not the production choices are least cost. A *production function* relates the most that can be produced from a given set of inputs. This allows the manager to measure the marginal product of each input. In the short run, some inputs are fixed. The *Law of Diminishing Marginal Returns* applies to the short run when some inputs are fixed. The long run production function deals with a period of time over which all inputs including capital can vary. *Scale economies* apply to the long run case where all inputs can be varied. Finally, this chapter discusses reasons for increasing or decreasing returns in the long run.

A. Production Functions in the Short Run

1. Each good or service produced requires inputs of time, materials, and capital. These resource inputs produce an output. If we listed the greatest output possible for any set of inputs, we would have described a production schedule, table, or function.

2. A *production function* is a schedule of maximum output from any set of inputs, X_i.

$$Q = f(X_1, X_2, ..., X_n)$$

3. Production is real. It is visible either in large scale on a factory assembly line or in smaller scale in an artist's workshop. Production can be measured in the number of cars assembled or the number of paintings completed.

4. Yet even in something as real as production, it is vital to a manager to have methods to measure efficiency and ways to think about improving the production process. Theory is useful when it helps organize thought in constructive ways.

5. In economics, *efficiency* generally refers to the *least cost* way to do an activity.

6. A production function with two inputs: $Q = f(K, L)$, where K is the amount of capital, and L is the amount of labor is used to illustrate issues in production.

7. A *Cobb-Douglas Production Function* relies on a multiplicative production model:

$$Q = A \cdot K^{\beta_1} \cdot L^{\beta_2}$$
Cobb-Douglas Production Function

8. The *short run* is defined as a period of time when one or more inputs are fixed. Capital, K, is thought to be relatively fixed in the short run, whereas labor, L, is thought to be variable.

9. In the *long run* all inputs are variable.

B. Production Functions with One Variable

1. In the short run, some factors of production are fixed. Suppose only labor, L, is variable. The short run production function is $Q = f(L)$.

2. *Average product of labor*, $AP_L = Q/L$; and the *marginal product of labor*, $MP_L =$ (change in Q)/(change in L) $= \Delta Q/\Delta L = \partial Q/\partial K$ for small changes in labor.

3. When MP is above AP, then AP must rise. When MP is below AP, then AP must fall. When MP equals AP, then AP is at a local maximum

4. The *production elasticity* for any input, X, $E_X = MP_X / AP_X = (\partial Q/\partial X) / (Q/X) = (\partial Q/\partial X) \cdot (X/Q)$, which is identical in form to other elasticities.

   a. When $MP_L > AP_L$, then the labor elasticity, $E_L > 1$. A 1 percent increase in labor will increase output by **more** than 1 percent.

   b. When $MP_L < AP_L$, then the labor elasticity, $E_L < 1$. A 1 percent increase in labor will increase output by **less** than 1 percent.

5. *Law of diminishing marginal returns* - holding one or more other factors fixed, increases in one factor of production will AFTER SOME POINT lead to diminishing marginal increases in total product.

6. Clearly this is a "short run" law, where at least one factor is fixed. There are cases, such as the promotional expenditures for high definition TV, however, that grow more productive as the market size grows.

7. *Three stages of production*:

    a. Stage 1:   average product rising.

    b. Stage 2:   average product declining (but marginal product positive).

    c. Stage 3:   marginal product is negative, or total product is declining.

C. Optimal Use of the Variable Input

1. Use more of an input, X, if the value of the production from that input is greater than the cost of using that input:

   a. *Marginal Revenue Product*: The amount that an additional unit of the variable input adds to total revenue. $MRP_X = MR_Q \cdot MP_X$

   b. *Marginal Factor Cost*: The amount added to total cost because of the use of one more unit of a variable input. $MFC_X = \partial TC / \partial X$.

2. Optimal Input Level: $MRP_X = MFC_X$.

D. Production Functions with Two Variable Inputs

1. *Production Isoquants* are the combinations of inputs that produce the same level of output.

   a. Isoquants of *Perfect Substitutes* are straight lines (*e.g.*, unskilled workers and robots).

   b. Isoquants of *Complementary Inputs* are right angles or L-shaped (*e.g.*, word processing typists and word processing computers). Production processes which require a fixed proportion of each input are complementary inputs that do not allow substitution.

   c. The usual isoquant shape is convex (or outward bulging) to origin.

2. *Marginal Rate of Technical Substitution*, $MRTS = MP_X / MP_Y$, which is slope of the isoquant. It is the rate of change of one input substituted for another input, holding total output constant.

3. *Isocost lines* are combinations of inputs that have the same total cost. If total cost is C_0, and the cost of X and Y are C_X and C_Y, then $C_0 = C_X \cdot X + C_Y \cdot Y$. The isocost line is best graphed with intercept, C_0 / C_Y, and slope, $- (C_X / C_Y)$:

$$Y = C_0 / C_Y - (C_X / C_Y) \cdot X$$

4. The efficient or *least cost production* combination has the lowest possible isocost line tangent to a given production isoquant. That is, the slope of the isoquant, MRTS, equals the slope of the isocost line, - (C_X/C_Y). Rearranging, we achieve:

Equimarginal Criterion: $MP_X/C_X = MP_Y/C_Y$

---

5. If the marginal product per dollar in X equals the marginal product per dollar in Y, then we have satisfied the problem of minimizing cost. The same rule applies when we maximize production subject to a given total cost. Both problems are *constrained optimization* that can be solved using Lagrangian multipliers (See Appendix 7A).

6. An increase in the cost of one input, X, will make $MP_X/C_X < MP_Y/C_Y$. To produce efficiently, the manager will wish to use more of Y, which now provides relatively higher marginal product per dollar than X. The shift to more Y and less X will raise MP_X and lower MP_Y, until the equimarginal criterion is satisfied.

E. Production Functions in the Long Run

1. All inputs are variable.

2. Increasing all inputs, increases the scale of production. We are quite interested in whether there are advantages or disadvantages to different scales of production.

3. Returns to Scale--The proportionate increase in output that results from a given proportionate increase in all the inputs used in the production process.

F. Production Functions and Returns to Scale

1. *Constant Returns to Scale* (CRS)--increasing all inputs by lambda percent, increases output **exactly** by lambda percent.

2. *Increasing Returns to Scale* (IRS)--increasing all inputs by lambda percent, increases output by **more** than lambda percent. This is also known as *economies of scale*.

3. *Decreasing Returns to Scale* (DRS)--increasing all inputs by lambda percent, **does not quite** increase output by lambda percent. Also known as *diseconomies of scale*..

4. A production function $Q = f(x, y)$ is *homogeneous of degree n*, if:

$$f(\lambda x, \lambda y) = \lambda^n \cdot f(x, y) \quad \text{for } \lambda \neq 0.$$

5. A Cobb-Douglas production function: $Q = A \cdot K^{\alpha} \cdot L^{\beta}$ -- can be IRS, CRS, or DRS. This function is homogeneous of degree = $\alpha + \beta$.
   a. If $\alpha + \beta = 1$, then CRS
   b. If $\alpha + \beta > 1$, then IRS
   c. If $\alpha + \beta < 1$, then DRS

G. Sources of Increasing and Decreasing Returns to Scale

1. Reasons for increasing returns to scale:

   a. *Specialization in the use of capital and labor.* Labor becomes more skilled at tasks, or the equipment is more specialized, less "a jack of all trades," as scale increases.

   b. Other advantages include: avoid inherent lumpiness in the size of equipment, quantity discounts, technical efficiencies in building larger volume equipment.

2. Reasons for decreasing returns to scale (or, why we don't have huge monopolies in every industry):

   a. *Problems of coordination and control* as it is hard to send and receive information as the scale rises.

   b. Other disadvantages of large size: slow decision ladder, inflexibility, and there are capacity limitations on entrepreneurial skills (there are diminishing returns to the C.E.O. which cannot be completely delegated).

H. Statistical Estimation of Production Functions

1. Statistically, a linear production function implies that the inputs are CRS and are perfect substitutes in production. These implications are unacceptable for most production processes.

2. The Cobb-Douglas production function: $Q = A \cdot K^{\alpha} \cdot L^{1-\alpha}$ must be CRS, because the sum of the exponents, $\alpha + (1 - \alpha) = 1$.

3. The later studies of Cobb and Douglas suggested a more general Cobb-Douglas production function which can be CRS, IRS, or DRS.

   $Q = A \cdot K^{\alpha} \cdot L^{\beta}$ general form of the Cobb-Douglas production function.

4. The Generalized Cobb Douglas implies:

    a. It is linear in logs: $\log Q = \log A + \alpha \cdot \log K + \beta \cdot \log L$

    This can be estimated using an OLS regression model.

    b. Each of the exponents are elasticities: α is the capital elasticity of output and β is the labor elasticity of output.

    c. $MP_K = \alpha \cdot Q/K$ and $MP_L = \beta \cdot Q/L$

5. Production functions for electrical generating capacity are particularly easy to estimate. Electrical plants produce primarily one output: electricity (and some steam heat), and because they are regulated, data is readily available on their total capital and variable expenditures (lumped together to be called labor for simplification purposes).

Suppose the log linear regression results for a sample of 25 utilities is:

$\log Q = -1.50 + .52 \log K + .65 \log L$
       (.65) (.12)   (.14)

$n = 25 \qquad R^2 = .954$

    a. sum of exponents ($\alpha + \beta$) reveals electrical utilities to be IRS: that is there does seem to be some economies of scale, since $.52 + .65 = 1.17 > 1$.

    b. output elasticities: If labor were expanded 10%, the coefficient on log K tells us that output expands about 6.5%. Also if we expanded capital by 10%, then output would expand by about 5.2%.

    c. If we had 10% more of both K and L, there would be about 11.7% more total output.

True and False Questions

Agree or disagree with the following statements, and correct the part that is erroneous.

1. Growth in the number of robots (a form of capital) will increase the marginal product of labor.

2. The law of diminishing marginal returns is applicable primarily to the long run production function where all inputs are variable.

3. When marginal product is at its maximum, average product is also at its maximum.

4. When marginal product is less than average product, then it must be that average product is declining.

5. If the production elasticity for labor is greater than 1, then $MP_L < AP_L$.

6. We should use relatively more labor if we learn that the marginal product per dollar of labor expenditures is less than a marginal product per dollar of capital expenditures.

7. If a production function is homogeneous of degree 0.94, then doubling all inputs will result in an increase in output of $2^{0.94}$, which is 1.9185. That means output rises only 91.85 percent even though inputs increased 100%.

8. If labor and capital have become more and more substitutable over time, then production isoquants have become more like right angles over time.

9. All production processes will exhibit diminishing marginal returns beyond some point.

10. All production processes will exhibit decreasing returns to scale beyond some point.

11. The law of diminishing marginal returns states that increases in the variable input reduce the total product.

12. The optimal input combination is where marginal products are equal.

13. If the labor elasticity of output is .65, then the anticipated increase in output for a 3% increase in labor would be approximately 1.95%.

14. If the capital elasticity of output is .40 and the labor elasticity of output is .60, and these are the only two inputs, then the production function displays increasing returns to scale.

15. If a firm has increasing returns to scale, then increasing all inputs by 1% will increase output by more than 1%.

Answers
1. True. Labor becomes more productive, the greater the amount of capital available.
2. Disagree. The law of diminishing returns applies when increasing one factor of production, holding one or more other factors of production constant. In the short run, some factors of production are constant. Hence, we can view the law of diminishing returns as predominantly a short run law.

3. Disagree. Marginal product hits its maximum before average product hits its maximum. In fact, at the maximum average product output, marginal product equals average product.
4. True.
5. Disagree. When the production elasticity for labor is greater than 1, then $MP_L > AP_L$.
6. Disagree. When $MP_L/C_L < MP_K/C_K$, then we should use relatively more capital compared with labor.
7. True.
8. Disagree. If labor and capital have become more and more substitutable over time, then production isoquants have become more like *straight lines* over time.
9. True.
10. Disagree. A production process can be constant returns to scale, for example, and never reach decreasing returns to scale.
11. Disagree. Increases in the variable input eventually reduce the marginal product of the input.
12. Disagree. Optimal input combination is where marginal products per dollar are equal.
13. True. The reason for the word "approximately" is that elasticities are best interpreted for very small changes in the input. Elasticities involve first derivatives that are precise only in the limit.
14. Disagree. The two elasticities sum to 1, which is constant returns to scale.
15. True.

Multiple Choice Questions

Fill in the missing spaces in the following table:

Variable input	Total product	Average product	Marginal product
4......		30	---
5......			20
6......	155		

1. What is the total product for 5 units of input in the fill-in-the blank table?
   a. less than 80
   b. 100
   c. 140
   d. 155
   e. none of the above

2. What is the *marginal product* for 6 units of input in the fill-in-the-blank table?
   a. 15
   b. 19
   c. 20
   d. more than 20

3. Which of the following is NOT a source of Decreasing Returns to Scale.
   a. problem of coordination and control.
   b. entrepreneurial capacity is fixed.
   c. inflexibility.
   d. cannot make fast decisions.
   e. specialization in the use of capital and labor.

4. The law of diminishing marginal returns:
   a. states that each and every increase in the amount of the variable factor employed in the production process will yield diminishing marginal returns.
   b. is a mathematical theorem that can be logically proved or disproved.
   c. is the rate at which one input may be substituted for another input in the production process.
   d. none of the above.

5. The combinations of inputs costing a constant C dollars is called:
   a. isocost line.
   b. isorevenue line.
   c. isoquant curve.
   d. marginal rate of technical substitution (MRTS).

6. The marginal product is defined as:
   a. total output divided by the amount of the variable input used in producing that output.
   b. the incremental change in total output that can be produced by the use of one more unit of the variable input in the production process.
   c. the percentage change in output resulting from a given percentage change in the amount of the variable input X employed in the production process with Y.
   d. (a) and (b)

7. Which of the following is never negative?
   a. marginal product
   b. marginal rate of technical substitution
   c. average product
   d. slope of the isocost lines
   e. production elasticity

8. If the average product curve is rising, the marginal product curve:
   a. must lie above the average product curve and must also be rising.
   b. must be above the average product curve.
   c. must be rising.
   d. must lie below the average product curve.

9. The law of diminishing marginal product indicates that, if a variable input is used in conjunction with a fixed input, there is a level of usage of the variable input beyond which:
   a. total product will decline.
   b. marginal product will decline.
   c. average product will decline.
   d. marginal product will rise.
   e. average product will rise.

10. Suppose that a firm uses two inputs: capital and labor. It has selected the levels of usage of capital and labor at which $MP_K = 50$ and $MP_L = 20$. If the cost of labor is $5 per unit and the cost of capital is $10 per unit:
    a. the firm should increase its usage of labor relative to capital.
    b. the firm is using the optimal (cost minimizing) combination of capital and labor.
    c. the firm should increase its usage of capital relative to labor.
    d. there is insufficient data to answer this question.

11. Consider a firm that produces its output using two inputs — K and L. The costs for these two inputs are, respectively, r and w. If the manager wishes to minimize the cost of producing a given level of output, the manager will use that combination of K and L for which:
    a. $MP_K = MP_L$
    b. $r = w$
    c. $MP_K = r$ and $MP_L = w$
    d. $MP_K/r = MP_L/w$

12. The short-run production decision provides for an optimal use of the variable input when:
    a. the marginal product of that input is at a maximum.
    b. the marginal revenue product equals marginal factor cost of that input.
    c. total costs are at a minimum.
    d. the marginal product of that input is zero.

13. If the average product curve is neither rising nor falling, then the marginal product curve:
    a. must lie above the average product curve and must also be rising.
    b. must be above the average product curve.
    c. must be rising.
    d. must equal average product.

14. You are an efficiency expert hired by a manufacturing firm that uses two inputs, labor (L) and capital (K). The firm produces and sells a given output. If the marginal product per dollar in labor were greater than the marginal product per dollar in capital, then:
    a. The firm is operating efficiently.
    b. This firm should increase the quantity of labor relative to capital.
    c. This firm should increase the quantity of capital relative to labor.

15. If the average product is greater than the marginal product for an input, then:
    a. the production elasticity is one for that input.
    b. the production elasticity is greater than one for that input.
    c. the production elasticity is less than one for that input.
    d. a 1% increase in that input will increase output more than 1%.

16. Examining output figures, a manufacturing firm which makes disposable paper cups finds that output per unit of input increased after the firm expanded the scale of its operations. This information is consistent with:
    a. constant returns to scale.
    b. increasing returns to scale.
    c. decreasing returns to scale.

17. Consider the following Cobb-Douglas production function for bus transportation:

$$Q = 2.3 \, L^{.45} F^{.20} B^{.30}$$

    Where L is labor, F is fuel, and B represents the number of buses
    a. The production function is constant returns to scale
    b. The production function is decreasing returns to scale
    c. The production function is increasing returns to scale
    d. The production is NOT homogeneous

18. The National Hardware Store Association (NHSA) is concerned with the decline in the number of small, family-owned hardware stores as the national chains continue to expand. The NHSA commissioned you to estimate a Cobb-Douglas production function with K measured in square feet of store, L the number of clerks, and Q the dollar volume of sales per store. The results were: $Q = A \cdot K^{.47} \cdot L^{.56}$.

a. You report that there are constant returns to scale in hardware stores.
b. The sad news is that there is decreasing returns to scale in hardware stores.
c. The decline of small stores may be due to increasing returns to scale in hardware stores.
d. Only linear functional forms can be used to find economies of scale.

Answers

Variable input	Total product	Average product	Marginal product
4	**120**	30	---
5	**140**	**28**	20
6	155	**25.8**	**15**

1.	c	10.	c
2.	a	11.	d
3.	e	12.	b
4.	d	13.	d
5.	a	14.	b
6.	b	15.	c
7.	c	16.	b
8.	b	17.	b
9.	b	18.	c

Worked Problems

1. The following three-input Cobb-Douglas production function over labor, L, capital, K, and materials, M, has the following form:

$$Q = 2.6 \cdot L^{.5} \cdot K^{.4} \cdot M^{.1}$$

a. Show that this production function is homogeneous of degree 1.

Answer: A production function is homogeneous of degree n, if increasing all inputs by λ, raises output by λ^n.

$$2.6 \cdot (\lambda L)^{.5} \cdot (\lambda K)^{.4} \cdot (\lambda M)^{.1} = 2.6 \cdot (\lambda)^{.5 + .4 + .1} \cdot L^{.5} \cdot K^{.4} \cdot M^{.1} = \lambda^1 \cdot 2.6 \cdot L^{.5} \cdot K^{.4} \cdot M^{.1}$$

This production function is homogeneous of degree 1.

b. Is this production function constant returns to scale, increasing returns to scale, or decreasing returns to scale?

> *Answer:* It is constant returns to scale, because all production functions which are homogeneous of degree 1 are constant returns to scale. Furthermore, the sum of the three exponents (.5 + .4 + .1) sum to 1, which shows that it is constant returns to scale.

2. A production process employs two inputs--labor (L) and raw materials (M). Output (Q) is a function of these two inputs and is given by the following relationship:

$$Q = 6 \cdot L^2 \cdot M^2 - .10 \cdot L^3 \cdot M^3$$

Assume that raw materials (input M) are fixed at 10 units.

a. Determine the total product function for input L, holding M = 10.

> *Answer:* Setting M = 10, we find that: $Q = 600 \cdot L^2 - 100 \cdot L^3$. This function is cubic in labor, holding raw materials constant. This becomes a "short run" production function, because some factors of production are fixed.

b. Determine the marginal product function for input L, holding M = 10.

> *Answer:* The marginal product can be found by taking the first derivative of the equation found in (a) above: $Q = 600 \cdot L^2 - 100 \cdot L^3$
>
> $MP_L = dQ/dL = \textbf{1200} \cdot \textbf{L} - \textbf{300} \cdot \textbf{L}^2$.
>
> Alternatively, we can find the marginal product by taking the partial derivative of the entire production function, and then substituting 10 for M.

c. Determine the average product function for input L, holding M = 10.

> *Answer:* The average product is Q/L. Since we are finding the average product where M = 10, we can use the equation in part (a), and then dividing by L.
>
> That is: $AP_L = Q/L = [600 \cdot L^2 - 100 \cdot L^3]/L = \textbf{600} \cdot \textbf{L} - \textbf{100} \cdot \textbf{L}^2$.

d. Find the number of units of input L that maximizes the total product function, holding M = 10.

> *Answer:* To maximize the total product function, we take the first derivative of the short run production function, and set that equal to zero. The short run production function in part (a) was: $Q = 600 \cdot L^2 - 100 \cdot L^3$. The first derivative is the marginal product found in part (b): $MP_L = dQ/dL = 1200 \cdot L - 300 \cdot L^2$.
>
> Hence, $1200 \cdot L - 300 \cdot L^2 = 0$, can be reduced to $1200 = 300 \cdot L$, which implies that **L = 4**.

e. Find the number of units of input L that maximizes the marginal product function, holding M = 10.

> *Answer:* The marginal product of labor, holding raw material constant was:
>
> $MP_L = 1200 \cdot L - 300 \cdot L^2$. To maximize MP_L, take the first derivative and set it equal to zero: $\partial MP_L/\partial L = 1200 - 600 \cdot L = 0$. The solution is: **L = 2**.

f. Find the number of units of input L that maximizes the average product function, holding M = 10.

> *Answer:* From part (c), the average product of labor is: $AP_L = 600 \cdot L - 100 \cdot L^2$.
>
> To maximize this figure, differentiate it with respect to L, and set it equal to zero.
>
> $\partial AP_L/\partial L = 600 - 200 \cdot L = 0$. Hence, **L = 3**.

3. Consider the following short-run production function for Superfast Hairdryers, Inc., where X is material inputs, and Q is output.

$Q = 10 \cdot X - .25 \cdot X^2$

Suppose the hair dryers are sold for $10 per unit to K-Mart. Also assume that the firm can obtain as much of the variable materials, input (X), as it needs at $20 per unit.

a. Determine the *marginal revenue product of materials*. (This is a function.)

Answer: Total revenue is:

$TR = P \cdot Q = 10 \cdot Q = 10 \cdot [10 \cdot X - .25 \cdot X^2] = 100 \cdot X - 4 \cdot X^2$. The marginal revenue by using a little more materials, X, is the derivative of TR with respect to X. $dTR/dX = 100 - 8 \cdot X$. The same answer can be found by finding the marginal product of X, and multiplying by the price of the final product, in this case, $10.

b.   Determine the *marginal factor cost* function.

Answer: Total factor cost, $TFC = 20 \cdot X$. Marginal factor cost is the derivative of cost, or $20.

c.   Determine the optimal value of X, given the objective is to maximize profits.

Answer: The optimal amount of X occurs where the marginal revenue product equals the marginal factor cost. From parts (a) and (b) we have:

$MRP = 100 - 8 \cdot X = 20 = MFC$. Therefore, **X = 10.**

d.   If the price of hair dryers were to rise, what happens to the optimal value of X employed to produce them?

Answer: Of course, the optimal use of X rises, if the price of hair dryers rises. The marginal revenue product curve shifts up. Given a constant MFC, then the optimal amount of X will be greater. The morale for workers in the hair dryer industry is this: whatever improves the desirability of Superfast Hairdryers, increases the need for more workers at the Superfast Hairdryer factories.

e. If the quantity of capital were to rise, what would happen to the marginal product of materials?

Answer: An increase in the quantity of capital will make the marginal product of X greater. In essence, each X will be more productive.

4. Consider the following production function for the bus transportation in St. Louis, Missouri:

$$Q = L^{\alpha} \cdot F^{\beta} \cdot B^{\phi}$$

where L = labor input in man-hours; F = fuel input in gallons; B = capital input in number of buses; and Q = output measured in millions of bus miles.

Suppose that the parameters (α, β, and ϕ) of this model were estimated using a log linear regression model with annual data for the past 25 years. The following results were obtained:

$\alpha = .45 \quad \beta = .20 \quad \phi = .24$

a. What type of <u>returns to scale</u> appears to characterize this bus transportation system (ignore the issue of statistical significance)?

> *Answer:* The sum of the exponents of the three inputs is .89, which is less than one. Ignoring statistical significance, it appears that there are slight decreasing returns to scale in this bus system.

b. Suppose that capital input (in buses) is increased by 10 percent next year (with the other inputs held constant). Determine the approximate percentage change in output.

> *Answer:* The capital elasticity of output is the exponent on buses, which is .24. A 10% increase in buses will increase output (that is ridership) by approximately 2.4%. This is approximate, since output elasticities are accurate for small changes in the inputs, as they are based on notions of calculus.

c. If Q = 1,000, and L = 10, what is the MP_L?

> *Answer:* The marginal product of labor, is the labor elasticity of output time the average product of labor: $MP_L = \alpha \cdot Q/L = .45 \cdot (1000/10) = 45$.

Net Sources

Production economics focuses on particular industries or particular firms. Firms on the Internet present marketing information, but little on costs of production or amounts produced. However, trade associations sometime offer information for studying the long run production function of the industry.

1. **National Information Center** (FDIC)   *www.ffiec.gov/nic/*
    Enter performance reports - summary ratios for banks. You may search for banks, based on their names. Three years of bank data on each bank is readily available. Issues such as the profitability of banks based on asset size, location, or nature of the customers (commercial, trust, *etc.)* can be explored.

2. **National Association of Home Builders**   *www.nahb.com/*
    Issues on lumber agreements, changes in regulations, wetlands, affordable housing, and other topics are discussed.

3. **PROJECT**:   *www.census.gov/statab/www/*
    The Statistical Abstract of the United States presents data on the growing expenditures in national health care since 1990. *National Health Expenditures* is available at: *www.census.gov/statab/www/part3.html.* Examine Medicare expenditures *versus* National health expenditures. How fast is each category growing? Why is this? Is it because of a high income elasticity for medical care, monopoly power in medical care, changes in the age of the population, or is it because of decreasing returns to scale in medical care?

Appendix 7A

Maximization of Production Output
Subject to a Cost Constraint

Managers wish to be as efficient as possible, as one way to improve profitability. To be efficient means to produce with as little cost as possible. We can characterize this efficiency goal as maximizing output, subject to a given budget to spend on inputs. Chapter 7 uses graphs to illustrate efficient production. This Appendix uses Lagrangian Multipliers.

A. Equimarginal (or Optimality) Criterion

1. Efficient use of inputs occurs when:

$$MP_X/C_X = MP_Y/C_Y$$

2. This equation means that the marginal product in X, per dollar spent on X equals the marginal product in Y, per dollar spent on Y.

3. Let the production function be: $Q = f(X, Y)$; and let the cost function be: $C = C_X \cdot X + C_Y \cdot Y$.

4. Max $L_Q = Q - \lambda \cdot (C_X \cdot X + C_Y \cdot Y - C)$.

5. Differentiating with respect to X, Y, and lambda yields:

   (i) $L_X = Q_X - \lambda \cdot C_X = 0$

   (ii) $L_Y = Q_Y - \lambda \cdot C_Y = 0$

(iii) $L_\lambda = C_X \cdot X + C_Y \cdot Y - C = 0$

6.   We know that Q_X and Q_Y are marginal products. Rearranging equation (i) yields: $\lambda = MP_X/C_X$. Similarly, the second equation shows that $\lambda = MP_Y/C_Y$. Hence, the two ratios are equal to each other.

7.   The same solution occurs if we attempt to minimize costs, subject to an output constraint. In that case, the Lagrangian is:

Min $L_C = C_X \cdot X + C_Y \cdot Y + \lambda \cdot [f(X, Y) - Q]$

Solving this Lagrangian produces the same equimarginal criterion.

Worked Problem

1.   Because of your business training, you have been hired as an efficiency expert by **Big Step Ladders, International**. You are working to *expand* production of utility ladders. After applying regression analysis to past data, you believe that the production function has a general Cobb-Douglas form:

$$Q = 4 \cdot K^{.5} \cdot L^{.5}$$

Labor costs of ladder assembly workers is $18 per hour, and capital costs are $108 per increment of a thousand dollars used in K (K is measured in thousand dollar units). You have been granted a budget to oversee of $266,400.

a.   Use Lagrangian multipliers to solve for the optimal amount of capital and labor at Big Step Ladders, International.

Answer: The Lagrangian problem is:

Max $L_Q = 4 \cdot K^{.5} \cdot L^{.5} - \lambda \cdot (18 \cdot L + 108 \cdot K - 266,400)$

Differentiating with respect to L and K shows that:

(i) $L_K = 2 \cdot K^{-.5} \cdot L^{.5} - \lambda \cdot 108 = 0$.
(ii) $L_L = 2 \cdot K^{.5} \cdot L^{-.5} - \lambda \cdot 18 = 0$.

Solving both of these equations in terms of lambda, we find:

$2 \cdot K^{-.5} \cdot L^{.5}/108 = 2 \cdot K^{.5} \cdot L^{-.5}/18$. Which can be written as:

$2 \cdot K^{-.5} \cdot L^{.5} / 2 \cdot K^{.5} \cdot L^{-.5} = 108/18$, or $K^{-1} \cdot L^{1} = 6$, or $L = 6 \cdot K$.

Substituting $L = 6 \cdot K$ into the cost constraint yields: $18 \cdot (6 \cdot K) + 108 \cdot K = 266{,}400$; which is: $216 \cdot K = 266{,}400$, or **K = 1,233.33**, and **L = 7,400**.

b. Find the maximum number of ladders that can be assembled with a budget of $266,400.

    Answer: These inputs will at most assemble, the following number of ladders:

    $Q = 4 \cdot K^{.5} \cdot L^{.5} = 4 \cdot (1{,}233.33)^{.5} \cdot (7{,}400)^{.5} = $ **12,084** ladders.

c. What is the economic meaning of lambda? What is its value?

    Answer: Lambda is the marginal product of relaxing the budget constraint by a dollar. Substituting L=7,400 and K=1,233.33 into equation (i) above yields:

    $2 \cdot (1{,}233.33)^{-.5} \cdot (7{,}400)^{.5} - \lambda \cdot 108 = 0$. That is, $\lambda = 4.8989/108 = $ **.045**. Alternatively, an additional \$100 will produce about 4.5 more ladders.

Appendix 7B

Production and Linear Programming

In this appendix, linear programming is used to determine the optimal *input* combinations from different production processes.

A. <u>Formulation of the Output-Maximization Problem</u>

1. Manufacturers have alternative production processes, some involving mostly labor, others using machinery more intensively.

2. The objective is to maximize output from these production processes, given constraints on the inputs available, such as plant capacity or union labor contract constraints.

3. The linear programming techniques apply to many different economic problems, including production issues. The critical step is to take primary information (as in a *story* problem) and form it into a linear programming problem.

4. DESK EXAMPLE: A manufacturer could use two processes. The first is labor intensive--it takes 1 machine-hour and 4 worker-hours to build one desk. The second process is capital (or machine) intensive--it takes 5 machine-hours and 2 worker-hours to construct one desk. The manufacturer has at most 16 machine-hours available per day, and at most 32 worker-hours available per day. The manufacturer wishes to maximize desks built. Set up the linear programming (LP) problem.

5. Max $Q_1 + Q_2$ subject to: $Q_1 + 5 \cdot Q_2 \leq 16$ the machine-hour constraint.

   $4 \cdot Q_1 + 2 \cdot Q_2 \leq 32$ the labor-hour constraint.

   Q_1 and $Q_2 \geq 0$ the non-negativity constraint.

6. Using graphical or computer software techniques, such as ForeProfit or LINDO, we find that the optimal solution is $Q_1 = 7.1111$ and $Q_2 = 1.7778$.

    a. This implies that both the labor-intensive and the machine-intensive processes were used.

    b. Given the relative abundance of labor to this desk manufacturer, it built most of the desks using that process.

7. Each production process can be illustrated as a ray from the origin. By combining several production processes, the firm achieves many alternative points on *isoquants*. Isoquants are the locus of all input combinations with the same level of output.

B. Profit-Maximization Problem

1. With constant returns to scale in each production process (which is assumed if we use linear production processes), and with constant costs for inputs and constant output prices, each unit of output is associated with a level of profits. The amount of profit from each production process may differ.

2. Production problems, such as the example of the desk manufacturer, can be changed into profit-maximization problems.

    EXAMPLE: Suppose labor costs $10 per man-hour and machinery costs $15 per hour. If the wholesale price of desks were $180, then the profit contribution of the first process would be $125 = [$180 - $15 - 4·$10].

    The profit contribution of the second process would be $85 = [$180 - 5·$15 - 2·$10].

3. The objective is: Max $\pi = 125 \cdot Q_1 + 85 \cdot Q_2$. This can be graphed as *isoprofit curves,* which are the locus of all output combinations with the same level of profit.

    EXAMPLE: To find the isoprofit line for the desk example, we know that the profit for one desk is $85 for process 2, using 2 labor hours and 5 machine hours. Since one desk using process 1 generates $125, to make $85 of profits requires only 68% of its 4 hours of labor and 1 machine hour.

    That is, 2.72 man-hours and .68 machine hours generates the same profit as 2 man-hours and 5 machine hours. Connecting these points reveals the slope of the isoprofit line.

4. In linear programming problems, labor, capital, or other inputs are constrained. The feasible region includes all input combinations that lie within these constraints.

5. The *optimal solution* occurs at the highest point of the feasible region that just touches the highest isoprofit line.

6. In the specific example of the desk manufacturer, with a maximum of 32 man-hours and 16 machine hours per day, profit , $\pi = 125 \cdot Q_1 + 85 \cdot Q_2 = 125 \cdot (7.1111) + 85 \cdot (1.778) = \$1,040$ per day in profit.

True and False Questions

Agree or disagree with the following statements, and correct the part that is erroneous.

1. A linear process ray from the origin assumes that output is produced in *fixed proportions* on inputs.

2. If labor is graphed on the vertical axis, and capital is graphed along the horizontal axis, a process ray that rises very rapidly is likely to be considered capital-intensive.

3. Linear programming can be applied to production problems because some inputs, particularly plant capacity, are inequality constraints.

4. A *production isoquant* graphs the feasible region for the inputs.

5. An increase in the allowable amount of each input will expand the feasible region.

6. A production problem may be converted into a profit-maximization problem.

7. Since one production process is always the most efficient, firms will end up using only one production process.

8. The *isoprofit line* shows the different input combinations that generate the same level of profit.

Answers
1. True.
2. Disagree. A steeply rising process ray would be labor-intensive.
3. True. In the short run, capacity may be fixed at a maximum level.

4. Disagree. The production isoquant gives the locus of all input combinations with the same level of output.
5. True.
6. True.
7. Disagree. Because of input constraints and different input requirements for each process, firms may well find it profitable to allow a combination of processes to exist, even if one process is technically more efficient. For example, students sometimes find long division by hand to be helpful for a few problems, even though we realize that calculators are more efficient.
8. True.

Multiple Choice Questions

Questions 1 through 6 all refer to a family-owned bead necklace operation as follows:

In Process 1, bead necklaces can be made entirely by hand. Each necklace takes 1 hour. Alternatively, in Process 2, a bead-threading machine process requires 20 minutes of machine time and 20 minutes of labor. Suppose bead necklaces are manufactured by a family with 16 hours of available time per day, and 8 hours of machine time.

1. The linear programming constraints are:
   a. $Q_1 + .333 \cdot Q_2$ ≤ 16 labor constraint
   $ .333 \cdot Q_2$ ≤ 8 machine constraint
   $ Q_1$ and Q_2 ≥ 0 non-negativity constraint

   b. $Q_1 + 20 \cdot Q_2$ ≤ 16 labor constraint
   $ 20 \cdot Q_2$ ≤ 8 machine constraint
   $ Q_1$ and Q_2 ≥ 0 non-negativity constraint

   c. $Q_1 + 20 \cdot Q_2$ ≤ 16 labor constraint
   $ .333 \cdot Q_2$ ≤ 8 machine constraint
   $ Q_1$ and Q_2 ≥ 0 non-negativity constraint

   d. none of the above.

2. What is the likely objective function for the family's bead necklace linear programming problem?
   a. Max Q_1
   b. Max $Q_1 + .333 \cdot Q_2$
   c. Max $Q_1 + Q_2$
   d. none of the above.

3. Which is correct of the bead necklace production problem.
   a. If there were exactly 8 hours of labor and 8 hours of machine time available per day, the maximum number of necklaces would be 24 per day.
   b. If there were exactly 8 hours of labor and 8 hours of machine time available per day, no necklaces would be entirely hand-made.
   c. When there are 16 hours of labor available and only 8 hours of machine time, it is optimal to use both hand-made processes and machine-made processes to make necklaces.
   d. all of the above.

4. Suppose that the family now has 24 hours of machine time available per day, but still has only 16 hours of labor available. What is the likely outcome?
   a. More necklaces will be made entirely by hand.
   b. Both labor and machine-time will be binding constraints.
   c. Machine-time will become slack.
   d. Both (a) and (b).

5. Suppose the profit associated with a hand-made necklace is $6, and the profit associated with a machine made necklace is $12. Set up the objective function for a profit-maximization problem.
   a. Max $Q_1 + 12 \cdot Q_2$
   b. Max $6 \cdot Q_1 + 12 \cdot Q_2$
   c. Max $Q_1 + Q_2$
   d. none of the above.

6. One hour of labor, with no machine time generates $6 of profit, according to question 5. How much labor and machine-time is needed using Process 2 to generate $6 of profit?
   a. 10 minutes of labor and 10 minutes of machine time.
   b. .167 hours of labor and .167 hours of machine time.
   c. 1/6 hours of labor and 1/6 hours of machine time.
   d. all of the above.

Answers
1. a
2. c
3. d (With 8 hours of labor and 8 hours of machine time, the best way to produce would be with process 2, which would achieve 24 necklaces. There is no slack labor or machine time, and nothing would be handmade.)
4. c
5. b
6. d

Worked Problem

1. **Ibbotson Associates** produces high quality financial data on domestic and international stock, bond, real estate, and money markets. Ibbotson has recently hired you as a manager of its international data collection operation. Data collection is exceptionally labor intensive, yet there are two data collection processes you may select for international monthly data.

   Process 1 takes 4 hours of labor and 2 hours of interconnection with international financial exchanges per country per month.

   Process 2 takes 20 hours of labor and 0 hours of interconnection with international financial exchanges per country per month.

   The data collection operation has 540 hours of useful labor-hours available per month. Because of the hardwired nature of computer interconnects, you have at most 50 hours of computer interconnections. Though it is not entirely correct, it is assumed that the difficulty of collecting data in all countries is identical.

   a. Your objective is to maximize the number of countries from which data is collected each month. Set up the Linear Programming problem.

      Answer: The objective is to maximize output from the two processes.

      Max $Q_1 + Q_2$ subject to:

      $$4 \cdot Q_1 + 20 \cdot Q_2 \leq 540$$
      $$20 \cdot Q_1 \leq 50$$
      $$Q_1 \text{ and } Q_2 \geq 0$$

   b. Find the optimal assignment between the two processes, and the maximum amount of data by country that your Data Collection Department could gather per month.

      Answer: With only two data collection processes, this problem can be readily solved graphically or may be solved using linear programming software.

      Graphically, the feasible region is 540 hours of labor on the vertical axis and 50 hours of computer interconnect time. Using 500 hours of labor achieves data collection from 25 countries using process 1. Using process 2 to collect data from 25 countries requires 100 hours of labor and 50 hours of computer time. Hence,

connecting these two observations is an *isoquant*.   The slope of the isoquant is - 8. However, this isoquant does not represent the greatest output possible.

At the corner point of 540 labor-hours and 50 computer-hours is the highest isoquant. An isoquant with a slope of -8 must hit the vertical axis at 940; that is, $L = 940 - 8 \cdot K$, where L is labor time and K is computer time. This isoquant is consistent with a total output of 47 countries with data collected, because using only labor $940/20 = 47$.

To find the exact assignment between process 1 and process 2, complete a parallelogram of the two *process rays* which achieve the corner point.   The process ray for process 2 is: $L = .50 \cdot K$. The process ray for process 1 is a vertical line from the origin.

From the corner point, construct a ray back to the vertical axis that is parallel to process ray 2. Since it has a slope of -.50, it will intersect the origin at $L = 440$. This shows that 22 countries will be collected manually with process 1, and 25 countries will be collected using process 2. Linear programming computer program yields results as follows:

LP routine - Primal solution results

Variable	Solution value	Contribution
Q1	*25.0*	*25.00*
Q2	22.0	22.00

Value of the objective function: Max OUTPUT = 47.00

LP routine - Dual solution results

Constraint	Shadow price	Contribution
Constraint 1	0.0500	27.0000
Constraint 2	0.4000	20.0000

Value of the objective function: OUTPUT = 47.000

The solution involves collecting data from 47 countries. The shadow price of time from both constraints is positive. Neither constraint is slack.

Chapter 8

Cost Analysis

Managers seek to produce the highest quality products at the lowest possible cost. Firms that are satisfied with the status quo find that competitors arise that can produce at lower costs. The advantages once assigned to being large firms (economies of scale and scope) have not provided the advantages of flexibility and agility found in some smaller companies. This chapter introduces cost concepts that are helpful in the task of finding lower cost methods to produce goods and services.

A. The Meaning and Measurement of Cost

1. Economic Cost *vs.* Accounting Cost

   a. The *Economic Cost* or *Opportunity Cost* of an economic good or service is the value of its next best alternative use. Economic cost, therefore, is subjective, as it depends on the alternatives one is examining. It is a measure of cost that helps in decision-making.

   b. Accountants have been trained to examine historical outlays of funds, as an objective measure of cost.

2. *Explicit vs. Implicit costs* (the costs borne by owner supplied resources).

3. Examples of Relevant Cost Concepts:

   a. **Depreciation Cost Measurement.** Accounting depreciation (*e.g.*, straight-line depreciation) tends to have little real-world relationship to actual loss of value, whereas to an economist the actual loss of value is the true cost of using machinery.

   b. **Inventory Valuation.** Accounting valuation depends on its acquisition cost, whereas economists view the cost of inventory as the cost of replacement.

   c. **Unutilized Facilities.** Empty space may appear to have "no cost", whereas economists view its alternative use (*e.g.*, rental value) as its opportunity cost.

147

d. **Measures of Profitability.** Accountants and economists view *profit* differently. Accounting profit, at its simplest, is revenues minus explicit costs. Economists include other implicit costs (such as a normal profit on invested capital).

    Economic Profit = Total Revenues - Explicit Costs - Implicit Costs

4. Marginal cost — the additional cost of the last unit produced

5. Fixed costs — those costs not affected by the quantity of goods or services produced.

6. Sunk costs — costs already incurred, which will not be altered by further decisions. Therefore, sunk costs are correctly ignored in making good economic decisions.

7. Two primary components of cost:

    a. input prices — amount spent to purchase inputs.

    b. productivity — how productive are those inputs.

8. Time, an important dimension of costs in the short run (SR) and long run (LR).

B. <u>Short Run Cost Functions — There are Fixed Costs</u>

1. Total cost function: Total Cost = Fixed Cost + Variable Cost

$$TC = FC + VC$$

2. Average total cost is: $ATC = TC/Q$.
   Average variable cost is: $AVC = VC/Q$.
   Average fixed cost is: $AFC = FC/Q$

3. So it must be that: $ATC = AFC + AVC$

4. The typical form is a U-shaped ATC curve with MC (marginal cost) which intersects ATC from below at its minimum.

5. In the SR, with some factors of production fixed, SR costs are influenced by the law of diminishing returns. Attempts to expand production in the SR tend to find declining marginal products for the variable inputs.

C. <u>Relation of Cost and Production Curves</u>

1. AP_L and AVC are inversely related.

2. MP_L and MC are inversely related.

D. <u>Theory of Long Run Cost Functions</u>

1. The Long Run Average Cost (LRAC) is an envelope of the short run average cost curves (SRAC). The long run (LR) cost is the lowest cost possible for any output.

2. Since, LR costs are least cost, they must be efficient; that is, obey the equi-marginal principle: $MP_X/C_X = MP_Y/C_Y$.

3. Long run marginal cost (LRMC) is more elastic than the short run marginal cost curve (SRMC). The LRMC is the derivative of the long run total cost curve.

E. <u>Economies and Diseconomies of Scale</u>

1. In the SR, costs are influenced by the law of diminishing returns, but in the LR we can expand all inputs.

2. If all input prices were constant, and the firm had constant return to scale production functions, the LRAC would be a flat line.

3. Economists tend to think that the LRAC is U-shaped. The first section is dominated by economies of scale which bring costs down. These economies include:

    a. **Product-specific economies** which include specialization and learning curve effects.

    b. **Plant-specific economies**, such as economies in overhead, required reserves, investment, or interactions among products (*economies of scope*).

    c. **Firm-specific economies** which are economies in distribution and transportation of a geographically dispersed firm, or economies in marketing, sales promotion, or R&D of multi-product firms.

4. The mid-section of the LRAC is thought to be flat, where most of the economies of scale and scope have been exploited, and there is no difficulty with the problems of very large size.

5. The last section of the LRAC is believed to be upward rising due to the problem of *diseconomies of scale*. These include transportation costs, imperfections in the labor market, and problems of coordination and control by management.

6. The **minimum efficient scale** (MES) is the smallest scale at which minimum per unit costs are attained. Note that any size larger than the MES is just as efficient as MES, so long as the firm does not expand to the point that the LRAC is upward rising.

7. Modern Schools of Business Management attempt to offer techniques to avoid diseconomies of scale. The introduction of profit centers, transfer pricing, and tying incentives to performance have tended to increase the MES and pushed out the point at which diseconomies of scale start to take effect.

8. Ford has developed an aluminum frame for its cars. The MES dropped from 500,000 frames made of steel to just 50,000 frames in aluminum. Steel is cheaper for large annual output, whereas aluminum is cheaper for smaller annual output.

True and False Questions

Agree or disagree with the following statements, and correct the part that is erroneous.

1. Average total cost is the sum of fixed cost plus variable cost.

2. "Sunk costs" is merely an alternative name for "fixed costs".

3. In cost theory, the "long run" is defined as when we are all dead.

4. An unused storage building has an opportunity cost of its next best alternative use.

5. We would expect LRAC to be typically lower than SRAC.

6. An increase in productivity, which increases the marginal product of labor, will tend to reduce marginal costs.

7. Procter & Gamble sometimes buys 60 seconds of TV advertising time, and divides it into two commercials of 30 seconds each for two different products. This is an example of a product-specific economy of scale.

8. It is often believed that the minimum efficient scale for the automobile industry is very large. This tends to create an industry with few firms.

9. Apparently there are few important sources of economies of scale in the cement mixing industry, since most cement firms are quite local.

10. If the cost per unit in the manufacture of tables declines as the size of the furniture manufacturer rises, then this is an example of an economy of scope.

Answers

1. Disagree. Average total cost is the sum of **average** fixed cost plus **average** variable cost.
2. Disagree. Sunk cost refer to costs borne in the past, whereas fixed costs are costs that do not change with the scale of the operation.
3. Disagree. In cost theory, the long run is when all inputs are variable so that we can produce at the lowest possible cost. John Maynard Keynes used the line, "in the long run, we are all dead", to criticize the Classical economists of his day that believed the economy would automatically correct itself from a depression *in the long run.*
4. True.
5. True.
6. True.
7. Disagree. This is a firm-specific economy of scale.
8. True.
9. True.
10. Disagree. This is an example of an economy of scale, not scope.

Multiple Choice Questions

1. Suppose that fixed costs is 100 and that average variable cost is $8 at an output of seven units. What is total cost at an output of 7?
   a. $56.
   b. $57.
   c. $156.
   d. $22.28

2. If marginal costs are less than average total costs as output increases, what *cannot* be true?
   a. Average total costs are rising.
   b. Average total costs have not yet reached their minimum point.
   c. Average fixed cost is decreasing.
   d. Average total costs are decreasing.

3. The short-run average cost curve is U-shaped because:
   a. diminishing returns will drive costs up before increasing returns will reduce marginal cost.
   b. whatever goes up must come down.
   c. as you produce more output, AFC declines; however, as plant capacity is reached, MC rises, driving average costs up again.
   d. U-shape cost curves only occur in the long run.

4. If marginal costs are greater than average total costs, then:
    a. average total cost curve is falling.
    b. average total cost curve is flat.
    c. average total cost curve is rising.
    d. average total cost curve is a minimum.

5. Which is not a reason for marginal cost curves to rise in the short run:
    a. because of the law of diminishing returns.
    b. because marginal products decline after a point in the short run.
    c. because marginal products and marginal costs are inversely related.
    d. because average fixed costs continuously decline in output.

6. In Japan, the top four brokerage houses handle over 80% of all stock sales. Small brokerage houses do not exist. From this information we could surmise:
    a. that brokerage services in Japan are highly competitive.
    b. that the minimum efficient scale for Japanese brokerage houses is quite large.
    c. that the Japanese do not like to trade stocks.
    d. that the long run cost curve for brokerage services is flat.

7. In the "short run":
    a. output is fixed.
    b. at least one input is fixed.
    c. all of the inputs are permitted to vary.
    d. there is no fixed cost.

In questions 8 and 9, suppose that a firm using two inputs (capital and labor) has selected the levels of usage of capital and labor at which $MP_K = 50$ and $MP_L = 20$.

8. If the price of labor is $4 per unit and the price of capital is $10 per unit:
    a. the firm should increase its usage of labor relative to capital.
    b. the firm is using the cost minimizing combination of capital and labor.
    c. the firm should increase its usage of capital relative to labor.
    d. there is insufficient data to answer this question.

9. If the price of labor is $5 per unit and the price of capital is $10 per unit:
    a. the firm should increase its usage of labor relative to capital.
    b. the firm is using the optimal (cost minimizing) combination of capital and labor.
    c. the firm should increase its usage of capital relative to labor.
    d. there is insufficient data to answer this question.

10. If TC is 10,000, and if output is 1,000, then:
    a. ATC = 10,000   c. ATC = 100
    b. ATC = 1,000   d. ATC = 10

11. In the short run, if the price is less than ATC but higher than AVC:
    a. the firm earns an economic profit.
    b. the firm earns a loss if it continues to operate, but a smaller loss than if it shut down.
    c. the firm should shut down in the short run.
    d. the firm should expand production.

12. Which is true concerning long run and short run cost curves:
    a. the long run marginal cost curve tends to be flatter that a short run cost curve.
    b. some factors of production are fixed in the short run.
    c. the long run costs represent the least cost combination of inputs to produce each output.
    d. all of the above.

13. We find that the long run average cost for electrical generation declines in the size of the plant (measured in megawatt hours). This indicates that:
    a. there exist plant-specific economies of scale.
    b. declining marginal product of labor.
    c. diseconomies of scale.
    d. imperfections in the labor market.

14. If $VC = 100 \, Q - 2 \, Q^2 + .1 \, Q^3$, find MC at an output of $Q = 10$. (Hint: Find the derivative and evaluate it at the appropriate output level.)
    a. $MC = 100$
    b. $MC = 90$
    c. $MC = 80$
    d. $MC = 10$

15. If the average product of labor suddenly rises, then:
    a. the average variable cost of output also rises.
    b. the fixed cost falls.
    c. the average variable cost of output declines.
    d. the total cost rises.

16. A U-shaped long-run average cost curve indicates the presence of
    a. decreasing and then increasing returns to scale.
    b. inefficient production.
    c. increasing and then decreasing returns to scale.
    d. natural monopoly.

17. You are given the following cost function: $TC = 1{,}500 + 300{\cdot}Q + 25{\cdot}Q^2$. From this cost we know:
    a. Fixed cost is 300.
    b. Average total cost is 1500/Q.
    c. Total cost declines as Q rises.
    d. Marginal cost is 300 + 50 Q

18. *Economies of Scope* refers to situations where
    a. per unit costs are unaffected when two or more types of products are produced.
    b. per unit costs are reduced when two or more types of products are produced.
    c. per unit costs are increased when two or more types of products are produced.
    d. there are increasing returns to scale.

19. If $TC = 321 + 55{\cdot}Q - 5{\cdot}Q^2$, then *average cost* at Q = 10 is:
    a. Less than 10
    b. Between 10 and 35
    c. Between 35 and 75
    d. More than 75

20. Which of the following is correct?
    a. Average total cost is the sum of average fixed cost plus average variable cost.
    b. "Sunk costs" is an alternative name for "marginal costs".
    c. We would expect the long run average cost (LRAC) curve to be rising in a declining cost industry.
    d. The minimum efficient scale for the concrete mixing firms must be very large.

21. The graph of short run average variable costs:
    a. always rises over output in the short run.
    b. always falls over output in the short run.
    c. rises at first and then falls over output in the short run.
    d. falls at first and then rises over output in the short run.

Answers

1. c	8. b	15. c
2. a	9. c	16. c
3. c	10. d	17. d
4. c	11. b	18. b
5. d	12. d	19. c (AC = 37.1)
6. b	13. a	20. a
7. b	14. b	21. d

Worked Problems

1. *Use the following information to answer questions a through c.*

Output	Fixed Cost	Variable Cost
0	$50	$0
5		20
10		35
15		55
20		80

a. Calculate the average total cost at an output of 20.

Answer: Average total cost is ATC = (TC)/Q = (FC + VC)/Q = (50 + 80)/20 = 130/20 = **$6.50**.

b. At an output of 10, what is total cost?

Answer: Total cost, at an output of 10, is: TC = FC + VC = 50 + 35 = **$85**.

c. What is the marginal cost as output is increased from 5 to 10 units?

Answer: Marginal costs are the change in total costs for a change in quantity. Increasing output from Q=5 to Q=10 increases cost by $15, for this 5 unit increase. Therefore, MC = $\delta TC/\delta Q$ = $15/5 = **$3**.

2. Consider the following <u>variable</u> cost function: $VC = 120 \cdot Q - 9 \cdot Q^2 + .25 \cdot Q^3$

   Fixed costs are equal to $180 and Q is output.

   a. Determine the **average variable cost function**.

   Answer: AVC = VC/Q = $[120 \cdot Q - 9 \cdot Q^2 + .25 \cdot Q^3]/Q = 120 - 9 \cdot Q + .25 \cdot Q^2$.

   b. Find <u>minimum</u> AVC quantity.

   Answer: AVC is at a minimum when the derivative of AVC with respect to Q equals zero. $\partial AVC/\partial Q = -9 + .5Q = 0$. Hence, Q = 4.5 is the output when AVC is at its lowest.

c. Determine the **marginal cost function**.

> *Answer:* Marginal cost is the derivative of total cost.
>
> $TC = FC + VC = 180 + 120 \cdot Q - 9 \cdot Q^2 + .25 \cdot Q^3$
>
> $MC = \partial TC / \partial Q = \mathbf{120 - 18 \cdot Q + .75 \cdot Q^2}$.
>
> Note that marginal cost is also the derivative of variable cost, since by definition, fixed cost does not change as output increases.

Net Sources

1. **Economies of scale in cash**   *www.spc.uchicago.edu/users/cbm4/mdfirms.html*

    Casey B. Mulligan, "Scale Economies, the Value of Time, and the Demand for Money: Longitudinal Evidence from Firms." *Journal of Political Economy*, 105(5), October 1997:1061-79, studied 12,000 firms. As firm size increased, cash holdings as a percentage of sales declined, which is an economy of scale.

2. Debate over deregulation of naturally monopolistic industries such as electricity is growing. One issue is whether economies of scale in the generation of electricity continue to exist. Several Internet sites of interest in this debate are:

    *   **The Electric Power Supply Association**   *www.epsa.org/*

        EPSA is the national trade association that seeks to bring the benefits of competition to all electricity customers.

    *   **American Public Power Association**   *www.appanet.org/*

        APPA is the national trade association representing more than 2,000 municipal and other state and local government-owned electric utilities.

    *   **The Federal Energy Regulatory Agency**   *www.ferc.fed.us/electric/electrc2.htm*

        The Office of Electric Power Regulation approves rates for wholesale electric sales of electricity and transmission in interstate commerce for private utilities, power marketers, power pools, power exchanges and independent system operators. The Commission acts under the legal authority of the Federal Power Act of 1935.

- **The Electric Power Research Institute**   *www.epri.com/*

    EPRI is one of America's oldest and largest research consortia, with some 700 members and an annual budget of about $500 million.

3. **PROJECT:** Use the **10-K Wizard** at   *www.tenkwizard.com/*
    Select a firm to examine their financial information on their 10-Q (Quarterly) or 10-K (Annual) filings. Go to their *financial statements*. Determine the firm's growth rate in operating revenues and the growth rate in operating expenses. Firms often change the nature of their business through mergers or divestitures, an easy type of firm to select is an electrical utility. Select your local electrical utility for your study.

Appendix 8A

The Cobb-Douglas Production Function
and the Long-Run Cost Function

Cost functions depend on the prices of inputs and the productivity of the inputs. We can see the relationships between cost and production functions in the long run by looking first at production functions with only one input, and then moving to two inputs.

A. Long Run Costs and Production Functions: One Input

1. Assume there is only one input, L. In the long run, total cost is: $TC = w \cdot L$, where w is the wage rate.

2. Assume that the one-input production function is Cobb-Douglas: $Q = L^{\beta}$.

3. Solving for L in the Cobb-Douglas production function, we find: $L = Q^{1/\beta}$.

4. Substituting this into the total cost function, we get: $TC = w \cdot Q^{1/\beta}$.

   a. This demonstrates that TC is a function of input prices (w) and output (Q).

   b. This also demonstrates that if the production function were constant returns to scale (ß=1), then TC rises linearly with output and average cost is constant.

   c. If the production function is increasing returns to scale (ß>1), then TC rises at a decreasing rate in output and average cost is declining.

   d. If the production function is decreasing returns to scale (ß<1), then TC rises at an increasing rate in output and average cost rises.

B.   Long Run Costs and Production Functions: Two Inputs

1. With two inputs, K and L, the long run cost is: $TC = w \cdot L + r \cdot K$, where w is the wage rate and r is the cost of capital, K.

2. Assume that the two-input production function is Cobb-Douglas: $Q = K^{\alpha} \cdot L^{\beta}$.

3. The manager attempts to minimize cost, subject to an output constraint. This is readily formed into a Lagrangian Multiplier problem.

$$\text{Min } L = w{\cdot}L + r{\cdot}K + \lambda{\cdot}[\,K^{\alpha}{\cdot}L^{\beta} - Q\,]$$

4. Differentiating with respect to L, K, and λ, and setting these derivatives equal to zero provides the least cost input combinations (L^* and K^*).

5. The derivatives are:

   a. $L_L = w + \lambda{\cdot}[\beta{\cdot}K^{\alpha}{\cdot}L^{\beta-1}] = 0$

   b. $L_K = r + \lambda{\cdot}[\alpha{\cdot}K^{\alpha-1}{\cdot}L^{\beta}] = 0$

6. The actual solution is less interesting than learning about the arguments of the solution:

   (i) $L^* = f(Q, w, r, \alpha, \beta) = Q^{(1/(\alpha+\beta))}{\cdot}(\beta{\cdot}r/\alpha{\cdot}w)^{(\alpha/(\alpha+\beta))}$

   (ii) $K^* = g(Q, w, r, \alpha, \beta) = Q^{(1/(\alpha+\beta))}{\cdot}(\alpha{\cdot}w/\beta{\cdot}r)^{(\beta/(\alpha+\beta))}$

7. Accordingly, Total Cost, $TC = w{\cdot}L^* + r{\cdot}K^* =$

$$TC = w{\cdot}Q^{(1/(\alpha+\beta))}{\cdot}(\alpha{\cdot}w/\beta{\cdot}r)^{(\beta/(\alpha+\beta))} + r{\cdot}Q^{(1/(\alpha+\beta))}{\cdot}(\alpha{\cdot}w/\beta{\cdot}r)^{(\alpha/(\alpha+\beta))}$$

8. While this expression is complex, there are several important conclusions that can be demonstrated:

   a. If the production function is constant returns to scale ($\alpha+\beta=1$), then $1/(\alpha+\beta)$ also equals one, and total cost rises linearly in output. That means that average cost is constant.

   b. If the production function is increasing returns to scale ($\alpha+\beta>1$), then $1/(\alpha+\beta)$ less than 1, and total cost rises at a decreasing rate in output. That means that average cost declines.

   c. If the production function is decreasing returns to scale ($\alpha+\beta<1$), then $1/(\alpha+\beta)$ is greater than one, and total cost rises at an increasing rate in output. That means that average cost rises.

   d. If w and r increase at the same percentage rate, then total cost will increase by that same rate. Note that ($\alpha{\cdot}w/\beta{\cdot}r$) is a ratio that does not change if w and r both rise by the same percentage rate. This shows that a doubling of all input prices would double LR cost.

True and False Questions

Agree or disagree with the following statements, and correct the part that is erroneous.

1. Long run cost curves refer to the cost of producing any given output using the least cost combination of inputs, assuming that all inputs are variable.

2. The greater the economies of scale, the more likely it is for average costs to rise in output.

3. If labor costs rise 10%, and capital costs rise 10%, then LR total costs will rise 20%.

4. If production functions are constant returns to scale, but as all firms expand production the prices of inputs rise with output, then average cost curves can rise due to rising input prices.

5. If prices of inputs are constant, doubling all inputs will more than double output if the production function is increasing returns to scale.

Answers
1. True.
2. Disagree. Average costs decline in output when there are economies of scale.
3. Disagree. LR total costs will rise by 10%, assuming that capital and labor are the only inputs.
4. True. Both production functions and input prices affect costs, as pointed out by the British economist, Professor Joan Robinson, in "Rising Supply Price," *Economica*, 1941.
5. True.

Multiple Choice Questions

1. Long run cost functions depend on all of the following, EXCEPT:
   a. whether the production function is increasing, decreasing, or constant returns to scale.
   b. the size of the fixed costs.
   c. the prices paid to inputs of production.
   d. the amount produced.

2. Long run average cost may rise in output for all of the following reasons, EXCEPT:
   a. the production function is constant returns to scale.
   b. the input prices are bid higher in input markets as all firms expand production.
   c. the sum of the exponents in the Cobb-Douglas production function sum to .89.
   d. the production function is decreasing returns to scale.

3. If there were three inputs in the long run cost function, which would most likely lead to long run total costs rising linearly in output?
   a. The wage rate for labor rises as the firm hires workers who live farther away from the factory.
   b. The production function is known to have decreasing returns to scale.
   c. The Cobb-Douglas production function is: $Q = A \cdot K^{.5} \cdot L^{.2} \cdot M^{.3}$.
   d. The exponents of the Cobb-Douglas production function sum to 1.445.

4. A sudden, but permanent, increase in productivity will:
   a. have no effect on long run total costs.
   b. will raise total costs.
   c. will raise average costs.
   d. will reduce total costs and average costs.

5. There are few nationally advertised concrete firms, whereas there are several nationally advertised manufacturers of windows. This is consistent with the view:
   a. that windows are more important than concrete.
   b. that there may be economies of scale in concrete manufacture.
   c. that there may be economies of scale in window construction.
   d. all of the above.

6. The National Hardware Store Association is concerned with the decline in the number of small, family-owned hardware stores as the national chains continue to expand. They commissioned you to estimate a Cobb-Douglas production function with K measured in square feet of store, L the number of clerks, and Q the dollar volume of sales per store. The results were: $Q = A \cdot K^{.47} \cdot L^{.56}$.
   a. You report that there is constant returns to scale in hardware stores.
   b. The sad news is that there is decreasing returns to scale in hardware stores.
   c. The decline of small stores may be due to increasing returns to scale in hardware stores.
   d. Only linear functional forms can be used to find economies of scale.

7. If all input prices double, long run cost would:
   a. rise by 50%
   b. double as well.
   c. stay constant, because in the long run, input prices are irrelevant.
   d. decline, because of increasing returns to scale.

Answers

1. b	5. c
2. a	6. c
3. c	7. b
4. d	

Worked Problem

1. Using a cross section of firms, the production function for furniture manufacturers in North Carolina has been found to be:

$$Q = K^{.5} \cdot L^{.6}$$

Wage rates in North Carolina are $18 per hour. The cost of capital, measured in $1000 units, is $90.

   a. You work for **Tryon Furniture**, which makes Shaker-style wooden chairs. You believe that this production function more or less fits your firm, and that the costs of labor and capital appear to be accurate. What is the optimal amount of labor and capital for any given amount of output (Q = chairs).

   Answer: Set the problem up as a Lagrangian Multiplier minimization problem:

   $$\text{Min } L = 18 \cdot L + 90 \cdot K + \lambda \cdot [K^{.5} \cdot L^{.6} - Q]$$

   (i) $L_L = 18 + \lambda \cdot (.6) K^{.5} \cdot L^{-.4} = 0$
   (ii) $L_K = 90 + \lambda \cdot (.5) K^{-.5} \cdot L^{.6} = 0$
   (iii) $L_\lambda = K^{.5} \cdot L^{.6} - Q = 0$

   Using (i) and (ii) to eliminate lambda, yields: $18/90 = (.6) K^{.5} \cdot L^{-.4}/(.5) K^{-.5} \cdot L^{.6}$. Simplifying this gives: $2L = 6 \cdot K$ or $K = .1667 \cdot L$. Substituting that into equation (iii) produces: $Q = 6^{.6} \cdot K^{1.1} = 2.93 \cdot K^{1.1}$.

   Therefore, $K^{1.1} = .34133 \cdot Q^{1/1.1}$. So, **$K^* = .3763 \cdot Q^{.9091}$**. This provides the same answer as when the exponents for the production function are inserted into equation 6(ii) on page 172. Similarly, substituting for K, produces $Q = .1667^{.5} \cdot L^{1.1} = .40824 \cdot L^{1.1}$. Hence, $L^{1.1} = 2.4494 \cdot Q$. So, **$L^* = 2.4494^{.9091} \cdot Q^{.9091}$ = 2.2579 \cdot Q^{.9091}$**, which is also what you get if you substitute exponents of the production function into equation 6(i) on page 172.

b. At Tryon Furniture, find the total cost of producing 3,000 chairs and the average total cost per chair.

> *Answer:* $TC = 18 \cdot L^* + 90 \cdot K^* = 18 \cdot 2.2579 \cdot Q^{.9091} + 90 \cdot .3763 \cdot Q^{.9091} = 74.5092 \cdot [3,000]^{.9091} = 74.5092 \cdot 1,448.94 = \$107,959.49.$
>
> Dividing TC/Q, that works out to an average total cost of about \$35.98 per chair. $[107,959.49/3000 = 35.98]$

c. At Tryon Furniture, find the average total cost per chair at 4,000 chairs. Explain why the average total cost changed.

> *Answer:* $TC = 18 \cdot L^* + 90 \cdot K^* = 18 \cdot 2.2579 \cdot Q^{.9091} + 90 \cdot .3763 \cdot Q^{.9091} = 74.5092 \cdot [4,000]^{.9091} = 74.5092 \cdot 1,882.06 = \$140,230.55.$ That works out to about \$35.06 per chair.
>
> The average total cost declines as the number of chairs increases at Tryon Furniture, because of the existence of economies of scale.

2. The following long run cost function was estimated in the dairy industry using a sample of 45 Wisconsin farms. "Log" is used to mean the natural logarithm.

$$\log TC = .4 + .93 \log Q + .23 \log F + .71 \log M + .02 \log W$$
$$(.29)(.03)(.44)(.033)$$

where TC is total farm costs excluding property taxes
       Q is the quantity of milk over a three-month period
       F is the price of feed supplements
       M is the price of medical treatments for the herd, and
       W is the county average wage rate for farm hands.
       (parentheses contain standard errors of the coefficients).

a. Does there appear (at first glance) to be increasing returns to scale?

> *Answer:* The coefficient on Log Q is less than 1. This shows, holding input prices constant, that a 1% increase in output leads to only a .93% increase in costs. There must be some increasing returns to scale in the dairy industry in Wisconsin.

b. You have noted that farms in Wisconsin with fewer than 10 milking cows made up 15% of all dairy farms in Wisconsin in 1940, but in 1990, there are no commercial dairy farms with fewer than 10 cows. What does this imply to you?

Answer: According to the "Survivorship Technique," the decline of small dairy herds demonstrates that they must have higher costs than other sizes. The survivorship technique is fully discussed in the next chapter. The evidence for increasing returns in part (a), which further substantiates this finding.

Chapter 9

Applications of Cost Theory

Managers must have reliable cost information to make good decisions. Correctly or incorrectly assigning costs, such as overhead, can make profitable product-lines appear unprofitable. Techniques for estimating costs in the short run and the long run are discussed, as well as break-even analysis and measures of the degree of operating leverage.

A. Estimating Cost Relationships

    1. Cost is function of output, input prices, and other productivity issues:
       $Q = f(Q, w, r, ...)$.

    2. Often multiple regression analysis based on historic data provides guidance as to the relationship between cost and a set of variables.

    3. Multi-product firms and multi-product plants present the problem of what goods are similar enough to be lumped together. The time series must have several observations. The length of each period depends on collecting many observations but with the presumption that the rate of production is constant through each period.

    4. The functional form chosen depends on whether we estimate total, marginal, or average costs, and whether it is a short-run cost or a long-run cost function.

B. Estimating Short Run Cost Functions

    1. Short run total costs are expected to be S-shaped, and short run average costs are expected to be U-shaped. Polynomial functions in Q allow for these shapes.

    2. If total cost is cubic, as in: $\mathbf{TC = a + b \cdot Q + c \cdot Q^2 + d \cdot Q^3}$, then:

        a. Marginal cost is quadratic: $MC = b + 2c \cdot Q + 3d \cdot Q^2$

        b. Average cost is: $AC = a/Q + b + c \cdot Q + d \cdot Q^2$

    3. An alternative functional relationship is logarithmic.

$$\ln TC = a + b \cdot \ln Q$$

     a. If total cost is logarithmic, and if b = 1, then there are constant returns to scale. A 1% increase in Q will increase TC by 1%, all else held constant.

     b. If total cost is logarithmic, and if b > 1, then there are decreasing returns to scale.

     c. With b < 1, and if the cost function is logarithmic, then there are increasing returns to scale.

4. The textbook examples of cost functions include food processing, where costs appeared to be constant after creating a weighted "index" of output from 14 different food products for a British firm. Another example involved electricity generation, where there is really only one output. Cost was a linear function of output, and the cubic and quadratic terms were generally insignificant.

5. In the "What went wrong with" section, Boeing uses new engineering diagrams for each Boeing 747 it builds. This raises the marginal cost of a new jet above its price. Boeing should consider customization of jets from a common platform to reduce costs.

C. Estimating Long Run Cost Functions

1. Long run costs can be estimated on a cross-section of plants or on a single plant that produced varying amounts of output. Both assume that the plant or plants are operating as efficiently as possible for that output.

2. Analysis of costs in multiple-product food processing found that costs were linear; hence marginal costs were constant.

3. A cross-section of electrical plants shows average cost rapidly declines until the minimum efficient scale, and then slowly rises.

4. *Engineering Cost Techniques.* An alternative to fitting lines through historical data points using regression analysis is to use knowledge about the efficiency of machinery. Some processes have pronounced economies of scale, whereas other processes (including the costs of raw materials) do not have economies of scale.

5. The *Survivor Technique* is to examine what sizes of firms are tending to succeed over time, and what sizes are declining. This is a sort of Darwinian survival test for firm size.

6. International competition to develop new technologies in computer chip memory has led to a series of joint research ventures. The research is so extensive and expensive,

there is an economy of two or more firms working together on it. Many of these joint ventures involve firms from different countries.

D. Break-even Analysis

   1. Break-even analysis is also known as *cost-volume-profit analysis.*

   2. With curved total revenue and total cost curves, we tend to find TWO break-even points. For most managerial decisions, however, the most profitable point is the more interesting output. It occurs between the two break-even points.

   3. While cost and revenue functions are nonlinear, over large regions, we may treat them as linear. For this analysis, assume linear costs and revenue functions.

      a. $TR = P \cdot Q$ where P is a constant price and Q is output.

      b. $TC = F + V \cdot Q$ where F is fixed costs and V is variable cost per unit.

      c. Earnings before interest and taxes $EBIT = TR - TC$, which excludes financing costs, interests, and taxes.

      d. Contribution margin $= (P - V)$

      e. Break-even Quantity, $Q_b = F / (P - V) = F / $ (Contribution Margin)

   4. The break-even sales dollar volume, $S_b = P \cdot F/(P - V) = F/(1 - V/P)$, where V/P is the variable cost ratio.

   5. If we attempt to achieve a *target profit*, the output that achieves that target profit is:

$$\text{Target Volume} = [F + target\ profit] / (P - V)$$

E. Break-even Analysis and Risk Assessment

   1. The output, Q, in break-even analysis can be viewed as stochastic, as when the manager is uncertain how many will sell. We can then ask, "What is the probability of not making positive profits?"

   2. The probability of having operating losses can be computed using: $z = (Q_b - Q)/\sigma_Q$, where Q_b is the break-even quantity, Q is the expected quantity, and σ_Q is the standard deviation of output.

3. Problems with break-even analysis include:
   a. nonlinear prices and costs occur in the real world
   b. some costs are partially variable and partially fixed
   c. multiple products have costs that depend on the *mix* of goods produced
   d. uncertainty
   e. useful for only a short term planning horizon

F. Operating Leverage

1. The **Degree of Operating Leverage** (D.O.L.) is an operating profit elasticity.

$$DOL = (\% \text{ change in EBIT})/(\% \text{ change in Q}) = \textbf{(P-V)Q} / \textbf{[(P-V)Q - F]}$$

2. The DOL is a measure of the importance of fixed cost. As F rises, other things equal, DOL rises. DOL is an elasticity: a one percent change in Q will increase EBIT by the DOL percent. DOL is greater than 1, for all profitable outputs.

3. At the break-even point, the DOL is infinity.

4. *Business Risk* is the variability of a firm's EBIT. It depends on the uncertainty of Q and the firm's Degree of Operating Leverage (DOL). Firms with greater inherent risk of variable output, may decide to produce with less fixed cost to moderate their overall business risk. Firms with greater certainty of sales, may elect to use greater amounts of fixed cost in their production decisions.

True and False Questions

Agree or disagree with the following statements, and correct the part that is erroneous.

1. The greater is the output sold, the greater is the DOL.

2. The greater is fixed cost, the greater is the DOL.

3. The shape of a cubic function, a polynomial of degree 3, is U-shaped.

4. If the total cost function is cubic, the marginal cost function is quadratic.

5. "Business risk" refers to the problem of having a lot of debt in the firm.

6. Other things equal, the larger is the contribution margin (P – V), the smaller is the breakeven quantity.

7. The 'Survivorship Technique' for finding the least cost size is to examine machinery closely.

Answers
1. Disagree. The DOL is greatest at the break-even point. As Q increases, the DOL declines closer and closer to 1. If there were no fixed costs, the DOL is always equal to 1.
2. True.
3. Disagree. A cubic function is S-shaped. A quadratic function, of degree 2, is U-shaped or ∩-shaped.
4. True.
5. Disagree. Business risk refers to the volatility of operating profits within the firm. Use of debt introduces financial risk of being in default of a debt payment.
6. True.
7. Disagree. The 'Survivorship Technique' looks at which firm sizes are becoming more prominent, and which firm sizes are disappearing over time. For example, larger banks are rapidly acquiring small banks . This fact leads one to conclude that the optimal size for a bank is a regional or super-regional bank at this time.

Multiple Choice Questions

1. If $TC = 123 + 55 \cdot Q - 5 \cdot Q^2$, then marginal cost at Q=4 is:
   a. 5
   b. 10
   c. 15
   d. 20

2. After estimating a TC regression, with independent variables of Q, Q^2, and Q^3, we discover that the quadratic and cubic terms were statistically insignificant, whereas the coefficient on Q was positive and significant. We conclude, therefore,
   a. that average cost is constant.
   b. that TC is linear.
   c. that there are no noticeable increasing returns to scale.
   d. all of the above.

3. The coefficient on Ln Q in a logarithmic total cost regression indicates an elasticity of TC with respect to output. If that coefficient:
   a. is greater than one, then demand is elastic.
   b. is greater than one, then the production function is increasing returns to scale.
   c. is greater than one, then the production function is decreasing returns to scale.
   d. is greater than one, then the production function is constant returns to scale.

4. When firms are operating close to their break-even point,
    a. their DOL is very large.
    b. their DOL equals 1.
    c. their DOL equals 0.
    d. their DOL is negative.

5. Suppose the expected output is 2300 and the standard deviation of output is 150. Determine the probability of having operating losses, if the break-even output is 2000.
    a. Since $z = -2$, the chances of having negative profits are only about 2.28%.
    b. Since $z = -1$, the chances of having negative profits are about 15.87%.
    c. Since $z = 0$, the chances of having negative profits are evenly split at 50%.
    d. Not enough information is provided to answer this question.

6. Instead, suppose that new information lowers the expected output to 2150, but that the standard deviation of output remains at 150. Determine the probability of having operating losses, if the break-even output is still 2000.
    a. Since $z = -2$, the chances of having negative profits are only about 2.28%.
    b. Since $z = -1$, the chances of having negative profits are about 15.87%.
    c. Since $z = 0$, the chances of having negative profits are evenly split at 50%.
    d. Not enough information is provided to answer this question.

7. Your firm manufactures air compressors. You must predict operating profits for the next year, but you anticipate a modest recession. In the past, mild recessions have led to a 10% reduction in quantity of compressors sold. You predict that operating profits will:
    a. Fall by 10%, regardless of the degree of operating leverage.
    b. Fall by less than 10%, because your firm uses some fixed costs.
    c. Fall by 13.5% if the degree of operating leverage is 1.35.
    d. Fall by 21.3% if the degree of operating leverage is .213.

8. Operating profits have been highly volatile in the department store industry. As an intern for a department store management headquarters, which of the following will tend to *reduce* the volatility of operating profits.
    a. increase the proportion of costs called fixed costs.
    b. identify ways to change fixed costs into variable costs, through short term leases, so that costs can be reduced when store sales slack off.
    c. reduce the quantity of products sold, as Q appears in the degree of operating profit formula: $(P-V) \cdot Q / [(P-V) \cdot Q - F]$.
    d. all of the above.

9. Wildly Wicked Webs creates plastic spider webs for Halloween. Fixed costs are $200,000 per year. Each plastic web has a price of $15. Variable costs are $10 each for the 60,000 units sold. Determine the degree of operating leverage.
    a. 0.45   c. 2.22
    b. 1.50   d. 3.00

10. Use data in question #9 to find the *break-even* quantity for Wildly Wicked Webs.
    a. 10,000
    b. 12,000
    c. 26,000
    d. 40,000

11. When total costs are estimated to be cubic, $TC = .078 + .891\,Q - .096\,Q^2 + .004\,Q^3$
    then a plot of the total cost curve would look like:
    a. an S-shaped curve.
    b. a U-shaped curve.
    c. a ∩-shaped curve.
    d. a Λ-shaped curve

12. Total cost is estimated using a quadratic form: $TC = C_0 + C_1\,Q + C_2\,Q^2$
    The regression results were presented as follows:

Predictor	Coeff	StdErr	T-value
Constant	500	100	5.0
Q	-5	2	-2.5
Q-squared	.2	.1	2.0

    R-square = .96
    Adj R-square = .95
    N = 45

    According to the results:
    a. Total cost is linear.
    b. At an output of 10, total cost is 400.
    c. At an output of 10, average total cost is 47.
    d. At an output of 10, fixed cost (500) is not statistically significant.

13. Cost analysis on a sample of 55 Wisconsin High Schools presents the following
    regression result:

$C = 10 - .4\,Q + .0001\,Q^2 + .1(\text{Teacher Salary}) + .9(\text{Number of Courses}) - 15(\text{Courses per teacher})$

$$R^2 = .557$$

where Q is enrollment and C is the operating expenditures per student. This
regression shows:
    a. That operating expenditure per student is CUBIC.
    b. That costs rise as teacher salaries INCREASE.
    c. That costs rise as the number of courses taught per teacher INCREASES.
    d. That 95% of the variation in cost is explained by these variables.

14. Leisure Products manufactures patio furniture. Its output is sold to wholesalers. Its cost per unit are estimated as follows:

Per unit
Direct Labor $6.00
Materials $3.00
Plant Overhead* $4.00

*The costs are allocated to each unit based on the projected production of 300,000 patio sets.

Leisure Products has commitments to sell all 300,000 sets. A new offer is made to purchase 50,000 additional sets at $12 per set to a wholesaler that is geographically distant from its current market. As the chief economic advisor to the firm, you suggest that:
   a. Leisure Products reject the $12 offer, since costs per unit are $13.00.
   b. Leisure Product think about the offer a while, and follow a stall tactic.
   c. Leisure Products accept the offer, since the incremental cost of the chairs is only $9.00, and this offer will generate a profit of $150,000.
   d. Leisure Products should give them an All or Nothing Offer, buy 350,000 patio sets or none at all.

15. Through mergers, the average size of banking firms has been growing rapidly this past decade. This evidence suggests that the cost function is downward sloping over the range of smaller-sized banks. This type of analysis is called:
   a. Regression Analysis using a cubic cost function
   b. Engineering cost technique
   c. The survivor technique
   d. Degree of operating leverage

16. Holding other factors constant, if fixed costs increase, the break-even output:
   a. increases
   b. decreases
   c. stays the same

Answers
1. c
2. d
3. c
4. a
5. a
6. b
7. c
8. b
9. d
10. d

11. a (Cubic functions have two curves, usually called S-shaped)
12. c (At Q=10, TC = 470, so average total cost is 47)
13. b
14. c
15. c
16. a

Worked Problems

1. After examining a cross section of 13 furniture manufacturers in North Carolina, you decide to estimate their long run cost function. You select a logarithmic functional form for total costs. Not all makers of furniture produce "chairs", but all output is measured in chair-equivalent units. For example, an end table may be counted *as if* it were a chair, but a sofa counts as 3 chairs.

Ordinary Least Squares Estimates

Dependent variable: TC Log

Independent variable(s):	Beta	t-statistic
Constant included	5.0548	6.8657
Q Log	0.8116	1.8163

Summary of `Goodness of fit' statistics:

Degrees of freedom = 10
R-Square = 0.61286
Adj R-Square = 0.46768

a. Write the functional equation for long run costs for furniture makers. Calculate the total cost for a furniture maker that builds 3,000 chairs.

Answer: Ln TC = 5.048 + .8116 Ln Q.   The ForeProfit software uses LOG to represent the *natural logarithm*.

We must first find the natural logarithm of 3000, which is Ln 3000 = 8.0063 (use your calculator). Therefore: Ln TC = 5.048 + .8116·[8.00636] = 11.5459.

Now we must find the anti-log of 11.5459. To do that, take the exponential of 11.5459. That is, $e^{11.5459}$ = **$103,359.44**. That is the total cost for 3,000 chairs according to this cost function.

b. Does it appear that North Carolina furniture makers experience constant returns to scale?

Answer: The coefficient on Ln Q is .8116, which is less than one. That means, a one percent increase in output leads to a less than one percent increase in costs, other things constant. That appears to demonstrate increasing returns to scale.

Those who are statistically minded may wish to test the hypothesis that the coefficient on Ln Q is equal to 1.

H_o: $\beta = 1$. The estimated t-statistic is: $t = (.8116-1)/\sigma = -.1884/.7352 = -.2562$.

We are not able to reject the hypothesis that there is constant returns to scale.

The standard error of the coefficient, σ, implicitly appears in the regression results. The regression results give the t-statistic on the hypothesis that the coefficient equals zero as $8.8657 = \beta/\sigma = .8116/.7352$. Hence, we used $\sigma = .7352$ to test the hypothesis that the coefficient equaled 1.

2. **Whiz Kids** offers computer classes to kids. Analysis of the cost structure shows that the fixed costs are $1300 per month, the variable cost per child is $9.00 per hour, and the price per hour is set at $15.

   a. What is the break-even number of hours of instruction sold per month?

   Answer: The break-even quantity occurs where TR=TC. That is: $Q_b = F/(P-V) = 1300/(15-9) = 1300/6 = 216.66$ hours of classes per month.

   b. If Whiz Kids plans on being open 8 hours a day, six days a week, assuming a 4.5 week month, what is the most number of kids one can handle on one computer a month?

   Answer: This is similar to engineering cost studies, as we calculate the number of hours per day, times six days a week, times 4.5 weeks per month. That is: $8\cdot6\cdot(4.5) = 216$ hours a month that the Whiz Kids store is open.

   c. Whiz Kids expects some hours to be peak times and other hours to be off-peak, so that the firm decided to have six computers in each store. If the number of kid-hours served per month becomes 480, what is the monthly operating profit, EBIT?

Answer: The monthly EBIT is TR - TC. TR is $15·480, and TC is ($1300 + $9·480). Hence, EBIT = (15-9)·480 - 1300 = 2,880 - 1300 = $1,580. The contribution margin is $6. So, $6 times 480 kids, minus the fixed cost is our operating profit per month in a store.

d. At 480 hours per month, what is the degree of operating leverage?

Answer: The DOL = (P-V)Q/[(P-V)Q - F] = (15-9)480/[(15-9)/480 -1300] = 2880/1580 =1.8228. A 1% increase in Q will generate a 1.8228% increase in operating profit.

e. Assuming that the summer offers the opportunity for more kids to have time for computer-assisted instruction, you forecast a 6% increase in customer hours. Use the operating profit elasticity estimated in (d) to forecast the percentage increase in operating profit expected.

Answer: The DOL is an elasticity. The elasticity is (% change in EBIT)/(% change in Q) = 1.8228. Since the denominator of the elasticity is given in the problem to be 6%, we must find the numerator. So, 6%·(1.8228) = 10.9367% increase in EBIT, or operating profit.

3. Economists working for the Petroleum Institute estimated a long run cost function for oil drilling rigs. Q is the quantity of oil drilled in a single well. A summary of the regression results appears below:

Dependent Variable: log (TC)
N=73

	Beta	T-value
Constant	-.36	0.48
log Q	.832	6.34
log w	.877	4.21
log r	.343	1.89

a. According to the regression results, does it look as if drilling is constant returns to scale, increasing returns to scale, or decreasing returns to scale? If the coefficient on the log Q were 1, it would indicate that a 1% increase in output increased cost by 1%, other things being equal. However, the coefficient does not equal one.

Answer: A 1% increase in output will increase cost by only .832%. There appears to be increasing returns to scale.

b. Test the hypothesis that the LR cost function is constant returns to scale; that is, the coefficient on Log Q equals 1, with a critical t = 2.

> *Answer:* Given the t-value and the beta on Log Q, we can compute the standard deviation of the coefficient on Log Q. The standard deviation of the coefficient on Log Q is **.1312**, because the t-value for the hypothesis that the coefficient is zero equals $(\beta - 0)/\sigma = .832/\sigma = 6.34$. Therefore, $\sigma = .1312$, because, $.832/.1312 = 6.34$.
>
> Therefore, the estimated t-statistic that the coefficient equals 1 is:
> t = (.832 - 1)/**.1312** = **-1.2805**. Hence, we cannot reject the hypothesis that petroleum drilling is constant returns to scale.

Net Sources

Economists study industries, costs, and the impact of market structure. There are several ways to find articles on costs in selected industries.

1. **RAND Journal of Economics (Search of Abstracts)**   *www.rje.org/*
   Search for any industry by a key word or phrase. For example, look at costs in the electricity and natural gas, search for "electricity and cost" or "gas and cost". The abstracts are free, but printing out the article requires a fee. Most college libraries carry the RAND Journal of Economics (formerly the Bell Journal of Economics).

2. **Breakeven Analysis**   *www.dinkytown.net/java/BreakEven.html*

   KJE Computer Solutions provides a breakeven chart that changes as you change any of the variables involved.

3. **Securities and Exchange Commission (Edgar)**   *www.sec.gov/edaux/formlynx.htm*

   Offers 10-Q SEC public filings for companies over the Internet. For example, to search for information on Rubbermaid, Inc., first select the type of form requested (try 10-Q), and the name of company (Rubbermaid), and the period of time (try since 1/1/1994). Select whichever date of filing you wish. Examine Rubbermaid's condensed statement of earnings, balance sheet, and statement of cash flows.

4. **PROJECT:** Calculate Rubbermaid's Degree of Operating Leverage using data from the SEC Edgar Form (address given in #3 above). Use recent quarterly filing information (10-Q). The DOL = $(P-V) \cdot Q/[(P-V) \cdot Q - F]$. The 10-Q filings do not give price or quantity data. Therefore, DOL can be calculated by finding the ratio:

$$DOL = (EBIT + F) / EBIT$$

EBIT is 'earnings before interest and taxes'. EBIT = TR −TC =[(P-V)•Q − F]. TR and TC are given in the 10-Q filing (the last page gives a summary of these numbers). Fixed cost is harder to find, but one heroic assumption is that "Selling, general, and administrative expenses," are likely to be primarily fixed. Using this as a measure of fixed cost, Rubbermaid's DOL can be estimated. If the number is less than one, you made an error.

Appendix 9A

The Learning Curve

The phrase, "learning by doing" has wide application in production processes. Workers and management become more efficient with experience. Ways to measure the effect of learning on costs are explored in this appendix.

A. The Learning Curve Relationship

1. The period of start-up of a new assembly line tends to be costlier than a line that has been in existence for some time. This is different from the idea of increasing returns to scale because it suggests that the amount of *past* production influences the cost of *current* production.

2. Intuitively, and objectively in many real-world examples, the cost of production declines as the accumulated past production, $Q = \Sigma q_t$, increases, where q_t is the amount produced in the tth period. Airline manufacturing, ship building, and appliance manufacturing have demonstrated the learning curve effect.

B. Learning Curve Relationship

1. Functionally, the learning curve relationship can be written as follows, where b is the rate of reduction in input cost per unit of output, a is the cost of the first input, and C is the input cost of the Qth unit:

$$C = a \cdot Q^b$$

2. Taking the (natural) logarithm of both sides, we get: **$\log C = \log a + b \cdot \log Q$**

3. When there are no data for a process, we must use analogies with other industries to come up with estimates for the parameters. However, when time series data is available, the learning curve can be estimated using ordinary least squares regressions.

4. The coefficient **b** tells us the extent of the learning curve effect.

a. If the coefficient **b**=0, then costs are at a constant level, at **a** per unit, because Q^0 always equals one.

b. If b > 0, then costs rise in output, which is exactly opposite of the learning curve effect.

c. If b < 0, then costs decline in output, as predicted by the learning curve effect.

C. The Percentage of Learning

1. The proportion by which costs are reduced through DOUBLING output is called the *percentage of learning*, L.

$$L = (C_2/C_1) \cdot 100\%$$

2. If the percentage of learning, L = 82%, then input costs decline 18% as output doubles.

True and False Questions

Agree or disagree with the following statements, and correct the part that is erroneous.

1. Learning by doing implies that total cost declines as a firm expands production.

2. If $C = 5 \cdot Q^{.5}$, then doubling output from Q=100 to Q=200 will demonstrate that L = 70.71%, and that input costs decline by 29.89% after doubling output.

3. Some college students report that they feel that they are more effective students and that their study time is more productive as juniors and seniors or graduate students than in their first year or two of college. This is a possible example of learning by doing.

4. There may be a point, after which, there are little or no benefits of learning by doing.

5. If the b-coefficient is insignificant in: log C = a + b·Log Q, then there are no apparent learning by doing effects.

Answers
1. Disagree. It implies that the cost per unit is reduced as the total amount produced, even in the past, rises. Total costs will undoubtedly increase if a firm expands production.

2. True. Plug in the output into the function. At Q_1=100, C_1=.5 (that is, C_1=5•[1/$\sqrt{100}$] =.5. At Q_2=200, C_2=.3535. The ratio of these costs in percentage terms is 70.71%.
3. True.
4. True. Some economists and social critics have felt that assembly-line work may become so tedious that productivity slips. This suggests that novelty and variety may offer a tradeoff with experience, after large amounts of output.
5. True.

Multiple Choice Questions

1. After the first year of operation, a management consultant devises a plan to pay monetary awards to assembly-line workers for expanded production. The incentive plan worked and output per worker increased.
   a. This is a clear example of learning by doing.
   b. The increased productivity is entirely due to the incentive scheme.
   c. The increased productivity may be due to the incentive scheme or learning by doing, or both. One cannot be certain.
   d. Monetary incentives at work are cruel. They make people work too hard.

2. The learning curve relationship was estimated at one firm to be: $C = .24 \cdot Q^{-.04}$.
   a. This firm could use this relationship for forecasting unit-input costs.
   b. The firm sees evidence of some learning by doing.
   c. The firm could calculate its percentage learning by doing from this.
   d. all of the above.

3. We would expect learning by doing to be most prevalent in WHICH industries:
   a. small motor assembly at Briggs & Stratton.
   b. designing computerized electronic data interchange programs for individual firms.
   c. acrylic paintings sold by top artists.
   d. writing Romance novels.

4. If doubling output reduced cost 6%, then we would predict that doubling output once again will:
   a. reduce cost by less than 6%.
   b. reduce cost another 6%.
   c. reduce cost by more than 6%.
   d. raise cost, as all of the advantages are extracted by the initial output expansion.

5. Examination of production costs sometimes shows "learning curve effects". By this we mean:
   a.   Costs rise due to "learning by doing".
   b.   Costs depend on how many units are produced per month.
   c.   Costs depend on the cumulative number of units produced over time.
   d.   Costs are U-shaped in the short run.

Answers

1. c
2. d
3. a [a reasonable argument can be made for each of the others; however, we anticipate that assembly-line, volume work would find **greater** *learning-by-doing* effects. Certainly all of the above show improvement by way of reduced time-cost as experience grows.]
4. b
5. c

Worked Problem

1. The **Tryon Furniture Company** began operation two years ago. Quarterly lumber costs and output measures were available over this period. Lumber prices did not remain constant, so data are available in both the dollars spent on lumber and the amount of lumber by the lineal foot. Scott Holcolm estimated the following regression using the amount of lumber in feet used to produce a chair (W), and the total number of chairs manufactured up to that moment. The data were:

WOOD Used Per Chair	Total CHAIRS Produced
13.50	600
13.00	1255
12.70	1910
12.50	3004
12.30	3678
12.10	4522
12.00	5744
11.95	6611

The OLS regression results were:

Dependent variable: Log WOOD

Independent variable(s):	Beta	t-statistic
Constant included	2.9345	18.7850
Log CHAIRS	-.0518	-2.6312

Summary of `Goodness of fit' statistics:

Degrees of freedom = 6
R-Square = 0.95705
Adj R-Square = 0.94989

a. Does there appear to be significant *learning by doing* effects in the use of wood? How do you explain using less wood per chair?

> *Answer:* Yes there are significant learning by doing effects. The coefficient on Log CHAIRS is negative and statistically significant at the .05 significance level. For 6 degrees of freedom, the critical t-statistic is 2.447, and the estimated t-statistic is greater at 2.6312 (we use the absolute value of the estimated t-statistic.)
>
> The reduced amount of wood probably indicates less waste of wood.

b. Estimate the *percentage of learning* for wood usage between Q=3000 and Q=6000 chairs.

> *Answer:* The cost at Q=3000 is:
> Log WOOD = 2.9345 -.0518·Log(3000) = 2.9345 -.0518·(8.0064) = 2.51977
> The anti-log is: $e^{2.51977}$ = 12.425
>
> The cost at Q = 6000 is:
> Log WOOD = 2.9345 -.0518·Log(6000) = 2.9345 -.0518·(8.6995) = 2.4839
> The anti-log is: $e^{2.4839}$ = 11.9875
>
> L = (C_2/C_1)·100% = (11.9875/12.425)·100% = **96.48%**. The percentage of learning is 96.48%.

c. By what percentage has wood usage declined between Q = 3,000 chairs and Q = 6,000 chairs?

> *Answer:* If L = 96.48%, then the wood usage declined by (1-.9648), which is .0352. That is, input cost of lumber falls by **3.52%** when the number of chairs produced doubles from Q=3,000 to Q=6,000.

Net Sources

Learning by Doing   *nicholas.www.media.mit.edu/people/nicholas/Wired/WIRED2-07.html*

Dr. Seymour Papert is the *Lego Professor of Learning Research* at MIT. (Don't laugh, it's true.) As an advocate of Learning by Doing in education, this is a short article entitled, *Learning by Doing: Don't Dissect the Frog, Build It,* from Wired. Students who use computers and the Internet are actually learning by doing, rather than memorizing facts, such as the date that Louis XVI died. (For those who want to know, on January 21, 1793 King Louis XVI was executed on the guillotine.)

PART IV - PRICING AND OUTPUT DECISIONS: STRATEGY AND TACTICS

Chapter 10

Prices, Output, and Strategy:
Pure and Monopolistic Competition

The eight chapters in Part IV demonstrate how the profit-maximizing price and quantity varies under different *market structures* and governmental regulation. The structure of a market depends on the number of buyers and sellers and on product differentiation or standardization. This chapter begins with *pure competition,* which is a standard against which other market structures are compared. When there are many firms, but the product is differentiated, the market is *monopolistically competitive.* This brand competition often involves advertising campaigns and promotional expenditures to stress tiny distinctions among products.

A. <u>The Relevant Market Concept</u>

1. A *market* is a group of economic agents that interact in a buyer-seller relationship. The number and size of the buyers and sellers affect the nature of that relationship.

2. A popular measure of concentration is the percentage of an industry comprised of the top 4 firms. Similarly, the market share held by the top 4 buyers is a popular measure of buyer concentration.

3. The *supply function* is the quantity of a good that sellers are willing to make available at all possible prices, during some time period. Supply is a function of the price of the good, the prices of inputs, and the technology available.

4. The *demand function* is the quantity of a good that buyers are willing to purchase at all possible prices, during some time period. Demand is a function of the price of the good, prices of complements and substitutes, income, expected futures prices, and tastes.

5. The *market demand curve* is the horizontal sum of all individual demand curves. The *industry supply curve* is the horizontal sum of all firm supply curves.

6. The relationship among firms is affected by:
   a. the number of firms and their relative sizes.
   b. whether the product is differentiated or standardized.
   c. whether decisions by firms are independent or coordinated (collusion).

7. On this basis, 4 market structures are defined:
   a. pure competition
   b. monopolistic competition
   c. oligopoly
   d. monopoly

B. Porter's Five Forces of Strategy

1. In his book, *Competitive Advantage,* Michael Porter lists five forces that determine competitive advantage. Each affects the likelihood of sustainable industry profitability.
   a. Substitutes (threat of substitutes can be offset by brands and special functions served by the product).
   b. Potential Entrants (threat of entrants can be reduced by high fixed costs, scale economies, restriction of access to distribution channels, or product differentiation).
   c. Buyer Power (threat of concentration of buyers).
   d. Supplier Power (threats from concentrated suppliers of key inputs affect profitability).
   e. Intensity of Rivalry (market concentration, price competition tactics, exit barriers, amount of fixed costs, and industry growth rates impact profitability).

2. The price-cost margin percentage (PCM) is: $PCM = (P - MC)/P$.

3. A price cut may help or hurt profitability depending on price elasticities and price cost margins. One way to think about this is to see how much quantity must change after a price cut to breakeven (from before the price cut). If the price cut were 10%, to breakeven the percentage change in quantity ($\Delta Q/Q$) must be large enough to satisfy the equation: **$PCM / (PCM - .10) < (1 + \Delta Q/Q)$**.

4. The larger is the price-cost margin percentage, the smaller will be the necessary quantity response to justify cutting price. If PCM is 80%, then $.8/(.8-.7) = 1.14$. Hence, a 10% cut in price must be offset by at least a 14% increase in quantity to breakeven in contribution.

5. Market share doesn't necessarily lead to high profits. The marketing attempt to maximize market share often leads to lower prices to increase sales, at the expense of profits.

C. Overview of Four Market Structures

1. Monopoly (Assumptions or Conditions)
   - (1) **one firm** (producing a specific product line)
   - (2) a perfectly differentiated product (low cross price elasticities with other products)
   - (3) substantial barriers to entry, such as absolute cost advantages, consumer loyalty, scale economies, large capital requirements, or legal barriers to entry

2. Monopolistic Competition (Assumptions or Conditions)
   - (1) many buyers and sellers
   - (2) **differentiated product**
   - (3) free entry and exit
   - (4) no collusion among the firms

   Each firm will view its demand curve as declining in its own price. A monopolistically competitive firm will have to have a pricing strategy, unlike a purely competitive firm.

3. Oligopoly (Assumptions or Conditions)
   - (1) **few firms**
   - (2) the products may be differentiated or standardized
   - (3) there is a noticeable degree of interdependence among the firms

   Many outcomes are possible in oligopolies, ranging from acting nearly competitively to acting like a monopoly.

4. Atomistic (or pure) Competition (Assumptions or Conditions for Pure Competition)
   - (1) a very large number of buyers and sellers
   - (2) homogeneous product (standardized)
   - (3) free entry and exit (no barriers)
   - (4) no collusion among the firms
   - (5) complete knowledge of all market information

   Each firm views its demand curve as perfectly elastic. We say that pure competition makes firms *price takers*.

D. Price and Output Under Pure Competition

1. Competitive firms attempt to maximize profits.

2. Competitive firms cannot charge more than the market price of others, since their product is identical to all others. Hence, competitive firms are price takers.

3. Total revenue, TR, is P Q, where price is given. Therefore, marginal revenue, MR, is price, P. Profit is total revenue minus total cost (π = TR - TC).

4. *Profit maximization* implies that each firm produces an output where Price = Marginal Cost (P = MC).

- To produce more than this quantity implies that P < MC, which is not the most profitable decision.
- To produce less than where P=MC, implies that P > MC, and the firm could increase profits by expanding output.

5. In short run, a competitive firm may earn economic profits. In the long run, entry pushes price down to the minimum point of the average cost curve, so that economic profits are zero.

E. Several Welcome Properties of Pure Competition

1. Since each firm produces where P=MC, there is no way to rearrange the total amount produced at lower cost than in pure competition.

2. In the long run, firms produce *efficiently* (least cost production) at the minimum point on their AC curves.

3. Political Decentralization of Power is an advantage of competition. Relations among small firms are impersonal or atomistic; therefore, they are without political power.

5. Prices will signal the true (marginal) cost to society (P = MC).

6. Economic profits in LR are zero. Definition of *economic profit* = accounting profit minus normal profits. Another way to view *economic profit* is revenue minus *economic costs* (which includes normal returns to owner supplied resources).

F. Monopolistic Competition

1. Monopolistic Competition is the market structure describing competitive firms that sell differentiated products.

2. Unlike pure competition, a monopolistically competitive firm has some limited discretion over price. If it raises price, it will lose some, but not all, of its customers.

3. Since there are many firms, and free entry, the equilibrium will end up with zero economic profits (just like competition). If profits were made, more firms would enter

until the firm's demand curve is just tangent to its AC. But, each firm will produce where marginal revenue, MR = MC, marginal cost (just like monopoly).

4. The equilibrium will not be at the lowest point of the firm's AC curve. ?

5. Some economists have criticized the model of monopolistic competition. They argue that not producing at the lowest point on the AC curve creates societal incentives to ? combine existing firms (either by merger or by several independent firms using the same factory) to achieve lower costs.

6. Note that when Sear's Kenmore appliances are built at a Whirlpool factory, they have exploited advantages of larger production runs.

G. Selling and Promotional Expenses

1. Promotional expenditures may shift upward the industry demand for the product. Advertising by Jiffy Lube may lead more people, in general, to change their oil.

2. Promotional expenditures may shift the percentage of the industry in favor of one firm over another. Advertising by one chocolate manufacturer may realign market shares without increasing overall chocolate consumption.

3. Profits and the Optimal Amount of Advertising

   a. Selling and promotional expenditures include warranties, quality assurance programs, customer service programs, as well as coupons and other selling promotions.

   b. Suppose the price is determined outside of the model, as with liquor prices in some States.

   c. We will expand promotional activities until the extra profit associated with the activity equals the extra cost of the promotion.

   d. This decision rule for Optimal Advertising is:

   Optimal when: Contribution = Marginal Cost of Advertising, *or*

   $$P - MC = k \cdot \Delta A / \Delta Q$$

   or *expand* advertising whenever $(P - MC)(\Delta Q / \Delta A) > k$

   ---

where, *contribution* (P – MC) is the marginal profit contribution of an additional sale, and the *marginal cost of advertising* is ($k \cdot \Delta A/\Delta Q$).

NOTE: That is, to sell one more unit of output will cost the price of the added message, k, divided by the marginal product of a dollar of advertising ($\Delta Q/\Delta A$). If a radio message costs $1000, and if that message yields 5 new items sold, then the marginal cost of advertising is $200, ($1000 /marginal product of advertising).

e. If it costs $200 to sell one more car (MCA=$200), and if the contribution of another car is $300 to profits, then we *should* expand promotional expenses.

H. The Net Value of Advertising

1. Advertising may be used to create monopoly power.

2. Advertising may extend the market for a product. If AC is declining, then advertising may reduce the prices of some products.

3. Price advertising reduces search costs of consumers who want to find the lowest price. Price advertising of legal or medical services sometimes reduces the average price that consumers end up paying.

4. Empirically, it seems that advertising tends to increase the demand elasticities of goods, since unadvertised products are found to be quite price inelastic.

True and False Questions

Agree or disagree with the following statements, and correct the part that is erroneous.

1. When the products are standardized, we can be sure that the industry will behave competitively.

2. When free entry exists, the atomistic or pure competitive model suggests that economic profit will always be equal to zero.

3. The notion of being a *price taker* competitive firm is that there is no pricing strategy because you cannot charge more than your competitors without losing all your customers.

4. When products are perfectly differentiated, we tend to view the firm as a monopoly.

5. The firm's demand curve in monopolistic competition is perfectly elastic.

6. In the long run, firms operate at the lowest point of their average cost curve in competition and in monopolistic competition.

7. If the marginal profit contribution of advertising is greater than the marginal cost of advertising, a manager should expand advertising.

8. All economists believe that additional advertising expenses raise prices that consumers must pay.

9. The profit percentage margin for Kellogg's cereal is high and the advertising elasticity of demand for cereal is high, it is not surprising that Kellogg spends 30% of every dollar of sales revenue in advertising.

10. Advertising is used to change the perception of goods so that they become more elastic.

Answers
1. Disagree. Oligopolies may have differentiated or standardized products. There are more characteristics than just "standardized" products to make an industry competitive.
2. Disagree. Economic profit will be zero in the long run, but in the short run, some firms may be making above normal economic profit.
3. True.
4. True.
5. Disagree. The firm's demand curve is downward sloping, but it is highly elastic.
6. Disagree. They do not operate at the lowest point of their average cost curve in monopolistic competition.
7. True.
8. Disagree. Price advertising may be helpful to consumers. If there are some economies of scale, a larger market for a product can help to reduce prices.
9. True. When both $[(P-MC)/P]$ and E^a are high, their product is high. The optimal amount of advertising is high.
10. Disagree. Advertising attempts to make the product more inelastic, so that customers want it at any price.

Multiple Choice Questions

1. For a typical competitive firm, the price in the long run equilibrium will tend to:
   a. " be greater than average cost
   b. be equal to average cost
   c. be less than average cost
   d. intermediate

2. A market where a large number of differentiated sellers comprise the entire industry is referred to as:
   a. monopolistic competition
   b. monopsony
   c. monopoly
   d. oligopoly
   e. competition

3. The **Nite Lite International** is a manufacturing company that makes night lights sold at hardware stores and drug stores. Night lights are sold in a highly competitive market directly to hardware stores at a *wholesale price* of $.49 each. The *retail price* of night lights varies, but the typical price is $1.19. You have just become the new president of Nite Light International and have learned that at the present level of production, marginal cost is about $.37. Being the fantastic economist that you are, your recommendation would be:
   a. to raise the price you charge for Nite Lites.
   b. to lower the price you charge for Nite Lites.
   c. to reduce output to reduce costs.
   d. to keep the price charged to hardware stores at $.49 for Nite Lites and try to expand the number of hardware stores that will sell our products.

4. Which of the following does NOT characterize monopolistic competition?
   a. products are standardized
   b. it is easy to enter this industry
   c. monopoly profits tend to disappear as entry occurs
   d. the demand curve of each firm is downward sloping

5. One virtue of competition is that the division of output produced across firms is efficient. Suppose that the marginal cost curves of two firms are:
$$MC_1 = 6 + 2\,Q_1 \quad \text{and} \quad MC_2 = 1 + 3\,Q_2$$
Suppose that the sum of the outputs of firm 1 and firm 2 equals 100, then the efficient output division in competition will be:
   a. firm one produces 50 and firm two produces 50
   b. firm one produces more than firm two produces
   c. firm two produces more than firm one produces

6. The existence of economic profits in an industry signifies that consumers want:
   a. more resources invested in the industry.
   b. fewer resources invested in the industry.
   c. no change in the resources invested in the industry.
   d. none of the above.

7. The demand function is given by $Q_D = 3000 - 10 \cdot P$, and the supply function is given by $Q_s = 300 + 5 \cdot P$. What is the competitive price and quantity in this industry?
   a. The price will be $1,200 and the quantity will be 180.
   b. The price will be $180 and the quantity will be 1,200.
   c. The price will be $100 and the quantity will be 2,700.
   d. The price will be $1,100 and the quantity will be 5,800.

In questions 8 and 9, suppose that a firm uses two advertising media, TV and radio. At the current level of advertising, marginal sales revenue generated from a 30 second TV commercial is $127,000. The cost of the TV commercial is $44,950. Let the marginal sales revenue generated from a 30-second radio commercial be $13,440. The radio commercial costs $1,800.

8. Presently, the firm should:
   a. expand TV commercials relatively more than radio commercials.
   b. expand radio commercials relatively more than TV commercials.
   c. realize that it is using the optimal combination of advertising media.
   d. know that the marginal sales revenue per dollar in TV is greater than the marginal sales revenue per dollar in radio.

9. Suppose that the cost of a radio commercial rises to $4,756.91. Then, the firm should:
   a. expand TV commercials relatively more than radio commercials.
   b. expand radio commercials relatively more than TV commercials.
   c. realize that it is using the optimal combination of advertising media.
   d. know that the marginal sales revenue per dollar in TV is greater than the marginal sales revenue per dollar in radio.

10. Which of the following is NOT a characteristic of an industry that displays atomistic or pure competition?
   a. free entry
   b. heterogeneous product
   c. many sellers
   d. free exit

11. For a competitive firm, if MC is below price:
   a. raise output to raise profit.
   b. reduce output to raise profit.
   c. raise price to raise profit.
   d. reduce price to raise profit.

12. In a competitive industry, if costs of production rise, we anticipate that:
    a. price will rise and quantity will stay about the same.
    b. price will rise and quantity will rise.
    c. price will rise and quantity will fall.
    d. price will decline to make up for the fact that costs rose.

13. A criticism of the monopolistic competition model is that:
    a. it ignores the fact that some products are differentiated.
    b. it says firms do not produce at their lowest AC point in the long run, so there are opportunities to earn more profits by firms producing products jointly.
    c. it says that there are positive economic profits in the long run.
    d. it shows that price is below marginal cost in the long run.

14. In the long run, if firms earn economic profit in a monopolistically competitive market, which of the following is most likely to happen?
    a. some firms will leave the market.
    b. firms will join together to keep others from entering.
    c. new firms will enter the market, thereby eliminating the economic profit.
    d. firms will continue to earn economic profit.

15. In the long run, the most helpful action that a monopolistically competitive firm can take to maintain its economic profit is to
    a. continue its efforts to differentiate its product.
    b. raise its price.
    c. lower its price.
    d. do nothing, because it will inevitably experience a decline in profits.

16. In which of these markets would the firms be facing the MOST elastic demand curve?
    a. perfect competition
    b. monopolistic competition
    c. pure monopoly
    d. oligopoly

17. In competition, marginal cost is the 'supply curve.' Therefore, an increase in labor costs in a competitive industry will
    a. Shift the demand curve to right
    b. Shift the supply curve up and to the left
    c. Shift the demand curve to the left
    d. Shift the supply curve down and to the right

18. Production of tin birdhouses is a highly competitive market. You sell birdhouses at a price of $2 per house. From the data below, how many houses (to the nearest hundred) should you produce per month.

Output in birdhouses per mo.	Total cost per mo. ($)
500	200
600	260
700	450
800	820
900	1,500

a. 600
b. 700
c. 800
d. 900

19. Marie's Party Baskets is an assembler of gift baskets with wine, cheese, and jam in a *competitive industry*. The linear regression provides the following annual demand curve:

$$P = 1246 - 30 \cdot Q$$

The marginal cost of a basket is $16. Find the *number of baskets* that Marie should make in a year.
a. $Q = 35$
b. $Q = 41$
c. $Q = 45$
d. $Q = 52$

20. Internet access has become a highly competitive market. The average cost is $20 per month and falling. The likely reason for the declining price for Internet access is
a. Entry into this industry, as firms see future growth prospects.
b. Governmental regulations that promote Internet use.
c. Reduced demand for Internet uses.
d. Higher costs for using the telephone.

Answers
1. b
2. a
3. d   (The wholesale price of $.49 is competitive. There is no reason to lower price).
4. a
5. b   (Find where $MC_1 = MC_2$ and where $Q_1 + Q_2 = 100$, which is $Q_1 = 59$ and $Q_2 = 41$)
6. a
7. b

8. b
9. c
10. b
11. a
12. c
13. b
14. c
15. a
16. a
17. b
18. b
19. b (Solve for 16 = 1246 - 30·Q)
20. a

Worked Problems

1. Determine the <u>decision rule</u> for optimal production in a competitive firm. The firm's <u>objective function</u> is profit: $\pi = TR - TC$

   where $TR = P \cdot Q$ and $TC = f(Q)$.

   Answer: To find an optimal quantity, differentiate the profit function with respect to quantity and set that equal to zero.

   $d\pi/dQ = dTR/dQ - dTC/dQ = P - MC = 0$.

   Hence, the quantity where **P = MC** is the optimal quantity to select.

2. Determine the optimal output, Q, for the following firm. Does the information show whether the firm is competitive, monopolistically competitive, oligopoly, or monopoly?

   $$\mathbf{TR = 14 \cdot Q}$$

   $$\mathbf{TC = 48 + Q + .5 \cdot Q^2}$$

   Answers: Profit, π, is: $\pi = 14 \cdot Q - 48 - Q - .5 \cdot Q^2 = -48 + 13 \cdot Q - .5 \cdot Q^2$.
   Hence, $d\pi/dQ = 13 - 1 \cdot Q^1 = 0$. That is, **Q = 13** will maximize profits.

   Furthermore, we realize that the firm is competitive, because the price is a constant $14 per unit.

3. Research at the National Institute of Mental Health (N.I.M.H) shows that the demand for voluntary psychiatric evaluations not covered by HMOs Medicaid, or Medicare depends on price. Using monthly data from thirteen cities, they find the following monthly demand function for first visits to a psychiatrist in Columbus, Ohio to be:

$$Q^d = 1,370 - 8 \cdot P + 4 \cdot I$$

where P is the price, and I is *per capita* annual income (in thousands of dollars) in the city. This month, Columbus has an I = 19.5. First visits involve a thorough medical and emotional evaluation.

The supply of voluntary psychiatric evaluations in Columbus is less well studied. However, it is believed to be:

$$Q^s = 28 + 2 \cdot P$$

Determine the likely market price and quantity of voluntary first visits to psychiatric doctors in Columbus. Assume that the voluntary first-visit market is competitive.

> *Answers:* The demand curve for voluntary visits in Columbus is found by substituting I=19.5 into the demand function.
>
> $Q^d = 1,448 - 8 \cdot P$ is the demand curve. Equilibrium in the market requires the quantity demanded to equal the quantity supplied.
>
> If $Q^d = Q^s$, then $1,448 - 8 \cdot P = 28 + 2 \cdot P$. This reduced to $1,420 = 10 \cdot P$, or **P = \$142.**
>
> At that price, the quantity demanded (and the quantity supplied) is **Q = 312.**

4. **Jaymar** is a manufacturer of slacks. During a recent experiment, Jaymar permanently lowered its price 15% at its own factory outlet mall near Michigan City, Indiana. It discovered that sales increased 24% over similar time periods before the price reduction. It is believed that no other variables, such as personal income or the prices charged by competitors, changed during this time period.

You were recently hired to help the promotions and sales department at Jaymar. Your best research shows that spending $1 of radio advertising in the nearby Chicago/Gary, Indiana market raises revenues at the outlet mall by $1.60. Your production department reports that the marginal cost of men's slacks is constant, and that the price of slacks will not change if you decide to expand radio advertising to Chicago and Northwest Indiana. Should you recommend to your firm to expand radio advertising?

> *Answer:* No. The marginal revenue of radio advertising is $1.60. But we also know that the price elasticity of demand for slacks, at the factory outlet mall is: $E_D = (24\%)/(-15\%) = -1.60$.
>
> According to the formula, we have achieved optimal outlays in an advertising medium when the absolute value of the price elasticity equals the marginal revenue of a dollar of advertising in that medium.

5. Main Furniture, a $24 million dollar small manufacturing firm of heavy-duty benches for malls and parks, finds that total revenue is: $TR = 15420 \cdot Q$ and total cost is: $TC = 4,500,000 + 20 \cdot Q + 5 \cdot Q^2$. What is the most profitable **quantity** of benches to build. (*Hint*: profit $\pi = TR - TC$).

> *Answer:* Differentiate profit with respect to Q, and set that equal to zero.
>
> $\pi = TR - TC = 15420 \cdot Q - 4,500,000 - 20 \cdot Q - 5 \cdot Q^2 = -4,500,000 + 15400 \cdot Q - 5 \cdot Q^2$.
>
> Differentiating, we find: $d\pi/dQ = 15,400 - 10 \cdot Q = 0$. Rearranging, we find Q = 15,400/10. Therefore, **Q = 1,540.**

Net Sources

Concentration Ratios by product type or industry are available in several places on the Internet. Most government sources are based on SIC codes for industries, without using firm names. Some industries analyze market shares using firm names, particularly the auto and computer industries.

1. **Computer Industry Forecasts at InfoTech Trends**   *www.infotechtrends.com/*

Products in the computer industry are analyzed by company name. Use their free search engine, to look for "market share". Quarterly data appear. For example, the market shares for PC and work station sales is given below. The 4-firm concentration ratio in 2000 is a competitive 29.5%. (*www.infotechtrends.com/cgi-bin/cif/sub_read.pl*)

<u>Market share of PC and workstation sales worldwide.</u>

	In 1999	In 2000
Compaq	13.5%	12.8%
Dell	9.7%	10.8%
HP	6.5%	7.6%
IBM	7.9%	6.8%
NEC	5.1%	4.3%
Gateway	4.0%	3.8%
All Others	53.3%	53.9%

2. **US Census Bureau**   *www.census.gov/mcd/mancen/download/mc92cr.sum*

This site provides tables based on the 1992 Census of Manufactures report, MC92-S-2, "Concentration Ratios in Manufacturing." Data are arranged by four-digit SIC industries. It gives 4-firm, 8-firm, 20-firm, and 50-firm concentration ratios and Herfindahl indices. For example, SIC 2111 (cigarettes) has a 4-firm concentration ratio of 93%, where SIC 2434 – (wood kitchen cabinets) has a 4-firm concentration ratio of only 19%. Which is more competitive? To look up numerical SIC designations, go to: *www.vivamus.com/InCodes/sic.html*

3. **PROJECT**: Select two manufacturing industries that you intuitively believe are relatively competitive. Based on the name of the industry, find their associated SIC codes using: *www.wave.net/upg/immigration/sic_index.html*. Use the Census Bureau's measure for 4-firm concentration (given in #2 above) as the measure of their concentration. Were their 4-firm concentration ratios less than 50%? Less than 20%?

Chapter 11

Competitive Markets Under Asymmetric Information

Pure competition assumed complete knowledge of all market information. In this chapter, this condition is relaxed. Often knowledge is unevenly distributed among firms and consumers. The concept of a "lemon" in the car market and adverse selection problem are only two of the interesting market phenomena when information is unevenly distributed (asymmetric) among the market participants.

A. <u>Asymmetric Information</u>

1. The seller of a used car knows more about the foibles of the car than the buyer. The buyer and seller have different information about the car.

2. Buyers may have to rely on "reputation" of the seller, rather than simply being able to assess the quality of the product.

3. *Incomplete Information* — uncertain knowledge of payoffs, choices, or types of opponents a market player faces.

4. *Asymmetric Information* — unequal or dissimilar knowledge among market participants.

B. <u>Incomplete Contracting and Incomplete Markets</u>

1. Insurance works when we can pool a group of possible events (like injuries at work) to reduce the risk of loss to any one party.

2. But some risks are catastrophic, like a nuclear accident. It is difficult to assess the likelihood or the damage; hence, insurance in this case is often unavailable.

3. Contracts can specify duties under several states of the world, but sometimes the outcomes are too numerous or unknowable for years. This creates incomplete contracts.

    a. *Full contingent claims contract* — specifies all possible future events.

    b. *Incomplete contingent claims contract* — not all possible future events are specified.

4. Due to incomplete contracts, some people take advantage of spirit of the contract. Accident insurance permits people to succumb to a *moral hazard* by acting recklessly.

C. Asymmetric Information in a Lemon's Market

1. *Search goods* — are products or services whose quality is best detected through a market search. This may involve looking at catalogs, reading Consumer's Report, or asking others their opinions.

2. *Experience goods* — are products and services whose quality is undetected when purchased. One must use it for a period, test it out over time (perhaps years) to reach a quality judgment.

3. To protect consumers, warranties and firm reputations are used to assure quality. Even "bonding" is used in some industries to assure quality.

4. But if someone is selling his or her car, isn't it likely that the car is no good? We think that the car is likely to be *a lemon*. The *cream puffs* (good cars) are traded to relatives.

5. Or, if one firm defrauds customers in an industry, how do the reputable firms signal that they are NOT like the fraudulent firm?

D. Adverse Selection and the Notorious Firm

1. A firm may decide to produce a High Quality or Low Quality product, and the buyer may decide to offer a High Price or a Low Price. The choices appear as a 2 by 2 matrix or game.

2. Since the firm fears that if it offers a High Quality product but that buyers only offer a Low Price, they only produce Low Quality products and receive Low Prices.

3. The *problem of adverse selection* leads to a belief of low quality products in the minds of the buyers because of asymmetric information between the market participants.

4. Examples: Bank lender and a new borrower — chances are that the new borrower is a deadbeat and omits previous defaults on his or her application.

E. Solutions to the Problem of Adverse Selection

1. *Regulations* can sometimes reduce adverse selection, as discussed in Chapter 18.

2. Long term relationships, or *reliance relationships*, between doctor and patient, or mechanic and customer create a mechanism to "punish" low quality behavior. Patients or customers that are unhappy, leave the relationship. They likely tell a dozen others about their experiences.

3. A "hostage mechanism" that is irreversible and irrevocable commitment. An example is like the promise to replace a handbag for the life of the customer, if the handbag is defective. This signals a quality handbag by the manufacturer.

4. *Brand names* are expensive capital investments. But the investment is at jeopardy if the firms begin to ship low quality products. "Their name is their bond."

5. *Nonredeployable assets* are assets that have little value in another other use. Firms that employ nonredepoyable assets or assets that are highly specific are most at risk if the firm decided to attempt to defraud its customers.

F. Cost Revelation in Joint Ventures and Partnerships

1. Potential partners have different information upon beginning a venture together, with each partner claiming higher costs for their share than their true costs. Even experience is not a perfect indicator since random cost disturbances do occur.

2. Some joint ventures never occur because of this behavior, even though both would benefit from the venture.

3. Some contractual ways to deal with asymmetric information include:

    a. Offer independent appraisals of the product.

    b. Offer warrantees as a signal of a good product.

    c. Offer leases with a high residual value.

    d. Offer a contingent payment if anything is amiss in the deal.

4   The *Clarke tax mechanism* creates incentives for partners to reveal the true costs.

    a. The mechanism is to assign probabilities to the revelation of costs of the partner.

    b. After the other partner's *expected costs* are covered, they receive the residual or net profit.

    c. Then each has an incentive to reveal their true cost.

G. Optimal Incentives Contract

1. An agreement about the payoffs and penalties the creates appropriate incentives is called an *optimal incentives contract*.

2. The penalty is often the termination of a contractual relationship. A breach of a contract leads to termination of the contract. If the contract creates a stream of profits, then a breach is a costly penalty.

3. The most common example: an employee who steals is fired! If the employee felt the employment at that firm was rewarding, the penalty of firing is severe.

H. Principal-Agent Problem in Managerial Labor Markets

1. Stockholders (principals) hire managers (agents) to run their firm. It is often claimed that managers have different incentives than owners. They may wish to be highly risk averse, for example.

2. Alternative labor contracts include paying a percentage of receipts due to this person's effort; profit-sharing by making the manager a shareholder; and paying a bonus on top of a salary when goals are exceeded.

3. Even profit-sharing arrangements have problems. If one employee loafs, he or she may still be rewarded by the profits created by others. Another *moral hazard* is the failure to comply with the expected (but unobservable) aspects of the agreement.

4. *Benchmarking* involves a comparison of similar firms, plants, or divisions. If employees are moved around, we can determine who, if any, were laggards at work.

I. Signaling and Sorting Managerial Talent

1. Applicants to positions know more about themselves than they reveal, which is the problem of asymmetric information. How do we know if an applicant highly risk averse or a risk taker?

2. A *Linear Incentive Contract* provides a combination of salary and (plus or minus!) a profit sharing rate.

   a. An offer that dominates all other offers will not help distinguish among applicants. This is a *pooling equilibrium*.

   b. An offer that distinguishes between behaviors is a *separating equilibrium*. For example, a risk averse person would tend to select an offer, which primarily paid a base salary, whereas the risk-loving individual would tend to select an offer with more profit sharing.

True and False Questions

Agree or disagree with the following statements, and correct the part that is erroneous.

1. Asymmetric Information involves uncertain knowledge of payoffs, choices, or types of opponents a market player faces.

2. Brand names or firm reputation can be used to substitute for a "bond" to insure that a firm delivers quality products.

3. Assets that are easily redeployable to other uses help to reduce the problem of adverse selection.

4. "If you're so eager to sell me your old snow thrower, then why are you buying a new one? Does this one really work?" These remarks go on inside the head of the buyer. They indicate an example of adverse selection.

5. *Moral hazard* involves a comparison of similar firms, plants, or divisions.

Answers
1. Disagree. *Incomplete Information* involves uncertain knowledge of payoffs, choices, or types of opponents a market player faces.
2. True.
3. Disagree. Nonredeployable assets help reduce the problem of adverse selection.
4. True. Adverse selection implies that there is a bias of low quality in the minds of the buyers due to asymmetric information.
5. Disagree. *Benchmarking* involves a comparison of similar firms, plants, or divisions. *Moral hazard* means that there is a failure to comply with the expected but unobservable aspects of the agreement.

Multiple Choice Questions

1. When the seller has an informational advantage over the buyer:
   a. we have asymmetric information.
   b. we have incomplete information.
   c. we face moral hazard.
   d. we are have full contingent claims contracts.

2. An "experience good" is one:
   a. that depends primarily on finding the lowest price.
   b. that involves a lot of time and effort to search for.
   c. whose quality is undetectable when purchased.
   d. that can be readily experienced simply by touching or tasting.

3. Used cars are thought to be "lemons", otherwise why do the sellers want to unload them? This indicates the
   a. problem of moral hazard.
   b. problem of adverse selection.
   c. principal-agent problem.
   d. incomplete information problem.

4. Some markets are left uninsured or under-represented in a competition market. An example is the so-called "orphan drugs," which are drugs that fight rare but life-threatening maladies. Use of strong drugs on very sick people has an unknown potential for liability with very little profit potential.
   a. This is an example of the problem of moral hazard.
   b. This is an example of the problem of adverse selection.
   c. This is an example of the principal-agent problem.
   d. This is an example of the problem of incomplete information.

5. There are methods employers can use to overcome the problem of asymmetric information with job applicants. One way to elicit information about *risk aversion* is:
   a. to ask if the person likes to take two steps at a time up a stairway.
   b. to offer two wage contracts, one weighted heavily to profit sharing and another weighted heavily to base salary.
   c. ask the applicants about their favorite authors, and whether they prefer cooked carrots or raw carrots.
   d. ask the applicants if they like to go to the horse track to gamble or if they would rather play horseshoes.

6. *Moral hazard* (a failure to comply with the expected but unobservable aspects of agreements) occurs in all of the following EXCEPT:
   a. Laws that require motorcycle drivers to wear helmets to reduce motorcycle deaths.
   b. Home fire insurance with replacement cost provisions to protect customers from inflation.
   c. "Orphan drugs" which are drugs to fight rare maladies, that few drug companies find economic to study.
   d. Anti-lock breaks are required on all new cars to reduce accidents due to locking of breaks.

7. In a job interview, if I ask you if you are willing to take risks to make the firm more profitable, you are very likely to say yes. But if I offer you a job which has a low base pay and a high bonus, I will likely find out whether you are a risk taker or not. We call this second type of offer:
   a. a pooling equilibrium.
   b. a comparative static equilibrium.
   c. a separating equilibrium.
   d. an unstable equilibrium.

8. Adverse selection leads to limited choice of lower quality attributes because of asymmetric information between buyer and seller.   Which of the following products are most likely to suffer greatest adverse selection?
   a. Golf shirts sold at The Master's golf tournament
   b. Ears of corn of the cob sold at a roadside stand
   c. Auto repair service
   d. Jewelry sold by Tiffany's

9. Brand names reduce the adverse selection problem because:
   a. It increases the problem of asymmetric information.
   b. Brand names create an insurance bond that is put at risk if it is found out that the firm sells inferior products.
   c. People like conspicuous consumption by putting cool logos on their cloths and purses.
   d. Adverse selection is illegal in America.

10. Which of the following is NOT an example of Moral Hazard?
    a. Motorcyclists who drive more recklessly after a state requires wearing of helmets.
    b. People who eat more after they purchase 'fat reduced' desserts.
    c. Divers who dive in shark infested waters after purchasing a bottle of shark repellant.
    d. Parents who continue to drive carefully after putting their kids in 'safety seats.'

11. As a member of the Compensation Committee, you consider what salary and bonuses should go to your talented CEO Greg Gregarious. Some of the performance of the firm is due to luck and some is due to hard work.   Good luck and Bad luck are a 50:50 probability.

		Good Luck	Bad Luck
Greg Gregarious	Works Hard	$4,000,000	$2,000,000
	Hardly Works	$2,000,000	$1,000,000

What is the GREATEST bonus you could bestow on CEO Greg?
   a. $1,000,000
   b. $1,500,000
   c. $2,500,000
   d. $3,000,000

Answers
1. a
2. c
3. b
4. d

5. b
6. c (There is little profit in making orphan drugs, but it is not due to moral hazard. Notice that in the other three choices, people will tend to alter their behavior if they wear helmets, have fire insurance, or know that their car has anti-lock breaks.)
7. c
8. c
9. b
10. d
11. b (Expected profit for hard work is $3 million. Expected profit for hardly works is $1.5 million. The difference between these is the most you 'd be willing to pay to get Greg to work hard.)

Worked Problem

1. A buyer is unsure whether the product is high or low quality. The buyer may offer either a low or a high price. The seller knows whether its product is low or high, but if it makes a high quality product, it must incur additional costs. The following is the experience good payoff matrix. This first number is the payoff to the seller, and the second number is the payoff to the buyer.

		BUYER	
		Offer High Price	Offer Low Price
SELLER	High Quality	25, 30	-10, 50
	Low Quality	30, -15	5, -10

a. What would the seller decide to do if he believed that the buyer would **always** offer a low price?

Answer: Assuming that the seller maximizes payoffs, he or she would decide to produce low quality goods, where the payoff is +30 rather than +25.

b. If the seller knew that the buyer 50% of the time would offer a low price and 50% of the time a high price, should the seller produce a low or high quality good? Assume that he maximizes expected payoffs.

Answer: The expected payoff of High Quality is .5(25) + .5(-10) = 7.5. The expected payoff of Low Quality is .5(30) + .5(5) = 17.5. Clearly, the seller continues to produce Low Quality goods.

c. If the buyer knew that the seller would produce High or Low Quality goods 50% of the time, and given that the buyer maximizes expected payoffs, what should she do?

Answer: The expected payoff of offering a High Price is .5(30) + .5(50) = 40. The expected payoff of offering a Low Price is .5(-15) + .5(-10) = -12.5. In this case, the buyer would offer the High Price.

d. Suppose that the buyer in this game promises to offer a High Price PLUS a bonus in 6 months if the good turns out to be good. If the bonus (in present value terms) is +10, the payoff matrix is changed to:

	BUYER	
	Offer High Price	Offer Low Price
High Quality	35, 20	0, 40
Low Quality	30, -15	5, -10

SELLER

Do these payoffs make the seller want to offer a High Quality good?

Answer: Yes. The payoff of High Quality is 35 now as compared with 30 for the low quality good. This is a side-payment designed to create an incentive to act properly. This is a very simplified example of "incentive compatible revelation mechanisms" which are discussed in the textbook.

Net Sources

1. **Blue Book for Used Cars**   *www.kbb.com/*

Kelly's Blue book provides estimates of the retail price of a used car and estimates of the selling price of a used car in trade or in sale.

2. **CEOs of Fortune 500 Firms**   *www.fortune.com/*

Browse the 'Full List' of the Fortune 500 list. The search by CEO. A list of the names of the Chief Executive Officers of the Fortune 500 firms, and a snapshot their firm performance is available at this site. Fortune magazine on-line has extensive articles on product strategies and firm performance.

3. **Executive Compensation**   *www.forbes.com/*

   Forbes magazine provides extensive data on CEO compensation. Go to Forbes on-line site and search for "Executive Compensation."

4. **PROJECT:** Examine the compensation for the top 800 CEOs in the country (in Forbes at: *www.forbes.com/ceos/*). By clicking the name of anyone on this list, we can find the amount of compensation due to bonus and due to salary. Did these firms perform well over the past few years that are at the top of the list of 800 firms?

Chapter 12

Price and Output Determination: Monopoly and Dominant Firms

Monopoly implies huge profits, great wealth, and indiscriminate power. Some monopolies now and in the past have been *robber barons*. Yet there also exist monopolies that are not especially profitable, as well as monopolies that are regulated by State Public Service or Utility Commissions. Some of these have had very low rates of return on invested capital. This chapter looks at the pricing and output decisions of unregulated monopolies and regulated monopolies (known as *utilities*).

A. Monopoly Defined

1. In monopoly, the *firm* and the *industry* demand are both the same. Since industry demand curves are downward sloping, a monopoly's demand curve is also downward sloping.

2. Although pure monopolies exist for many (narrowly defined) products, there is some substitution available with nearly similar products.

3. For example, Windows by Microsoft is close to a monopoly; whereas *Excel* by Microsoft has a number of successful spreadsheet competitors. Therefore, the degree of monopoly power varies with the ease consumers have to switch to alternatives. Some near monopolies, like Intel, find competitors Hitachi and AMD taking away market share.

B. Source of Market Power

1. **Legal restrictions** of entry create market power. These include copyrights & patents.

2. **Control of critical resources** creates market power. *Market power* and *monopoly power* is frequently used interchangeably. When Alcoa had exclusive access to bauxite deposits, it effectively could exclude potential competitors from entering the aluminum industry.

3. **Government-authorized franchises**, such as provided to cable TV companies gives exclusive regions to be served by one firm. In British history, entire countries have been granted exclusive territories, as in the East India Company's authority in India.

4. **Economies of size** allow larger firms to produce at lower cost than smaller firms. Small firms would tend to disappear, as they would be unprofitable to operate. This creates a *natural monopoly*.

5. **Brand loyalty and extensive advertising** makes entry into these markets highly expensive. The well-known product has some market power, because of its high recognition value to consumers, especially if they were generally pleased with its performance.

C. The Monopoly Price and Monopoly Output

1. Because the monopoly demand curve is downward sloping, *marginal revenue* is less than price. Graphically, the marginal revenue curve is below the demand curve.

2. In the case of a linear demand curve, the marginal revenue curve is twice as steep. That is, if $P = a - b \cdot Q$, then $MR = a - 2b \cdot Q$.

3. Profit maximization occurs at the quantity where **MR = MC.** This is readily proven. Profit, $\pi = TR - TC$. Differentiating with respect to quantity and setting that equal to zero reveals: $MR - MC = 0$, or $MR = MC$. Several numerical examples appear in the Worked Problems.

D. Monopoly *vs.* Competition

1. In monopoly, the output is reduced. Indeed, monopolists restrict production in order to raise price.

2. Competitive firms in the long run produce at the lowest point of their AC curves. This does not tend to occur in monopolies.

3. The monopoly price, $P > MC$. In monopoly, no longer does price accurately signal cost, whereas in competition, $P = MC$.

4. Other comparisons that are sometimes made include:

a. Some monopolies have had a history of discrimination.

b. Some monopolies have been resistant to technological changes and thus have been less than progressive.

c. Some monopolies have been wasteful by not attempting to minimize costs.

5. These criticisms of monopoly can sometimes be made of competition, oligopoly, or monopolistic competition, but historical examples of monopoly fit several of these objections remarkably well.

E. The Importance of Price Elasticity and Monopoly

1. Marginal revenue is a function of the price elasticity. This appears in Chapter 3 (also page 49 in the Study Guide) to be:

$$MR = P(1 + 1/E_D).$$

2. A profit maximizing monopolist produces a quantity where MR = MC. By substitution, then, the formula for profit-maximizing output in monopoly is:

$$MC = P(1 + 1/E_D)$$

3. NOTE: a profit-maximizing monopolist will never operate in the inelastic region of its demand curve. If demand were inelastic, the firm should raise price. This will raise total revenue, and will tend to reduce costs as the firm will be selling and producing fewer units. Hence, the formula works only when demand is in the elastic region.

4. When MC = 1, and E_D = -2, then the *optimal monopoly price* is P = $2. If the elasticity were E_D = -5, then the optimal monopoly price drops to P = $1.25. At the extreme, if $E_D = -\infty$, then P = MC. As demand becomes more elastic, the optimal monopoly price becomes closer and closer to MC.

F. Monopoly, Economic Profits, and Efficiency

1. The optimal monopoly price does not necessarily mean that P > AC, or that the firm is earning *economic profits* (that is, above normal profits). One could have the absolute monopoly to produce a good that few people want, and find that owning this monopoly is worthless.

2. Whereas competitive firms will tend in the long run to operate at the lowest average cost, least cost production may or may not occur in monopoly. Monopolies are not forced by competition to be as efficient as possible.

3. Monopolies may decide to set prices lower than optimal in the short run, called *limit pricing*, to discourage entry of new firms.

G. Regulated Monopolies

1. Examples include:
   a. Electrical Power Companies
   b. Natural Gas Companies
   c. Communications companies (*e.g.*, local telephone companies)

2. There is an economic rationale to regulate these sorts of industries.

3. Each of these industries has economies of scale in distribution and to a lesser extent in production. Consequently, they all have declining average cost curves, so they are viewed as *naturally monopolistic*.

4. With declining AC, MC must be at each output below AC. If there were no regulation, P = MC would lead to losses, since P = MC < AC means losses.

5. Regulation implies that entry is blocked, to prevent competition. In exchange for this protection, a maximum price is set at a rate hearing. Of course, the firm would like a monopoly price and consumers would like the competitive price. What tends to happen is that the regulated price is the AC-price. The AC-price covers all costs and it produces a normal profit.

6. Regulation helps to prevent **duplication of services**. If electrical companies were to compete, there may be duplicate electrical wires run through neighborhoods as is the case in Lubbock, Texas.

7. Regulation allows many forms of **price discrimination** to occur where customers are not paying prices in proportion to cost. Electrical utilities charge different prices to residential customers than to commercial or industrial customers. Telephone companies charge different prices to businesses than to homeowners.

8. Regulated monopolies are permitted a *fair* rate of return, so they have an incentive to overinvest in assets whose regulated return is greater than their cost of capital.

H. The Regulatory Process

1. Each state has Public Utility Commissions or Public Service Commissions who determine entry into the industry, jurisdictional disputes, and set a fair rate of return on the rate base.

2. Each Commission has a staff (including some economists, lawyers, and accountants).

3. If a company wants higher rates, it petitions the Commission for a specific amount of money. A quasi-judicial "rate case" hearing occurs before an administrative law judge. Evidence from the firm, the staff, and others determines if rate relief is justified or not.

4. The revenue (R) must cover all operating costs (C) plus a permissible rate of return (k) on the rate base (V-D), where D is the accumulated depreciation and V is the value of the firm's assets.

$$R = C + (V - D) \cdot k$$

5. Price discrimination is commonplace in utility regulation. The justifications for it are:

   a. *Cost Justification*: it may cost less to sell to big users, since there is only one transmission line to service.

   b. *Demand Justification*: it may cost more to sell to users who use the service at peak times. The peak demand level determines the size of a utility's required output.

6. *Block pricing* refers to prices that depend on the amount used. Generally, this meant *declining block pricing* whereby the rates declined with the amount purchased.

7. *Peak-Load Pricing* occurs when the price is set higher at the peak times and lower on the off-peak times. Long-distance telephone rates are lower at night than in the day, since use of the phone lines are typically lower at night.

True and False Questions

Agree or disagree with the following statements, and correct the part that is erroneous.

1. A profit-maximizing monopolist produces output where marginal cost is equal to the price.

2. Monopolies tend to waste resources more, at least historically, than in competitive industries.

3. A profit-maximizing monopolist produces output where price is greater than marginal cost.

4. If the price elasticity is $E_D = -.75$, and MC = 10, then the optimal monopoly price will be: P = -30.

5. Monopolies tend to practice more discrimination, at least historically, than is typically found in competitive industries.

6. Marginal revenue is less than the price for simple monopolies.

7. Marginal revenue is always twice as steep as the demand curve.

8. If price is set equal to marginal cost in a naturally monopolistic industry, then there will be losses (negative profits), because P < AC.

9. In a rate case, the regulated monopolist would wish to show that its operating costs are high, its rate base is high, and that it needs a high *fair* rate of return on its rate base.

10. In a rate case, consumer advocates would wish to show that the rate base is too large, that operating costs are too high, and that the permitted return is too high.

11. Peak load pricing of electricity generally leads to higher prices for electricity late at night.

Answers
1. Disagree. The optimal output occurs where marginal cost is equal to *marginal revenue*.
2. True.
3. True.
4. Disagree. When demand is inelastic, the firm should raise its price. The formula does not apply to the inelastic region of the demand curve where MR is negative.
5. True.
6. True.
7. Disagree. For a monopolist, MR is twice as steep as a *linear* demand curve. For nonlinear demand curves, MR is below a downward sloping demand curve. If the firm's demand curve were perfectly elastic, MR equals price.
8. True.
9. True.
10. True.
11. Disagree. Higher prices occur during peak times. This is usually during the daytime hours and during some seasons, such as the summer peak air conditioning months.

Multiple Choice Questions

1. The inverse demand curve facing a monopolist is: $P = 300 - 14 \cdot Q$, where P is price and Q is output. Let marginal cost be: $MC = 2 \cdot Q$. The profit maximizing **output** for this monopolist is:
    a. less than twelve.
    b. more than twelve, but less than nineteen.
    c. more than nineteen, but less than thirty.
    d. more than thirty.

2. Using the same demand curve as in question 2, but setting marginal cost at a constant rate [**MC = 20**] determine the monopolistic **price**.
   a. P = 10
   b. P = 100
   c. P = 160
   d. none of these

3. Which of the following is NOT a problem with monopoly?
   a. the price does not signal true cost.
   b. monopolists typically force customers to purchase more than they want to.
   c. a monopolist may not produce at the lowest point of its average cost curve.
   d. the quantity produced is typically less than in pure competition.

4. The monopolistic producer:
   a. faces severe pressure to keep costs low.
   b. maximizes the public interest.
   c. faces many good substitutes for his product.
   d. has a powerful incentive to restrict output.

5. The monopolist maximizes profits by producing where marginal cost equals marginal revenue. At that output:
   a. this causes marginal cost to be more than price.
   b. this causes marginal cost to equal price.
   c. this causes marginal cost to be less than price.
   d. this causes a 50:50 probability that marginal cost to be either more than or less than price.

6. The ultimate success of monopoly in the long run depends on its ability:
   a. to promote its product.
   b. to manipulate consumers.
   c. to reduce costs.
   d. to prevent entry of rivals.

7. Which of the following is NOT considered a consequence of monopoly?
   a. high prices
   b. restriction of output.
   c. huge profits.
   d. least cost production.

8. Which of the following is never negative?
    a. marginal revenue
    b. marginal product
    c. average product
    d. profit

9. In the case of pure monopoly:
    a. one firm is the sole producer of a good that has no close substitutes.
    b. the firm's profit is maximized at the price and output combination where marginal cost equals marginal revenue.
    c. the demand curve is always elastic at the optimal monopoly price.
    d. both a and b.

10. The demand curve facing the firm in _____ is the same as the industry demand curve.
    a. pure competition
    b. pure monopoly
    c. monopolistic competition
    d. oligopoly

11. Most electrical utilities offer different rates to commercial users, industrial users, and residential users. This pricing arrangement is:
    a. price discrimination.
    b. red lining.
    c. graft.
    d. illegal.

12. If a monopolist finds that its marginal costs have gone up, it will
    a. expand output.
    b. increase price.
    c. further restrict output.
    d. both (b) and (c).

13. In natural monopoly, AC continuously declines due to economies in distribution or production creating increasing returns to scale. If price were set equal to marginal cost, then:
    a. price would equal average cost.
    b. price would exceed average cost.
    c. price would be below average cost.
    d. all three are possible.

14. Peak-Load Pricing in regulated industries tend to:
    a. Charge a high price to big users of the product.
    b. Charge a marginal cost price plus a cost for capacity on the peak times.
    c. Charges a capacity cost to all users on and off-peak.
    d. Induce customers to buy during the peak periods.

15. Land's End estimates a demand curve for turtleneck sweaters to be:

$$Log\ Q = .41 - 2\ Log\ P + 1.6\ Log\ Y$$

where Q is quantity, P is price, and Y is a measure on national income. If the marginal cost of imported turtleneck sweaters is $11.50. The optimal monopoly price would be:
    a. P = $23
    b. P = $26
    c. P = $27
    d. P = $34

16. Declining cost industries
    a. have marginal cost curves above their average cost curve
    b. are the ones said to be naturally monopolistic
    c. are industries where the average cost curve continuously rises
    d. are ones where the AC for 100 units is lower than the AC for 130 units produced

17. A state utility commission regulates the Public Service Company of the Southwest. The firm has total assets of $100,000,000. The demand curve is:

$$P = 1700 - .01 \cdot Q,$$

where P and Q are prices and quantities of megawatt hours. The firm faces a cost function:
$$TC = 7,000,000 + 12 \cdot Q$$
The commission has ordered that the firm receive a price of <u>$200 per megawatt</u>. What profit is the commission permitting?
    a. At P = $200, Q = 200,000 and profit is $30,000,000, for a rate of return on assets of 30.6%.
    b. At P = $200, Q = 180,000 and profit is $26,800,000, for a rate of return on assets of 26.8%
    c. At P = $200, Q = 150,000 and profit is $21,200,000, for a rate of return on assets of 21.2%
    d. At P = $200, Q = 100,000 and profit is $11,800,000, for a rate of return on assets of 11.8%

Answers
1. a   (actually, Q=10, because, MR = 300 - 28·Q = 2·Q implies 300 = 30·Q)
2. c   (MR = 300 –28·Q = 20, so Q=10. Hence, P = 300 - 14(10) = $160)
3. b
4. d
5. c
6. d
7. d
8. c
9. d
10. b
11. a
12. d
13. c
14. b
15. a
16. b
17. c   (Solve the demand equation at P = 200, to find Q = 150,000. Total revenue is 200•150,000, or $30,000,000. Total cost is 7,000,000 + 12•150,000 or 8,800,000. Hence, profit is $21,200,000.)

Worked Problems

1. Examine the following diagram for a *naturally monopolistic* industry below. Give the price that best fits the alternative regulatory outcome in the blanks provided.

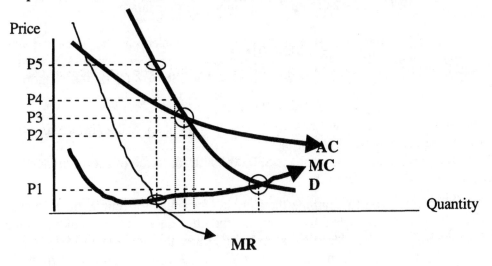

The price would be:

a. _____, if the government elected to prevent entry, subsidize losses in the industry, and impose a price ceiling which only covered marginal costs.

b. _____, if the government decided to grant exclusive rights to a territory, but did not indicate an effective price ceiling.

c. _____, if all firms were allowed to bid on the franchise, and the bidding process was not rigged so that the winning bid covered all costs. Select the likely winning bid.

d. _____, if a firm were granted an exclusive territory, but the firm was regulated to achieve only a fair rate of return on their assets, and to cover costs.

> *Answers:*   (a) is P1, where P = MC. Notice this will create losses. Unless the government subsidizes the firms sufficiently, no output will be available.
>
> (b) is P5, is the highest price possible, given an output where MR = MC.
>
> (c) is P3, the average cost price. Prices higher than P3 will encourage more bidders to join the franchise bidding competition. Prices lower than P3 generate losses.
>
> (d) is also P3. Regulated prices cover all costs and a fair return on investment. This is equivalent to an average cost price.

2. Suppose the demand curve is estimated to be: P = 140 - 3·Q. It is known that marginal cost is upward rising: MC = 4 + 2·Q. Find the monopoly price and quantity.

> *Answer:*   The marginal revenue curve is twice as steep as the linear demand curve; hence, MR = 140 - 6·Q. A monopolist produces where MR = MC. Therefore, 140 - 6·Q = 4 + 2·Q implies that 136 = 8·Q, or the monopoly quantity is **Q = 17**.
>
> To find the monopoly price, substitute Q=17 into the demand curve. We find, P = 140 - 3·(17) = 140 - 51 = **$89**.

3. **Rollins Trucking** hires you to examine their pricing structure for rentals of their cabs and trailers. You have requested five years of monthly data for your study, which includes the monthly number for trailers rented (Q) and the average monthly rental prices per day (P). Using data from the *Survey of Current Business*, you collect monthly data on industrial production (X), producers price index (W), and a measure of income (Y). Employing a log linear model, you find the following output:

Dependent Variable: Log Q
N = 60

	Beta	**T-value**
Constant	-0.22	0.89
Log P	-2.81	3.11
Log X	1.13	2.42
Log W	0.57	1.45
Log Y	4.12	3.18

a. Given that the marginal cost of a rental day for this large firm is $85, what is the optimal monopoly price to suggest for Rollins?

> *Answer:* The coefficient (beta) on Log P is the price elasticity. Therefore, E_D = -2.81.
>
> For the optimal monopoly price, we must solve: $MC = P(1 + 1/E_D)$. Substituting for MC and the price elasticity shows: $85 = P(1 + 1/(-2.81))$, or $85 = P(.644)$, consequently, **P = $131.96** is the optimal monopoly price.

b. It is expected that the price elasticity is cyclical over the year. Using eleven dummy variables for months 1 to 11 (Jan. to Nov.), the results changed to the following. The dummy variables, Di, are 1 in the i-th month, and zero thereafter. Determine the optimal monopoly price in JUNE, if the marginal cost is $85.

Dependent Variable: Log Q		N=60
	Beta	T-value
Constant	0.96	1.59
Log P	-2.79	2.88
Log X	1.09	2.34
Log W	0.43	1.08
Log Y	4.02	3.07
D1·Log P	-0.55	0.88
D2·Log P	-0.23	0.32
D3·Log P	0.15	2.02
D4·Log P	0.52	2.22
D5·Log P	0.65	3.13
D6·Log P	0.77	6.19
D7·Log P	0.75	3.09
D8·Log P	0.54	1.48
D9·Log P	0.58	2.16
D10·Log P	-0.45	2.10
D11·Log P	-0.65	0.78

Answer: June is the sixth month. The coefficient on D6·Log P is +.77, whereas the coefficient on Log P is -2.79. Therefore, the price elasticity in JUNE is E_D = -2.79 + .77 = -2.02. June has a lower price elasticity (in absolute terms) than the omitted month of DECEMBER.

Using the optimal monopoly price formula once again we find: $MC = P(1+1/E_D)$, or 85 = P(1 + 1/(-2.02)) = P(.505), This means that P = $168.33. The optimal monopoly price rises in months that are less elastic, and declines in months that are relatively more elastic.

4. Find the optimal monopoly price and quantity if demand is: $P = 133 - 4·Q - Q^2$ and MC = 5.

    Answers: Because demand is nonlinear, we are unable to use the fact that MR is twice as steep as a LINEAR demand curve. Instead, we must calculate MR.
    $TR = P·Q = [133 - 4·Q - Q^2]·Q = 133·Q - 4·Q^2 - Q^3$. Therefore, $MR = dTR/dQ = 133 - 8·Q - 3·Q^2$. Setting MR and MC equal yields:

    $133 - 8·Q - 3·Q^2 = 5$, or $-3·Q^2 - 8·Q + 128 = 0$. By applying the *quadratic rule*, we find that roots of this equation. By the quadratic rule, we find that the roots Q = $[-b ± \sqrt{b^2 - 4ac}]/2a$ or Q = $[8 ± \sqrt{64 - 4(-3)·128}]/(-6)$. This simplifies to: Q = $[8 ± \sqrt{1600}]/(-6) = [8 ± 40]/(-6)$. Q = 5.33 or -8. Since only outputs in the positive range make sense, **Q = 5.33**.

    The optimal monopoly price would be: $P = 133 - 4·(5.33) - (5.33)^2 =$
    133 - 21.32 - 28.4989 = **$83.27**, which is the highest price possible to sell 5.33 units.

5. Suppose demand for CD players using the following double log regression model:

    $$\log Q = 4 + 1.7 \log I - 2.1 \log P$$

    If MC is $100, what is the optimal monopoly price for CD players?

    Answer: The price elasticity is E_D = -2.1.
    Therefore, P(1 + 1/(-2.1)) = 100.
    This simplifies to: P(.5238) = 100, or P = **$190.91**.

Net Sources

1. **Antitrust Division of the Department of Justice**   *www.usdoj.gov/atr/index.html*

   Provides information on recent and on going cases, such as the Microsoft case.

2. **Federal Trade Commission**   *www.ftc.gov/*

   The Federal Trade Commission seeks to ensure that the nation's markets function competitively, and are free of undue restrictions. The Commission attempts to eliminating acts or practices that are unfair or deceptive. For an orderly discussion of antitrust laws, read "Promoting Competition, Protecting Consumers: A Plain English Guide to Antitrust Laws" at: *www.ftc.gov/bc/compguide/index.htm*

3. Auctions involve one-of-a-kind or rare items which are clear examples of monopoly. The value of rare items is determined by what people would pay for it. Go to the following two sites.

   - **Sotheby's Auction of Books and Manuscripts**   *www.sothebys.com/*

   Bidders can bid online through a web-based bid sheet, or they can bid by email, FAX, or phone. The highest bid buys the described "lot", if that bid is above the *reserve price*. The reserve price tends to be considerably lower than the lowest auction estimate. For example, the first edition of *Tarzan of the Apes*, by Edgar Rice Burroughs, printed in 1914, was listed as: Auction Estimate $1500-2000. If $500 were the reserve price, and if all bids were less than $500, then no winning bid would be awarded.

   - **eBay**   *www.ebay.com/*

   eBay is the world's first and biggest person-to-person online trading community. It's a place to find the stuff you want to buy or an outlet to get rid of stuff by selling it to the highest bidder.

   - **Christie's International**   *www.christies.com/*

   Christie's International does not offer an Internet-based auction; however, rather detailed descriptions of upcoming auctions and their locations are presented.

4. **PROJECT:** Pick two or three destinations that are about the same distance from the closest airport nearest you. For finding distances, use Yahoo Maps! *maps.yahoo.com/py/maps.py*. Suppose you live near Chicago, and find that the state capitols: St. Paul, Minnesota; Columbus, Ohio; and Jefferson City, Missouri were

approximately the same distance. The question is: How many airlines fly to these cities from Chicago? Which destination is cheapest? To find the number of airlines who fly to a destination, use *travel.yahoo.com/*. Click 'book a flight,' then select 'all flights so that I can build my own itinerary'. After entering to Departure and Arrival locations, the number of flights will appear for the day requested. Be sure to click the "I've changed my mind button," before leaving, so that you don't book a flight you didn't want. (It is generally more expensive to fly to cities served by only one airline.)

Chapter 13

Price and Output Determination: Oligopoly

When there are only a few firms in an industry, each firm must consider the *reaction* of the other firms to any decision it makes. If one firm introduces new products or lowers its price, will rival firms make similar moves? Since there are a variety of different possible reactions, behavior in oligopolies runs the gamut from highly coordinated monopolistic practices to behavior hardly distinguishable from pure competition. This chapter examines Cournot oligopoly model, price leadership models, and collusive behavior in oligopolies.

A. Oligopolies: the Airline Industry

1. There are only a few major U.S. airlines, after a series of bankruptcies to Eastern Airlines, Continental, and TWA. Soft drinks and cereals are also oligopolies.

2. Airline prices are complex, depending on advance purchases, round trip prices over a weekend, and nonstop service. Often American Airlines has acted as a *price leader*. When it changes its prices, it must consider the likely responses by rivals.

B. Oligopolies in the United States

1. When there are only a few firms in an industry, the *market share* of the top couple of firms is large. In tobacco, Phillip Morris is a *dominant firm*, selling 49% of the cigarettes. In gasoline, the top firm's market share is slightly less than 9%, with each of the top 9-firms having at least a 5% market share.

2. Firms may have a small part of the national market share, but be dominant firms within a smaller geographical region.

3. Models of behavior in oligopoly allow for varying degrees of interdependent behavior. At one extreme, each pricing or output action is coordinated (collusion); whereas, at the other extreme, interdependencies are ignored, as in the Cournot oligopoly model.

C. Cournot Model: Ignoring Interdependencies

1. A two-firm oligopoly is called a *duopoly*. An example would be Coke and Pepsi.

2. The Cournot model is based on a simple assumption of no reaction. If Coke expands production, Coke assumes that Pepsi *will not change its output*..

3. The Cournot assumption assumes away conscious interdependencies.

4. Economists like the Cournot model because the "solution" is between the pure competitive and the pure monopoly solutions. Furthermore, if there were *three* firms, the solution becomes closer to the competitive price and output. This fits the belief that the more firms in an industry, the closer we come to pure competition.

5. The Cournot model is criticized because of the unrealistic view that duopolists think the rival firm will not change output, even though they are repeatedly shown that they do change output. Normally, we would expect some "learning" from past actions.

6. If $P = 100 - Q$, where $Q = Q_1 + Q_2$. Suppose marginal cost is zero for both firms.

   a. In **competition**, $P = MC$, implies that output is 100, and price is $0.

   b. In **monopoly**, $MR = MC$, implies that output is 50, and the price is $50.

   c. In **Cournot duopoly**, solve $d\pi_1/dQ_1 = 0$, and $d\pi_2/dQ_2 = 0$.

   $$\pi_1 = P \cdot Q_1 = 100 \cdot Q_1 - Q_2 \cdot Q_1 - Q_1^2 \quad \text{and} \quad \pi_2 = P \cdot Q_2 = 100 \cdot Q_2 - Q_1 \cdot Q_2 - Q_2^2$$

   So, $d\pi_1/dQ_1 = 100 - Q_2 - 2 \cdot Q_1 = 0$ (i)
   and $d\pi_2/dQ_2 = 100 - Q_1 - 2 \cdot Q_2 = 0$ (ii)

   Two equations and two unknowns can be solved. We find $Q_1 = Q_2$.

   Substituting this result into equation (i) above, we find $100 - 3 \cdot Q_1 = 0$, so that $Q_1 = 33.33$, and $Q_2 = 33.33$. This means **Q = 66.66** and price is **$33.33**. This solution is between the competitive and monopolistic solution.

D. Cartels and Other Forms of Collusion

1. *Cartels* are formal agreements to coordinate pricing, output, or other decisions. Except for specific industries that are exempted from the Sherman Antitrust Act, cartels are illegal in the U.S. Cartels are legal in some countries.

2. *Collusion* usually refers to hidden and illegal agreements to set prices, output levels, or geographic regions among firms.

3. Oligopolistic industries may attempt to collude to restrict output and raise prices. But collusion does not always succeed. Executives of Archers-Daniels-Midland went to prison in 1996 after being convicted of price fixing of lysine (a growth hormone for livestock).

4. Six factors influence whether collusion is likely to succeed or fail:

  1. Number and Size Distribution of Sellers. Collusion is more successful with only a few firms or if there exists a dominant firm.

  2. Product Heterogeneity. Collusion is more successful with products that are standardized or homogeneous. With heterogeneous products, each producer views itself as a separate monopoly.

  3. Cost Structures. Collusion is more successful when the costs are similar for all of the firms in the oligopoly.

  4. Size and Frequency of Orders. Collusion is more successful with small, frequent orders.

  5. Secrecy and Retaliation. Collusion is more successful when it is difficult to give secret price concessions, as when the government is the purchaser and the winning bid is published.

E. Profit Maximization and the Division of Output

  1. The objective is to maximize *industry* profits, rather than simply firm profits.

  2. The optimal monopoly price and quantity for the industry occurs where the industry MR = ΣMC, which is the sum of the firms' marginal cost curves.

    • Let $\Sigma MC = MC_0$, a particular level of cost equal to industry MR.

    • If each firm "pretends" it is competitive with price, $P = MC_0$, then the oligopoly has optimally assigned output to each member firm.

  3. The consequence of collusive oligopolies or cartels is lower output, higher prices, and greater industry profits.

  4. The difficulty with this solution is that each oligopolistic firm will *desire* to sell more than their assignment. They realize that their cost is less than price, so selling additional units will raise their profit. But if each firm raises output, the collusive agreement will fall apart.

  5. Examples of cartels include Siemens *vs.* Thomson-CSF electronics companies, the NCAA for negotiations of TV college sports contracts (prior to 1984), and the OPEC oil cartel.

F. Price Leadership

1. Many industries exhibit a pattern where one or a few firms set the price that the other firms tend to copy. This may be *dominant firm price leadership* or *barometric price leadership.*

2. **Barometric Price Leadership Model**

   a. Perhaps one firm in an industry is unusually aware of the changes in cost and demand conditions in that industry.

   b. If that barometric firm sees cost rising, it raises its price first.

   c. This would occur in competition but might have the appearance of collusion. It is not necessarily bad!

   d. It may also be that the "leader" is merely the first to announce changes in list prices, without really being the first to change the actual prices.

   e. Where might we expect to see barometric price leadership?
      i.   many firms.
      ii. diverse costs in the industry.
      iii. good forecasting ability, for example, in a good location, or have "modern management".

   f. EXAMPLES: announcements of changes in the Prime Lending Rate, by Citibank, are likely barometric price leadership. Some airline price changes appear consistent with barometric price leadership.

3. **Dominant Price Leadership Model**

   a. Suppose one firm has a dominant market share [over 40% of the market share], such as Intel has in some computer chips.

   b. No direct price and quantity collusion is possible.

   c. Dominant firm expects the other (follower) firms to match the dominant firm's price, P_L, but the follower firms produce where their $\Sigma MC_F = P_L$.

   d. The dominant firm finds its demand curve, net of the followers' supply. The leader's demand curve, $D_L = D - \Sigma MC_F$, which could be described as a net demand curve.

e. The dominant firm acts like a *monopolist* with respect to the leader's demand curve, D_L. It equates $MR_L = MC_L$. Numerical examples appear in the "Worked Problems".

G. Kinked Oligopoly Demand Curve Model

1. There was widespread belief that oligopolies were price rigid in the Great Depression.

2. Suppose price cuts cause price wars. In that case, price decreases do not increase sales by much since all begin to cut price.

3. Suppose price increases are not followed. The firm that bravely raises price loses customers.

4. These *asymmetrical* responses create a "kinked" demand at the *prevailing price* currently charged.

5. The marginal revenue curve has a break in it, which implies that some changes in marginal cost will not alter the price.

6. The sole prediction: Oligopolies will have rigid prices because of this alleged kink.

H. Criticism of the Kinked Oligopoly Model

1. The theory does not explain where the *prevailing price* came from.

2. Empirical tests on oligopolies by Nobel Prize winner George Stigler found no evidence for kinks.

3. Other theories also expect that oligopolies will have rigid prices, *e.g.,* it is costly for an illegal cartel price agreement to be changed, which creates price rigidity without a kink.

4. The kinked demand model may work best for pricing behavior in the short run for new industries. For older industries, the kink is a barrier to profit maximization. Firms are in the business of maximizing profits, and should find ways around these alleged kinks.

I. Oligopolistic Rivalry and Game Theory

1. A type of mathematics was developed by Von Neuman & Morgenstern to describe risk averse behavior. It uses the language of *games*, where groups make decisions.

2. Simplest is a 2-person game. We assume:
   a. Each player knows his own and his opponent's alternatives.
   b. Preferences of both players are known.
   c. Single period game.

3. A *zero-sum game* is like poker, what one person wins the others lose. In *non-zero sum games*, some strategies can be better for the whole group than other strategies.

4. The "game" is to select the strategy alternative that maximizes the players' *security level* (minimum payoff). This is the MAXIMIN strategy. [Max of the Minimums]

J. The Prisoner's Dilemma

1. The prisoner's dilemma. There are two suspects, but the one who confesses first will implicate the other, and will thereby receive clemency in exchange for the confession.

2. In *noncooperative games*, the suspects are not permitted to communicate.

3. In the *noncooperative solution* to the Prisoner's Dilemma both suspects confess.

4. In a *cooperative game*, both players can communicate; if they could cooperate, they would both be better off.

5. However, even in a cooperative game, there is the potential for the "Double Cross" in prisoner's dilemma. Note that the cooperative solution is unstable.

6. *Duopoly* acts like a prisoner's dilemma game. Prediction: Duopoly games end in perfect competition because it is impossible to trust the opponents!

7. Duopoly Game: the payoff matrix below displays only the payments to "Firm B".

| | Firm A: | |
	Small Output	Large Output
Firm B: Small Output	100	10
Firm B: Large Output	150	20

8. The minimum payoff for Firm B is 10 if it produces a small output; the minimum payoff is 20 if it produces a large output. If firms systematically attempt to maximize their security level, Firm B will produce a **large amount**. So also will Firm A.

True and False Questions

Agree or disagree with the following statements, and correct the part that is erroneous.

1. Collusion is harder to achieve if the costs of the firms in the group are similar.

2. An oligopoly is a small group of firms that colludes to raise price.

3. Industry A has five equal-sized firms, whereas Industry B has five firms, but the largest firm has a 40% market share. Other things being equal, we would more likely expect to see collusion succeeding in industry B.

4. It is more difficult to coordinate collusion for mature industries than industries that are relatively new.

5. We would expect more collusion among firms in industries that produce nearly identical items, compared to industries that produce made-to-order products.

6. In the kinked demand curve theory, we expect rivals to copy price increases, but not to copy price cuts.

7. In cooperative games, the communication between the players assures that they will achieve the best, or cooperative solution.

8. In a sequential form game, each player makes a decision in turn, whereas in a normal form game, all players make decisions simultaneously.

9. Barometric price leadership does not result in lower total output, whereas dominant firm price leadership involves the dominant firm restricting output and raising the price for the entire industry.

10. In the theory of dominant price leadership, we would expect to find that the market shares of the firms in the industry never change.

Answers:
1. Disagree. When costs are similar, it is easier to get firms to agree on a price for the industry.
2. Disagree. An oligopoly is an industry with only a few firms. Whether the firms collude to raise price or do not collude does not change the fact that it is an oligopoly.
3. True.
4. Disagree. Mature industries have greater social affiliations, and members of the industry know each other relatively well. This makes collusion more likely.
5. True.
6. Disagree. They copy price cuts, but do not follow price increases.

7. Disagree. They *could* achieve a cooperative solution, but one of the players may double-cross the rivals to earn a higher payoff.
8. True.
9. True.
10. Disagree. We would expect the dominant price leader's market share to decline over time as the follower firms expand production.

Multiple Choice Questions

1. Which of the following does NOT describe oligopolies?
   a. The rivals react to business decisions made by other firms.
   b. The firms are price-takers.
   c. There are just a few firms.
   d. The products may be either homogeneous or heterogeneous.

2. Compared to the competitive price and output, when oligopolistic firms collude in order to maximize their joint profits, their actions generally lead to:
   a. a larger output and a lower price.
   b. a smaller output and a lower price.
   c. a smaller output and a higher price.
   d. a larger output and a higher price.

3. According to the kinked demand curve analysis, the demand curve of an oligopolistic firm is generally:
   a. inelastic above the current price.
   b. elastic above the current price.
   c. unit elastic at the current price.
   d. elastic below the current price.

4. In the kinked demand curve model, if marginal cost rises, then:
   a. it is possible for prices not to rise, unlike the competitive model.
   b. price does not change, if the marginal cost intersects the marginal revenue curve in its discontinuous section.
   c. price rises, if the marginal cost intersects the marginal revenue curve above its discontinuous section.
   d. all of the above are correct.

5. The kinked demand curve model of oligopoly provides one explanation why:
   a. high entry barriers characterize oligopoly.
   b. prices do not always immediately respond to changed cost conditions.
   c. oligopoly firms are able to earn long-run economic profits.
   d. typically there are few firms in an oligopoly industry.

6. In a Cournot duopoly, we would expect the price and the quantity in the market to closely resemble:
   a. competition.
   b. monopoly.
   c. prices near the monopoly prices, and quantities near the competitive output.
   d. prices and quantities between the monopoly and competitive amounts.

7. In the Cournot duopoly model, firm A assumes that firm B:
   a. does not change firm B's output, even if firm A expands output.
   b. does not change firm B's price, even if firm A cuts its price.
   c. will always copy firm A's price decisions.
   d. will always copy firm A's output decisions.

8. In a two-firm oligopoly that has decided to jointly maximize profits, we would expect that the output:
   a. would be split fifty-fifty.
   b. would be greater than the monopoly quantity.
   c. would be set where the sum of their MC's equal the industry's MR.
   d. would be determined by a federal mediator.

9. Military commanders have orders in battles to consider what the enemy is capable of doing, and then to select the command decision that avoids the worst outcomes. This thinking is identical to:
   a. game theory.
   b. Cournot duopoly.
   c. dominant price leadership.
   d. kinked oligopoly demand.

10. Barometric price leadership exists when
    a. one firm in the industry initiates a price change and the others may or may not follow.
    b. one firm imposes its price on the rest of the industry.
    c. all firms agree to change prices simultaneously.
    d. one company cuts price below cost.

11. The Prisoner's Dilemma model can be used to explain why:
    a. oligopolists tend easily to achieve collusion in "one shot" games.
    b. oligopolies face zero-sum games.
    c. oligopolists are suspicious that other players may double cross them.
    d. oligopolists can rely on cooperative behavior by all parties.

12. A game is considered to be noncooperative if:
    a. it is not possible to negotiate with the other participants.
    b. it is not possible to enforce any agreement between participants.
    c. participants have symmetrical payoffs.
    d. both (a) and (b) are required for noncooperative games.

13. With dominant price leadership, the large firm:
    a. sets the price and determines how much output each firm is permitted to produce.
    b. sets the price and supplies the residual demand.
    c. sets a price that is lower than would result from active competition in the industry.
    d. is essentially a price taker.

14. When a "Strategy Game" involves more than two players:
    a. there is no equilibrium.
    b. coalitions can be formed and break up as the game continues.
    c. the game cannot be zero sum.
    d. the game can last only one period.

15. The kinked demand curve results from the assumption that
    a. competitors match price cuts but not price increases.
    b. competitors match price increases but not price cuts.
    c. there is product differentiation.
    d. there are no cost changes.

16 Assume that pricing at marginal cost would result in a competitive industry output of 600 units. For a **Cournot** oligopoly with two firms ($N = 2$), the equilibrium industry output would be
    a. 600 units.
    b. 400 units.
    c. 225 units.
    d. 125 units.

17. Alchem (L) is a price leader in polyglue. The other 10 firms are follower firms (F). Demand for the total market of polyglue is $Q_T = 5000 - .25 P$. The supply curve for the follower firms is $Q_F = .25P - 500$. Alchem, the leader, is attempting to determine its *net demand curve* or leader's demand curve, where $Q_L = Q_T - Q_F$. Find Alchem's demand curve, in this dominant firm price leadership model.
    a. $Q_L = 4500 + .50 P$
    b. $Q_L = 5500 + .50 P$
    c. $Q_L = 5500 - .50 P$
    d. $Q_L = 1000 - .25 P$

18. A barometric price leader will display *which* of the following:
    a. The price leader may have good forecasting abilities
    b. The price leader may be in a good location to be aware of changes in demand or cost in the industry.
    c. The price leader may only be announcing changes in its price list, but real price changes had occurred earlier.
    d. All of the above.

19. Collusion is more likely to succeed when
    a. the cost of production is identical for all firms in the oligopoly.
    b. the products sold are highly differentiated.
    c. it is easy secretly to sell products without the other firms learning about it.
    d. there are quite a few firms in the oligopoly

20. Two manufacturers of the same product must decide independently whether to build a new production facility. The profit payoff matrix is:

		FIRM 2 Don't Build	FIRM 2 Build
FIRM 1	Don't Build	**5, 5**	**0, 10**
FIRM 1	Build	**10, 0**	**4, 4**

The payoffs for Firm 1 given first in each pair in the matrix.
    a. if Firm 1 uses a maximin strategy, it will decide to "Don't Build".
    b. there is no dominant strategy.
    c. {Don't Build, Don't Build} is the likely solution.
    d. Firm 2's maximin strategy is to Build.

Answers
1. b
2. c
3. b
4. d
5. b
6. d
7. a
8. c
9. a
10. a
11. c
12. d
13. b

14. b
15. a
16. b
17. c (The leader's demand is $Q_L = Q_T - Q_F = [5000 - .25P] - [.25P - 500] = 5500 - .50P$)
18. d
19. a
20. d

Problems or Short Essays

1. There are two primary sellers of rolls of crepe paper. We will call them **Bunting International** and **Partytime Now, Ltd.** Costs in the crepe paper business are highly uniform and constant. Marginal cost for Bunting and Partytime is 20 cents per roll. Some years ago, Bunting made an informal offer to acquired Partytime, but worried that the U.S. Justice Department would rule it a *per se* violation of the Sherman Antitrust Act. Partytime angrily rebuffed Bunting's informal merger offer. Ever since, the two firms have never been able to cooperate, much less collude. Partytime has even refused to join the trade association of party favor manufacturers because Bunting is a member.

   The market demand for crepe paper is: $P = 120,000,000.20 - 2 \cdot Q$.

   a. What is the quantity of crepe paper sold if Bunting and Partytime were competitive firms?

      Answer: In competition, $P = MC$. Hence, they would sell at a price of 20¢. The number of rolls of crepe paper would be found by substituting .20 for P in the demand curve. Therefore, $Q = 60$ million rolls of crepe paper.

   b. What is the quantity of crepe paper sold if Bunting and Partytime were to act as a single monopolist?

      Answer: In monopoly, $MR = MC$. Given a linear demand curve, $MR = 120,000,000.20 - 4 \cdot Q = .20$. Hence, a monopolist would only sell $Q = 30$ million rolls of crepe paper.

   c. What is the quantity for each firm, if they behave according to the assumptions of Cournot?

      Answer: In the Cournot model, each firm separately maximizes profit. The profit function for one firm is:
      $$\pi_1 = P \cdot Q_1 - .20 \cdot Q_1 = 120,000,000.20 \cdot Q_1 - 2 \cdot Q_2 \cdot Q_1 - 2 \cdot Q_1^2 - .20 \cdot Q_1$$
      and $\pi_2 = P \cdot Q_2 - .20 \cdot Q_2 = 120,000,000.20 \cdot Q_2 - 2 \cdot Q_1 \cdot Q_2 - 2 \cdot Q_2^2 - .20 \cdot Q_2$

      Solve $d\pi_1/dQ_1 = 0$, and $d\pi_2/dQ_2 = 0$.

So, $d\pi_1/dQ_1 = 120{,}000{,}000 - 2 \cdot Q_2 - 4 \cdot Q_1 = 0$
and $d\pi_2/dQ_2 = 120{,}000{,}000 - 2 \cdot Q_1 - 4 \cdot Q_2 = 0$

Two equations and two unknowns can be solved. We find $Q_1 = Q_2$. Substituting this into either of the above equations reveals, $120{,}000{,}000 - 6 \cdot Q_1 = 0$, so that $Q_1 = 20$ million and $Q_2 = 20$ million. This means that $Q = 40$ million rolls of crepe paper.

2. Price is a signal in oligopolistic industries of actions and intents. Often a leader announces the price. Other firms generally assent to the leader's price. We considered *dominant price leadership* and *barometric price leadership*. In addition, we looked at a *kinked demand curve oligopoly* and an *oligopoly that maximizes joint profits*. Given the facts below, which type best hypothetically describes each of the following industries?

a. De Beers diamond prices are sometimes listed in the London <u>Financial Times</u>. Other diamond merchants pay close attention prices charged by De Beers, frequently using it as their price for standard weights and cuts and clarity. We see a slow, but steady increase in the market share of several rival diamond merchants in India, Hong Kong, and the United States.

   Answer: The diamond market, according to this information, appears to fit the dominant price leadership model. Prices of the leader are matched, but there is no intention of rival producers in India, Hong Kong, U.S., or even the former Soviet Republics to restrict their output.

b. Tuition at leading private Ivy League universities has been rising faster than the inflation rate for some years. Tuition increases for the succeeding year at Harvard are announced traditionally prior to tuition decisions at Princeton, Brown, or the University of Pennsylvania. Tuition fees vary across schools somewhat, but the percentage increases are often nearly identical.

   Answer: Harvard is the oldest university in the United States, and tends to be a natural leader. It is likely that Harvard is a barometric price leader. As the costs of faculty, libraries, and laboratories rise nationally, Harvard may express those cost increases in their percentage tuition increase tolerably well. Since tuition differs remarkably across schools, it is unlikely a collusive oligopoly. However, the practice of sharing information on scholarships granted to new admissions had the effect of reducing some types of competition among the schools.

c. Cocoa prices are determined in an international market, with only a few major "governmental" producers and few major buyers appearing to be close to a bilateral oligopoly model. Brazilian prices are matched quickly by Colombian and other "governmental" sellers. Market share among the several major producers has been remarkably stable over time, and the costs of production are relatively constant, except for periodic outbreaks of fungus or frost.

Answer: The few national producers of cocoa have great incentives to maximize joint profits. Stable market shares would occur if the several countries had consciously decided to divide the market along pre-set market shares. At least this evidence is consistent with an effectively managed oligopoly behaving like a single monopolist.

3. Kinked demand curve theory predicted price rigidity for oligopolies, especially industries with homogeneous products and with equal size market shares. Give an alternative explanation of why oligopolistic industries, which produce a relatively homogeneous product, would display price rigidity.

Answer: In the kinked demand model, firms expect different responses to price increases versus price cuts. This creates the break in the marginal revenue curve. When costs move up or down a little, the price remains the same.

But suppose the firms have secretly met to set prices and outputs for the members of an illegal collusion. When costs move up or down a little, it is much too dangerous to meet frequently to re-set prices for the members. The price rigidity itself may be a clue that collusion, not a kink, is at work.

4. Two competing firms (duopolists) have the entire market for a given product and must determine their advertising strategies for the coming period. The payoffs (profits) for Firm A are shown in the following table (the payoff or profit to Firm B is equal to $50,000 minus the payoff to Firm A):

Firm B
Advertising Strategy

Firm A Advertising Strategy		1	2
	1	25,000	15,000
	2	20,000	35,000

a. What strategy (1 or 2), maximizes Firm A's security level; that is, what is Firm A's *maximin strategy?*

Answer: Strategy 2, because the worst that could happen is $20,000; whereas with Strategy 1 the payoff could be only $15,000. Students may wish to look at page 712 in the textbook to better understand a maximin strategy.

b. What strategy (1 or 2), maximizes Firm B's security level; that is, what is Firm B's *maximin strategy?*

Answer: Strategy 1, because the worst that could happen is ($50,000 - $25,000), whereas with Strategy 2 the payoff could be as low as ($50,000 - $35,000).

c. Are the firm solutions in equilibrium; that is, can either firm improve their outcome knowing what choice that the other firm is going to select?

Answer: They are not in an equilibrium, since Firm A would change strategies to improve its payout. For example, if Firm A "knows" that Firm B will pick Strategy 1, Firm A should switch from Strategy 2 (with a payoff of $20,000) to Strategy 1 (with a payoff of $25,000). This will further induce Firm B to change its Strategies. No single solution will dominate.

d. Would you describe this as a *zero-sum game* or a *non-zero sum* game, and why?

Answer: It is a non-zero sum game, since the payments sum to $50,000. However, it is a "constant sum" game, since the payoffs sum always to $50,000. In zero-sum games, the payoffs sum to zero. Poker games are zero-sum, since the winnings of one player are the losses of the other players.

5. Borateem is the dominant firm price leader in the borax market (a laundry additive similar to bleach). All five other manufacturers [follower (F) firms] sell borax products at the same price as Borateem. Borateem cannot prevent the other firms from selling as much as they wish at the established price. Borateem supplies the remainder of the demand itself. The *inverse* total demand for Borateem is given by the following function ($Q_T = Q_L + Q_F$), where quantity is measured in cases of Borateem:

$$P = 200 - 4 \cdot Q_T$$

Borateem's marginal cost function for manufacturing and selling Borateem is:

$$MC_L = 4 \cdot Q_L$$

The aggregate marginal cost function for the other manufacturers of borax products is:

$$P \equiv \Sigma MC_F = 8 + 4 \cdot Q_F$$

a. Since followers are expected to produce where price equals their marginal cost, write Q_F as a function of P.

    Answer: The supply curve of the followers would be: $Q_F = -2 + .25 \cdot P$. This comes from solving the aggregate marginal cost function for the follower firms in terms of the quantity for the followers, Q_F.

b. From the inverse demand curve, we know that $Q_T = 50 - .25 \cdot P$. Calculate the leader's demand curve, which is $Q_L = Q_T - Q_F$.

    Answer: $Q_L = Q_T - Q_F$. Substitute $(50 - .25 \cdot P)$ for Q_T and substitute $(-2 + .25 \cdot P)$ for Q_F. This implies that $Q_L = 52 - .50 \cdot P$.

c. Borateem has some monopoly power with respect to its leader demand curve. Find Borateem's marginal revenue function.

    Answer: Marginal revenue is twice as steep as its linear (inverse) demand curve. The word *inverse* in this problem means that it is written with price as the dependent variable instead of quantity as the dependent variable.

    First, we rearrange the answer to part (b). $P = 104 - 2 \cdot Q_L$. This is a linear inverse demand curve. Therefore, $MR = 104 - 4 \cdot Q_L$, which is twice as steep.

d. **How much** borax additives should Borateem produce and what **price** should Borateem charge? HINT: Set MR equal to MC for the leader.

    Answer: Equating MR and MC we find: $MR = 104 - 4 \cdot Q_L = MC_L = 4 \cdot Q_L$. This reduces to $104 = 8 \cdot Q_L$, or $Q_L = 13$. At that quantity, go back to the leader's inverse demand curve: $P = 104 - 2 \cdot Q_L = 104 - 2 \cdot (13) = 78$. Therefore, P = \$78.

e. If Borateem has a 58.1% market share today, what will you predict concerning its market share:
    (i) over time?
    (ii) in an economic boom period?

Answer: (i) We would predict that Borateem's market share would decline as other follower firms expand production.

(ii) In economic booms, we predict that Borateem's market share would rise.

Net Sources

1. **The Aluminum Industry**   *www.aluminum.org/*

Price leadership models for industries with dominant firms typically point to the steel industry (US Steel) or the aluminum industry (Alcoa). The Aluminum Association is the trade association for U.S. producers of primary aluminum, recyclers and semi-fabricated aluminum products. It provides extensive aggregate production statistics of the industry. Production by Alcoa of primary aluminum can be found at its homepage at: *www.alcoa.com/*. The amount of aluminum produced by Alcoa appears in their Investor section: *www.alcoa.com/investor/financialhighlights/aluminumproductship.asp.*

2. **The Steel Industry**   *www.steelworld.com/* also *www.steelnet.org/*

Dominant firm price leadership models predict the withering away of the dominance of the leader overtime. The "Steelworld" site offers statistics, such as the, "Top 25 Steelmakers of Crude Steel Worldwide," at *www.steelworld.com/stat.htm#24*. The "Steelnet" site is the Steel Manufacturers Association. For US Steel, go to: *www.usx.com/corp/ussteel/index.htm.*

3. **PROJECT:** The Prisoner's Dilemma can be played online against a computer. Your computer opponent is Albert. Albert can be assigned the following strategies: Golden Rule, Brazen Rule 1 & 3, Iron Rule, and a question mark. You may play for several rounds, amassing years in prison. See if you can determine your best strategy against each of Albert's strategies at: *www.princeton.edu/~mdaniels/PD/PD.html*

Chapter 14

Game-Theoretic Rivalry: Best-Practice Tactics

Increasing attention in business is being given to tactics and strategy to achieve competitive advantages. This chapter predicts rival firm behavior as if they were games. Sometimes being the first-mover offers advantages. Sometimes credible threats or matching the actions of rival firms affect opponents' behavior. These issues are addressed for firms in oligopolistic industries, where the interdependence among firms is most keenly felt.

A. Business Strategy Games

1. The speed of change in business requires one's best efforts.

2. When oligopolistic rivals alter their products or pricing, our firm must react or adapt. The best approach would be *proactive behavior* that could anticipate actions.

3. A *sequential game* is one in which there is an explicit order of play. A *simultaneous game* occurs when all players must chose their actions at the same time.

4. A sequential example is when one firm has announced a price cut, your decision to respond or not is sequential.

5. A *game tree* is like a decision tree. It is a schematic diagram of decision nodes (or *focal outcomes*).   Decision trees provide opportunities to make decisions. If a manufacturer alters its product, then the retailer than must decide whether to continue to sell the product or to discontinue it. The *best reply response* is the one in the firm's best interest.

6. Solving a game is similar to the thought process in board games like chess. One way to solve a decision problem is to use *end-game reasoning*, where we start with the final decision and use *backward induction* to find the best starting decision on the game tree.

7. When all players make their best reply responses (so changing their choices cannot improve their position) then the game is in a *Nash Equilibrium.*

8. Since game trees have several branches, we can examine the concept of equilibrium in each part of the tree, called a *subgame.*

B. Business Rivalry as a Sequential Game

1. The first to introduce a product, lower price, *etc.*, often achieves recognition and an advantage, called a *first-mover advantage*. In some decisions, being the first achieves profit, whereas being second may mean losses.

2. When games last several periods, the actions by firms in one period can be punished or rewarded in future period. If a new firm enters a market, the threat is that the incumbent firm may drop prices down to levels that are unprofitable.

3. A *credible threat* is an action that is perceived as a possible penalty in a noncooperative game. Its existence sometimes induces cooperative behavior.

4. A *credible commitment* is a mechanism for establishing trust (such as a reward for good behavior) in a noncooperative game.

5. Mechanisms for credible threats and commitments include:

    a. *Contractual side payments*, but side payments may violate antitrust laws.

    b. Use of *nonredeployable assets* such as reputation. Failing to perform one's commitments can be punished by the threat of loss of the value of these assets.

    c. Entering *alliance relationships* that would fall apart if any party violated their commitments.

    d. Using a "hostage mechanism" that is irreversible and irrevocable can deter breaking commitments. Examples are "double your money back guarantees," and "most favored nation" clauses.

C. Underline: Excess Capacity, Scale of Entry, and Entry Deterrence

1. Building excess capacity can deter entry. Potential entrants know that the price can be driven down to near zero if they entered, and the incumbent firm began a price war.

2. The building of extra capacity is an action in a sequential game, often with the intent of forestalling entry. This is called a *precommitment game*.

3. Customers may be inclined to buy from the newest firm or from incumbent firms. Several customer-sorting rules include:

    a. *Brand loyalty to incumbents* — that favors incumbents and first-movers.

b. *Efficient rationing* – customers prefer low prices. This is favorable at times to low-cost entrants.

c. *Random rationing* – customers buy from incumbents or entrants randomly, so long as the price is the same.

d. *Inverse intensity rationing* – the most price sensitive customers buy up all of the capacity of the low priced producers. An example might be People Express airline that was the low price provider (now defunct!).

4. If the minimum efficient size is large, then entrants must leap to a large scale if they wish to enter a market.

   a. incumbent firms may *accommodate* the entrant, allowing a niche.

   b. incumbent firms may take *entry-deterring actions*, such as cutting their prices at any threat of entry.

5. The *theory of contestable markets* holds that, with no barriers to entry, even a monopolist must be aware that charging higher prices will encourage entry. Hence, a contestable market will tend to have zero economic profits and competitive prices.

D. Simultaneous Games

1. A sealed bid auction is a simultaneous game.

2. A *dominant strategy* is the best decision, no matter what anyone else does. It is an action (strategy) that is better in each "state of the world."

3. A *Nash equilibrium strategy* occurs when all players make their best reply responses (so changing their choices cannot improve their position).

4. When no Nash equilibrium exists, it is useful to hide one's strategy by randomly changing strategies. This is a mixed Nash equilibrium strategy.

E. Escape From Prisoner's Dilemma: Repeated Games

1. If the games are repeated, as they typically are in the duopoly problem, there is greater expectation that firms will achieve the cooperative solution.

2. Each firm "shows" by its behavior each period that it wants to cooperate. Firms that expand production "show" that they do not want to cooperate. These games may include:

   a. a *grim trigger strategy* which has an infinitely long punishment.

b. alternatively, the punishment can last for a period. For multi-period games, there usually is some period of punishment that can induce cooperation.

4. For non-infinite lived games, if you are one period before the end, the best strategy is to act noncooperatively. Yet this logic works for two periods before the end, and tends to unravel a cooperative, multi-period game.

5. Some game theorists have wondered if the slight defections could go unpunished, called a *trembling hand trigger strategy*. If the rival acts noncooperatively once, perhaps you can forgive. But fool me twice, and then watch out!

6. Games often involve more than two players. When there are 3 or more players, *coalitions* of players can "win" the game. These *n*-person games have complex solutions.

True and False Questions

Agree or disagree with the following statements, and correct the part that is erroneous.

1. Sealed bid auctions for contracts are used in many governmental purchasing requests for proposals. These are examples of sequential games, when there are only a few potential bidders.

2. After several decision focus points, the branches reveal the payoffs in a game tree.

3. If customers sort themselves according to random rationing, then the best strategy is always to be the first-mover. Incumbency means everything.

4. The grim reaper strategy is the one that involves infinitely long punishments.

5. It is usually believed in infinite-lived Prisoner Dilemma games that cooperation can be achieved.

6. In inverse intensity rationing, customers are sorted so that most price sensitive customers buy up all of the capacity of the highest priced producers.

Answers
1. Disagree. This is an example of a simultaneous game.
2. True.
3. Disagree. In random rationing, low prices attract customers. Incumbency is valueless.
4. Disagree. Infinitely long punishments are found in the grim *trigger* strategy. The trigger is finding that someone has not lived up to his or her commitments.

5. True.
6. Disagree. In inverse intensity rationing the most price sensitive customers buy up all of the capacity of the *low* priced producers.

Multiple Choice Questions

1. Noncooperation in games can be overcome by:
   a. offering a credible commitment.
   b. creating a credible threat.
   c. entering into alliance relationships
   d. all of the above.

2. A game tree is drawn which shows all of the final payoffs. Using this game tree, we can often determine our best strategy by:
   a. deductive logic.
   b. backward induction.
   c. the trembling hand trigger strategy.
   d. treating a sequential game as if it were a simultaneous game.

3. The behavior of games depends heavily on customer sorting (buying) decisions. Which is NOT a customer-sorting rule:
   a. extreme brand loyalty.
   b. efficient rationing.
   c. the hostage mechanism.
   d. inverse intensity rationing.

4. A dominant strategy means that:
   a. the action is domineering.
   b. the game is far more complex than can be described by a matrix of payoffs.
   c. involves coercion, as in the hostage mechanism.
   d. an action that is best, no matter what anyone else does.

5. Suppose a duopoly is involved in a pricing game (high or low price). A "hostage mechanism" perhaps is too colorful a term for a type of strategy used to establish commitment. Which of the following is an example of a hostage mechanism.
   a. prices are stamped on the packages as "suggested retail prices."
   b. prices are widely advertised in the Sunday editions of the local newspaper.
   c. prices are randomly changed up and down each day.
   d. double-your-money-back guarantees to customers if they don't receive the lowest price.

6. Which of the following is **not** important for a good strategy in a repeated game so as to get to a cooperative, or monopolistic, result?
   a. Belief that the game is very likely to continue in future periods.
   b. Small chance of being misunderstood in one's actions.
   c. Ability to punish cheating.
   d. The gain from cheating on a cooperative agreement with the other players is huge.

Consider the following payoff matrix for questions 7 and 8. The first payoff in each pair is for Target.

Big-K
Advertising Strategy

Target	modest	high
modest Advertising Strategy	35, 35	15, 50
high	50, 15	20, 20

7. According to these figures,
   a. Big-K has a dominant strategy of choosing a high advertising strategy.
   b. Target has a dominant strategy of choosing a high advertising strategy.
   c. none of the above are true.
   d. both (a) and (b) are true.

8. In the game described by the Target *vs.* Big-K payoff matrix in question #7, it appears that:
   a. in a multi-period game, the eventual solution would be Big-K with a high advertising strategy and Target with a low advertising strategy.
   b. the cooperative solution for the entire industry would be { modest advertising, modest advertising }.
   c. this game is an example of large-scale entry with accommodation.
   d. this is a game that uses the concept of a sequential game.

9. Game trees illustrate sequential games where one firm makes an offer to a client, and then the other firm comes up with an offer. What method do we use to try to *solve* the best strategy in such sequential games?
   a. Flip a coin.
   b. We look to the end result of each branch of the tree, and eliminate branches that end in bad outcomes.
   c. We select the maximin strategy pairs.
   d. We randomize our decisions to fool the other firms.

Questions 10-13 refer to the following table. Greek letters represents the payoffs for both firms. The payout to Firm A is the bold number in the bottom left of each box, whereas the payout to Firm B is in the upper right corner of each box.

Firm A \ Firm B	Cuts Price 20%	Maintains Price	Raises Price 20%
Cuts Price 20%	-10 α / **-10**	-20 ß / **+10**	-35 Γ / **+25**
Maintains Price	+5 π / **-5**	0 Σ / **0**	-15 σ / **+5**
Raises Price 20%	+30 μ / **-40**	+5 τ / **-15**	+10 Φ / **+10**

10. Suppose that both Firm A and Firm B cut prices 20%. Is this a *Nash equilibrium*?
   a. Yes, there is no improvement possible by changing their pricing strategies.
   b. No, Firm A should change its pricing strategy to "Maintains Price."
   c. No, Firm B should change its pricing strategy to "Raises Price 20%."
   d. No, Firm B should change its pricing strategy to "Maintains Price."

11. If both firms pursue a maximin strategy (examine the worst case in each strategy, and pick the best among these), they will end up:
   a. in the box that includes cell α.
   b. in the box that includes cell ß.
   c. in the box that includes cell Γ.
   d. in the box that includes cell π.

12. If both firms cooperated, they could improve upon the noncooperative outcome. Which is the cell with the best possible outcome:
   a. in the box that includes cell Γ.
   b. in the box that includes cell Σ.
   c. in the box that includes cell Φ.
   d. in the box that includes cell ß.

13. Suppose that the pricing decision for these two firms mentioned above is a *sequential game*. Firm B has announced a price cut. Because profit-maximizing Firm A knows for sure that B cuts price, Firm A would:
   a. cut its price as well.
   b. maintain its price.
   c. raise its price.
   d. cut its production.

14. Burger King is contemplating a response to McDonald's salads sold in plastic glasses. McDonalds is considering another *Monopoly* ™ game. Examine the game for Burger King and McDonalds given below.

McDonalds

		New *Monopoly* ™ Game	No New Game
Burger King	New BK Salad Shaker	50, 80	100, 90
	No New BK Salad	60, 100	90, 120

Which of the following is correct?
a. The maximin strategy for Burger King is to offer a New BK Salad Shaker.
b. The maximin strategy for McDonalds is to start a New *Monopoly* ™ Game.
c. The strategy pair: {No New BK Salad, New *Monopoly* ™ Game } is a Nash equilibrium.
d. The strategy pair: {New BK Salad Shaker, No New Games} is a Nash equilibrium.

15. Consider a game between Lem and Zelda, given in the following diagram. What is Lem's Maximin strategy? In each pair, Zelda's number comes first.

		Lem			
		L1	L2	L3	L4
Zelda	Z1	34, 40	31, 48	5, 20	88, 10
	Z2	20, 33	39, 30	8, 120	15, 49

Lem's maximin strategy is:
a. L1
b. L2
c. L3
d. L4

Answers

1. d	4. d	7. d	10. b	13. b
2. b	5. d	8. b	11. d	14. d
3. c	6. d	9. b	12. c	15. a

Worked Problem

1. Massive cigarette advertising on television was commonplace until laws prohibiting such advertising were introduced in the early 1970's. Imagine prior to such legislation that there were only two brands: Camels and Marlboros sold by duopolists in a two person, non-zero sum game. The two "strategy choices" were limited advertising (low) and massive advertising (high). How might prohibitions on advertising affect the cigarette industry in the short run, and in the long run using a Prisoner's Dilemma sort of argument.

   Answer: Both cigarette companies realize that the cost of advertising was higher than the benefits achieved from it, at least in the short run. Advertising chiefly shifted customers from one brand to another. If either went to a low advertising strategy, the would lose customers to the other firm.

   This is a simple two-person game. With Marlboro's profits given first in each pair, a payoff matrix might look like:

Camel
Advertising Strategy

		low	high
		low	high
Marlboro Advertising Strategy	low	high, high	highest, lowest
	high	highest, lowest	low, low

The governmental prohibition essentially forced the brands to the cooperative solution of *{ low advertising, low advertising }*. The short run effect achieved cooperative behavior, with the government assuring that TV advertisements were prohibited. Accordingly, we predict that the short run impact would be higher profits earned by these firms.

In the long run, however, the brands may find that overall cigarette smoking declines. The effect of an advertising campaign wears off slowly over time. To the extent that advertising changes behavior, or at least associates smoking with the semblance of strength, maturity, confidence, or sexual attraction, then the cigarette firms lost in the longer run.

2. Consider the famous *Prisoner's Dilemma* game. But this time, let's apply it to the former Yugoslavia. There are many players in this conflict, but for simplicity let the two players be the U.S. and the Bosnian Serbs.

The U.S. can select a policy of "talking tough but doing nothing," or "air strikes with eventual ground forces." The Bosnian Serbs can select the policy of "continuing to expand territory," or "retreat from occupied areas."

Though these are hardly the only strategies, and the only major players, suppose this two-person non-zero sum game looks like the following, where the payoffs for the U.S. are shown in the following table in the upper triangle, the payoffs or profit to Bosnian Serbs are in the lower triangle.

Bosnian Serbs

	B1: Expand Territory	B2: Retreat
United States US1: Attack	-723,000 / -892,000	+515,000 / -300,000
US2: Do nothing	-328,000 / +430,000	+920,000 / -997,000

a. In this formulation, does the U.S.A. have a *dominant strategy*. [If so, is it Strategy US1 or US2?]

   Answer: Yes, the dominant strategy for the US is US2: Do nothing. Whether the Serbs use B1 or B2, the US is better off it picked US2.

b. Determine the Bosnian Serb's best strategy. [Strategy B1 or B2?]

   Answer: Since the US has a dominant strategy, they can presume the US will take it. The game is far simpler now. The Serbs must pick between +430,000 and -997,000. Clearly, they pick B1: expand territory.

c. Suppose the players talked, and trusted each other, would any combination of strategies be described as the *cooperative solution*?

   Answer: Given the payoffs, the sum of the two payoffs is highest if the US attacks and Bosnian Serbs retreated. The US gets worldwide recognition for its effective solution to the problem, but perhaps the US feels obligated to extend foreign aid to rebuild bombed cities as the US did in Europe after World War II in the Marshall Plan.

Net Sources

A growing group of economists, political scientists, and management experts are thinking and using game-theoretic concepts. Books and courses are designed around game theory, tactics, and business strategy.

1. **Al Roth's Page**   *www.economics.harvard.edu/~aroth/alroth.html*

   Introductory and advanced material by a Professor Roth, from Harvard. Extensive links to topics on game theory.

2. **International Journal of Game Theory**   *fismat.dima.unige.it/citg/ijgt/issues.htm*

   Index of all previous articles and abstracts. This site shows the wide variety of topics to which game models apply. For a visually more interesting site for the International Journal of Game theory, go to: *www.tau.ac.il/ijgt/*

3. **PROJECT**: Test your end-game reasoning and decision-making skills at the following address: *mayet.som.yale.edu/~nalebuff/java/threenumbers.html*. By trying several different series of three numbers, you must uncover the hidden rule that organizes them. After you make your guess, the example shows how you should have proceeded. This decision-making test comes from the homepage for the book, *Co-opetition*, by Adam M. Brandenburger and Barry J. Nalebuff. The homepage for *Co-opetition* is:
                    mayet.som.yale.edu/coopetition/index2.html

Appendix 14A

Capacity Planning and Pricing Against a Low-Cost Competitor: A Case Study of Piedmont Airlines and People Express

Piedmont Airlines and People Express present a case study of the reaction to entry of a low-cost firm. Deregulation in 1979 permitted new entry, and People Express was the first to enter the highly competitive airline industry.

A. Airline Entry Strategy

1. People Express tried a new strategy of a uniform low-price in the mid-Atlantic states in 1981. They cut costs by adding seats and eliminating all 'frills'. Low cost flying would compete with driving.

2. People could enter with scale of their entry. Should it be large scale or small scale, measured by having large planes or small 30-seat planes? Their decision would be based on what People Express thought would be the reaction of rival firms, particularly Piedmont Airline.

3. The response that Piedmont Airline could make would be either 'match' the low price of People Express, or to accommodate them, keeping only the customers who like the 'frills' of full service.

4. This strategy game can be written as a decision tree. The best final outcome (or subgame) being if People Express entered at large scale and Piedmont accommodated.

B. Large Scale Entry Deterrence of a Low-Cost Competitor

1. By 1985, Piedmont faced with more routes likely to compete with People Express the decision tree is more complex (14A.2 in the textbook). Piedmont can match low prices of People Express or accommodate.

2. People Express entered with large scale (120 seat planes). Piedmont matched their low price. But Piedmont, as the incumbent firm, tended to get most of the travelers to select Piedmont.

3. People Express did not see that with too many seats on a route, more of the passengers would take their rival. A price war ensued, and ultimately People Express lost too much money to continue operations

True and False Questions

Agree or disagree with the following statements, and correct the part that is erroneous.

1. If a new entrant faces an incumbent firm that always matches their price, then brand loyalty can be a big problem for the new entrant.

2. Looking at a decision tree, the subgame with the highest payout for the firm is the one you will always take.

3. Piedmont Airline entered in 1981.

Answers
1. True.
2. Disagree. The firm cannot select the subgame that will occur, as it depends on the other players (firms). Hence, the firm selects the path that will lead to its best result regardless of the choices of the rival. For example, in Figure 14A.2, selecting *Large Capacity* leads to the highest payout for People Express if Piedmont accommodates. But Piedmont didn't. Hence, picking *Small Capacity* would lead to a higher payout since we can predict that Piedmont would accommodate under that choice.
3. Disagree. People Express entered in 1981 after the airline industry was deregulated in 1979.

Multiple Choice Questions

1. When the payoffs are presented in a game tree form, a branch of the tree is: Filene's is
   a. a subgame.
   b. a probability.
   c. a variance.
   d. an expectation.

2. Suppose the question is whether to enter with BIG or SMALL capacity. If you enter with BIG your payoffs are either {100 or 700} depending on the rival's action. If you enter SMALL, your payoffs are either { 50 or 200 }.
   a. Enter SMALL because you will get 200.
   b. Enter SMALL because you never get a negative payoff.
   c. Enter BIG because your expected payoff is likely higher than if you enter SMALL.
   d. Enter BIG because of your hope that you get 700.

Look at an expansion of the game presented in Question 2, where the payoffs are given first for the Rival firm and then for your firm.

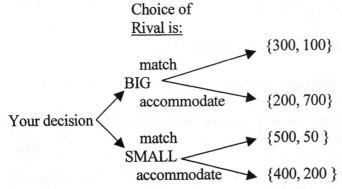

Choice of Rival is:

3. Given the game tree above, your decision should be:
   a. go BIG as your rival will surely match your price and you get 100.
   b. go BIG as your rival will surely accommodate and you get 700.
   c. go SMALL as your rival would surely match giving you 50.
   d. go SMALL as your rival would then surely accommodate giving you 200.

4. The following decision tree exists regarding future profits, where the probabilities of good and bad results are uncertain:

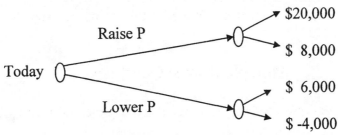

   a. The decision should be to lower price.
   b. The decision should be to raise price.
   c. The decision tree indicates that either price increase or price decrease is the same.
   d. The decision tree shows that the end point of lower price is the best.

Answers

1. a
2. c
3. a (If you go BIG the rival will match (300 > 200) and you get 100, but if you go SMALL your rival will match (500 > 400) and you get only 50. Because 100 > 50, you should go BIG).
4. a (If your raise price, all payoffs are greater than if you lower price. Raising price dominates lowering price here.)

Worked Problem or Short Essays

1. Yahoo!, Amazon, eBay and other Internet companies became household names in the past few years. In part, this was due to massive advertising and excite in the financial press over their stock price explosion.

   a. Use economic reasoning to explain the rapid drop in the share prices of these firms in 2000 and 2001.

   Answer: New entrants easily copied the technology and business plan adopted by the first firms. NBCi, Ask Jeeves!, and iWon entered the web portal business drawing off some customers to Yahoo! Barnes & Noble, Book-Club.net, and the American Book Center offered competition to Amazon. Even eBay found competition from Yahoo Auctions. The new entrants could match prices of the incumbent firms. As investors saw that the business model produced little profits, stock prices declined.

   b. The cost of getting price information is reduced. MySimon, PriceSCAN, and BizRate searches for the lowest price for all sorts of products. What is the impact of price searching technology on Amazon and other e-tailers?

   Answer: The more customers know about price, the harder it is to have large margins. Technology has improved price competition to the benefit of the customers but at the cost of lower profits for the sellers.

Net Sources

1. **Yahoo!**   *www.yahoo.com/*

2. **Amazon**   *www.amazon.com/*

3. **eBay**   *www.ebay.com/*

4. **The American Book Center**   *www.abc.nl/*

5. **NBCi**   *www.nbci.com/*

6. **mySimon**   *www.mysimon.com/*

7. **Ask Jeeves!**   *www.ask.com/*

8. **Barnes & Noble**   *www.bn.com/*

Chapter 15

Organizational Form, Governance, and Mechanism Design

Coordination and control are problems for all business organizations. The larger the organization, typically the problems increase. Contracts help insure performance, but most contracts are incomplete. Goods are allocated in free markets by using prices. However, there are alternative allocative mechanisms that are adopted, such as waiting in line (queues) and auctions. This chapters discusses why alternative mechanisms for allocation exist, and the impact of these methods on the markets where we find them.

A. The Role of Business Contracting in Cooperative Games

1. The amount of advertising and service offered by manufacturers and retail distributors can be viewed as a game. The outcome can be sub-optimal; that is, it is not value maximizing. The cooperative solution sometime yields better payoffs.

2. To get to a value-maximizing solution, the manufacturer may have to consider side payments or credible commitments to the retailer.

3. *Contracts* between players are binding that specifies actions by both parties. Contracts must assign penalties for not living up to the agreement. These payments are part of a several step sequential game. If the retailer decides to discontinue providing service for the product the manufacturer produces, then the contract can provide economic sanctions that make this decision unattractive.

4. A *vertical requirements contract* is one in which the firms in successive stages of production agree to payments and/or penalties for taking an action. If the manufacturer spends a large amount to advertise the product, the distributor promises to promote the product as well.

5. An alternative to contracts between two parties is *vertical integration*. If the retailer and manufacturer merge, then both interests are reflected in a decision to discontinue advertising or service.

6. *Spot markets* present few incentive or informational problems. The purchase of a dozen ears of corn at a roadside stand or the sale of electricity at a spot rate off the grid, are examples of spot markets. The products are relatively standardized and sold for immediate delivery.

B. Governance Mechanisms and the Problem of Moral Hazard

1. Doing business in markets involves the cost of contracts. Establishing a price for a product or service involves a cost.

2. *Transaction cost economics* — involves the issue of finding the lowest cost organizational structure. In some cases it is cheapest to vertically integrate and avoid markets. In other cases, firms create quasi-prices, known as *transfer prices*, to create market-like pricing in a multi-divisional firm. Still others find that market relationships work best, by buying and selling at arm's length prices.

3. When only *incomplete contracts* are possible, it is often the best to integrate the operations within a firm.

4. *Moral hazard* occurs when parties change their behavior due to contracts. This is especially true when the people's effort is hard to observe.

5. Consider a borrower-lender contract. A reliable borrower, once given money in a loan, may elect to invest in high risk projects. To avoid this moral hazard, the bank may insist on costly monitoring or governance actions, forcing the borrow to submit frequent financial data.

C. Alternative Organizational Forms

1. The nature of the product and the assets that produce it, affect the choice of organizational form.

2. A *reliant asset* is a non-redeployable durable asset. Specialized equipment or specialized (specific *vs.* general) knowledge cannot be transferred to other uses.

   a. Rental cares are redeployable, so we may expect use of spot market rentals.

   b. A paper-cup-making machine is non-redeployable, so we may expect long term rental agreements.

3. Markets with reliant assets one party could "hold-up" the other party. The choice of organization will require explicit contracts. The likely outcome is *franchise contracts*. At the extreme, if the asset has only one use, as in a bauxite mine, the likely organizational form is *vertical integration*, where the aluminum firm acquires the mine.

4. *Relational contracts* are promissory agreements of coordinated performance. A jet charter company is a good example, where long term relationships matter.

5. *Vertical integration* is a way to avoid transaction costs, such as moral hazard, in arm's length dealing. The two stages of production is merged: the producer ships goods to the next stage of the same firm.

6. If each stage of production has some monopoly power, the profits can be higher by merging the two stages. The optimal price for the final good maximizes profits, where successive stages of monopoly can lead to price higher than the one that maximizes profits.

D. The Concept of an Optimal Mechanism Design

1. What is the best way to divide a deceased individual's estate? What mechanism will encourage open communication and a fair division? This is the type of issue discussed in finding an optimal design.

2. Fair division of a *decaying prize* problem. Suppose the division of an award between two parties shrinks each time one party refuses the agreement. The incentive is created to agree to a 50:50 split; otherwise, the prize may get smaller.

3. Filling customer orders from those waiting in line is the *service queue* problem.

   a. *First-come, first-served* — leads some inefficient use of time, with some spending the night waiting for the ticket office to open. The people with the lowest cost of time get the tickets. Wealthier people can purchase these tickets at premium prices.

   b. *Last-come, first-served* — removes the incentive to wait in line. The best strategy is to show up anytime, whenever the ticket window is open. But someone arriving just after you can preempt you. This may lead to costs of bribing late arrivals to leave. Also, the power of custom leads to a preference for the fairness of first-come, first-served.

   c. *Stratified lotteries* — advanced reservation tickets are assigned different prices than last minute walk-ups. Price discrimination is discussed in Chapter 16.

E. Auction Design and Information Economics

1. Auctions are used to allocate oil and mineral rights, to Monday Night Football.

2. Auctions types include:

   a. *Simultaneous* bidding — such as open outcry at estate auctions. Information about other bidders valuation is revealed in the process. This leads to "price discovery" of the value of the item.

b. *Sequential* bidding — such as private placement for newly issued securities.

c. Bid prices can be *discrete* or *continuous* — by agreed increments, as in 1/8 or 1/16 for stocks or any price.

d. Bids can be *sealed* or *posted* — sealed bids make them anonymous and secret to other bidders, whereas posted means all know what you have bid

e. Bids can be *one-time-only* or *multiple rounds*.

3. In English auctions, the prices rise as more bids arrive.

4. In Dutch auctions, a high price is announced, and if no one agrees, the auctioneer lowers the price until the first bid arrives. Dutch auction often allows the bidder to buy some of the lot at that price. If mineral rights to 1,000 acres of land were auctioned, the winning bid may elect to purchase less than 1,000 acres or rights.

5. Reservation prices — the minimum acceptable bid.

F. Winner's Curse in Asymmetric Information Bidding Games

1. If the true value of an item is not known, but bidders have a distribution of values that they are willing to pay, the winning bid is very likely to be higher than the true value. The regret for the bidder is that he or she paid too much: the winner's curse.

2. If everyone is aware of the winner's curse, then all would bid less than what they think is its true value. This problem has led some auctions to award the highest bidder with the second-best price in a sealed bid auction. Even though you won, the price was a bit lower than what you paid.

G. Information Revealed in Common-Value Auctions

1. Common-value auctions are ones where the bidders have identical valuation of the item when information is complete.

2. For simultaneous, sealed-bid auctions, the bidder offers prices below their expected value. No information is conveyed to competitors.

3. For simultaneous, *open-bidding* auctions, information is revealed by the bids of others. One variation is multiple rounds.

4. Bidding for broadcast spectrum bidding, the FCC used 112 rounds over a four-month bidding period.

H. Strategic Underbidding in Private-Value Auctions

1. Private-value auctions are where bidders have different valuations for the item, even when information is complete.

2. The highest value bidders may wish to wait-and-see in *English open outcry auctions*.

3. In *sealed-bid auctions*, this strategy does not work. Even with sealed bidding, the fear of the winners curse may lead to underbidding.

3. A *Vickery auction* — is a way for getting sealed bids to equal to their private value. A good example of a Vickery auction is the second-highest sealed bid auctions.

4. *Second-highest sealed bid*s are used to reduce underbidding. Knowing that you pay less than bid helps to move bid closer to one's private value.

5. As the number of bidders rises, the percentage underbid tends to decline. Vickery shows the optimal underbidding is $1/N^{th}$ the true value, with N the number of bidders.

True and False Questions

Agree or disagree with the following statements, and correct the part that is erroneous.

1. A highest-bid sealed bid auction could also be described as a simultaneous English auction.

2. A good example of a reliant asset is a rental car.

3. Vertical integration is one solution to the hold-up problem when dealing with reliant assets.

4. Last-come, first served queuing system for allocating tickets will lead to long lines and long waits.

5. The winner's curse is that the winner has to pay for what he or she bid on.

6. The purpose of the second highest sealed bid (as the price paid by the winning bidder) is to the make the bid-price lower.

7. A yarn maker merges with a maker of socks is a horizontal merger.

8. If a highly competitive market exists in yarn, there is little incentive for a maker of socks to backward integrate by purchasing the yarn maker.

Answers
1. True.
2. Disagree. There is a good market for used cars, so a car is easily redeployable. Reliant assets are non-redeployable.
3. True.
4. Disagree. First-come, first-served methods lead to lines and long waits; whereas last-come, first-served creates discourages waiting in line.
5. Disagree. The winner's curse is that the winning bid is very likely to be higher than the true value.
6. Disagree. The purpose is to overcome the problem of the winner's curse, so that bidders will bid closer to the value of the item.
7. Disagree. This is a vertical merger.
8. True. Only when the yarn maker also has market power does there appear benefits for the vertical merger.

Multiple Choice Questions

1. Filene's, a Boston department store, offers prices of close-out merchandise in the basement with prices that decline with time. The price tag on an oriental rug may say $200 until June 15; $150 if after June 15 but before August 30; $100 after August 30, *etc.* In essence, Filene's is using:
   a. an open outcry auction.
   b. a Dutch auction.
   c. a sealed bid auction.
   d. an English auction.

2. First-come, first-served is a method to allocate scare items, such as tickets to a Lilith Fair concert. This method:
   a. tends to make for long queues of waiting fans.
   b. is perceived as a fair method of allocation, but tends to allocate tickets to those with lower cost of time.
   c. is somewhat inefficient, as the time wasted could be avoided if the price were allowed to allocate tickets.
   d. all of the above.

3. Bidding by television networks for the Olympics is often fierce. The number of minutes of commercials is somewhat fixed, and the rate the winning network charges depends on the number of advertisers wanting to buy ad time and the rates charged for other TV slots. The bidding is a sealed bid auction. The outcome of this auction:
   a. may lead to the winner's curse.
   b. could create a dominant strategy.
   c. would be called the maximin solution.
   d. should represent the lowest possible price that anyone would pay.

4. Which is likely to be a *reliant asset*?
   a. cars that are available at a Hertz rent-a-car agency.
   b. a paper-cup-making machine rented by a manufacturer of paper cups.
   c. a photocopying machine rented by a Kinko's photocopying shop.
   d. office furniture rented by a law firm.

5. Which of the following is NOT correct about auctions.
   a. Stocks and futures contracts historically are bid in *discrete* units.
   b. The traditional auctioneer at an estate sale uses an *English* auction style.
   c. A *Dutch* auction is another way of saying the second-highest sealed bid.
   d. Government contracts are often awarded based through *sealed bid* auctions.

6. Auctions are used in place of markets when the items traded are unique (*e.g.*, a Ming vase or a right to drill for oil). Which of the following examples are typically sold using Vickery auction methods?
   a. For-sale-by-owner houses
   b. Household furnishings
   c. Oil drilling rights
   d. Old Master paintings

7. In English outcry auctions, the bidding
   a. starts low and rises until the highest bidder wins.
   b. is done in secret "sealed bids" which are opened at a specified time.
   c. begins with a very high price, and is reduced until the first person takes it.
   d. is accomplished by giving the price of the second highest bid to the highest bidder.

8. Vertical integration of a yarn producer and a sweater maker works best when
   a. the yarn maker charges a price above its marginal cost to the sweater maker.
   b. the yarn maker charges a price at its marginal cost to the sweater maker.
   c. the yarn maker charges a price below its marginal cost to the sweater maker.
   d. the yarn maker does not allow any of its yarn to be used in sweater making.

Answers
1. b
2 d
3 a
4. b
5. c
6. c
7. a
8. b

Worked Problem or Short Essays

1. Your firm wants to rent land from the city on a 40-year lease basis. The rental is arranged as a sealed-bid auction, with the reservation rental $10,000/year. Comparable sites for your firm rent for $30,000 per year, which is the private value your firm places on this site.

   a. There are likely to be three bidders, who are the major developers in your area. What bid would you suggest if the developers cannot collude?

      Answer: Vickery's model shows that the optimal underbid is a function of the number of bidders. With three bidders, the underbid should be $1/3^{rd}$ less than the private value of the site. Your bid should be $20,000/year without collusion, which maximizes the bidders expect profit from participating in the auction.

   b. If the developers collude, what is the likely bid?

      Answer. If the three developers collude, then one developer will likely submit the minimum $10,000/year bid, and the other two refrain from bidding.

2. Auctions are used in place of markets often when the items traded are unique (*e.g.*, a Ming vase or a right to drill for oil).

   a. What is the difference between a "sealed bid" and an open outcry auction? How will it affect the bidding, and what does it do to the problem of "the winner's curse"?

      Answer: A sealed bid does not permit much 'learning' about the value others place on an item. This lack of price discovery can lead to a greater sense of regret than with an open outcry auction. Open outcry forms are more likely to involve psychological influences of a 'bidding frenzy.'

   b. Houses sold by owners are typically sold in an informal "Dutch auction" style whereas most auctions of household furnishings are "English auctions." What is meant by this distinction? Auctions often use "reservation prices" at which price no transaction will occur. Can you explain this phenomenon?

      Answer: Houses are reduced in price over time, when they don't sell at the original asking price. Households furnishing sold at estate sales begin at low prices and move up. The reservation price prevents sales at auctions at ridiculously low prices that anger the sellers.

c. Oil auctions and auctions of valuable postage stamps have often been transacted at the second highest bid. RFPs (requests for proposals for service contracts) have sometimes been transacted at the second lowest bid. Why? Why not at the highest or lowest bid?

> *Answer:* The second-best bid gives an incentive to the bidder to bid the their value but no more than their value, knowing that they will receive at least that or higher for their payment. This reduces the fear of the winner's curse.

Net Sources

1. **Sotheby's Auction**   *www.sothebys.com/*

2. **Christie's International**   *www.christies.com/buy/index.html*

3. **Yahoo! Auctions**   *auctions.yahoo.com/*

4. **eBay**   *www.ebay.com/*

5. **PROJECT:** Using Yahoo! Auctions' site at *auctions.yahoo.com*, examine the price, the number of bidders, and the time remaining for items in the "Antiques, Art, & Collectibles," category. Examine the price action over a few days. Consider, if you were to bid on one of the items, would you want your bid turned in several days in advance, or would you prefer to wait until the last few hours of bidding?

Chapter 16

Pricing Techniques and Analysis

Value-based pricing is advocated over *cost-based* in this chapter. Also firms charge different customers different prices, which is known as *price discrimination*. Price differences tend to be set with respect to their price elasticity. This chapter also looks at pricing within a firm called *transfer pricing*. Pricing techniques that are used by many multi-product firms, such as *full-cost pricing* and *target return pricing* are discussed in this chapter.

A. Proactive Value-Based Pricing

1. The price of the product cannot be the last issue in the design and cost-specifications of a product. If the price doesn't fit what customers are willing to pay, then the product may not be profitable to produce.

2. Customer value is the focus for pricing, not just the costs associated with the product. The pricing of Apple Computers, for example, was above other computers, even as their market share continued to decline.

3. It may be more profitable to refuse some orders and accept others by differentially pricing products. Pricing peak demand above off-peak demand, is a simple form of *differential pricing*. Toll bridges could charge more in the rush hour.

B. Price Discrimination

1. *Price discrimination* — goods, which are not priced in proportion to their marginal costs, even though they are technically similar.

2. Necessary Conditions:

    a. must be able to separate or segment customers to prevent *arbitrage* — *i.e.,* buying cheaply in one segment to sell at higher prices in another market.

    b. differences in price elasticity must exist in different markets.

    c. there must be some monopoly power, otherwise P = MC in all markets would effectively eliminate price discrimination.

3. Price discrimination is hard to accomplish with *goods*, since arbitrage of goods is easy. Hence, it is difficult to segment markets of goods. However, *services* are easier to price discriminate. For example, it is impossible to sell a low price appendectomy operation you received at the Student Health Service to another.

4. The *purpose* of price discrimination is to earn greater profits by selling at the most a customer would be willing to pay for each item. In simple monopoly, the price was the same for all customers. A price discriminating monopolist can charge different prices to different customers.

C. First Degree Price Discrimination

1. Each customer is charged the most he or she would be willing to pay. The result of first-degree price discrimination is more production and more profits.

2. EXAMPLE: Hospitals ask you what health insurance you have as you are wheeled in on a stretcher. Hence, the pricing of surgery could include the "the most the HMO or Blue Cross would be willing to pay."

D. Second Degree Price Discrimination

1. With Second Degree Price Discrimination, units are "grouped" and prices are set for groups of units.

2. An example of second-degree price discrimination is "block rate setting". The price for the first group is greater than the next group. Some 1-900 calls have a different price for the first few minutes than subsequent minutes of long distance calling.

3. Block rates traces out area under the demand curve. Historic examples: telephone rates and foreign film festivals, where the first film costs more than subsequent films.

4. Other examples include all-or-nothing offers that make customers purchase large quantities of a product or none at all. An example of this is candy bars sold at movie theaters — note that only large bars are available!

E. Third Degree Price Discrimination

1. Charge different groups of customers different prices. They charge the highest prices to *most inelastic* demanders.

2. The marginal revenue is a function of the price elasticity, E_D. $MR = P(1 + 1/E_D)$.

If the marginal cost is the same in two markets, $MC = P_1 \cdot (1 + 1/E_{D1}) = P_2 \cdot (1 + 1/E_{D2})$. Consequently, the ratio of their prices is a function of their respective elasticities:

$$P_1/P_2 = (1 + 1/E_{D2})/(1 + 1/E_{D1})$$

3. If $E_{D1} = -10$ and if $E_{D2} = -2$, then $(1 + 1/E_{D2})/(1 + 1/E_{D1}) = .90/.50 = 1.80$. Therefore, $P_1 = 1.80 \cdot P_2$. That is, the more elastic market 1 has a LOWER price. If marginal cost were $10. The price in market 1 would be 11.11, whereas the price in market 2 would be $20.

4. EXAMPLES: Twilight movie prices *vs.* Prime nighttime prices; or firms that charge different prices in two different countries.

5. Graphically, third degree price discrimination requires finding the marginal revenue in each market segment and equating that to marginal cost to find the optimal quantity to sell in that segment. In effect, each segment is a separate monopoly.

F. Pricing of Multiple Products

1. Many firms sell a whole array of products. Choosing to produce one more product is an economic decision based on the expected revenues and expected added costs of the new product.

2. Some **new** products induce customers of the firm's old products to switch to the new style product, which cannibalizes the original product. In this case, the demand for the several products is highly **interdependent**. These erosion effects will be examined.

    a. With two products: $TR = TR_A + TR_B$.

    b. When the products are interdependent, $MR_A = \partial TR_A/\partial Q_A + \partial TR_B/\partial Q_A$ and $MR_B = \partial TR_A/\partial Q_B + \partial TR_B/\partial Q_B$.

    c. The interdependency terms are $\partial TR_B/\partial Q_A$ and $\partial TR_A/\partial Q_B$.

    b. When the signs of these partial derivatives are positive, the products are *complementary*. When the signs are negative, the products are *substitutes*. When they are zero, the products are *independent*.

3. For the moment, assume that the demand for each product in the firm is **independent**: the products are neither substitutes nor complementary.

   a. For firms with excess capacity, one option is to invade new markets.

   b. The order to enter new markets is in order of their profitability.

   c. A firm will continue to enter new markets until the marginal profitability of a new product is zero.

   d. With multiple products, the firm will set the firm marginal cost equal to firm marginal revenue. This *equal marginal revenue* (EMR) acts like the marginal cost for the firm. For each product, the firm produces where the EMR equals the product's marginal revenue.

G. Pricing of Joint Products

   1. *Joint products* are interdependent in the production products, as in producing both beef and hides from slaughtered cattle.

   2. Some joint products occur in *fixed proportions*, as in one hide and 500 pounds of beef from a steer. Since there are separate demands for the two products, the demand for "steers" is the vertical sum of the demand for hides and 500 pounds of beef.

      a. The marginal revenue for steers, therefore, is the sum of the MR for hides and the MR for beef. The profit-maximizing quantity of steers is where this total MR intersects the MC of steers.

      b. The price for each product is the most that would be paid for that profit-maximizing quantity of steers.

      c. Sometimes the MR of one of the products is negative at the profit-maximizing quantity of steers. Suppose hides have negative MR, then the firm should sell only the number of hides up to the point where MR equals zero, and hold some of the hides back as excess product.

   3. Some joint products occur in *variable proportions*, as when the output of a chemical process is various proportions of product X and Y.

      a. If the products X and Y are sold in competitive markets, their prices are fixed. Hence, in product space, the firm will know its *isorevenue lines*, which will be straight lines.

    b.   The firm knows also the output combinations available for a given cost, its *isocost lines*.

    c.   Therefore, the objective for any given isocost line is to find the maximum isorevenue line obtainable. This will maximize profits. These points occur where the ratio of the product prices equal the ratio of their marginal products. The point of tangency between the isocost and isorevenue curve that has the highest profit is the one the firm should select.

H. Transfer Pricing

1. Large firms have an exceedingly complex problem of coordination and communication. Charging "prices" for goods transferred from one division to another in a vertically integrated firm serves several functions:

    a.   <u>A measure of marginal value of the resource</u>: a product that is broken "costs" the division that breaks it the price of the product. No *free* goods.

    b.   <u>A performance measure of the total value of resources used</u>: each division can be a profit center, and evaluated, when appropriate transfer prices exist.

2. Disagreements between divisions on transfer prices are natural. The division "selling" a product wants a HIGH price; the "buying" division wants a low price.

3. The correct transfer price is the one that would occur if there had been a *competitive market price* for the good or service transferred.

4. If *external markets for the good exist*, the transfer price typically should be the price the buying (or selling) division could buy (sell) it externally. This procedure tends to be somewhat objective and tends to reduce disagreements across divisions.

5. If *no external markets exist*, then the marginal cost of production of the good should be the transfer price.

I. Pricing in Practice

1. Profit-maximization as the goal leads to finding outputs where $MR = MC$, and a price that solves: $P(1 + 1/E_D) = MC$. Instead, surveys of managers show that other pricing methods are actually in use.

2. Most firms produce more than one product. One way to streamline pricing is the common practice of manufacturing firms of charging a markup, over ATC at a normal level of capacity, (AC_n), or standard costs. **$P = AC_n + $ Markup.** This is the

simplest version of a markup pricing method, which does not look at all like marginal cost pricing.

J. **Full-Cost Pricing Techniques**

1. In full-cost pricing, the price should cover all costs at a standard or normal output plus a return on the investment made in the business. If a return on owner-supplied resources is considered an implicit cost, then the price covers the *full-cost* of the products.

2. For example, a full-cost price may attempt to achieve a *target return on investment*, π, which is given in the following target pricing rule:

$$P = vc_L + vc_M + vc_{mk} + F/Q + \pi \cdot K/Q$$

where vc_L, vc_M, and vc_{mk} are the variable costs **per unit** of labor, materials, and marketing; F/Q is average fixed cost; and $\pi \cdot K/Q$ is the desired or target profit rate on investment times the amount of the investment, divided by the standard or normal amount of output, Q.

3. Advantages of target rate of return on investment pricing:

a. *Price stability* based on cost standards. Changing prices is not free, and in oligopolies, price changes may evoke unknown responses.

b. Well suited to industries with *price leaders*.

c. It is improves *planning* of expected profits.

K. **Full-Cost Pricing versus Marginal Analysis**

1. Economists suggested that P=MC in competitive markets, and that price is a function of MC and the price elasticity in other markets. There seems little room for fixed costs.

2. The allocation of fixed costs to different products tends to be relatively arbitrary. If a new product is profitable, and fixed costs are not altered by its introduction, there is no fundamental duty that the new product should be "assigned" a share of the fixed cost (or overhead).

3. Furthermore, if costs are constant, average cost and marginal costs are identical. In that case $MC = AVC = P(1 + 1/E_D)$. This can be rearranged to show: $P = AVC \cdot (1 + [-1/(E_D + 1)])$, which shows that the "markup" is $[-1/(E_D + 1)]$. If $E_D = -3$, the markup is 50%.

L. Other Pricing Strategies

1. *Skimming* is pricing of a durable product, like a new electronics product, where the price is set high at first. After all of those customers are satisfied, the strategy is to lower the price over time to attract additional customers.

2. *Prestige Pricing* is pricing to increase the perceived value to potential customers. Purchasers of these prestige items (such as BMWs) show off their conspicuous consumption to everyone, because the prices of these products are known to be high.

True and False Questions

Agree or disagree with the following statements, and correct the part that is erroneous.

1. If a convenience store in the inner city sells a can of peaches for 99 cents, and if the same brand of peaches is sold in the suburbs for 89 cents by that convenience store chain, then we have ample evidence to prove *price discrimination*.

2. With first-degree price discrimination, the monopolist will restrict output even more than would a simple monopolist.

3. Suppose a used-car salesmen asks you the most you would be able to pay for a car and, unthinkingly, you answer truthfully, $4,800. Suppose, amazingly, that $4,800 is exactly the price for the car that you are presently examining. Then, the used-car salesman has effectively used first degree price discrimination on you!

4. A sale on men's slacks at T.J. Maxx, where if you buy the first pair at full price, you can buy the second pair at half price, is an example of second-degree price discrimination.

5. Charging a different price for tickets to movies at twilight than after 6 o'clock is an example of second-degree price discrimination.

6. Barbers charge less to cut the hair of five-year-old kids than they do to those who are twenty-five years old. Assuming that cutting the hair of a kid takes just as much time, we suspect a form of third degree price discrimination. If that were the case, we suspect that the price elasticity of kids is lower in absolute value than for those who are *twenty-something*.

7. If the introduction of Jello Pudding Pops (pre-made pudding in plastic containers) reduces the sales of Jello Instant Pudding and Pie Filling, then the two products would be examples of interdependent products.

8. Beef and hides are *joint products*. When the demand for beef rises, holding the demand for hides constant, the optimal price for hides will rise and the optimal price for beef will rise.

9. With *full-cost pricing* using a target return of π%, the firm is assured to receiving that percentage return on investment of π%.

10. Ford Motor finds that it is selling more drive trains to the replacement market, and that the external price for drive trains has risen. However, the Ford assembly divisions do not want to "pay" higher transfer prices for drive trains. Nevertheless, economic theory says that the transfer price should rise.

Answers
1. Disagree. If the costs to sell the products differ, then there may be a cost justification for the price difference. Absent a cost reason, this would be price discrimination.
2. Disagree. In first degree price discrimination, output will tend to be larger than in a simple monopoly.
3. True. But he will say that you were a great negotiator, and that nobody has ever talked him down to such a low price before.
4. True.
5. Disagree. This does not group units. It is an example of third degree price discrimination, however.
6. Disagree. This pricing policy only makes sense if kids are more price elastic than adults are. Since kids hair can more readily be cut at home, they have more substitutes to a professional hair cut. This would "explain" why kids appear to be more price sensitive to the price of haircuts than adults are.
7. True.
8. Disagree. The optimal price for hides will fall, while the optimal price for beef will rise. If hides were in excess before the shift in beef demand, the optimal hide price will remain unchanged.
9. Disagree. That profit is earned if all the costs remain as expected and if the firm sells the normal amount of output, Q. If the firm sells less than expected, they could well earn less than π%. They could also earn more, if they sell more than expected.
10. True.

Multiple Choice Questions

1. Which of the following would be most able to employ first-degree price discrimination?
   a. a chiropractor in a relatively small community.
   b. a fast-food franchise.
   c. a water company with thousands of customers.
   d. a retail toy store.

2. Which of the following is NOT a necessary condition for effective price discrimination?
   a. the elasticity of demand for the product must not be perfectly elastic.
   b. you must be able to segment customers.
   c. the customers must be totally unaware of the discrimination.
   d. each firm must have some monopoly power, *i.e.*, a downward-sloping demand curve.

3. Blue jeans manufacturers sell slacks to both women and men with only slightly different costs of materials, sewing, and design. Assume that the costs are identical for slacks sold to both genders. If manufacturers believe that men are more price elastic than are women, we would expect to see:
   a. men to have a perfectly inelastic demand.
   b. women to have a perfectly inelastic demand.
   c. men to pay a lower price for blue jeans than women.
   d. women to pay a lower price for blue jeans than men.

4. Miller Lite and Miller High Life beer are heavily advertised brands. Miller brewery also manufactures several other lesser-advertised brands of beer. It may be that advertising differentiates a product, which reduces the number of close substitutes for it. If that were so, then:
   a. the advertising reduces the demand for Miller Lite and Miller High Life.
   b. the advertising lowers the absolute value of the price elasticity of Miller Lite and Miller High Life.
   c. the advertising raises the absolute value of the price elasticity of Miller Lite and Miller High Life.
   d. the advertising prevents price discrimination between the advertised and unadvertised beers.

5. Some electric utilities offer one rate to commercial users, and a different rate to residential users. This is an example of:
   a. third degree price discrimination
   b. declining block pricing
   c. second degree price discrimination
   d. monopoly abuse

6. In price discrimination, the user group with relatively inelastic demand will be charged a _____ rate than the user group with the relatively elastic demand.
   a. higher
   b. lower
   c. the same
   d. not certain

7. One interpretation of the commonly observed phenomenon that the prices of newly introduced electronic products (VCR's, microwaves, compact disc players) tend to get lower over time is:
   a. It is known as predatory price cutting
   b. It is prestige pricing.
   c. It is skimming.
   d. It is third degree price discrimination.

8. If the absolute value of the price elasticity for grocery items were higher than the price elasticity of jewelry, the optimal markup on grocery items would be:
   a. twice as large as jewelry's markup.
   b. somewhat larger than jewelry's markup.
   c. about the same, it is based only on cost.
   d. somewhat smaller than jewelry's markup.

9. Pricing set by $P = [w \cdot L + \pi \cdot K]/Q$, where Q is the "normal" amount produced, and (π) is a desired rate of return, is just one simple example of:
   a. price lining
   b. full-cost pricing
   c. prestige pricing
   d. marginal cost pricing

10. Which of the following is influenced by the selection of a *transfer price* between the production and the marketing divisions.
    a. The measured profit performance of the production division.
    b. The measured profit performance of the marketing division.
    c. The measure of the marginal value of the product produced in the production division, in the case of accidental breakage.
    d. all of the above are influenced by the choice of a transfer price.

11. If a firm produces complementary goods A and B, then the derivative of TR_A for the two-product firm with respect to product B will involve
    a. a positive term, $\partial TR_A / \partial Q_B$.
    b. a negative term, $\partial TR_A / \partial Q_B$.
    c. all cross terms will be zero.
    d. the same as the rates that maximize profits in the absence of complementary goods.

12. For products produced jointly in fixed proportions, output should be increased until the sum of marginal revenues for the products equals
   a. average total cost of the product package.
   b. average variable cost of the product package.
   c. marginal cost of the product package.
   d. None of the above.

13. First degree price discrimination is most likely to be used
   a. at hospitals
   b. at grocery stores
   c. at take-out restaurants.
   d. at hardware stores

14. Second degree price discrimination involves charging different prices based on
   a. geographic area.
   b. characteristics of consumers.
   c. the use to which the product is put by the customer.
   d. the amount of the product purchased by a customer.

15. Necessary conditions for price discrimination include all but one of the following.
   a. The firm must have some control over price.
   b. The firm's markets must be separable.
   c. The firm must have declining long run average costs.
   d. The elasticity of demand must vary among markets.

16. The Kirby vacuum salesman comes to resident's homes to demonstrate the power of the Kirby vacuum. The price is stated to be $1,837. However, the salesman can lower the price based on trade-ins, cash payments, and other considerations. The price charged to any two people is likely to differ. The actual price paid by anyone who buys one is likely to be:
   a. the marginal cost of production.
   b. close to the most that the consumer would be willing to pay.
   c. a price that maximized consumer surplus.
   d. a price that is below the manufacturer's average cost of production.

17. Kohl's Foods occasionally permits shoppers who have purchased at least $10 worth of other grocery items to purchase America's Choice milk, their store brand, at 88¢ per gallon. This is similar to:
   a. First degree price discrimination.
   b. Third degree price discrimination.
   c. Marginal cost pricing.
   d. Two part pricing.

18. Some Internet-based stock trading firms are offering FREE trades for the first 10 to 25 trades in a given year. This approach differs from two-part pricing, where the customer pays to become a member. Here, the firm essentially 'pays' to get a member, as new customers are hesitant about this new service. What must be true for this approach to work in the long run?
   a.   Customers must find the trial experience attractive.
   b.   Customers must become loyal to the firm so that they will continue to trade there after the trial period.
   c.   Customers may be enticed by advertising of other financial products that are shown on the stock-trading firm's homepage.
   d.   All of the above would help explain this phenomenon.

19. The Green Bay Packers sells only season tickets. No individual tickets are sold. This is:
   a.   First degree price discrimination.
   b.   Second degree price discrimination.
   c.   Third degree price discrimination.
   d.   Cost-plus pricing

Answers:

1. a	6. a	11. a	16. b
2. c	7. c	12. c	17. d
3. c	8. d	13. a	18. d
4. b	9. b	14. d	19. b
5. a	10. d	15. d	

Price Discrimination Matching Questions

For each example of pricing, match the (possible) example of price discrimination with the type of price discrimination being practiced.
   a.   First-degree Price Discrimination
   b.   Second-degree Price Discrimination
   c.   Third-degree Price Discrimination
   d.   Not Necessarily Price Discrimination

1.   Charging a lower price for drinks to people wearing skirts on "skirts night" at the bar.

2.   A restaurant in an isolated spot on the coast of Maine which sells only complete meals at a fixed price (a so-called *prix fixe*) with opportunity to select *à la carte* choices.

3.   Country club memberships cost a great deal at the Augusta National Golf Course, but members must still fork over some more cash for greens fees for each round of golf.

4. Medical operations for highly unique maladies, where there are no set fees.

5. The practice of requiring movie theaters (and others) to rent several films from the distributor, rather than renting each movie separately.

6. Selling tickets in the orchestra region of the Metropolitan Opera for $55 and selling tickets in the upper balcony for $28 to listen to Luciano Pavoratti.

7. Bank loans at prime rate for financially secure firms, but charging a higher rate to the riskier commercial clients.

8. Charging more for cosmetics and astringents designed exclusively for men by **Clinique** (a cosmetics firm), than for nearly identical products designed for women.

Answers
1. c (Two groups are charged different prices.)
2. b (The food items are grouped into one price.)
3. b (The so-called *two-part pricing* effectively charges more to those who golf more.)
4. a (The price will reflect the patient's ability to pay.)
5. b (The grouping of movies is second degree, it is called *block booking.*)
6. c (The "cost" of the Opera is no higher in the orchestra region than the balcony, we merely charge more to those who are closer. Ushers must attempt to enforce that balcony ticket holders do not "crash" the high-priced seats.)
7. d (Prices may reflect cost differences in default rates.)
8. c (Since the costs are the same, it must be third degree price discrimination.)

Worked Problems

1. The price elasticity of demand for a textbook sold in the United States is estimated to be -2, whereas the price elasticity of demand for books sold overseas is -3. Assuming that a profit-maximizing price discriminator sells the books, determine the ratio of prices in the U.S. to the prices charged overseas for these books.

   Answer: $P_{us}/P_o = (1 + 1/E_{Do})/(1 + 1/E_{Dus}) = (1 + 1/(-3))/(1 + 1/(-2)) = .6667/.50 = 1.3334$. This means that $P_{us} = 1.3334 \cdot P_{overseas}$, or U.S. prices are 33.33% higher than textbook prices overseas.

2. If the price elasticity in the jewelry business for a reputable retail outlet was: $E_D = -2.333$, what is the optimal percentage markup on average variable cost according to economic theory? You may assume that the average variable cost equals marginal cost for the jewelry sold at this outlet.

Answer: According to economic theory, a monopolist would select a price such that $MC = P(1 + 1/E_D) = P[(E_D + 1)/E_D]$. If $MC = AVC$, then $P = AVC \cdot (E_D/(E_D+1))$. Using $E_D = -2.333$, we find $P = AVC \cdot (-2.333/-1.333) = AVC \cdot 1.7502$. The optimal markup is 75.02%.

This problem can be also solved by realizing that $P = AVC \cdot (1 + m)$, with the markup, $m = -1/(E_D + 1) = -1/(-1.333) = .7502$, which is also a 75.02% markup.

3. Suppose the inverse demand for beer for a typical Milwaukee Brewer fan at *Stormin' 'N Vukes* bar near Miller Park in Milwaukee is:

$$P = 4.25 - Q$$

a. Assume that the marginal cost of beer is a constant 25 cents at Stormin' 'N Vukes. Given the monopoly power attached to the nick-names of the ex-Milwaukee Brewer co-owners, they could charge a **cover charge**. What is the MOST consumer surplus that the owners might extract with a cover charge if they served 25-cent beer? [*Hint*: draw the demand curve and cost curve and calculate the area of a triangle above price.]

Answer: If they charged 25 cents for beer, a typical Brewer fan would decide to buy 4 beers according to the demand curve given. To show that to yourself, substitute .25 for P into the demand curve, and Q must equal 4.

Drawing the demand curve, we see that a Brewer fan who buys 4 beers would have been willing to pay more than $.25 per beer. The area above the price but below the demand curve is the consumer surplus. The base of that triangle is 4, the height of the triangle is also 4, because the intercept is 4.25 but the price is .25. The formula for solving the area of triangle is one-half the height times the base. Consequently, a typical Brewer fan would at MOST be willing to pay an $8 coverage charge to buy $.25 beer at Stormin' 'N Vukes bar. The total profit per customer would be $8.00, since the beer is sold at cost.

b. Suppose the owners of *Stormin' 'N Vukes* bar tried an alternative pricing scheme to extract consumer surplus from their patrons. In this scheme, the price for the first beer is $3.00 [they might stamp your wrist in blue ink with the brewer logo to signify that you have purchased your first beer]. The price charged becomes only $1.25 per beer thereafter. Given the inverse demand for beer given above, what PROFIT per person can this scheme extract? The cost for each beer to the bar is 25 cents.

Answer: This is a form of block pricing, which is a second degree price discrimination. The profit for the first beer would be $3.00 minus $.25 (the cost of the beer) or $2.75. Similarly, the profit for subsequent beers would be $1.00. With the demand curve given as P = 4.25 - Q, we see that a patron would be willing to purchase at most 3 beers, since the third beer would solve the demand curve, as in: $1.25 = $4.25 - 3, so Q = 3. The profit per customer would be ($2.75 + $1.00 + $1.00), or $4.75 per customer.

c. Suppose the bar decides to use a simple monopoly price. How many beers will a typical customer consume? What is the simple monopoly price? And what is the profit per person of monopoly pricing without price discrimination?

Answer: The marginal revenue curve is twice as steep as the demand curve. Hence, MR = 4.25 - 2·Q = .25 = MC. This shows that Q = 2 is the monopoly quantity.

If the bar sells two beers to a typical customer, the most that they would be willing to pay would be on the demand curve. Since, P = 4.25 - Q, the price per beer at Q=2 is P = $2.25.

The profit for a simple monopolist would be $2.00 per beer. Because they sell two beers, the total profit per customer would be $4.00. The two alternative pricing schemes of 25¢ beer with a cover charge, or the block pricing approach provided greater profits than simple monopoly pricing.

4. Pricing and costing decisions in the real world differ in various ways from the theoretical optimal pricing decision rules taught in managerial economics classes. In each of the following sections, **determine the optimal price from economic theory**:

a. A firm estimates its demand curve, for a product whose marginal cost is $5.37, to be:

$$\log Q = .45 - 1.87 \log P + 1.45 \log I$$

Answer: We should use the profit-maximizing formula, MR = MC. In elasticity form that is: MC = P[1 + 1/E_D]. The double log regression shows that the price elasticity it E_D = -1.87, because it is the coefficient on log P. Therefore, P[1+1/(-1.87)] = 5.37; so **P=$11.54**. Clearly this is not a competitive model, because price is well above marginal cost.

b. A production facility produces motor controllers. These controllers are boxed and sold to other firms for $87.50, and are transfer priced at $84.00 to their motor assembly division. Marginal cost is $82.00. What should the transfer price be?

Answer: When an **external** market exists, transfer at that price, P = $87.50.

c. A third degree price discriminating monopolist wishes to price women's blue jeans differently from men's. The demand elasticity for women is believed to be -2.34, whereas the demand elasticity for men is -3.46. Let the fabric and production cost for imported jeans be $8.23 for both types of garments. Find the profit-maximizing prices for both types of jeans.

Answer: Use $MC = P_{men} \cdot [1 + 1/E_{Dmen}] = P_{women} \cdot [1 + 1/E_{Dwomen}]$. If $MC = 8.23$, then by substituting the price elasticities we find that $P_{women} = \$14.37$; and $P_{men} = \$11.58$. The more elastic group ends up with the lower price.

5. Cost-plus pricing and target return pricing are relatively inflexible over the business cycle. Economists suggest that the price is a function of the price elasticity and marginal cost. Explain how "optimal markups" on marginal cost would behave over a business cycle, and how this differs from a fixed markup on average cost over a business cycle.

Answer: As demand becomes more elastic and costs become lower in business declines, an optimal markup and optimal prices would decline in recession. As business improves in the boom times and demand becomes less elastic, and upward cost pressure arises, an optimal markup would increase and prices increase.

6. Transfer pricing within a firm is a politically sensitive issue--some divisions *want* a high price, as when they are selling products to other divisions, whereas other divisions *want* a low price, as when they are *buying* products from other divisions. As a manager, explain how transfer prices OUGHT to be determined.

Answer: If an external market exists, the transfer price should be that price. If no external market exists, the transfer price ought to be the marginal cost of production at an output that a profit-maximizing firm would select if it did not have divisions.

7. A pharmacy in Austin, Texas has discovered through trial and error that a 10% price cut in mascara generally results in a 24% increase in <u>TOTAL REVENUE</u> attributable to mascara. Use the implied price elasticity of demand for cosmetics from this information to determine the **optimal percentage markup** on costs for mascara.

Answer: If TR increases by 24% when price declines 10%, then output must have grown by 34%. This makes the price elasticity, $E_D = -3.4$. The optimal markup is a function of the price elasticity. The markup would be: $-1/(E_D + 1) = -1/(-3.4+1)$, so the optimal markup is 41.66 percent.

8. Some movie theater operators own both theaters that show first-run movies, and other budget theaters that show older movies or movies that are not newly released. The cost of renting the movies are not identical, and the price elasticity of the customers at the first-run and budget theaters are different. The accountant for the theaters reports that the average cost per customer to show first-run movies is $1.83, and the cost per customer to show budget movies is $.99.

You have studied the demand patterns for first-run and budget movies using log-linear regression models over the past 18 months. Though the t-statistics are low, we find price elasticities of -1.8 for first-run movies and a price elasticity of -7.7 for budget flicks. Find the *optimal monopoly prices* for both types of theaters. Round up to the nearest 25 cents. Do the prices you find reflect price discrimination or not?

> *Answer:* For first time movies, we solve: $MC = P[1 + 1/E_D]$. This would be $1.83 $= P[1 + 1/(-1.8)]$ implies that $P = \$4.1175$ which rounds up to the nearest 25 cents at **$4.25** for first run movies.
>
> For budget movies we also solve: $MC = P[1 + 1/E_D]$. In this case, $.99 = P[1 + 1/(-7.7)]$. Solving for P, we find $P = 1.1378$, which round up to the nearest 25 cents at **$1.25** for budget movies.
>
> These prices reflect both cost difference AND price discrimination. The prices differ by much more than their minor cost differences.

9. **Transfer pricing** disagreements within firms can be settled quite simply when well functioning external markets exist for the intermediary products in a vertically integrated firm. But even external markets present difficulties, as when firms sell at a variety of prices in the external market due to different degrees of monopsonistic buying power in different markets.

Suppose that **Consolidated Sugar Company's** problem is the pricing of cane juice from its farming division (F) to sell to its sugar processing division (P). Assume that Consolidated has some market power in the final good, sugar, and that one unit of cane juice is converted into one unit of processed sugar. Consolidated purchases some of its cane juice from independent farmers, but the price it pays varies depending on its monopsonistic power in different markets and countries. Hence, the Farming Division wants to use the highest price Consolidated ever purchased caned juice ($100 per 100 weight), whereas the Processing Division wants to buy at the lowest price it ever paid ($11 per 100 weight). As a manager in the central office of Consolidated, how would you mediate the dispute?

> *Answer:* To mediate the transfer pricing dispute, use the marginal cost of cane juice from the farming division, which approximates the competitive price for the

intermediate good even though there does not exist a perfectly competitive market price for cane juice.

10. **Filene's Basement** has opened in Gurnee Mills Mall, the largest manufacturers' close-out mall in Illinois, just north of Chicago. Filene's Basement is an offshoot of **Filene's**, a Boston department store, which has a famous basement in which it auctions off products by discounting prices over time for clothing, rugs, and other soft goods. Each item in Filene's Basement provides a price label with a series of prices and the actual dates that these prices will become effective. The prices decline over time. The highest price is for the first eleven days. If a customer buys the merchandise after eleven days the price is lowered, usually about 25 percent, until the seventeenth day. A discount of 50 percent applies to merchandise eighteen to twenty-three days old. The fourth price is discounted 75 percent for merchandise purchased between the twenty-fourth day to the twenty-ninth day. The merchandise is turned over to charity on the thirtieth day. Because the store views most of the merchandise sent to the basement as surplus, there is limited selection of sizes or styles.

a. Can you determine what Filene's pricing strategy accomplishes? Please describe the customers that you suspect make up the different customer segments.

Answer: The objective is to unload old merchandise within a month. The method is a form of an auction, sometimes called a Dutch auction, where the price begins high and comes down. The first to buy it (or raise one's hand, in an auction) gets the merchandise. Furthermore, the attraction of Filene's Basement brings customers to the Department Store, who may decide to shop "upstairs" after checking for any bargains in the basement.

The customers who come to the bargain basement are known to be quite price sensitive. Furthermore, the most price sensitive will wait until the twenty-fourth day to buy their products. Others, uncertain if the products will still be available later, will buy sooner. They reveal themselves to be somewhat less price elastic.

b. Some close-out retailers have tried adopting Filene's strategy for surplus merchandise, but no store has adopted it for new merchandise. Can you suggest why?

Answer: The products must be surplus goods. The "value" is zero and must be gotten rid of somehow. This cannot be true for new products.

Net Sources

1. **Robinson-Patman Anti-Discrimination Act**   *www.law.cornell.edu/uscode/15/13.html*

You can read the law forbidding some forms of price discrimination. Paraphrased, it includes the lines: "It shall be unlawful...to discriminate in price between different purchasers of commodities of like grade and quality...where the effect of such discrimination may be substantially to lessen competition or tend to create a monopoly in any line of commerce, or to injure, destroy, or prevent competition...Provided, That nothing herein contained shall prevent differentials which make only due allowance for differences in the cost of manufacture..."15 USC Section 13

2. **Transfer Pricing: Outline**   *www.intltaxlaw.com/shared/transfer/onepage.htm*

An excellent guided reading of the Internal Revenue Code No. 482 on Transfer Pricing. By Tax attorney Bradley A. Smith. Multinational firms have been able to reduce taxes by having controlled off-shore corporations. The tax authorities attempt to prevent tax avoidance. The regulations dictating transfer pricing are extensive.

3. **Trade Expert**   *www.tradeport.org/*

Trade Expert, from TradePort Partners, LLC, in Los Angeles, is a tutorial on topics related to exporting. Go to the section, "Focusing on the Details: Quotes, Terms, and Delivery." Click the section labeled, "Preparing Price Quotations" for advice about *cost-plus pricing* in export products at: *www.tradeport.org/ts/trade_expert/details/quotes/price_meth.html*

4. **PROJECT:** Filene's Department Store is a chain of stores presently owned by Value City Department Stores (ticker VCD). The close-out, discount, or outlet store approach gained popularity in many areas of the country; however, Filene's Basement went through bankruptcy proceedings in 1999 and was acquired by Value City in 2000. Examine the earnings, stock price history, and related announcements about sales and earnings for Filene's Basement or Value City. Get on Yahoo! Finance at: *quote.yahoo.com* and enter the ticker VCD. Given what you read, does this look like an attractive investment or not to you?

Appendix 16A

Revenue Management

Revenue Management relates to products that are highly perishable: the value of a hotel room's rental disappears if no one rents it for the night. Management in most *service* industries involves forecasting the demand for the service, price discriminating among customers to maximize profit, and reducing prices if necessary to fill vacancies. An additional problem is *overbooking*, which reduces the chance of having empty rooms but increases customer dissatisfaction if everyone actually shows up. This appendix examines these service industry issues.

A. The Concept of Revenue Management

1. This appendix develops theory, tools of analysis, and jargon for managerial economics in service industries. *Revenue Management* is the problem of the disappearing inventory, known also as yield management.

2. The language of revenue or "yield" management originally came from the *food service* industries, but it can be used in airlines, hotels, or any other service industry with highly perishable products.

3. The "yield" from a 64 oz. jar of juice in a restaurant could be eight glasses of juice at 8 oz. each, but the yield typically ends up being much lower.

4. Construction of additional capacity is expensive. When demand is low, much of the that capacity will be idle.

5. A retail ski clothing store must balance the problem of too little inventory losing customers (a "spill" or a "stockout" due to shortages) or too much inventory not selling by the end of the season (a "spoil").

B. Revenue Management Decisions

1. *Proactive Pricing Decisions*. Managers attempt to maximize profits by anticipating late arriving demand and rival firm response.

    a. Since service industries are able to price discriminate, the manager must forecast demand by market segments.

    b. If price discrimination is practiced, the price must equate MR in each segment, and "sell" all of the seats or hotel rooms; that is, reduce spoilage to a minimum.

2. *Capacity Reallocation.* Managers must be flexible to change their predicted sales by market segment as information arrives.

    a. If an airline price discriminates between business and non-business travelers, and if too few business travelers have booked tickets compared to the amount expected, then more non-business tickets should be released.

    b. Forecasting of ticket sales by segment becomes critical. The forecast will have a time dimension, which will be the moment the service perishes.

    c. Capacity reallocation can be short run, as in switching proportions of customer segments, or long run, as in *conversion* or hotel rooms into offices or condos or conversion of passenger airlines into freight delivery.

3. *Optimal Overbooking.* Managers who want to reduce spoilage may authorize reservation clerks to sell more seats (or hotel rooms) than are available. This combats spoilage due to "no shows".

    a. The greater the overbooking, the lower are the costs of spoilage.

        • *Spoilage* — is an inventory of rooms or seats on a plane NOT sold. If capacity is large, compared to mean demand, an airline or hotel will have high spoilage.

    b. The greater the overbooking, the greater are the costs of spillage or oversells, including giving free travel to some customers, making customers unhappy by finding that they have no seat or "no room in the inn."

        • *Spillage* — is the excess demand that cannot be met. If the service industry has low capacity, the spillage will be great, as customers leave the hotel or airline unable to get a room or an airplane seat.

    c. Since the two costs go in opposite directions, the sum of these costs has a minimum with the optimal amount of overbooking.

    d. Since business travelers tend to a large extent to be repeat customers, the cost of spillage (oversells) may be very high. The optimal amount of overbooking for this market segment may well be lower than for non-business clients.

True and False Questions

Agree or disagree with the following statements, and correct the part that is erroneous.

1. Yield management applies quite well to the problems facing managers of the **Avis** or the **Hertz** rent-a-car companies.

2. In the airline industry, *spoilage* refers to the unhappiness the travelers feel when they are bumped from a flight because of overbooking.

3. At **Disney M.G.M. Studios**, *spillage* would refer to customers who would be turned away on busy days because the capacity of the Studio grounds is limited.

4. The greater the amount of capacity available at **American Airlines**, the lower is the likely amount of spoilage.

5. For a price discriminating airline, if the demand for business travelers were to expand, a proactive price discriminator would expand the number of seat assignments to business travelers and likely raise business traveler ticket prices.

6. If customers become angrier or even violent when they are bumped from their flights due to overbooking, the likely response will be that the optimal expected load factor will rise.

Answers
1. True.
2. Disagree. Spoilage refers to the lost revenue of any seat not occupied after the plane takes off. This revenue is lost forever.
3. True.
4. Disagree. Other things equal, an increase in capacity raises the expected amount of spoilage; that is, unoccupied seats. In airlines, they refer to the percent of a plane that is filled as the "load factor". Added flights tend to reduce load factors.
5. True.
6. Disagree. Higher spill costs will tend, other things equal, to reduce the expected load factors as airlines decide to reduce their percentage of overbooking.

Multiple Choice Questions

1. Reservations for dinner, at some restaurants, are overbooked. This will:
   a. reduce spoilage.
   b. increase the expected number of tables that are filled (higher load factors).
   c. increase the likelihood of spillage.
   d. all of the above.

2. Yield management issues apply best in _____.
   a. the baby food manufacturing industry.
   b. the aerobic dance instruction industry.
   c. Harley Davidson Motor Company's manufacturing of motor cycles.
   d. the plate glass industry.

3. When a hospital expands to have additional beds, the problem of:
   a. spillage increases.
   b. spillage decreases.
   c. spoilage decreases.
   d. spillage and the problem of spoilage cancel out.

4. As computers and electronic data transfer systems increase a manager's ability to forecast room reservations at hotels, then we would expect:
   a. less price discrimination.
   b. static product offerings.
   c. faster inventory reallocations across segments.
   d. additional spillage.

5. If an airline price discriminates between business and non-business travelers, and if it finds that both business and non-business demand increases, we expect:
   a. price discrimination to disappear.
   b. higher prices for business travelers and higher prices for non-business travelers.
   c. higher prices for business travelers but lower prices for non-business travelers.
   d. lower prices for business travelers but higher prices for non-business travelers.

6. If the demand for tickets grows exponentially, then we could forecast the number of tickets sold using:
   a. a semi-log forecasting model, as in: $Log(Ticket) = \alpha + \beta \cdot t$.
   b. a double log forecasting model, as in: $Log(Tickets) = \alpha + \beta \cdot Log(T)$.
   c. a linear forecasting model, as in: $Tickets = \alpha + \beta \cdot T$.
   d. a naive forecasting model, as in: $Tickets_{t+1} = Tickets_t$.

Answers
1. d
2. b
3. b   (Spillage, or excess demand, decreases. With more beds, spoilage, or wasted beds, should also increase):
4. c
5. b
6. a   (The semi-log form estimates the percentage rate of change, $\beta\%$, in answer a.)

Worked Problem

1. **Ramada** has hired you to join its central headquarters. You are given extensive data on hotel occupancy rates by weekdays and weekends at all Ramada Inns. In scanning the data, you notice that Ramadas in large cities have a greater drop in occupancy rates during weekends, though all Ramadas have lower load factors on the weekend.

Present your recommendations on the following, given this information:

a. What *proactive price discrimination* modifications would you suggest should be test marketed? You are apprised that business conventions are charged a lower price than other business travelers, and that vacation travelers tend to use family coupons to reduce their prices for a night's stay, distributed in national magazines.

> *Answer:* We can suspect that business travelers tend to congregate in large cities. The data suggests that there are bigger load factor swings in large cities due to the greater percentage of business clients, rather than non-business clients. The present pricing system tends to reduce hotel prices for "business conventions" or for coupons used by family travelers. Ramada should try to provide super-low prices, through coupons useful for weekends at select Big City hotels. One marketing idea would be to view the weekend as a "Romantic Weekend Away" for couples.

b. The New Orleans Ramada competes for large conventions that periodically come to that city. You observe that the spillage is great on those convention times. Give your recommendations on a proposed 10% expansion of this Ramada, and what issues an expansion would improve or worsen.

> *Answer:* The problem of spillage on the peak times would be reduced, but at the expense of greater problems with spoilage. Marginal capacity expansions are warranted as long as the expected incremental revenue minus marginal cost exceeds the marginal cost of additional capacity.

> *Arguments against an expansion include:* (1) The off-peak times would have greater expense, simply because of the larger staff, electricity, and other operating and non-operating expenses associated with a bigger hotel; (2) it is already known that this Ramada does not always run at full capacity, so prices might have to be lowered to all market segments to fill the additional rooms; and (3) the convention business is highly competitive, so one way to win more conventions is to reduce prices further to conventioneers. This makes the expansion less profitable than it might at first appear.

> *Arguments for the expansion include:* (1) Revenues during the busy seasons would be larger, (2) the New Orleans Ramada may be able to house bigger convention

groups that formerly went to the Marriott or other hotels, (3) size is itself an attraction that customers appear to like, and (4) the expansion may help preclude other hotels in the area from expanding first.

c. Over the past eighteen months, the average number of rooms occupied has been 565, with a standard deviation of 35. There are, at most, 600 rooms, under the current configuration. The distribution of room occupancy is somewhat negatively skewed, since we cannot observe observations greater than 600 or smaller than zero. But we can ignore the skewness. Using applied statistics, what is the probability of having a day with 600 or more reservations?

Answer: The z-statistic normalizes this distribution to the unit normal. Then, $z = (600 - 565)/35 = 35/35 = 1.0$. Looking at the z-table in the textbook (called the Values of the Standard Normal Distribution Function), we find that 84.13% of the distribution is below 600. Therefore, 15.87% of the time, the number of reservations will exceed 600.

d. The plan is to expand the hotel to 660 rooms. Because of the larger size, the mean number of rooms will rise, it is believed, to 615 rentals per night, but the standard deviation will rise to 40. What is the likelihood of exceeding 660 rooms, after the new expansion project?

Answer: The $z = (660 - 615)/40 = 45/40 = 1.12$. The z-score for 1.12 is .8665, which is the probability of being less than 660. Therefore, the probability of exceeding the larger size hotel in reservations is [1 -.8665] = .1335, or only 13.35%. A larger facility will have greater spoilage and the percentage of the days in which it is "booked up" will be smaller.

Net Sources

1. **Ramada Inn** *www.ramada.com/*

As with most hotel chains and resorts, extensive information about the facilities and locations are available on the internet. In the past, tens of thousands of booklets had to be printed and often became out-of-date. Booking of hotel reservations via the Internet, or by finding appropriate phone numbers via the Internet is becoming the norm rather than the exception. Look at Ramada's homepage. Find at least seven examples of price discrimination.

2. **SABRE** *www.sabre.com/*

Booking of airline tickets fits the issues involved in yield or revenue management. SABRE Group Holdings is a leader in the electronic distribution of travel-related products and services.

3. **Revenue Management** *www.abovetheweather.com/home.asp*

An AltaVista site that provides dozens of examples of firms that use revenue management, lists of revenue management consultants, and articles that are related to this area of economics.

Chapter 17

Government Regulation

Corporations are legal entities that exist because governments allow them to exist. Governments impose many restrictions (regulations) on firms concerning *mergers, patents, licensing, subsidies,* and *business conduct.* The stated intention of a government is to set restrictions that promote social welfare, but restrictions typically benefit particular groups or individuals. This chapter explores the impact of government on competition and on markets that are imperfectly competitive.

A. <u>Market Performance, Market Conduct, and Market Structure</u>

1. The *Coase Theorem* argues that, if the transaction costs for private contracting between parties are very low, the problems of externalities will be resolved without governmental regulation.. Even if governments and the courts can assign property rights or duties however they wish, the solution is unaffected whenever transaction costs are low.

2. Good market *performance* depends on:

   a. *Efficient resource allocation.* Resources go to produce items that consumers most desire and resources are not wasted.

   b. *Technologically progressive.* Producers would adopt new technologies quickly.

   c. *Promote full employment.* Producers do not "waste" labor, since unused labor services are perishable.

   d. *Equitable distribution of income.* Production resources should be organized to encourage an equitable income distribution.

3. Market *conduct* refers to actions taken by firms. These include:

   a. *Pricing behavior.* Is pricing collusive or competitive?

   b. *Product policy.* Do product quality and styling vary or are they consistent?

   c. *Sales promotion and advertising.* Do firms advertise extensively or only a little?

d. *R&D and innovation strategies.* Do firms spend a great deal on R&D?

e. *Legal tactics.* Do firms use patents and licensing to restrict entry?

4. *Market structure*

a. *Seller and buyer concentration in a market.* The fewer the sellers, the closer we get to a monopoly structure. Similarly, the fewer the buyers, the closer we get to *monopsony*, or just one buyer who dictates the price.

b. *Product differentiation.* Markets with many firms, which sell standardized products fits, the model of pure competition. A market structure of highly differentiated products may be monopolistically competitive.

c. *Conditions surrounding entry conditions.* The ease of entry and exit are market structure determinants.

B. Contestable Markets and the Structure-Performance Relationship

1. Economists have used the notion that the structure influences conduct and performance in an industry, though there are feedback effects of performance and conduct to structure. This is the central paradigm in the economic field known as *industrial organization.*

2. The idea of *contestable markets* is applied in markets with scale economies. A *perfectly contestable market* has many "potential entrants" with the same cost functions as the incumbent firms. They enter or not depending on the incumbent's price, which causes the incumbent firms to set prices equal to marginal costs.

C. Threat of Entry

1. **Demand conditions.** It may be possible to limit entry of new products by keeping prices low. Limit entry pricing requires either absolute cost differences or product differentiation AND buyer loyalty.

2. **Control over input supplies.** Forestalling purchase of inputs creates market power, but all the monopoly profits can be extracted at one level without so-called "extending monopoly power".

3. **Legal barriers.** Law is the ultimate source of monopoly power over time.

4. **Scale Economies.** If the minimum optimal size is very large, it is difficult to enter at that large size. But if this is not added cost to the new entrant, perhaps NOT a true barrier to entry.

5. **Large capital requirements** are barriers similar to scale economies; so not necessarily a "barrier". If cost of capital rises with the size of project, new entrants may find high costs to entry.

6. **Technological barriers.** If you have a special skill which others cannot acquire, this is a barrier. But "giving away" these skills would lower the incentives to discover better and cheaper methods of production. This is the argument FOR patents.

D. Market Concentration

1. Concentration ratio sum the market shares of the largest 4, 8, 20, 50 firms. A four-firm concentration ratio (4CR) of 80 says that the top 4-firms comprise 80% of sales.

2. Herfindahl-Hirschman Index (HHI) is: $HHI = \Sigma\ S_i^2$, which is the sum of the squares of the market shares of all firms in the industry. HHI is near zero when there are countless tiny firms. When an industry approaches monopoly, the HHI goes to one.

E. Antitrust: Government Regulation of Market Conduct and Structure

1. In *trusts*, the voting rights to the several firms are conveyed to a legal trust to manage the group of firms as if it were one firm. This tends to create monopoly.

2. *The Sherman Antitrust Act (1890)* outlawed monopolies *per se* and attempted monopolization.

3. *The Clayton Act (1914)* extended the list of conduct that was anti-competitive:
   a. price discrimination.
   b. tying contracts force customers to buy added products with one product.
   c. purchasing shares of competing firms.
   d. corporate directorship interlocks occur when the same people are in directorships of competing firms.

4. The Federal Trade Commission was established in 1914 to prohibit unfair methods of competition.

5. The Robinson-Patman Act (1936) aimed at pricing behavior that tended to lead to monopoly. Section 2(a) makes illegal price discrimination that lessens competition. In Section 2(b) permits a cost defense for meeting competition against the charge of price discrimination. Section 2(d) prohibits discounts for having the buyer provide merchandising services to the seller.

6. The *Celler-Kefauver Antimerger Act* (1950) restricted mergers through asset acquisition when the acquisition "may be substantially to lessen competition."

7. The *Hart-Scott-Rodino Antitrust Improvement Act* (1976) requires notification by large firms to the Justice Department of impending mergers.

F. Regulatory Constraints

   1. Operating controls appear in environmental pollution and product quality and safety issues. The government, for example, mandates that automobile manufacturers must sell cars with seat-belts and must attain certain emissions standards for their fleet.

   2. EXAMPLE: The Palladium Metal-Casting numerical example uses a simple monopoly model. Adding an additional fixed cost (to reduce smoke) lowers profit and ROI (return on investment) without changing the price. If the operating controls raise variable costs, the output and price changes in the directions you would expect: higher prices and lower output.

G. The Deregulation Movement

   1. The airline and trucking industries have been deregulated. They are no longer "infant industries" needing the government's protection, nor do they demonstrate important economies of scale.

   2. Deregulation of long-distance occurred, in part, due to technological changes in transmitting phone messages by microwave. AT&T was further divided into seven regional companies and a long-distance company.

H. Government Support to Business

   1. Governments historically have "helped" some companies, by restricting or eliminating competition.

   2. *Licensing* of professions (or businesses) restricts those without the license for undertaking some tasks. The stated reason for licenses is to protect the populace from quacks or charlatans. It succeeds in this in part, but at the expense of conferring monopoly power on the group with the licenses.

   3. *Patents* of ideas or processes restricts use of the idea or process to those that the patent-holder allows. The stated reason for the patent is to reward discoveries of useful processes or ideas. It, however, grants a monopoly position to the holder of the patent. Without patents, firms would tend to keep their discoveries secret.

   4. *Restrictions on price competition* occur when governments acquiesce to requests to reduce price competition.

a. The *Robinson-Patman Act of 1936* was written in the Great Depression, and attempts to prevent chain stores such as A&P from charging low prices (that would hurt other small firms).

b. Restriction of price competition hurts the consumers but helps the firms.

6. *Import Quotas and Import Tariffs* help domestic firms from competing with foreign producers. This will tend to raise prices that consumers must pay and raise profits for the domestic firms assisted by the quotas.

7. *Government Subsidies* are cash payment or special tax treatments that can directly benefit specific firms. National examples include Amtrak, Federal National Mortgage Association, and the FDIC. Local examples include firms that are forgiven of property tax payments for a specific number of years to locate a factory in a district.

8. *Government Promotion* occurs when the government spends money on research & development or on the benefits of particular life styles or practices. The U.S. government has variously promoted atomic energy, alternative energies, highway construction to promote the auto industry, mortgage lending to promote home ownership, use of condoms to reduce the spread of AIDS, and spraying of DDT to fight mosquitoes.

9. *Tax as a Regulatory Tool.* Particular industries can be encouraged or discouraged if the government provides tax incentives or added excise taxes. Oil depletion allowances have benefited the petroleum industry, whereas excise taxes on liquor have been modestly discouraging to the alcohol business. *Enterprise zones* are low tax regions to encourage businesses to locate in central city locations.

True and False Questions

Agree or disagree with the following statements, and correct the part that is erroneous.

1. The "stated reason" for licensing of a profession often is to prevent quacks and charlatans from injuring the public.

2. Often the actual effect of a regulation, such as licensing, is to raise prices customers must pay and to restrict entry.

3. The *Coase Theorem* says that if transaction costs are very low, only the government can correctly determine who should be allowed to pollute, and who should be protected from pollution.

4. Without patents, there would be no new discoveries.

5. A criticism of the Robinson-Patman Act is that it tends more to discourage price competition by large chains of stores against small stores than it really does to prohibit price discrimination.

6. There really is no way for the government to give cash directly to a firm.

7. When a government imposes operating controls to reduce particulate emission from smokestacks from a monopoly, if the new equipment raises only the firms fixed cost, then price and output will not change.

8. Pure Competition is a *market structure* with many buyers and sellers, easy entry and exit, and a homogeneous product.

9. An industries pricing behavior, product policy, amount of advertising, R&D, profits, and legal tactics determine our judgment about the industry's performance.

10. A large capital requirement makes entry more difficult, but is not technically an "entry barrier" since all of the firms face the same disadvantage.

11. A market is perfectly contestable, if the cost functions of the potential entrants are higher than the cost functions of the incumbent firms in the industry.

Answers
1. True.
2. True.
3. Disagree. If transaction costs are low, regardless of who has "property rights" the optimal solution will tend to occur. Suppose residents have a right to clean air, then polluters could compensate those who are injured to allow pollution to continue. Suppose factory owners have a right to pollute, if the damage done by the pollution is large, those injured would compensate the factory not to pollute.
4. Disagree. Without patents, discoveries would still be valuable up until the time that others began to copy them; or discoveries may be kept a trade secret.
5. True.
6. Disagree. Direct government subsidies have gone to airlines, Amtrak, and other firms.
7. True. Go back to see the example of the foundries that make palladium: fixed costs rise which lowers profit, yet they select the same profit maximizing price.
8. True.
9. Disagree. This list applies to *market conduct* rather than *market performance*. "Good" market performance depends on efficient allocation of resources, technologically progressive, promotes full employment, and leads to equitable income distributions.
10. True.
11. Disagree. The cost functions of the two should be the same; otherwise this introduces entry barriers.

Multiple Choice Questions

1. An organization of sellers designed to coordinate their supply decisions so that their joint profits will be maximized is called a:
   a. monopoly
   b. savings and loan association
   c. regulatory agency
   d. cartel

2. Which of the statements, S_1 and S_2, are correct?

   S_1 Both the Clayton Act and the Robinson-Patman amendment deal with price discrimination.

   S_2 The Sherman Antitrust Act prohibits monopolies and attempted monopolization.

   a. Both S_1 and S_2 are true
   b. S_1 is true but S_2 is false
   c. S_1 is false but S_2 is true
   d. Both S_1 and S_2 are false

3. Which of the statements, S_1 and S_2, are correct?

   S_1 The Celler-Kefauver Antimerger Act of 1950 restricted mergers through asset acquisition when the acquisition substantially lessens competition.

   S_2 The Hart-Scott-Rodino Antitrust Improvement Act of 1976 required large firms to notify the Antitrust Division of the Justice Department about proposed mergers.

   a. Both S_1 and S_2 are true
   b. S_1 is true but S_2 is false
   c. S_1 is false but S_2 is true
   d. Both S_1 and S_2 are false

4. If the voting rights to several firms are conveyed to a legal entity to manage the group as if it were one firm, the organization is:
   a. a joint venture
   b. a joint product
   c. a trust
   d. a conglomerate

5. The ratio of the sales of the four largest firms in an industry divided by the total sales of the entire industry is called:
   a. the four-firm concentration ratio
   b. the four-firm market power ratio
   c. the four-firm sales/output ratio
   d. the four-firm inventory/sales ratio

6. In the case of natural monopolies, if the producing firm were broken into several smaller competing firms, which of the following could be expected to occur?
   a. Each of the smaller firms would have higher per unit production costs.
   b. Each of the smaller firms would be able to take advantage of economies of scale.
   c. A price equal to marginal cost would result in normal profits.
   d. None of the above would result from competition in a natural monopoly.

7. AT&T agreed to divest its local operating companies in 1982 into seven regional Baby Bells and a long-distance company. AT&T, as the long distance company, can set its own prices for long distance calls. This event is an example of:
   a. the Coase Theorem.
   b. re-regulation of the communication industry.
   c. deregulation of the communication industry.
   d. operating controls of governmental regulation.

8. The *capture theory of regulation* predicts that industries have incentives to keep regulators aware of their interests, but consumers have only a diffuse interest in the activities of regulatory bodies. Over time, the regulators end up acting on behalf of the industry. The *consumer protection theory of regulation* holds that consumers are highly visible and political, so that regulators end up siding with the point of view of consumer groups. Which of the following is true about the performance of a regulated industry?
   a. Prices tend to be close to marginal costs, if consumer protection view is correct.
   b. Prices would be well above marginal costs, if the capture theory of regulation were correct.
   c. Marginal revenue would be approximately equal to marginal cost if the capture theory of regulation were correct.
   d. All of the above are correct.

9. Which of the following governmental regulations would tend to raise profits for the U.S. domestic automobile industry?
   a. An increase in the excise tax on gasoline, to encourage drivers to be ecologically concerned.
   b. A ruling by the National Highway Traffic Safety Board that automobile bumpers must withstand an 8 mile per hour crash with a fixed pole without buckling.
   c. A quota on foreign automobile imports below last year's voluntary import quota.
   d. A truthful disclosure act, that says that automobile manufacturers must give a written accounting to all purchasers on car parts that are likely to break down.

10. Food and Drug Administration hired you to decide which drugs will be permitted to be sold. Be honest with yourself, which of the following will probably be your likely actual behavior?
    a. Allow almost any drug to be sold, and reduce the time of testing of drugs for safety to an absolute minimum.
    b. Allow only new drugs that are very different from the existing drugs, because you want doctors and patients to have access to variety.
    c. Create high costs and long lead times for any new drug to be approved, since you want to be absolutely sure than no new drug ever is permitted to be sold that potentially could kill someone.
    d. Create an *orphan drug* advocacy group, that would allow potent drugs, possibly dangerous drugs, to be tested on humans with rare but life-threatening diseases, before there is convincing evidence that they are safe.

11 Consider two industries X and Y, both have eleven firms. The following data presents their market shares of total industrial sales in descending order.

    Industry X: .22, .21, .10, .09, .08, .07, .06, .05, .05, .05, .02

    Industry Y: .25, .18, .11, .10, .07, .07, .06, .06, .05, .03, .02

    According to the data:
    a. Industry X is more concentrated according to the four-firm concentration ratio.
    b. Industry Y is more concentrated according to the four-firm concentration ratio.
    c. Both industry have the same degree of concentration according to the four-firm concentration ratio.

12. The Coase Theorem argues:
    a. that regulation solves the problem of moral hazard by making people obey.
    b. when the cost of contracts is low with full information between parties involved, voluntary bargaining will lead to the proper result in questions of externalities.
    c. only judges can determine the proper result of nuisances or tort claims in externalities.
    d. a coin flip is the best way to determine property rights in all circumstances.

13. Antitrust laws develop over time. Which of the following made an actual monopoly or attempted monopolization illegal?
    a. The Sherman Antitrust Act
    b. The Clayton Act
    c. The Robinson-Patman amendment to the Clayton Act.
    d. The Cellar-Kefauver Antimerger Act.

Answers

1. d
2. a
3. a
4. c
5. a
6. a
7. c
8. d
9. c
10. c [The *agency problem* is that administrators fear being blamed for permitting sale of drugs that are discovered, years later sometimes, to lead to cancer, blindness, or death, but they are seldom blamed for not allowing a drug to be permitted that could have helped someone.]
11. b
12. b
13. a

Problems or Short Essays

1. The idea of *contestable markets* changes the focus of antitrust enforcement from the actual number of firms in an industry to the number of *potential entrants* into an industry. How would the following major international developments affect potential entrants, and the structure-performance relationship?

   a. The **North American Free Trade Agreement** was designed to widen the U.S. free trade zone among the states, to include all of Canada and Mexico. What is this treaty doing to industrial performance?

      Answer: A larger market can support more firms. In addition, the larger North American market offers greater opportunities for potential entry of U.S. firms into Mexico and Canada, and greater opportunities for potential entry of Mexican and Canadian firms into the U.S. By increasing potential entry, we move closer to perfectly contestable markets and we will tend to increase competition in North America, keep prices closer to marginal cost, promote allocative efficiency, promote equity in income distributions, and ultimately tend to promote full employment.

   b. Before the *contestable markets* theory, economists viewed most mergers with suspicion that it would increase market concentration and tend to become more like a monopoly. How would the contestable markets theory alter this suspicion?

Answer: Mergers would still increase measured market concentration, but if the conditions for easy entry were available in a particular horizontal merger, some economists would feel a horizontal merger would not materially alter the conduct or performance of the industry. The Department of Justice has taken a more liberal view of horizontal mergers in the past dozen years.

2. The stated reason for automobile and highway safety improvements is to reduce traffic fatalities and injuries. Unfortunately, the existence of safety requirements, such as seat belts, air bags, or guardrails along the road may affect people's behavior. Explain how it might be possible that safety equipment required by the government could **raise** the number of highway deaths. Is it likely?

   Answer: If the existence of safety equipment tends to make people feel "safer" they may drive faster or more recklessly. The net effect could be more traffic fatalities. However, the more likely result is that people's behavior becomes only slightly altered, so that the safety equipment results in a net reduction in traffic fatalities. This question reminds us that the *intention* of a regulation can be, and sometimes is, thwarted by people altering their behavior after the regulation.

3. Truthful disclosure regulations are designed to eliminate misrepresentation of products or services. Nevertheless, some auto mechanics or doctors have "sold" services that the client did not really need.

   a. Apart from the actions of government regulation, discuss the importance of implicit long-term contracts to reduce fraud and misrepresentation.

      Answer: Often the customer implicitly promises to return to the same doctor, dentist, or auto mechanic, so long as they feel that they were treated properly. This acts like an unwritten contract for repeat business. Doctors, dentists, or auto mechanics who want to maintain implicit long-term contracts with patients or customers are motivated to provide appropriate levels of service. They know that excessive services "sold" will tend to become known by clients over time, and that they will lose the repeat business of these clients.

   b. How might the frequency of fraud change in doctor-patient relationships as families and doctors become more transient?

      Answer: The likelihood of repeat business declines when the customers move frequently. Therefore, we would expect greater fraud (that is, excessive sales of services) in communities that are transient than in less transient communities.

   c. What is the importance of brand names in the likely amount of fraud?

Answer: Brand names require a large amount of advertising by the company. This advertising is intended to have a long life. Misrepresentation of the product, even without governmental regulations on truthful disclosure, will damage the value of this advertising. Therefore, it is expected that highly advertised products will have lower levels of fraud and misrepresentation than unadvertised products, other things equal.

d. What is the importance of posting the year a firm was established for customers to see?

Answer: Firms that have lasted over time have a reputation that they want to keep. Long-lived firms will tend to have lower levels of misrepresentation than firms that are new. We sometimes use the term "fly by night" to describe fraudulent firms, because they have very little personal capital invested in the firm, and are more inclined to mislead or misrepresent their products.

4. The "problem of moral hazard" occurs when people behave differently after taking out an insurance policy. For example, if we heavily insure the driver, the driver may tend to become somewhat more reckless. This moral hazard problem occurs with governmental regulations, as well. Explain the moral hazard problems facing banking and savings and loan executives because of the FDIC, the Federal Deposit Insurance Corporation.

Answer: For many years, banks and savings and loans have had very low capital-asset ratios. This would make the bank unable to pay depositors if a larger than expected number asked for their money at one time. Therefore, bankers would have to take very conservative lending decisions. But because of governmentally sponsored insurance of deposits, investors were willing to deposit funds in low-asset banks. The "protection" of insurance led some bankers and savings and loan executives to lend aggressively, and forego conservative banking practices. When a number of the risky loans failed, some of these banks had to close.

Recently, the government is asking banks with low-asset ratios to pay higher insurance fees. This action will reward banks that are sound, and give incentives to less well financed banks to alter their behavior in the direction of less risky banking practices.

5. When the government determines regulations, politicians want to benefit their constituents. Politicians want firms to help some customers at the expense of other customers. This is known as *cross-subsidization*, in which service is extended to two regions (or products), but one region pays more than what it costs to serve it, and the other region pays less. Can you think of examples of governmental regulations that promote cross-subsidization?

a. The U.S. Post Office charges the same price for a stamp throughout the U.S.

Answer: In general, mail to Hawaii and Alaska is subsidized. Mail sent short distances across town subsidizes longer haul mail.

b. Electrical generating companies are permitted to charge different prices to residential, commercial, and industrial users. They are generally not permitted to charge higher rates to rural residential customers than urban residential customers.

Answer: Price discrimination across the classes occurs. The commercial and industrial customers subsidize residential customers. Rural customers cost more to send service, yet they pay the same rate per kilowatt-hour. Therefore, urban customers subsidize rural customers.

Net Sources

1. **Legal Information Institute**   *www.law.cornell.edu/*

A handy site from the Cornell Law School, which provides access to Supreme Court decisions, the full U.S. Code, and the U.S. Constitution. If you wanted to read about the Glass Ceiling Act (1991), the Sherman Antitrust Act (1890) click on the U.S. Code. Perhaps you want to read about the Napster decision, search for it. Use the common names of these Acts (Glass… or Sherman…) that are arranged alphabetically. If you find yourself engrossed in this site, you may wish to consider going to Law School. If you find reading law vexing, perhaps the law is not for you.

2. **Nobel Prize in Economics**   *nobelprizes.com/nobel/economics/alpha.html*

The Nobel Prize winners in economics are listed. Click on the 1991 winner, Ronald Coase. Find out more about his contributions to the problem of regulation. Other Nobel laureates that worked in the area of governmental regulation included George Stigler, and James Buchanan, Jr. A fun Nobel Prize trivia quiz appears at:

www.almaz.com/nobel/cgi-bin/quiz.cgi

Appendix 17A

Economic Externalities and Market Failure

Private enterprise will fail to achieve an efficient allocation of resources when some of the benefits or some of the costs fall on others. These *externalities* are examined in this appendix, and remedies for them are suggested. There may also be inefficiency in governmentally produced goods as well.

A. <u>The Importance of Externalities</u>

1. Private enterprises as well as government enterprises generate externalities.

2. Externalities exist when third parties receive benefits or bear costs arising from economic transactions in which they are not a direct participant.

3. Alternatively, externalities occur when there are interactions in the utility functions of individuals, but where some activity is outside of one of the individual's control.

4. Public sector externalities occur, for example, when one community discharges incompletely treated sewage into a stream, but the discharge injures other communities downstream.

B. <u>Types of Externalities</u>

1. Production Externalities:

   a. *External Production Economies* — expansion generates benefits to other firms.

   b. *External Production Diseconomies* — expansion generates uncompensated costs on other firms.

2. Consumption Externalities:

   a. *External Consumption Economies* — an increase in use of this product increases the utility of others.

   b. *External Consumption Diseconomies* — an increase in use of this product results in uncompensated costs on others.

3. *Public Sector Externalities*: Government action can produce both economies and diseconomies. Governments as well as private firm have been known to dump garbage into streams and lakes.

C. Coase's Railroad and Coase's Theorem

1. Coal burning railroads tended to make fires along the tracks. The issue is who is responsible for the damage. Should the railroad company protect farmers from firm as a form of duty? Should the farmers have to protect their crops from firm?

2. At first, this question seems obvious. But it really is an example of *property rights*. Who has property rights is a question of assignment of these rights.

3. If we give rights to the railroad, then the farmers will spend money to protect their crops with fencing if that is cheap enough, otherwise they will accept as natural some fire damage. They may even pay the railroad not to go through their area.

4. If we give rights to the farmers, then the railroad will spend money to protect the farmer's crops if that is cheap enough, or they will contract with the farmers to subsidize them for any fire damage.

5. So long as the costs for contracting is low, the exact assignment of the rights does not affect the outcome: whether the fencing is constructed or not. This is known as *Coase's Theorem.*

6. When transaction costs are high, however, then who has property rights matters. For example, the farmers may find it hard to organize together against a wealthy railroad company.

D. Possible Solutions to the Externalities Problem

1. *Solution by Prohibition.* Abolishing the externality will reduce the externality, but it may entail a waste of resources. The optimal elimination of pollution, is where the costs of the last bit of removal of pollution equaled the marginal benefits. Prohibition may lead to excessive reduction of some types of externalities.

2. *Solution by Directive.* Set maximum allowable pollution standards, to reduce, but not necessarily eliminate an externality. It is difficult to set the "correct" standard, and the assignment of "pollution rights" will typically be arbitrary.

3. *Solution by Voluntary Payment.* Pay a polluter to reduce pollution.

a. In the spirit of Coase, a community could pay a firm to reduce pollution, but citizens will tend to understate their desire to reduce the pollution and not contribute.

b. A *Pareto Optimal* decision makes someone better off and makes no one worse off.

3. *Solution by Merger*. If one firm injures another through externalities, merging the two firms will encourage them to determine what is best for the whole enterprise.

4. *Solution by Taxes and Subsidies*. Tax activities that have external diseconomies and subsidize activities that have external economies. One way would be to meter the amount of pollution, and impose an "emission charge" on the polluter.

5. *Solution by Sale of Pollution Rights*. Give owners a limited right to pollute. If firms are not using all of their pollution rights they may "sell" their rights to firms which have been unable to reduce pollution to the limited allotment of pollution rights. Like product markets, those who need them the most will purchase these rights.

6. *Solution by Regulation*. Requiring specific safety equipment such as seat belts installed in cars, as an example.

True and False Questions

Agree or disagree with the following statements, and correct the part that is erroneous.

1. Firms will tend to extend an activity up to the point where their direct private marginal cost equals their direct private marginal benefit.

2. If a third party bears a cost, but is not being compensated for that cost, this form of externality is called an *external economy*.

3. Externalities occur in the private sector of the economy, but because the government is "owned" by everyone, the government does not produce externalities.

4. If your neighbor plants a colorful, flower garden in her front yard, she has created a indirect marginal benefit for you.

5. According to Coase, it may be possible for you to reward your neighbor (with praise or presents) to expand her flower garden to the point where the marginal social and private cost and benefits were equal.

6. The "solutions" to externalities are many. If you received a limited allotment of pollution rights, you would use up all of your rights.

7. Zoning ordinances prohibit bars from being built near schools, churches, or synagogues. This is the only way to keep bars from being built near these areas.

8. The optimal solution to air pollution is to prohibit all air pollution.

Answers
1. True.
2. Disagree. This is an *external diseconomy*. If we used utility functions to describe the problem, it would be an external consumption diseconomy.
3. Disagree. One municipality may create externalities on other neighboring municipalities. The federal government creates externalities as well.
4. True.
5. True.
6. Disagree. While you might do that, you would realize that these pollution rights could be sold. If the value of the money from the sale is greater than the value of the added pollution, then you would prefer to sell some of your pollution rights.
7. Disagree. The schools, churches, and synagogues could use voluntary payment to ask potential bar owners to move. One problem with this; however, is that some potential bar owners may purposefully plan to build near a school merely to extort a payment from the PTO or local School Board.
8. Disagree. The air can clean itself of some, perhaps low, amounts of air pollution. It is not typically optimal to prohibit an activity. The optimal amount of pollution occurs when the marginal cost of reducing pollution further equals the marginal benefit to society of allowing more pollution.

Multiple Choice Questions

1. Which of the following activities likely generates total social marginal benefit greater than direct private marginal benefit?
   a. Complimenting your fellow employees.
   b. Picking up litter that is blowing along the street.
   c. Contributing money to the National Multiple Sclerosis Society to find a cure for MS.
   d. all of the above.

2. Which of the following activities likely generates total social marginal cost greater than direct private marginal cost?
   a. Time spent planning a stock purchase.
   b. Time spent smoking in a crowded bus station.
   c. Time spent building a workbench in your basement.
   d. Time spent raking leaves into your own compost pile.

3. As the world becomes more crowded,
    a. externalities will naturally expand.
    b. social benefits will whither away.
    c. the world becomes more Pareto Optimal.
    d. the need for governmental regulation will disappear.

4. Which of the following activities likely generates social marginal benefits *greater* than direct private marginal benefit?
    a. Complaining about your fellow employees.
    b. Littering, as a low cost manner for disposal of paper.
    c. Contributing money to the National Multiple Sclerosis Society to find a cure for MS.
    d. All of the above.

5. Which of the following activities likely generates social marginal costs greater than direct private marginal cost?
    a. Time spent planning a stock purchase.
    b. Time spent smoking in a crowded bus station.
    c. Time spent building a workbench in your basement.
    d. Time spent raking leaves into your own compost pile.

6. As the world becomes more crowded,
    a. externalities will naturally expand.
    b. social benefits will whither away.
    c. the need for governmental regulation will disappear.
    d. according to the Coase Theorem, external benefits always increase.

7. Autos cause auto emissions. To stop auto emissions entirely would be through a prohibition on using cars. This 'solution to externality' is:
    a. too drastic, as it ignores the benefits to society of having transportation.
    b. suboptimal, as the optimal amount of pollution is where the social marginal cost of pollution equals the social marginal benefit.
    c. ignoring the fact that the environment can naturally clean up some emissions.
    d. all of the above.

Answers
1. d
2. b
3. a
4. c
5. b
6. a
7. d

Matching Externality Solutions With Examples

Select the letter of the solution to externalities that fits the description or example.

    a. *Solution by Prohibition*
    b. *Solution by Directive*
    c. *Solution by Voluntary Payment*
    d. *Solution by Merger*
    e. *Solution by Taxes and Subsidies*
    f. *Solution by Sale of Pollution Rights*
    g. *Solution by Regulation*

1. _____ Minimum fleet miles per gallon standards given to automobile companies.

2. _____ Zoning ordinances that do not permit construction of multi-family apartments in a village.

3. _____ The 1990 Clean Air Act which gives the owner a transferable right to pollute up to specific limits.

4. _____ Requiring crib manufacturers to allow less than 4 inches between each bar on the crib to prevent a baby from sticking his or her head through the bars.

5. _____ Florida allowed the Walt Disney Co. to purchase a huge track of land for its Disney World operation, to avoid some external economies that occurred when it built on a small track of land at Disneyland in Anaheim, California.

6. _____ Patent holders frequently license others to use their process or idea.

7. _____ The continuation of passenger trains was deemed to have greater social benefits than the private benefits, as modern passenger trains can move people with less aggregate pollution. To keep Amtrak alive, the government periodically infuses it with more money.

Answers
1. b
2. a
3. f
4. g
5. d (Merger integrates the private interests of both parties. Owning large tracks of land helped Disney integrate all beneficial externalities associated with higher land values near the park).
6. c
7. e

Worked Problems

1. A homeowner must decide on the optimal amount of insulation to install in the attic. After reading about insulation at the local library, the following direct private marginal benefit curve for R-value insulation was determined:

$$MB_P = 90 - 3 \cdot R$$

where R is the R-value of the insulation that is installed. As higher and higher R-value is installed, the marginal benefit of still more of it diminishes.

After several trips to hardware stores, the added cost of increasing the R-value was found to be:

$$MC_P = 2 \cdot R$$

a. Determine the optimal amount of R-value insulation.

   Answer: The private decision is to add insulation until the private marginal benefit equaled the private marginal cost. This means: $MB_P = 90 - 3 \cdot R = 2 \cdot R = MC_P$. This implies that the attic will have an R-value of **R = 18**.

b. If all homeowners have relatively low amounts of attic insulation, the whole region will have to build larger gas pipelines and electrical power plants. Suppose that there is an indirect social marginal benefit of:

$$MB_I = 2.5 \cdot R$$

   Find the total social marginal benefit function, and the social optimal amount of R-value insulation.

   Answer: The total social marginal benefit function is: $MB_T = MB_P + MB_I$. Therefore, $MB_T = 90 - 3 \cdot R + 2.5 \cdot R = 90 - .5 \cdot R$. The socially optimal amount of R-value occurs when $MB_T = MC_T$. Assuming that there are not indirect marginal costs of insulation, then $90 - .5 \cdot R = 2 \cdot R$. Hence, the socially optimal amount of R-value in the attic is **R = 36**.

c. Since the socially optimal R-value is twice as large as the privately optimal amount of insulation, what advice would you give to the government to move closer to the socially optimal amount. You may use any of the following seven "solutions to externalities."

> 1. *Solution by Prohibition*
> 2. *Solution by Directive*
> 3. *Solution by Voluntary Payment*
> 4. *Solution by Merger*
> 5. *Solution by Taxes and Subsidies*
> 6. *Solution by Sale of Pollution Rights*
> 7. *Solution by Regulation*

Answer: Each residence must meet minimum standards for safety, otherwise cities or counties can condemn properties as unlivable. In addition, many communities require that houses receive a certificate of compliance before they are able to be sold.

Of the methods listed above, the solution by regulation or the solution by directive seems to fit this problem best. An announcement could be made that all new houses will have to meet an R-value standard. This is the solution by directive. The old housing stock may have to be given a lesser requirement and a longer time period to achieve this (lower) standard. Similar to laws that say motorcyclists must wear helmets, this law might say that all homes within the decade must have R-value insulation in the attic at least equal to R = 36 (or perhaps R= 22).

2. *Universal service* is the goal that all people would have access to local telephone service, because access to a telephone is critical to reach medical or police services. In the U.S., the telephone companies are privately owned, but regulated. How would you go about deciding how to achieve universal telephone service, given your choice of governmental policies, controls, or regulations?

Answer: First, we would need to know the magnitude of the problem. If there are only a few pockets of the populace that are without access to telephones, the government policy could be targeted with direct cash subsidies or vouchers to those who cannot afford telephones.

This program may be connected with general assistance or programs for the mothers with dependent children or the aged. One problem with this approach is that some low income people would decide to drop telephone service, and then request assistance to get telephone service re-started.

If the problem were wide spread, then the issue is getting telephone installation charges low, and getting monthly "basic service" charges down to a minimum. The regulatory commissions would have to seek ways for phone companies to have "life line rates" for minimum service. One way would be to expand the degree of price discrimination, by cross-subsidizing basic service by higher business telephone fees, higher fees for call-waiting, and other telephone special features.

Net Sources

1. Environmental Protection Agency   *www.epa.gov/*

The EPA administers over a dozen laws on the environment. These include:
- National Environmental Policy Act of 1969 (NEPA)
- The Clean Air Act (CAA, 1970)
- The Clean Water Act (CWA, 1977)
- Comprehensive Environmental Response, Compensation, and Liability Act (CERCLA or Superfund, 1980)
- The Emergency Planning & Community Right-To-Know Act (EPCRA, 1986)
- The Endangered Species Act (ESA, 1973)
- The Federal Insecticide, Fungicide and Rodenticide Act (FIFRA,1972)
- The Oil Pollution Act of 1990 (OPA, 1990)
- The Pollution Prevention Act (PPA , 1990)
- The Resource Conservation and Recovery Act (RCRA, 1976)
- The Safe Drinking Water Act (SDWA, 1974)
- The Superfund Amendments and Reauthorization Act (SARA)
- The Toxic Substances Control Act (TSCA, 1976)

PART V - LONG-TERM INVESTMENT DECISIONS AND RISK ANALYSIS

Chapter 18

Long-Term Investment Analysis

Assets that will last for more than one year form the central character of a firm. Earlier chapters dealt with short-run price and output decisions, but long-term investments in assets offer the opportunity to change production technology or even change industries. This chapter discusses *capital budgeting techniques*, including the tools of *internal rates of return* and *net present value*. Other topics covered include the *capital asset pricing model* and other methods to estimate the cost of capital. The chapter concludes with techniques of *cost-benefit analysis* for examining public projects.

A. <u>The Nature of Capital Expenditure Decisions</u>

1. *Capital Expenditures* are cash outlays that are expected to generate flows of future cash benefits.

2. The steps in capital budgeting are:

   a. *Generate alternative investment projects.* These alternatives may be projects to: (1) reduce costs; (2) improve the firm's demand; (3) create future growth; or (4) to meet legal requirements.

   b. *Estimate the cash flows for each project.* Cash flows should be estimated (1) on an *incremental* basis, (2) on an *after-tax* basis using the firm's marginal tax rate, (3) include all *indirect effects*, (4) exclude *sunk costs*, and (5) measured in terms of their *opportunity costs*. The formula for net cash flows (NCF) is:

$$NCF = (\Delta R - \Delta C - \Delta D)\cdot(1 - t) + \Delta D$$

   where ΔR is the difference in revenues; ΔC is the difference in operating; and ΔD is the difference in depreciation due to the project. Since depreciation is not a cash outlay, it is added back in the end.

   c. *Evaluate and choose the best ones.* The decision to accept or reject a project will involve its net present value or its internal rate of return.

d. *Review investment decisions after they have been implemented.* This review will help to provide information on the effectiveness of the selection process.

B. Internal Rate of Return and the Net Present Value Rule

1. *Internal Rate of Return* (IRR) is the discount rate (r) where the net present value of future net cash flows equals the projects net investment (NINV).

$$\sum_{t=1}^{n} \{ NCF_t/(1+r)^t \} = NINV$$

2. If the IRR is greater than the firm's required rate of return, then the project should be accepted. If not, the project should be rejected.

3. *Net Present Value* (NPV) is the present value of all net cash flows, including the initial outlay, discounted at the firm's required rate of return, k, and n is expected life of the project.

$$NPV = \sum_{t=1}^{n} \{ NCF_t/(1+k)^t \} - NINV$$

4. If the NPV is positive, accept the project. If it is zero or negative, reject the project.

5. Both NPV and IRR give the same answer for independent projects; however if two projects are *mutually exclusive*, the two rules can give conflicting rankings.

6. The rules have different *implied reinvestment rates*. IRR assumes that the cash flows are reinvested at the IRR, whereas the NCF rule assumes that cash flows are reinvested at the firm's cost of capital (which is the required rate of return). The reinvestment assumption of the NPV seems more likely to most analysts.

C. Estimating the Firm's Cost of Capital

1. The *Cost of Debt* Capital is $k_i = k_d \cdot (1 - t)$, that is the after tax cost of the debt. The cost of the debt is the average cost of debt of the firm, which can be found by finding the internal rate or return on all of the debt.

2. The *Cost of Equity* Capital is $k_e = D_1/V_0 + g$, where D_1 is the dividend per share next period, V_0 is value of the firm, and g is the constant compounded growth rate expected for dividends.

3. The cost of equity is derived from a dividend valuation model assuming a constant perpetual growth in dividends. This is approximately true for many utility stocks.

4. Alternatively, the cost of equity can be derived from the *capital asset pricing model* (CAPM).

5. The *security market line* (SML) depicts the risk-return relationship for all securities. Investors can earn a risk free rate, r_f, and a premium for holding risk.

6. Risk that is unique to the security is *unsystematic*. The variability of returns that affects all securities is *systematic risk* or nondiversifiable risk.

7. The CAPM holds that investors can hold a diversified portfolio, so that there will be no reward for holding unique risk. Only systematic risk will be rewarded through earning higher returns.

8. One measure of systematic risk is the firm's beta, ß. Beta is the regression coefficient between the returns of an individual security and the returns on the market.

9. According to CAPM, the cost of equity is: $k_e = r_f + ß(k_m - r_f)$.

10. In addition to the cost of equity and the cost of debt, there is a *cost of external capital*. This includes the flotation costs of new shares. If we subtract these external costs from the value of the firm we can modify the cost of equity (k_e') to be: $k_e' = D_1/V_{net} + g$, where V_{net} is the value of the firm net of these costs.

D. Weighted Cost of Capital

1. The costs of financing a new project must be taken in light of the firm's long-range target capital structure. Using E to reflect equity, and D for debt, the weighted cost of capital, k_a, is:

$$k_a = [E/(D+E)] \cdot k_e + [D/(D+E)] \cdot k_i$$

2. This weighted cost of capital is the discount rate that should be used to evaluate projects with risks similar to the firm on the whole. Projects that have no risk should be discounted at the risk-free rate. Very risky projects should have a higher discount rate.

E. Cost Benefit Analysis

1. Cost-benefit analysis is the public sector counterpart to capital budgeting. Cost-benefit analysis is also applicable to personal decisions people must make.

2. Cost-benefit analysis may be applied to an entire program. To determine the *optimal size* of a program, then we would use *marginal cost, marginal benefit analysis*.

3. Steps in Cost-Benefit Analysis are (1) determine the objective function to be maximized, (2) find the constraints on the analysis, (3) count the costs and the benefits of the decision, (4) determine an investment criterion to use, and (5) find an appropriate discount rate.

4. The objectives may include:

   a. *Pareto Optimality* which allows all decisions where someone is made better off, without making anyone worse off.

   b. *Kaldor-Hicks criterion* which allows all decisions where there is the "potential" of Pareto improvement, even though someone actually becomes worse off. If the "gain" is greater than the "loss", the gainers could potentially compensate the losers.

5. Constraints on cost-benefit analysis include:

   a. *Physical constraints.* Limited by available technology.

   b. *Legal constraints.* Laws on property rights.

   c. *Administrative constraints.* Must be able to hire qualified administrators.

   d. *Distributional constraints.* Must not harm or help any group more than a pre-specified level.

   e. *Political constraints.* What is possible is sometimes different from what is best.

   f. *Financial or budget constraints.* Pre-specified budgets which limit programs.

   g. *Social and religious constraints.* Cultural and religious considerations affect types of programs the community will accept.

6. Social projects involve costs and benefits. These include both direct and indirect costs, and direct and indirect benefits. For example, the indirect benefits of a campaign against glaucoma include reduced expenditures for social security disability payments to the blind.

7. *Pecuniary benefits* should not be counted, as they tend to be pure transfers. Pecuniary benefits result from lower prices paid for inputs. The input producers receive less revenue and the project yields the benefit, but that was a transfer.

8. *Intangibles* are recognizable impacts but are hard to measure, such as aesthetic aspects, but should be included in the project.

9. The appropriate rate of discount generally should be the return that resources would earn in the private sector. Advocates for a project, however, will want a low rate (to

make projects look better). Similarly, enemies of public projects will ask for high social rates of discount (to make public projects appear to be negative NPV projects).

F. Cost Effectiveness Analysis

1. In *cost-effectiveness analysis* we ask what are the costs associated with various alternative means for reaching a given objective. We know we must fight crime, but what is the cheapest way to do it?

2. *Constant-cost studies* specify the output for a given cost from alternative programs.

3. *Least-cost studies* alternative programs to achieve a given goal are examined in terms of cost.

4. *Objective-level studies* estimate the cost of achieving several performance levels of the same objective. The higher the performance objective, the higher is the cost.

True and False Questions

Agree or disagree with the following statements, and correct the part that is erroneous.

1. **S.C. Johnson** is considering expanding their production of **Raid** bug spray in Eastern Europe. The project includes expanding their facilities in the Ukraine. The capital budgeting manager for the project, Svetlana Stankov, who lives in Kiev, decides to include the $45,000 of the money she already spent to analyze interest in expanding this popular anti-cockroach spray. Do you agree with her?

2. Svetlana Stankov determines that the Raid facility should be built in Kiev or in Budapest, but not in both. This is a *mutually exclusive* project decision.

3. If Svetlana finds that the Kiev facility has a higher NPV than the Budapest facility, then it cannot be that the IRR in Budapest is greater than the IRR in Kiev.

4. It is determined that S.C. Johnson's weighted cost of capital is 10.34%. Svetlana has found that the IRR of the Kiev facility is 14.55%. She can be confident that its NPV will be positive.

5. Because of concerns about the convertibility of currency in Eastern Europe, the Kiev project is not expected to generate cash flows for three years. Svetlana uses a fifteen-year time horizon for the new facility. Using internal rates of return estimates, she is implicitly assuming that the cash flows after three years are reinvested at S.C. Johnson's cost of capital.

6. If the internal rate of return on debt for S.C. Johnson does not change, but the government raises the marginal corporate tax, then the cost of debt, k_i, will fall.

7. The higher the constant dividend growth rate for a firm, other things equal, the lower is its cost of equity capital.

8. According to the Capital Asset Pricing Model, the cost of equity financing is a function of the firm's beta.

9. If a public project has marginal costs of $44,000, and marginal benefits of $33,000, then the size of the project should be increased.

10. If I give up my chance to go to graduate school in business this year so that my younger sister can attend college, then this is an example of *Pareto Optimality*.

11. Suppose you were wildly optimistic about the stock market for next year. You would then prefer stocks with low betas (ß) to stocks with high betas.

12. A prime example of a Pareto Optimal exchange from the rich to the poor is Robin Hood.

Answers
1. Disagree. The $45,000 is *sunk costs*, and should not inhibit the decision to expand the Raid production facility near Kiev.
2. True.
3. Disagree. For mutually exclusive projects, the IRR and NPV can disagree.
4. True.
5. Disagree. The IRR assumes reinvestment of the cash into projects that earn the IRR.
6. True. The after tax cost of capital declines.
7. Disagree. As *g*, the growth of dividends rises, then k_e also rises.
8. True.
9. Disagree. The scale of the project should shrink because the marginal costs are greater than the marginal benefits.
10. Disagree. This example follows the *Kaldor-Hicks criterion* if the benefits for the younger sister are greater than the costs to the older sibling who delays attending graduate school. In that case, the younger sister could "potentially" compensate the lost wages due to the delay in graduate studies in business. This is not Pareto Optimality.
11. Disagree. If the stock market rises, high beta stocks will benefit proportionally more than low beta stocks.
12. Disagree. The rich are made worse off, so it cannot be a Pareto exchange that helps some without hurting others.

Multiple Choice Questions

1. If the present value of future net cash flows (at a 12% discount rate) is equal to the net investment, then:
   a. the project has a 12% internal rate of return.
   b. the project has a zero net present value if the discount rate is 12%.
   c. the project should be accepted so long as the required discount rate is less than 12%.
   d. all of the above.

2. If net investment is $100, and if the present value of future net cash flows at a 10% discount rate is $120, then:
   a. the project has a 10% internal rate of return.
   b. the project has a net present value of $20.
   c. the project should not be accepted.
   d. all of the above.

3. A municipal official knows that crime must be fought. When he or she determines the amount of crime reduced for a given budget for public safety using alternative techniques, this is an example of:
   a. *Cost-effectiveness analysis*
   b. *Constant-cost studies*
   c. *Least-cost studies*
   d. *Objective-level studies*

4. If the present value of benefits are greater than the present value of costs:
   a. then we should do the project.
   b. then we should not do the project.
   e. then we should do the project if nobody objects.
   d. then we should wait to see if somebody else does the project.

5. If the present value of benefits are less than the cost of a public project for high rates of discount, but the present value of benefits are greater than the cost of the public project for low discount rates, then we:
   a. should do the project.
   b. should not do the project.
   c. should use a discount rate that resources would earn in the private sector.
   d. should use the average discount rate between the high and low.

6. If the internal rate of return on all debt for a firm is 11%, and if the firm's marginal tax rate is 34%, then the cost of debt capital is:
   a. 11%.
   b. between 9% and 11%.
   c. 7.26%
   d. 3.74%.

7. If **Hershey's** board of directors have raised their dividend annually at a rate averaging 8%, and if the dividend yield anticipated on the stock over the next 12 months is 2.4%, then:
   a. the cost of debt financing is 10.4%.
   b. the cost of equity financing is 10.4%.
   c. we must know the stock's beta.
   d. none of the above.

8. If the acceptance of Project A makes it impossible to accept Project B, then :
    a. they are contingent projects.
    b. they are mutually inclusive projects.
    c. they are complementary projects.
    d. they are mutually exclusive projects.

9. Calculate the *net cash flow* from the following information:
    ⇒ depreciation expense is $4,000 per year
    ⇒ the marginal corporate tax rate is .30
    ⇒ yearly revenues are $10,000
    ⇒ other operating expenses are $5,000 with no fixed costs
    a. NCF = $10,000
    b. NCF = $10,700
    c. NCF = $4,700
    d. NCF = $4,600

10. The cost of debt financing is usually considered cheaper than the cost of equity financing because:
    a. equity holders are paid off first, if the firm goes bankrupt.
    b. debt holders are residual claimants on funds after the equity holders are paid off.
    c. there is a tax advantage for equity financing.
    d. debt financing is less risky, because debt holders are paid off first.

11. If the company's "beta" is ß = 1.23, this shows us that:
    a. The firm moves counter-cyclically to the business cycle.
    b. The firm is unaffected by the business cycle.
    c. The firm follows the business cycle perfectly.
    d. The firm swings in the same direction as the overall stock market, but the swings are even greater.

Answers
1. d
2. b
3. b
4. a
5. c
6. c
7. b
8. d
9. c
10. d
11. d

Matching Concepts

Pick the letter of the most relevant example

1. _____ Pareto Optimal
2. _____ Kaldor-Hicks Criterion

a. Robin Hood
b. one brother giving up college for his brother.
c. rules allowing people to paint their living rooms any color that they want.

Answer:
1. c
2. b

Worked Problems

1. Suppose a project to increase worker awareness of hazards on the job requires an initial $1,000 expense. In one year, the project is likely to provide one fewer accidents for a gain of $2,000. By the second year, however, additional costs are incurred of $510. The project's *net cash flow* can be summarized as:

    -1,000; +2,000; -510

    a. Suppose the cost of capital is .50. Calculate whether or not to accept the project according to the *net present value*.

      Answer: The net present value is the present value of the future net cash flows minus the net investment: $NPV = 2000/(1.5) + (-510)/(1.5)^2 - 1000$. This reduces to NPV= 1333.33 -226.66 -1000 = **106.67**. Because the NPV is positive, we should proceed with the worker awareness program.

    b. Calculate the *internal rate of return* (IRR) and compare that return to 50%. Should you accept this project?

      Answer: The internal rate of return is the rate, r, that equates the present value of future expected net cash flows with net investment. This problem can be solved at least three ways:

      (1) *Trial and Error:* Because we know that the NPV is positive with a 50% discount rate, we must try larger discount rates. Try $r = .60$. In this case, the present value of expected net cash flows is: $PV = 2000/(1.6) - 510/(1.6)^2 = 1250 - 199.21 = 1050.78$, which is larger than the net investment of $1,000. Hence, we must try a still larger discount rate. Suppose we try $r = .70$. Again, the present value is: $2000/(1.7) - 510/(1.7)^2 = 1176.47 - 176.47 = 1000$. This is exactly equal to the net investment. Hence, $r = .70$ is the internal rate of return. This approach works best by using successive approximation.

(2) *Analytical*: For problems with only two or three cash flows, it is often possible to solve for r explicitly. The problem is to find a root of a polynomial, which is quadratic in this example. $0 = -1000 + 2000/(1+r) - 510/(1+r)^2$. If we multiply $(1+r)^2$ to both sides we get: $0 = -1000 \cdot (1+r)^2 + 2000 \cdot (1+r) - 510$. This factors out to: $0 = -1000 - 2000 \cdot r - 1000 \cdot r^2 + 2000 + 2000 \cdot r - 510$. This reduces to: $0 = -1000 \cdot r^2 + 490$. Hence, $r^2 = -490/(-1000) = .49$. Taking the square root of both sides reveals, **$r = .70$**.

(3) *Calculator:* Enter the cash flows (CF_i) and compute the IRR. This is clearly the fastest method.

2. Given the following seven pieces of information, calculate the *weighted cost of capital* for this firm. Not all of the information is required in the calculation. Find, k_a.

   1. debt-equity ratio is 30:70; that is, percentage of debt is = .30
   2. marginal tax rate is .50
   3. interest rate on borrowing is .12
   4. number of shares is 200,000
   5. inflation rate is .06
   6. the dividend yield is .05
   7. the constant rate of growth of dividends is .15

   Answer: The cost of debt capital, $k_i = .12 \cdot (1 - .50) = .06$.

   The cost of equity capital must use the dividend discount method because there is no information concerning the capital asset pricing model. The cost of equity capital, $k_e = D_1/V_0 + g$ which is the dividend yield plus the growth rate of dividends. This is $.05 + .15 = .20$.

   The weighted cost of capital, $k_a = [E/(D+E)] \cdot k_e + [D/(D+E)] \cdot k_i = .70 \cdot (.20) + .30 \cdot (.06) = .14 + .018 = \mathbf{.158}$.

3. Suppose shareholders demand a return of 20 percent. If the present share price is $40.00, and if a dividend of $2.00 is expected one year hence, what does the market feel the price of the stock will be a year from now?
   Answer: To achieve a 20% return, the shareholder would have to receive $8 payoff from a $40 investment, because $.20 \cdot \$40 = \$8$. But we know that $2 is received as a dividend. Therefore the shareholder expects that the shares will sell for $46 in one year, with a $2 dividend.

4. Given the following eight pieces of information, calculate the *weighted cost of capital* for this firm. Not all of the information is required in the calculation. Find, k_a.

   1. the risk free interest rate is .04
   2. the market's rate of return is .12

    3. total debt is 750 million
    4. total equity is 250 million
    5. marginal tax rate is .34
    6. interest rate on borrowing is .11
    7. the firm's beta is, $ß = 1.1$
    8. the dividend growth rate is .02

Answer: The cost of debt financing is: $k_i = .11 \cdot (1 - .34) = .0726$.

The cost of equity financing is: $k_e = r_f + ß(k_m - r_f) = .04 + 1.1(.12 - .04) = .04 + 1.1(.08) = .04 + .088 = .128$.

The weighted cost of capital is: $k_a = [E/(D+E)] \cdot k_e + [D/(D+E)] \cdot k_i = [250/1000] \cdot .128 + [750/1000] \cdot .0726 = .032 + .05445 = .08645$, or **8.645%**.

5. **V.F. Corporation** is exploring new uses for denim material. It is believed that denim may work well in furniture recovering. Given **Lee Jeans** brand appeal, V.F. has developed the following spreadsheet of numbers for selling a **Lee Everlast Furniture Fabric** through major material dealers. V.F. expects that this business has comparable risk to is other soft goods businesses in jeans and lingerie, and that V.F. believes its cost of capital is 10.5%. Should V.F. launch its new line of **Lee Everlast Furniture Fabric**? The initial outlay of money is $98,000. V.F.'s marginal tax rate is .40 (which includes state taxes). For this venture, V.F. expects no salvage value for the project after 5 years, as this project is expected to be merely a "fad".

6.

Categories:	Time 1	Time 2	Time 3	Time 4	Time 5
New Revenues	107,000	135,000	199,000	210,000	101,000
New Expenses	68,000	39,000	36,000	45,000	55,000
Depreciation	24,500	24,500	24,500	24,500	0

Answer: First we calculate the net cash flows in each period. These rely on the formula that NCF = (new revenues - new expenses - depreciation)$\cdot(1 - t) +$ depreciation. These are $NCF_1 = 33,200$; $NCF_2 = 67,400$; $NCF_3 = 107,600$; $NCF_4 = 108,800$; and $NCF_5 = 27,600$.

The NPV $= 33,200/(1.105) + 67,400/(1.105)^2 + 107,600/(1.105)^3 + 108,800/(1.105)^4 + 27,600/(1.105)^5 - 98,000 = $**$156,723.**

Certainly, the NPV is quite positive. Even if costs were higher or sales lower, it appears that this Lee Everlast Furniture Fabric should be started. Its internal rate of return is 56.4%, which is quite a bit higher than the V.F.'s cost of capital.

Net Sources

1. **Kiplinger's Financial Calculator**   *www.kiplinger.com/tools/index.html*

   Extensive financial calculations in the form of questions. By filing in information requested, the calculation is made for you. Examples questions: What is my return if I sell my stock? How long it will take to be a millionaire? What's my yield to maturity on the bond?

2. **CNN Financial Network Page**   *cnnfn.cnn.com*

   A useful guide to what is happening in financial markets. Pop in for a quick review of the day's business and market news.

3. **PROJECT: Memphis Area Teacher Credit Union calculators**   *www.matcu.com*

   Automobile buy or lease questions are complicated by the unknown amount of driving you expect to do, what happens to auto prices over time, and your likelihood of wanting to keep the same car after the term of the lease. These questions require self analysis. But some questions are readily calculated as annuities or a capital leases. For the question: How much car can I afford go to: *www.matcu.com/calculators/personal.htm* For the question: What would be my lease payment on a $22,000 car for a 24-month lease, when the residual value of the care is $14,000 at 8%, go to:

   www.matcu.com/calculators/lease.htm

   For a review of the advantages of buying versus leasing, see:

   www.autoflex.com/lease/facts.html

Web Chapter A

Optimization Techniques

Depending on the problem, the highest value or lowest value is the optimum. In golf, lowest is best, whereas in bowling the highest number of pins is best. The mathematical tools to find the best value, are *optimization techniques*. Finding the least cost input combination to produce a given output, the most profitable output, or the maximum net present value for a given amount of investment funds are all optimization problems. This chapter discusses calculus and Lagrangian multipliers, which provide the tools for discovering rules for optimal decision making. The chapter shows how an *objective function*, such as profit, can be optimized leading to *decision rules* which managers can use.

A. Optimum Can Be Highest or Lowest

    1. Plane flights can be described as a complex mathematical equation. Finding the maximum flying range for the Stealth Bomber is an *optimization problem*. Calculus teaches that when the first derivative is zero, the solution is an optimum.

    2. The original study showed that a controversial flying wing design optimized the bomber's range, but the original researchers failed to find that their solution in fact *minimized the range*. It is critical that managers make decision that maximize, not minimize, profit potential!

B.   Types of Optimization Techniques

    1. Most economic problems have some budget or resource constraints. Maximizing utility with unlimited funds means that you could have everything, but economic problems require tradeoffs forced on us by the limits of our money, time, and energy.

    2. A standard format for optimization involves an *objective function* and one or more constraints, b. Both maximization and minimization problems are given below.

Maximize $y = f(x_1, x_2, ..., x_n)$ *Minimize $y = f(x_1, x_2, ..., x_n)$*

Subject to $g(x_1, x_2, ..., x_n) \leq b$ *Subject to $g(x_1, x_2, ..., x_n) \geq b$*

3. This standard format suggests that there is only one objective, *y*. However, sometimes problems involve several different objectives, in which case there are multiple decision variables (such as the student's objective of finding the *biggest* apartment for less than $350 per month, that is also *closest* to the college campus). Another important issue is that most decisions are made in the presence of uncertainty, which is missing in this standard format.

4. Large companies, such as **Union Pacific Railroad, American Airlines**, or **AT&T** work constantly to improve their sophisticated constrained optimization problem. Union Pacific needs to schedule train cars on time to pick up freight but with the least wasted travel (empty backhauls). American Airlines needs to minimize the cost of flying their published schedule, subject to FAA and union regulations. AT&T needs to route billions of calls with the least cost.

5. *Unconstrained Optimization* is a relatively simple calculus problem that can be solved using differentiation, such as finding the quantity that maximizes profit in the function $\pi(Q) = 16 \cdot Q - Q^2$. [The answer is $Q = 8$.]

6. *Constrained Optimization* involves one or more constraints. When there are inequalities (as when you must spend less than or equal to your total income), mathematical programming can be used. Linear programming applications are encountered in Chapter 10. Most often, managers know that some constraints are binding, which means that they are equality constraints. *Lagrangian multipliers* are used to solve these problems. Lagrangians are discussed in Appendix 3A, following this chapter.

C.   Differential Calculus

1. The simplest case is when the objective, *Y*, is a function of one variable, *X*. $Y=f(X)$.

2. The first derivative of *Y* is the slope of *Y* for very small changes in *X*. We write the first derivative as *dY/dX*.

$$dY/dX = \lim_{\Delta X \to 0} \Delta Y/\Delta X$$

3. *Marginal profit* $(\Delta\pi/\Delta Q)$ is a discrete version of the idea of a derivative, $d\pi/dQ$, indicating very small changes in Q.

D. Rules of Differentiation

1. A CONSTANT. The slope of a constant, $Y = a$, is zero. Hence, *dY/dX = 0.*

EXAMPLE: if $Y = 3$ then $dY/dX = 0$.

2. A LINE. The slope of a line, $Y = aX$, is a. Hence, $dY/dX = a$.

EXAMPLE: if $Y = 3X$ then $dY/dX = 3$.

3. POWER FUNCTIONS. The slope of $Y = aX^b$ changes in X. Hence, $dY/dX = abX^{b-1}$.

EXAMPLE: if $Y = 3X^2$ then $dY/dX = 6X$.

4. SUM RULE. The derivative of $Y = f_1(X) + f_2(X)$ is: $dY/dX = df_1/dX + df_2/dX$.

EXAMPLE: if $Y = 5X + 3X^2$ then $dY/dX = 5 + 6X$.

5. PRODUCT RULE. The derivative of the product of two functions, $Y = f(X) \cdot g(X)$ is: $dY/dX = (df/dX) \cdot g(X) + (dg/dX) \cdot f(X)$.

EXAMPLE: if $Y = (5X) \cdot (3X^2)$ then $dY/dX = 5((3X^2) + (6X) \cdot (5X) = 45X^2$.

6. QUOTIENT RULE. The derivative of the ratio of two functions, $Y = f(X)/g(X)$ is: $dY/dX = [(df/dX) \cdot g(X) - (dg/dX) \cdot f(X)]/[g(X)]^2$.

EXAMPLE: if $Y = (3X^2)/(5X)$ then $dY/dX = [(6X) \cdot (5X) - (5) \cdot (3X^2)]/(5X)^2 = 3/5$.

7. CHAIN RULE. The derivative of a function of functions, $Y = f(Z(X))$ is: $dY/dX = (dY/dZ) \cdot (dZ/dX)$.

EXAMPLE: if $Y = (3 \cdot X + 5)^2$ then $dY/dX = 2(3 \cdot X + 5) \cdot (3) = 18 \cdot X + 30$. Note that we can view $Z = (3X + 5)$, and $Y = Z^2$, so first find dY/dZ, and multiple it to dZ/dX.

E. Applications of Calculus in Managerial Economics

1. MAXIMIZATION PROBLEM: Profit maximization supposes that there is some output level that is the most profitable. A profit function might look like an arch, rising to a

peak and then declining at even larger outputs. A firm might sell huge amounts at very low prices, but discover that profits are low or negative.

2. At the maximum, the slope of the profit function is zero. The *first order condition* for a maximum is that the derivative at that point is zero. If $\pi = 50 \cdot Q - Q^2$, then $d\pi/dQ = 50 - 2 \cdot Q$, using the rules of differentiation. Hence, $Q = 25$ will maximize profits.

3. MINIMIZATION PROBLEM: Cost minimization supposes that there is a least cost point to produce. An average cost curve might have a U-shape. At the least cost point, the slope of the cost function is zero. The *first order condition* for a minimum is that the derivative at that point is zero. If $C = 5 \cdot Q^2 - 60 \cdot Q$, then $dC/dQ = 10 \cdot Q - 60$. Hence, $Q = 6$ will minimize cost.

4. The first order condition is the same for a maximum and a minimum. It is a necessary condition for an optimum. To find whether the point is a local maximum or a local minimum, we need a second condition.

5. SECOND ORDER CONDITION: To find a second derivative $d^2\pi/dQ^2$, we simply differentiate twice. The rules are:

   a. If the second derivative at an optimum is NEGATIVE, then it is a MAXIMUM.

   b. If the second derivative at an optimum is POSITIVE, then it is a MINIMUM.

   NOTE: $d^2\pi/dQ^2 = -2$, in the *profit example* above, which is negative at $Q=25$. This substantiates that the solution is indeed a maximum. And in the *cost example*, $d^2C/dQ^2 = +10$, which is positive at $Q=6$. This shows that $Q=6$ is a minimum cost solution.

F. Partial Differentiation and Multivariate Optimization

1. We now consider optimization for functions with several variables: $Y = f(X_1, X_2)$.

2. Most business decisions involved several different variables. A production function depends on the size of the plant, material, labor, and other variables.

3. *Partial differentiation* is like a controlled experiment where one variable is increased, holding the other variables constant. The rules for partial differentiation are identical to the rules for differentiation of one variable, as long as all the other variables are treated *as if* they were constants.

4. If $Y=f(X, W)$, the partial derivative of Y with respect to X is written as: $\partial Y/\partial X$.

EXAMPLE: $Y = 3X \cdot W - 2W$. The partial derivatives are: $\partial Y / \partial X = 3W$ and $\partial Y / \partial W = 3X - 2$.

5. To solve maximization or minimization problems with several variables, we find the first order conditions for each variable, set them equal to zero, and find the solution to the system of equations. Suppose you wish to find the optimum of the following equation:

EXAMPLE: $Y = X^2 - X \cdot W + W^2 + 2X + 2W + 24$

$\partial Y / \partial X = 2X - W + 2 = 0$ and $\partial Y / \partial W = -X + 2W + 2 = 0$.

Therefore $2X - W + 2 = X + 2W + 2$, so $X = W$. Substituting $X=W$ into one of the first order conditions, we find $X = -2$, $W = -2$, and $Y = 20$.

6. By trying other values of X and W (for example $X=0$ and $W=0$) we find that all other solutions lead to higher values for Y. The solution we found was a **minimum**. There are precise second order conditions for multivariate problems involving matrix algebra, but it is often possible to inspect the function to find if a solution is a local minimum or maximum. However, the case of the Stealth Bomber optimization problem shows that errors have been known to occur.

G. International Import Restraints

1. Import quotas of Japanese automobiles are inequality constraints. Added constraints will affect decisions.

2. A Japanese manufacturer will shift more production to U.S. assembly facilities and increase the price of cars exported to the U.S. We may also expect that the exported cars will be "top of the line" models, and we expect U.S. manufacturers to raise domestic car prices.

True and False Questions

Agree or disagree with the following statements, and correct the part that is erroneous.

1. The attempt by firms to produce the greatest output from a given total budget is an example of an unconstrained optimization.

2. If the first order condition holds, then we know that the solution is a maximum.

3. If the first derivative of a function of one variable is zero at a point, and the second derivative at that point is positive, then we have found a local minimum.

4. The first derivative of the profit function, $\pi = TR - TC$, with respect to Q is: $d\pi/dQ = MR - MC$.

5. Partial differentiation is used when differentiating equations of only one variable.

6. The first derivative of Y with respect to X, where $Y = 45 + 6 \cdot X^3$, is $dY/dX = 18 \cdot X^2$.

7. The function $Y = 6 \cdot X - X^2$ is at a minimum when $X = 3$.

8. Suppose as a plant foreman you wish to maximize the output of motor control devices built at your plant, but your budget constraint for labor is fixed. If top management cuts your budget for labor, you expect that the maximum number of motor control devices that you will be able to make will decline.

9. Average profit is the first derivative of the total profit function with respect to output, Q.

10. Marginal cost is the first derivative of the total cost function with respect to output, Q.

11. Suppose that $Y = X^3 - X \cdot W + W^4$. The partial derivative of Y, with respect to W is: $\partial Y/\partial W = 3X^2 - X + 4W^3$.

Answers
1. Disagree. It would be a constrained optimization. The firm could spend no more than the allotted budget.
2. Disagree. If the first order condition holds, then we know that the solution is an extreme, either a maximum or a minimum.
3. True.
4. True.
5. Disagree. Partial differentiation is used for multivariate functions.
6. True.
7. Disagree. When $X = 3$, the second derivative is negative. Hence, $X = 3$ is a MAXIMUM for the function.
8. True.
9. Disagree. Marginal profit is the first derivative of the total profit function.
10. True.
11. Disagree. The partial derivative is: $\partial Y/\partial W = - X + 4W^3$.

Multiple Choice Questions

1. Use calculus to find the marginal profit function from the following profit (π) function:

$$\pi = -100 + 30 \cdot Q + 10 \cdot Q^2 - 2 \cdot Q^3$$

Calculate what the marginal profit is when Q equals 2.
 a. less than $20
 b. $40
 c. $44
 d. $46
 e. more than $47

2. Determine the optimum X for the function below, and determine if that solution is a minimum or a maximum.

$$Y = 150 + 720 \cdot X - 3 \cdot X^2$$

 a. X = 120, which is a maximum
 b. X = 120, which is a minimum
 c. X = 240, which is a maximum
 d. X = 240, which is a minimum

3. Which of the following statements are true:
 a. Some polynomial functions (*e.g.*, cubic) can have both a minimum and a maximum.
 b. There may be more than one local maximum.
 c. An upward sloping straight line does not have any point where the first derivative equals zero.
 d. all of the above.

4. A small manufacturing firm of heavy-duty benches for malls and parks finds that total revenue is: TR = 1498·Q and total cost is: TC = 4,500 + 20Q + 5Q^2. What is the most profitable number of benches to build. (*Hint*: remember π = TR - TC).
 a. less than 10.
 b. more than 10 but less than 200.
 c. more than 200 but less than 1000.
 d. more than 1000 benches.

5. Suppose Y = 42X·W + 5·W - 3W·X^2 - 38. The partial derivative of Y with respect to X is:
 a. 42W + 5 - 6W·X − 38   c.   42W
 b. 42W - 6W·X   d.   6W

6. Your wage income (I) is the product of your wage rate per hour (W) times the number of hours you work (H).

$$I = W \cdot H$$

Wage rates tend to be a positive function of schooling, $W = W(S)$, meaning that more schooling tends to increase your wage rate. What is less well known is that hours of work tend also to be a positive function of schooling (many medical doctors, for example, work in excess of 60 hours per week). Hence, $I = W(S) \cdot H(H)$. Using the *product rule*, the derivative of income with respect to schooling is:
   a. $dI/dS = dW/dS + dH/dS$
   b. $dI/dS = W \cdot H$
   c. $dI/dS = (dW/dS) \cdot H + (dH/dS) \cdot W$
   d. $dI/dS = (dW/dS) \cdot (dS/dH)$

7. If the first derivative of Y with respect to X is: $dY/dX = -2 \cdot X^2$, then the second derivative is:
   a. -2
   b. $-2 \cdot X$
   c. $-4 \cdot X$
   d. $-2 \cdot X^2$

8. Suppose that profit comes from two products, A & B. The profit function is:

$$\pi = 50 \cdot A + 40 \cdot B - A^2 - B^2$$

then, the optimal profit occurs:
   a. When $\partial \pi / \partial A = 0$ and $\partial \pi / \partial B = 0$.
   b. When $\partial \pi / \partial A = 50 - 2 \cdot A = 0$ and $\partial \pi / \partial B = 40 - 2 \cdot B = 0$.
   c. When $A = 25$ and $B = 20$.
   d. When all of the above occur.

9. Suppose that profit is a function of sales revenue (R), costs (C), and advertising (A). The advertising budget affects sales and costs. Using functions we say:

$$\text{profit} = R(A) - C(A)$$

To find the marginal impact of advertising on profit.
   a. we set $R(A) = C(A)$.
   b. take the derivative of profit with respect to advertising.
   c. use the chain rule.
   d. use the product rule.

10. Suppose total profit has the function: $\pi = 30 \cdot Q - Q^2$. Then which of the following is true?
    a. Average profit at $Q = 5$ is 25.
    b. Marginal profit at $Q = 5$ is 25.
    c. Average profit is maximized at $Q = 30$.
    d. all of the above.

11. The chain rule is especially helpful for which of the following functions, when you want to find the derivative of Z with respect to X.
    a. $Z = 25 \cdot X + 3 \cdot X^2$
    b. $Z = (25 \cdot X) \cdot (3 \cdot X^2)$
    c. $Z = [25 \cdot X + 3 \cdot X^2]^5$
    d. $Z = 25 \cdot X / 3 \cdot X^2$

12. Often firms which to MINIMIZE things such as costs, defects, and customer complaints. When we can formulate these "bad" outcomes into a function, the way to determine the LOWEST is:
    a. take the derivative and set it equal to zero, and check that the second derivative is positive.
    b. take the derivative and set it equal to zero, and check that the second derivative is negative.
    c. take the average of the function and set it equal to zero.
    d. assume that there are no costs, no defects, and that all customers are satisfied.

13. Which derivative below is CORRECT?
    a. If $Y = 2X^2$ then $dY/dX = 2X$.
    b. If $Y = 5X + 2X^2$ then $dY/dX = 5 + 4X$.
    c. If $Y = (2X^2)(5X)$, then $dY/dX = 10X^3$
    d. If $Y = 3X$, then $dY/dX = X$.

14. Total revenue involves the price, P, and quantity, Q. But price itself is a function of quantity, $P = f(Q)$. Hence, $TR = f(Q) \cdot Q$. Using the rules of differentiation (specifically, the *product rule*), what is marginal revenue?
    a. $MR = f(Q)$
    b. $MR = [df(Q)/dQ]Q + f(Q)$
    c. $MR = Q$
    d. $MR = [df(Q)/dQ]Q$

Answers
1. d $(d\pi/dQ = 30 + 20 \cdot Q - 6 \cdot Q^2 = 30 + 20 \cdot 2 - 6 \cdot 2^2 = 30 + 40 - 24 = 46)$
2. a $(dY/dX = 720 - 6 \cdot X = 0$, so $X = 120$. Note that $d^2Y/dX^2 = -6$ is negative)
3. d

4. b (actually, 147.8 benches)
5. b
6. c (the product rule shows that higher schooling can have multiplicative effects on income by raising both the wage rate and the hours worked. It is suspected that higher wages make leisure time appear more expensive, so many higher wage individuals work long hours)
7. c
8. d
9. b
10. a
11. c (this is a function $[25 \cdot X + 3 \cdot X^2]$ within a function, $[\cdot]^5$)
12. a
13. b (note that the derivative for 13a. is 4X)
14. b (marginal revenue depends on the impact of quantity on price and on quantity)

Problems or Short Essays

1. Use calculus to find the *decision rule* for most profitable production for a competitive firm. Assume that the *objective function* involves profit maximization, $\pi = P \cdot Q - C(Q)$ and that P is price, Q is quantity, and total cost C(Q) is an increasing function in quantity.

2. Trees appear to grow more rapidly in their "formative" years and then grow at progressively slower rates thereafter. Their growth can be modeled as a cubic growth function, and the value of their wood similarly is cubic, where V is the value of a tree in dollars, and y is the number of years of growth.

$$V = -50 + 14 \, y + 40 \, y^2 - .8 \, y^3$$

   a. Find the value of the tree in year 25.

   b. Find the marginal value of allowing the tree to grow an additional year, given you are in year 25 of the tree's growth.

   c. Find the value of tree in year 26.

   d. If the relevant interest rate is 10%, and the tree is in year 25, is it better to harvest the tree or to let it grow one more year?

3. Find the derivatives (dY/dX) of the following equations:
   a. $Y = 1/X$
   b. $Y = 120 - 24X + X^2$
   c. $Y = 5 \cdot (6X + 4)^5$

Answers

1. The first order condition is $d\pi/dQ = P - dC/dQ = 0$. Hence, $P = dC/dQ$ assures that this is an extreme point. We call dC/dQ, *marginal cost*. Therefore, decision rule for the most profitable quantity to produce is where PRICE EQUALS MARGINAL COST. The second order condition involves $d^2\pi/dQ^2$, which equals $-d^2C/dQ^2$. The second derivative of the cost function is positive for upward rising cost functions, so $-d^2C/dQ^2$ is negative.

2. a. $V = -50 + 14 \cdot 25 + 40 \cdot 25^2 - .8 \cdot 25^3 = \$12,800.00$.
    b. $dV/dy = +14 + 80\,y - 2.4\,y^2 = 14 + 80(25) - 2.4(625) = \$514$.
    c. $V = -50 + 14 \cdot 26 + 40 \cdot 26^2 - .8 \cdot 26^3 = \$13,293.20$.
    d. Harvest it now, since the increase in value is only about 4%, whereas the interest rate is 10%. Parts (a) and (c) indicate that the tree's value grows $493.20, whereas the calculus version in part (b) suggests $514. The slight difference between the two is caused by calculus assuming an *instantaneous* change in time, whereas the comparison over a whole year is an incremental change. In either case, $500/$12,800 yields only about 4%.

3. a. $-1/X^2$ (by using the quotient rule)
    b. $-24 + 2X$
    c. $25 \cdot (6X + 4)^4 (6) = 150 \cdot (6X + 4)^4$ (by using the chain rule)

Worked Problems

1. **Account Temps, Inc.**, a firm which supplies qualified temporary accounting and bookkeeping employees to firms, has determined that profits in their Peoria, Illinois operation rises as the number of on-call accountants rises. The more accountants who are willing to work for Account Temps, the more assignments they will be able to fill. However, there are costs to recruiting more qualified on-call candidates. These costs include screening and advertising.

Consequently, the profit function in Peoria is:

$$\pi = -3,500 + 341 \cdot L - .5 \cdot L^2$$

How many accountants should the Peoria office recruit to be their on-call workers? What is the amount of profit at the optimal number of on-call accountants.

Answer: Profit is maximized when the first derivative of profit equals zero. In this problem. That occurs when $d\pi/dL = 341 - L = 0$.

Hence, **L = 341** is the solution which gives the optimal number of accountants. The second derivative at L = 341 is: $d^2\pi/dL^2$ = -1, so the solution L= 341 is a local maximum for Account Temps in Peoria.

Total profit at L = 341 would be: π = -3,500 + 341·341 - .5·341^2 = **$54,640.50**.

2. You are considering starting your own economic consulting operation, which you plan to call **MacroCon, Ltd.** Your firm will "sell" economic newsletters that foretell the macroeconomic future for GNP, interest rates, stock prices, gold prices, and the value of the dollar versus the Yen.

Demand for the MacroCon Newsletter is expected to be: Q = 581 - P, where Q is the number of newsletters sold and P is the price.

The costs of producing newsletters is: TC = 35 + 20·Q + .5·Q^2.

a. Find total profit function, and find the first derivative of total profit with respect to quantity.

Answer: Total Profit (π) is total revenue minus total cost. Total revenue is price times quantity, P·Q. By substituting (581 - Q) for P, we find total revenue equals: (581 - Q)·Q. That is, total revenue is 581·Q - Q^2. Therefore, total profits is:

π = TR - TC = 581·Q - Q^2 - 35 - 20·Q -.5·Q^2 = -35 + 561·Q -1.5·Q^2

dπ/dQ = 561 - 3·Q = 0. Hence, **Q = 187**, is the quantity with maximum profit.

b. What is the optimal price to sell these MacroCon Newsletters?

Answer: The optimal price would be the highest price that one could sell 187 newsletters. Looking at the demand curve, Q = 581 - P, that means if Q=187, the price would be **$394**.

c. If the price were $394 and the number of newsletters sold by MacroCon were 187, would MacroCon be profitable?

Answer: Surprisingly, Yes. Total Profits at MacroCon would be:
π = -35 + 561·Q -1.5·Q^2 = -35 + 561·187 - 1.5·(187)^2 = $52,418.50.

Alternatively, total revenues would be ($394)·187 = $73,678. Total costs would be: TC = 35 + 20·187 + .5·187^2 = $21,259.50. Hence, profits are the difference between revenues and expenses, which is $52,418.50.

Net Sources

Math-related sites spring up and disappear as their web-masters move from job to job. The following sites may disappear over time. You may enjoy them, or follow their embedded links to others.

1. **Animation**: Graphical techniques to understand calculus are available. One that students enjoy uses animation at: *www.math.psu.edu/dna/graphics.html*

2. **Sample Tests:** Math teachers are making useful web sites for reviewing concepts and taking tests. One site includes material that is pre-calculus as well as a derivative test. You can find it at: *www.geocities.com/CapeCanaveral/Launchpad/2426/*

3. **Calculus@Internet Library**: Access to software, books, problems, and anything related to calculus is at: *www.calculus.net*

4. **PROJECT**: Graphing linear, quadratic, and cubic functions is in economics. These are together called polynomial functions. Review polynomials at:
math.usask.ca/readin/grpo.html

Appendix to Web Chapter A

Constrained Optimization and Lagrangian Multipliers

Most economic applications of optimization recognize that our time, money, energy, and resources are limited. Scarcity of resources is the essential constraint on maximizing utility, profit, or output. This appendix discusses methods to optimize in the face of binding or equality constraints. Web Chapter B looks at optimization when the constraints are inequalities through the use of linear programming.

A. Substitution and Constrained Optimization

1. For simple constrained optimization problems, the *resource constraint* can be **substituted** back into the objective function. This method assumes that all of the resources in the constraint must be used, with nothing left for the future.

2. EXAMPLE: Let U represent happiness or utility. U is a function of two goods, H (for housing) and A (for all other goods). Let the utility function for a typical person be:

$$\text{Maximize } U = H \cdot A + 14 \cdot A$$

Utility would be maximized if a person had infinite A, or some A and infinite H. But reality restricts people to a budget: $36,000 = \$1000 \cdot H + \$1 \cdot A$. In this budget, each unit of H costs a thousand dollars and each unit of A costs a dollar.

3. To solve the constrained optimization, first solve for H using the budget constraint: $H = 36 - .001 \cdot A$. Substitute this H into the objective function. The problem is reduced to one variable, A.

$$\textit{Maximize } U = 50 \cdot A - .001 \cdot A^2$$

Differentiating with respect to A and setting equal to zero shows that the optimal amount of all other goods, A, is $25,000, which leaves $11,000 for housing, H.

B. Lagrangian Multiplier Techniques

1. An artificial variable is created for each constraint in the Lagrangian multiplier technique. This artificial variable is traditionally called lambda, λ.

2. LAGRANGIAN OBJECTIVE FUNCTION: The traditional structure of a Lagrangian Multiplier objective function is:

   Max L = *objective function* - λ·*constraint*

   or Min L = *objective function* + λ·*constraint*

3. The constraint or constraints are arranged so that they form expressions equal to zero. For example, the budget constraint in the utility maximization problem above would be re-arranged to be: $1000 \cdot H + A - 36000 = 0$.

4. Multiplying anything to zero arrives at a zero product. For example, lambda times zero is zero. Therefore, subtracting $\lambda \cdot (1000 \cdot H + A - 36000)$ from the objective function cannot alter the equation.

5. Max $L = H \cdot A + 14 \cdot A - \lambda \cdot (1000 \cdot H + A - 36000)$

   $$L_H \equiv \partial L / \partial H = A - 1000 \cdot \lambda = 0$$

   $$L_A \equiv \partial L / \partial A = H + 14 - 1 \cdot \lambda = 0$$

   $$L_\lambda \equiv \partial L / \partial \lambda = 1000 \cdot H + A - 36000 = 0$$

6. Solving the three first order conditions above, we find $H = 11$ (measured in thousand dollar units), $A = 25{,}000$, and $\lambda = 25$.

7. The *economic meaning of lambda* is:

   Lambda equals the marginal (*objective function*) of (*relaxing the constraint*)

8. In the problem here, lambda is the marginal (*utility*) of (*income*). That means, if the person had an extra dollar of income, his or her utility would increase 25 units.

9. If the problem was maximization of a production function, subject to budget constraint, lambda would be the marginal product for an added dollar of resources. If the problem were minimization of cost, subject to a set quantity of output necessary to be constructed, then the lambda would be the marginal cost of production. The value of lambda, therefore, is often as important as the exact solution to the problem.

True and False Questions

Agree or disagree with the following statements, and correct the part that is erroneous.

1. The Lagrangian multiplier technique is the only technique able to solve constrained optimization problems.

2. The Lagrangian multiplier lambda, λ, equals zero at the optimum.

3. Only one constraint can be binding using the Lagrangian multiplier technique.

4. The solution to a Lagrangian multiplier problem can be found by solving a system of first order conditions for each variable and lambda.

Answers
1. Disagree. Substitution, Lagrangian multipliers, and even linear programming are alternative methods used to solve constrained optimization problems.
2. Disagree. The Lagrangian multiplier typically is nonzero at the optimum, since it indicates the value of having more of the constraint. Lambda would be zero only if the constraint were non-binding.
3. Disagree. Several constraints can be used, using several Lagrangian multipliers. For example, during vacations families find that money and time, and sometimes energy or patience, are all binding constraints.
4. True.

Multiple Choice Questions

1. If a shipping firm wished to minimize the delay-time of its customers, but was constrained to a particular budget:
   a. the problem is unconstrained maximization.
   b. the lambda would be the marginal product.
   c. the lambda would be the marginal delay-time reduction of an added dollar spent to improve on-time delivery.
   d. the solution would be zero delay-time for any level of budget.

2. If a firm wished to maximize total units produced, subject to a binding budget constraint on money, and a binding time constraint on one of its producing machines:
   a. there would be two different lambdas.
   b. one lambda would be the marginal product of an added dollar in the budget, and the other lambda would be the marginal product of more time available on the machine.
   c. more time or more money would allow the total number of units produced to increase.
   d. all of the above.

3. The profit contribution of Leading Edge's lap top (L) computer is $221 and the profit contribution of its desk top (D) computer is $389. Because of limited facilities, the firm can only house 140 workers in an hour. Each lap top takes .85 hours to construct, whereas each desk top takes 1.15 hours to construct. Therefore, the Lagrangian Objective Function for an hour of factory time would be:

a. Max $L = 221 \cdot D + 389 \cdot L + \lambda \cdot [.85 \cdot D + 1.15 \cdot L - 140]$
b. Max $L = 221 \cdot L + 389 \cdot D - \lambda \cdot [.85 \cdot L + 1.15 \cdot D - 140]$
c. Min $L = .85 \cdot L + 1.15 \cdot D + \lambda \cdot [221 \cdot L + 389 \cdot D - 140]$
d. Max $L = .85 \cdot D + 1.15 \cdot L - \lambda \cdot [221 \cdot D + 389 \cdot L - 140]$

4. The economic meaning of the value of the lambda on problem 4 is:
a. the marginal product of labor.
b. the marginal profit of another worker-hour.
c. the marginal revenue of selling one more item.
d. the marginal cost of labor.

5. A factory manager is given a fixed labor and materials budget. She is told that her bonus will depend on the amount of orders fulfilled (output). We can best describe this as an optimization problem, where she is:
a. Maximizing the labor and materials budget, subject to a fixed output constraint.
b. Minimizing output, subject to a fixed labor and materials budget.
c. Maximizing output, subject to a fixed labor and materials budget.
d. Minimizing the labor and materials budget, subject to a fixed output constraint.

Answers
1. c
2. d
3. b [we wish to maximize profit subject to the worker constraint per hour]
4. b
5. c

Worked Problems

1. Solve this Lagrangian multiplier problem:

$$\text{Max } L = X \cdot Y - \lambda \cdot [20 \cdot X + 10 \cdot Y - 400]$$

a. Solve for the optimal X and Y

Answer: Differentiate the Lagrangian problem with respect to X, with respect to Y, and with respect to lambda. Set each one equal to zero to find the maximum.

(i) $L_X = Y - \lambda \cdot 20 = 0$

(ii) $L_Y = X - \lambda \cdot 10 = 0$

(iii) $L_\lambda = 20 \cdot X + 10 \cdot Y - 400 = 0$

The first two equations can be used to solve for X and Y. If $Y = \lambda \cdot 20$ from (i) and $X = \lambda \cdot 10$ from (ii), then the ratio of these two equations is:

$Y/X = 2$. Substituting $Y = 2 \cdot X$ into equation (iii) we find:

$20 \cdot X + 10 \cdot (2 \cdot X) - 400 = 0$. Or, $40 \cdot X = 400$, or **X = 10**. If $X = 10$, then for equation (iii) to hold, it must be that **Y = 20**.

b. Solve for lambda.

   Answer: Substitute $X = 10$ and $Y = 20$ into **either** (i) or (ii). In equation (i) for example, $20 - \lambda \cdot 20 = 0$, implies that lambda equals **1**.

c. If the objective, X·Y, were total product and if the constraint was the budget spent on two inputs, X and Y, then what would be the economic meaning of lambda?

   Answer: Lambda would be the **marginal product** of relaxing the budget constraint by one dollar. Remember: Lambdas represent the marginal (what ever the objective function is) of relaxing (whatever the constraint represents).

d. What is the value of objective function at the optimal number of X and Y?

   Answer: The objective is X·Y. At $X = 10$ and $Y = 20$, the maximum is $10 \cdot 20 =$ **200**.

e. If the constraint were relaxed to 401, find the new optimal X and Y, and the value of the objective function?

   Answer: The solution is nearly identical to part (a). The new Lagrangian Problems is: Max $L = X \cdot Y - \lambda[20 \cdot X + 10 \cdot Y - 401]$ Differentiate the Lagrangian problem with respect to X, with respect to Y, and with respect to lambda. Set each one equal to zero to find the maximum.

   (iv) $L_X = Y - \lambda \cdot 20 = 0$

(v) $L_Y = X - \lambda \cdot 10 = 0$

(vi) $L_\lambda = 20 \cdot X + 10 \cdot Y - 401 = 0$

The equations (iv) and (v) can be used to solve for X and Y. If $Y = \lambda \cdot 20$ from (iv) and $X = \lambda \cdot 10$ from (v), then the ratio of these two equations is $Y/X = 2$.

Substitute $Y = 2 \cdot X$ into equation (vi). We find

$20 \cdot X + 10 \cdot (2 \cdot X) - 401 = 0$. Or, $40 \cdot X = 401$, or $X = \mathbf{10.025}$. If $X = 10.025$, then for equation (vi) to hold, it must be that $Y = \mathbf{20.05}$.

In that case $X \cdot Y = 201.00125$. Notice that at the optimum, the objective has increased from 200 (in part c) to approximately 201 in this question. We knew that this would happen, since part b found that lambda equals 1. The marginal increase in the objective function from a unit relaxation of the constraint was about one unit. It is not exact, since Lagrangian multipliers are based on calculus which is exact only for changes that in the limit approach zero.

2. An efficiency expert is working to reduce costs in production. The production function depends on the amount of labor, L, and capital, K, used. The production function has been found to be:

$$Q = 7 \cdot K^{.4} \cdot L^{.6}$$

Labor costs \$14 per hour, and capital costs \$98 per increment of a thousand dollars used in K. The firm has contracts to produce 7000 items.

a. Write the equation for the constraint that you must produce 7000 units, arranged in the form that the expression equals zero.

   Answer: The constraint is: $7 \cdot K^{.4} \cdot L^{.6} = 7000$. By rearranging, we can write the constraint as equal to zero:

   $7 \cdot K^{.4} \cdot L^{.6} - 7000 = 0$.

b. Write the objective function for reducing costs.

   Answer: Reducing cost, **C**, means that we are minimizing the cost function, as in:

   Minimize $C = 14 \cdot L + 98 \cdot K$

c. Write the Lagrangian multiplier equation in the traditional format.

Answer: $\text{Min } L = 14 \cdot L + 98 \cdot K + \lambda \cdot (7 \cdot K^{.4} \cdot L^{.6} - 7000)$

d. Solve for the optimal L and K.

Answer: Differentiate the Lagrangian function with respect to L, K, and lambda:

(i) $L_K = 98 + \lambda \cdot 7(.4) \cdot K^{-.6} \cdot L^{.6} = 0$ these reduce to   } $L = 10.5 \cdot K$

(ii) $L_L = 14 + \lambda \cdot 7(.6) \cdot K^{.4} \cdot L^{-.4} = 0$ }

(iii) $L_\lambda = 7 \cdot K^{.4} \cdot L^{.6} - 7000 = 0$

Substitution for L = 10.5·K into the production constraint (iii) ($7 \cdot K^{.4} \cdot [10.5 \cdot K]^{.6} = 7000$), yields the solution: **K = 243.94.** If L is 10.5 times larger than K, we find that **L = 2561.37.**

e. Solve for lambda.

Answer: Lambda is found by substituting K=243.94 and L=2561.37 into either first order condition (i) or (ii) in part d. **Lambda = -8.538.**

f. Give an economic interpretation of lambda. Remember that the objective is to <u>minimize</u> cost and that the constraint was to produce 7000 units.

Answer: Lambda is the marginal cost of *relaxing* the output constraint. That is, if we had only to produce 6999 units, costs would be lower by about $8.54.

g. What is the cost of the 7000 units?

Answer: Cost = 98(243.94) + 14(2561.37) = **$59,765.30.**

3. Semiannual sales, S, at **PolyCard Holiday Greetings**, is a function of promotional expenditures, E, and time store is open, T. Budget for expenditures and time open is: $30,000 = 4 \cdot E + 10 \cdot T$

Regression analysis suggests that:

$S = 400 \cdot E \cdot T - 3 \cdot T - 4 \cdot E$, where E is dollars spent over 6 months, and T is hours open over 6 months.

a. Set up Lagrangian problem in good form for maximizing sales at PolyCard subject to a budget constraint.

Answer: $\text{Max } L = 400 \cdot E \cdot T - 3 \cdot T - 4 \cdot E - \lambda[4 \cdot E + 10 \cdot T - 30000]$

b. Solve for optimal E and T at PolyCard Holiday Greetings.

Answer: Differentiate the Lagrangian with respect to E, T, and lambda:

(i) $L_E = 400 \cdot T - 4 - \lambda \cdot 4 = 0$
(ii) $L_T = 400 \cdot E - 3 - \lambda \cdot 10 = 0$
(iii) $L_\lambda = 4 \cdot E + 10 \cdot T - 30000 = 0$

Equations (i) and (ii) can written as ratios to eliminate lambda, as in:

$(400 \cdot T - 4)/(400 \cdot E - 3) = 4/10$. This can be further reduced to show:

(iv) $T = .4 \cdot E + .007$. Equation (iv) is then substituted back into the budget constraint, equation (iii).

$4 \cdot E + 10 \cdot T - 30000 = 4 \cdot E + 10 \cdot (.4 \cdot E + .007) - 30000 = 0$. So, $8 \cdot E = 29,999.93$. Therefore, $E = 3749.99$ or about **3750**. That means that $T = 1500.0035$ or about **1500**.

E = 3750 and T = 1500

c. Solve for optimal lambda. Give an economic interpretation of lambda at PolyCard.

Answer: lambda = 149,999 is **marginal sales** from a relaxation of the budget. It appears that a slight increase in the budget would lead to a phenomenal increase in sales.

The large marginal sales number occurs because sales, as a function of promotional expenditures and time, increases in both variables. Typically, we would expect sales to rise at declining rates in both variables.

Net Sources

Discussion of Lagrangians on the Internet is less common than calculus. They appear as parts of classes in economics, engineering, or quantitative business courses.

1. One that may appeal to students who want to read about the economic and geometric interpretations of Lagrangians is:

   mat.gsia.cmu.edu/QUANT/notes/node25.html#SECTION0051

2. **ForeProfit:** Software libraries for complex problems are available, but they generally are not free. Users of the McGuigan/Moyer/Harris textbook have access to software, *ForeProfit*, which has a linear programming package, regression package, and tools for forecasting. For information on the textbook, authors, slide presentations, and ForeProfit, go to the web site for the textbook at:

   mcguigan.swcollege.com

Web Chapter B

Linear Programming Applications

Constrained Optimization problems frequently occur in economics. Examples include maximizing output from a given budget, or minimizing cost of a set of required outputs. Lagrangian multiplier problems required binding (equality) constraints, whereas a number of business problems have *inequality constraints*. This chapter also examines the problem of capital rationing.

A. <u>Profit Maximization Problem Using Linear Programming</u>

1. Managers are faced with constraints of production capacity, time, money, raw materials, budget, space, and other restrictions on choices. These constraints can be viewed as *inequality* constraints; that is, a manager wishes to maximize the profit from a mix of products sold, but the capacity to produce the goods is fixed.

2. A "linear" programming problem assumes a *linear objective function*, and a series of *linear inequality constraints*. Linearity implies:

   a. constant prices for outputs (as in a perfectly competitive market).

   b. constant returns to scale for production processes.

3. Typically, each *decision variable* also has a non-negativity constraint. For example, the time spent using a machine cannot be negative.

4. Linear programming problems can be solved using graphical techniques, SIMPLEX algorithms using matrices, or using software, such as ForeProfit software.

5. In the graphical technique, each inequality constraint is graphed as an equality constraint. The *Feasible Solution Space* is the area that satisfies all of the inequality constraints.

6. The *Optimal Feasible Solution* occurs along the boundary of the Feasible Solution Space, at the extreme points or corner point.

7. The corner point that maximizes the objective function is the Optimal Feasible Solution. There may be several optimal solutions. Examination of the slope of the

objective function and the slopes of the constraints is useful in determining which is the optimal corner point.

8. One or more of the constraints may be *slack*, which means it is not binding.

9. Each constraint has an implicit price, the *shadow price* of the constraint. If a constraint is slack, its shadow price is zero.

10. Each shadow price has much the same meaning as a Lagrangian multiplier.

B. The Dual Problem

1. Each linear programming problem (the primal problem) has an associated dual problem.

2. EXAMPLE: A maximization of profit objective function, subject to resource constraints, has an associated dual problem. The dual problem is a minimization of the total costs of the resources, subject to constraints that the value of the resources used in producing one unit of each output be at least as great as the profit received from the sale of that output.

3. THEOREM: The Duality Theorem: the maximum value of the primal (profit max problem) equals the minimum value of the dual (cost minimization) problem.

4. The resource constraints of the primal problem appear in the objective function of the dual problem.

Primal: Maximize $\pi = P_1 \cdot Q_1 + P_2 \cdot Q_2$ subject to:

$c \cdot Q_1 + d \cdot Q_2 \leq R1$ The budget constraint, for example.

$e \cdot Q_1 + f \cdot Q_2 \leq R2$ The machine scheduling time constraint.

where Q_1 and $Q_2 \geq 0$ Nonnegativity constraint.

Dual: Minimize $C = R1 \cdot W_1 + R2 \cdot W_2$ subject to:

$c \cdot Q_1 + e \cdot Q_2 \geq P_1$ Profit contribution of product 1.

$d \cdot Q_1 + f \cdot Q_2 \geq P_2$ Profit contribution of product 2.

where W_1 and $W_2 \geq 0$ Nonnegativity constraint of shadow prices.

5. The solutions to primal and dual problems may be solved graphically, so long as this involves two dimensions. With many products, the solution involves the SIMPLEX algorithm, or software available in ForeProfit or LINDO.

C. Cost Minimization Problem Using Linear Programming

1. Multi-plant firms want to produce with the lowest cost across their disparate facilities. Sometimes, the relative efficiencies of the different plants can be exploited to reduce costs.

2. A firm may have two mines that produces different qualities of ore. The firm has output requirements in each ore quality. Scheduling of hours per week in each mine has the objective of minimizing cost, but achieving the required outputs.

3. If one mine is more efficient in all categories of ore, and is less costly to operate, the optimal solution may involve shutting one mine down.

4. The dual of this problem involves the shadow prices of the ore constraints. It tells the implicit value of each quality of ore.

D. Capital Rationing Problem

1. Financial decisions sometimes may be viewed as a linear programming problem.

2. EXAMPLE: A financial officer may want to maximize the return on investments available, given a limited amount of money to invest. The usual problem in finance is to accept all projects with positive net present values, but sometimes the capital budgets are fixed or limited to create "capital rationing" among projects.

3. The solution involves determining what fraction of money allotted should be invested in each of the possible projects or investments. In some problems, projects cannot be broken into small parts. When this is the case, integer programming can be added to the problem.

True and False Questions

Agree or disagree with the following statements, and correct the part that is erroneous.

1. If the primal problem is a maximization problem, then the dual is also a maximization problem.

2. The solution of a linear programming problem usually occurs at a corner point.

3. If the shadow price of a constraint is positive, then the constraint is slack.

4. All primal problems are maximization problems.

5. The dual of a dual problem is the primal problem.

6. At the optimum, all the constraints must be slack.

Answers
1. Disagree. The dual will be a minimization problem, if the primal problem is a maximization problem.
2. True. The solution of a linear programming problem will be at the edge of a feasible region, at a corner point.
3. Disagree. If the shadow price of a constraint is positive, then the constraint is binding.
4. Disagree. The primal or the dual may be a maximization problem. If the primal is a minimization problem, its associated dual will be a maximization problem.
5. True.
6. Disagree. At the optimum point, at least one constraint must be binding.

Multiple Choice Questions

1. The **CC-Express Line** is a private passenger van line to a major Chicago airport. CC-Express has constraints on the number of vehicles, the number of bus drivers, and time it takes to drive from Chicago's North-side or its South-side. If CC-Express finds that its bus-driver constraint is not binding:
   a. the dual variable for bus drivers will be greater than zero.
   b. the optimal solution will involve zero bus drivers.
   c. there cannot be a feasible solution.
   d. there will be some bus drivers with nothing to do.

2. In the profit maximization problem discussed above, if **CC-Express Line** hired more van drivers:
   a. profit would rise.
   b. the slackness problem would disappear.
   c. the feasible solution would grow.
   d. the optimal feasible solution would not change.

3. If all the constraints are binding, then:
   a. all constraints have non-zero shadow prices.
   b. the solution will be in the midpoint of the feasible space.
   c. the value of primal will be greater than the value of the dual problem.
   d. all dual variables are zero.

4. If a primal problem has three variables and four constraints, then the dual problem has:
   a. seven shadow prices.
   b. five shadow prices.
   c. four shadow prices.
   d. three shadow prices.

5. Graphical solutions profit maximization linear programming problems:
   a. are difficult if there are more than two independent variables.
   b. involve finding corner points.
   c. can be solved using the slope of the objective function *versus* the slopes of the sides of the feasible space.
   d. all of the above are correct.

6. If a primal problem has three variables and four constraints, then the dual problem has:
   a. seven constraints.
   b. four constraints.
   c. three constraints.
   d. no more than two constraints.

7. If the primal problem has resource constraints, so that the inequalities are (≤), less than or equal to constraints, then the *dual constraints* are:
   a. equality constraints.
   b. are (≥), greater than or equal to constraints.
   c. are (≤), less than or equal to constraints.
   d. it depends entirely on the problem.

8. In a linear programming problem, if all of the constraints are slack, then:
   a. we probably have not found the optimal feasible solution.
   b. we have certainly found multiple optimal feasible solutions.
   c. the constraints are impossible, so there is no feasible space.
   d. all of the above.

9. Linear programming is difficult to apply for decision problems that involve:
   a. monopoly power, where the prices depend on the amount sold.
   b. constant returns to scale.
   c. perfectly competitive input and output markets where the prices are given.
   d. both (a) and (c).

10. A "capital rationing" problem involves the problem of:
   a. too little food for people, where "capital" is derived from the Latin for the word "head".
   b. too many positive net present value investments, but only a limited amount of investment funds are available to use to fund these investments.
   c. too few machines to produce output, and too many workers.
   d. all of the above are capital rationing problems.

Answers
1. d
2. d
3. a
4. c
5. d
6. c
7. b
8. a
9. a
10. b

Worked Problems

1. Graphical Approach: Operating profit, π, depends on the composition of sales of two products, Q_1 and Q_2. Because of limited budget, machine scheduling time, and energy, there are three production constraints. The linear programming problem is:

Maximize $\pi = 4 \cdot Q_1 + 3 \cdot Q_2$ subject to:

$Q_1 + 2 \cdot Q_2 \leq 100$ The budget constraint.

$2 \cdot Q_1 + Q_2 \leq 80$ The machine scheduling time constraint.

$3 \cdot Q_1 \quad \leq 90$ The energy constraint.

where Q_1 and $Q_2 \geq 0$

a. What is the optimal solution for Q_1 and Q_2.

Answer: Graph Q_1 along the vertical axis and Q_2 along the horizontal axis. The slope of the profit function is -3/4 because: $Q_1 = \pi/4 - (3/4) \cdot Q_2$.

Each of the three constraints can be written as equalities and put in the form of equations of lines.

Budget: $Q_1 = 100 - 2 \cdot Q_2$

Time: $Q_1 = 40 - .5 \cdot Q_2$

Energy: $Q_1 = 30 - .333 \cdot Q_2$

The slope of the profit function is between the slopes of the budget and time constraints. These must be binding. Equating the budget and time constraints reveals: $100 - 2 \cdot Q_2 = 40 - .5 \cdot Q_2$, which is, $60 = 1.5 \cdot Q_2$. Hence, $60/1.5 = Q_2 = 40$. Therefore, $Q_1 = 20$.

b. What is the optimal operating profit?

Answer: We substitute the optimal solutions for Q_1 and Q_2 into the objective function:

Profit $= 4 \cdot 20 + 3 \cdot 40 = 80 + 120 = \$200$.

c. Are any constraints slack?

Answer: Yes. The energy constraint is slack. Since $Q_1 = 20$, we find that there are 30 units of energy that are slack.

2. Given the linear programming problem (the PRIMAL) in problem #1, answer the following questions concerning the dual.

a. Write out the objective function to the DUAL with W_1, W_2, and W_3 as the shadow prices.

   Answer: Minimize $C = 100 \cdot W_1 + 80 \cdot W_2 + 90 \cdot W_3$

b. Write out the inequality constraints for the DUAL problem.

   Answer: $W_1 + 2 \cdot W_2 + 3 \cdot W_3 \quad \geq 4$

   $2 \cdot W_1 + W_2 \quad\quad\quad \geq 3$

   where W_1, W_2, and $W_3 \quad \geq 0$

c. Imagine that the shadow prices on the constraints were $W_1 = 0.6667$, $W_2 = 1.6667$, and $W_3 = 0.0000$, how many constraints are slack? What is the value of the dual objective function using these values for the dual variables?

   Answer: The energy constraint is slack because its shadow price is zero.

   $C = 100 \cdot .6667 + 80 \cdot 1.6667 + 90 \cdot 0 = 66.67 + 133.33 = 200$.

   The solution is identical to problem 1.

d. If increasing the amount of resources in the second constraint from 80 to 81 would cost you $1.50, would it be a good decision, given the shadow prices in part (c)?

> *Answer:* Yes. The "value" of an extra unit of resource is $1.67, whereas it costs you $1.50. Expanding the time resource has greater value than cost.

e. If increasing the third constraint to 91 costs you only $2, would it pay to do it? [Hint: look at the shadow prices.]

> *Answer:* Do not do it. The value of the third (energy) resource is zero. We already have slack energy.

3. Use Economist's Toolkit, Lindo, ForeProfit or other LP software (See the Net Sources at the end for where to find these). Operating profit, π, depends on the composition of sales of three products, Q_1, Q_2, and Q_3. Because of limited budget, machine scheduling time, and energy, there are three production constraints. The linear programming problem is:

Maximize $\pi = 4 \cdot Q_1 + 3 \cdot Q_2 + 2 \cdot Q_3$ subject to:

$Q_1 + 2 \cdot Q_2 + Q_3 \leq 100$	The budget constraint.
$2 \cdot Q_1 + Q_2 \leq 80$	The machine scheduling time constraint.
$3 \cdot Q_1 + Q_3 \leq 90$	The energy constraint.
where Q_1, Q_2, and $Q_3 \geq 0$	The non-negativity constraints.

You have used ForeProfit software to calculate the following results:

LP routine - Primal solution results

Variable	Solution value	Contribution
Q1	25.0	100.00
Q2	30.0	90.00
Q3	15.0	30.00
Value of the objective function:	Max PROFIT = 220.00	

a. What is the optimal solution for Q1, Q2, and Q3.

> *Answer:* Using the computer output, the solution is given: $Q_1 = 25$, $Q_2 = 30$, and $Q_3 = 15$.

b. What is the optimal operating profit?

> *Answer:* The optimal operating profit is found by substituting the optimal values of output into the objective function.
>
> $\pi = 4 \cdot 25 + 3 \cdot 30 + 2 \cdot 30 = 100 + 90 + 30 = \$220$. We see that the LP results give the "contribution" to profit from each of the three goods.

c. Are any constraints slack?

> *Answer:* Substitute the optimal solution into each of the three constraints.
> $25 + 2 \cdot 30 + 15 \quad = 100$ The budget constraint is an equality.
> $2 \cdot 25 + 30 \qquad\quad = 80$ The machine scheduling time constraint is an equality.
> $3 \cdot 25 \quad + 15 \qquad = 90$ The energy constraint is an equality.
> No constraint is slack.

4. Given the linear programming problem (the PRIMAL) in problem #3, answer the following questions concerning the dual. Use this computer output.

LP routine - Dual solution results		
Constraint	Shadow price	Contribution
Constraint 1	1.3333	133.3333
Constraint 2	0.3333	26.6667
Constraint 3	0.6667	60.0000
Value of the objective function:	PROFIT = 220.00	

a. Write out the objective function to the DUAL with W_1, W_2, and W_3 as the shadow prices.

> *Answer:* Minimize $C = 100 \cdot W_1 + 80 \cdot W_2 + 90 \cdot W_3$. This is identical to the objective function for the dual to problem #1.

b. Write out the inequalities for the DUAL problem.

> *Answer:*
>
> $W_1 + 2 \cdot W_2 + 3 \cdot W_3 \geq 4$
>
> $W_1 + W_2 \geq 3$
>
> $W_1 + W_3 \geq 2$
>
> where W_1, W_2, and $W_3 \geq 0$

c. Use the computer output to determine which of the primal constraints were slack.

Answer: All of the shadow prices are positive; therefore none of the constraints were slack.

Net Sources

1. **Economists Toolkit**   *www.swcollege.com/bef/mcguigan/mcguigan.html*

The *Economist's ToolKit*, developed by Robert Ritchey of Texas Tech University, performs regression analysis, forecasting, linear programming, and capital budgeting analyses. This software is useful to help demonstrate key concepts in the course. ISBN: 0-324-00761-2. To download a free version go to "Learning Resources" at the website for the McGuigan, Moyer, and Harris textbook given above.

2. **ForeProfit**   *www.swcollege.com/bef/mcguigan/mcguigan.html*

Joseph Kreitzer of the University of St. Thomas developed the ForeProfit software, revised for this edition of McGuigan, Moyer, and Harris' Managerial Economic. This DOS-based, free standing, user-friendly software provides on-screen help and user diagnostics. It can be used to solve problems in regression analysis, forecasting, linear programming, capital expenditure, and cost-benefit analysis. ISBN:0-324-00757-4 . An educational version 1.1 can be downloaded for free.

3. **PROJECT:** Michael A. Trick provides a bond investment linear programming problem, and solves it using LINDO, a linear programming package. The example is at: *mat.gsia.cmu.edu/mstc/decomp/node1.html*. This problem involves five bonds of various quality ratings, different types of issuers (government, agency, municipal), different maturities (in years), and yields. The solution, given in the Internet site, uses bonds A, C, and E. Use the same data in the problem, but change the maturity on the Agency bond B from 15 years to 5 years. Does your solution change? Why or why not? Those who wish to use LINDO rather than Economists Toolkit or ForeProfit can download a free trail version of LINDO that can handle 50 constraints and up to 100 variables at: *www.lindo.com.*

Appendix A

Time Value of Money

This appendix covers basic analysis of the value of cash flows over time. This includes present value, future value, annuities, and perpetuities.

A. Present Value and Future Value

1. *Present Value* is the amount you could sell a future cash flow today.

$$PV = FV_n / (1 + r)^n$$

Techniques:

   a. *Financial Calculator*. Enter the FV, the interest rate, and the number of periods. Then compute the PV.

   b. *Tables*. Look up the **present value interest factor** in Table 4. Then multiply FV·**PVIF**, which gives the PV. NOTE: the $PVIF(r, n) = 1/(1 + r)^n$

   EXAMPLE: if we receive $100 in 9 years, what is its PV, if the discount rate is 8%? The answer is: $PV = \$100 \cdot PVIF(8\%, 9) = \$100 \cdot (.50025) = \$50.025$.

   c. *Logarithms* can be used to solve for PV. By taking the logarithm of both sides of $PV = FV_n / (1 + r)^n$, we can find the PV.

   EXAMPLE: In the previous example, $PV = 100/(1.08)^9$. So, $Ln\ PV = Ln(100) - 9 \cdot Ln(1.08) = 4.60517 - 9 \cdot (.076961) = 3.9125$. To anti-log, we take the exponential. Therefore $PV = e^{Ln\ PV} = e^{3.9125} = \$50.02489$. Notice that the result from the table is rounded.

2. *Future Value* is how much an investment will be worth at time n in the future, compounding at rate r.

$$FV_n = PV \cdot (1 + r)^n$$

B. Solving the Interest or Growth Rate

1. There are four pieces of information in both the FV and PV formulas. Given any three of them, we can solve for the missing information.

2. If we know FV, PV, and n, we can find r. For example, we will sell our U.S. Savings Bond for $50 in 7 years. The bond cost us $37.50. What is the implied interest rate using PVIF(r, 7)?

   Answer: We know that $37.50 = $50 \cdot \text{PVIF}(r, 7)$. Therefore, $37.50/50 = \text{PVIF}$, or $.75 = \text{PVIF}(r, 7)$. Examining Table 4 we find that $\text{PVIF}(4\%, 7) = .75992$, and that $\text{PVIF}(5\%, 7) = .71063$. The implied interest rate is between 4% and 5%. The solution requires interpolating between these numbers. Using a calculator, the exact solution is 4.195%.

3. Similarly, if we know FV, PV, and r, we can solve for n.

C. Present Value of a Series of Equal Payments (Annuity)

1. An *annuity* is a series of payments of a fixed amount (C).

2. The Present Value of an Annuity is:

   $$\text{PVAN} = C/(1 + r) + C/(1 + r)^2 + ... + C/(1 + r)^n$$

   $$\text{PVAN} = (C/r)[\, 1 - 1/(1 + r)^n \,]$$

3. Table 5 gives Present Value of an Annuity Interest Factors, **PVIFA**. The PVIFA $= (1/r)[\, 1 - 1/(1 + r)^n \,]$. Using Table 5 we solve:

   $$\text{PVAN}_0 = C \cdot \text{PVIFA}(r, n).$$

4. For a given annuity, it is possible to solve for the interest rate. For example, a stream of automobile payments of $250 per month for 24 to borrow $2,630 for a used car. What is the interest rate?

   Answer: $2,630 = 250 \cdot \text{PVIFA}(r, 24)$. This reduces to: $10.52 = \text{PVIFA}(r, 24)$. Looking up Table 5 shows that $10.5288 = \text{PVIFA}(\mathbf{8\%}, 24)$. The answer is 8%. This may also be calculated directly with a financial calculator.

D. Present Value of a Series of Unequal Payments

1. If the payments or cash flows vary, the present value is:

$$PV_0 = \sum_{t=1}^{n} PMT_t/(1+r)^t = \sum_{t=1}^{n} PMT_t \cdot PVIF_{r,t}$$

The $PVIF_{r,t}$ are the present value interest factors from Table 4.

E. <u>Concluding Formulas For Added Knowledge</u>

1. A *Perpetuity* is an infinte annuity. The present value of an infinite annuity, $PVAN_0 = C \cdot PVIFA(r, \infty)$ simplifies to:

   $PVAN = C/r$

2. A growing perpetuity (*e.g.* utility stock dividend growing at rate g)

   $PVAN = C/(r - g)$

3. Compounding (semiannually, quarterly, monthly, daily, etc., **m** periods per year)

   $PV_0 = FV_t/(1 + r/m)^{mt}$

4. For infinitely compounded: $FV_t = PV \cdot e^{rt}$ or $PV = FV_t \cdot e^{-rt}$

True and False Questions

Agree or disagree with the following statements, and correct the part that is erroneous.

1. The longer is the number of periods, n, the larger is the present value interest factor, PVIF.

2. The longer is the number of periods, n, the larger is the present value of an annuity interest factor, PVIFA.

3. If we know the present value, the interest rate, and the number of periods, then we can calculate the future value.

4. Given the size of the annuity payments, the number of payments, and the present value of the annuity, we can determine the interest rate.

5. It is impossible to calculate the present value of a *negative* cash flow.

Answers
1. Disagree. The $PVIF = 1/(1+r)^n$, as n rises, PVIF falls.

2. True. As the number of annuity payments increases, PVIFA rises.
3. True.
4. True.
5. Disagree. If the cash flow is negative, the present value will also be negative. For example, if I owe $100 in one year, and the current interest rate on personal borrowing is 7%, then the present value of that money owed is: PV = -100/(1.07) = $93.46. My creditor may well prefer to receive $93.46 now, rather than waiting for the $100.

Multiple Choice Questions

1. The future value of $200 in two years at an interest rate 15% is:
   a. $200.00
   b. $224.75
   c. $230.50
   d. $264.50

2. If the interest rate is 12%, what is the present value of $1000 if you receive the money in two years from now?
   a. $1000.00
   b. $797.19
   c. $1254.44
   d. $756.14
   e. $892.86

3. If the interest rate rises, the present value of a future return will:
   a. rise.
   b. remain unchanged.
   c. fall.
   d. There is insufficient information provided to answer this question.

4. A firm is considering the purchase of a particular piece of machinery. The purchase price of the machine is $26,000. The machine is expected to produce a stream of income of $10,000 per year for three years. At the end of the third year, the machine will have a scrap value of $5,000. The relevant rate of interest is 10%. What is the net present value of this machine?
   a. $28,625
   b. $2,625
   c. $9,000
   d. -$337

5. As the winner of Super Bingo, you have a choice of receiving one of the following prizes. From the point of view of present value, which should you choose? Assume that the relevant rate of interest for discounting is 8%.
   a. An immediate lump sum of $42,000.
   b. A payment in two years of $50,000.
   c. An annuity for seven years of $8,600 per year.
   d. A payment of $24,000 immediately, a payment of $12,000 in one year, and a final installment of $10,000 in two years.

Answers
1. d
2. b
3. c
4. b (NPV = -26,000 + 10,000/1.1 + 10,000/(1.1)^2 + 15,000/(1.1)^3 = 2,625. Also the IRR is 15.259%)
5. c (Using tables the present values are: a is $42,000; b is $42,867; c is $44,775.04, and d is $43,684.56. If you use a financial calculator the answers are more exact.)

Worked Problems

1. The earnings of MacroTronics have been growing tremendously. Five years ago, they earned $.53, but this year they earned $1.32. What is MacroTronic's annual compounded growth rate?

   Answer: Earnings can be thought of as a present value problem, which equate the present (five years ago) earnings to the future (now). $.53 = $1.32·PVIF($r$, 5). Dividing both sides by $1.32, we find: .401515 = PVIF(r, 5). Using Table 4, we find PVIF(**20%**, 5) = .40188. Earnings have been growing at a 20% annually compounded rate.

2. Find the future value of $100, at a simple annual rate of 40%, compounded semi-annually, in one year.

   Answer: The interest rate for each 6-month period is 20%. There are two periods. Therefore, FV = $100·(1.20)^2 = $144. The extra $4 dollars represent interest on the $20 earned in the first 6-month period, since 20% of $20 is $4.

3. You decide to borrow for a car. You will need $5,000. Unfortunately, because of several loan defaults in your credit history, the best rate you can find is 1% per month for 25 months. What will be your payment per month?

Answer: This is an annuity problem, since a constant stream of car payments are an annuity. You realize that $5,000 = C·PVIFA(1%, 25) = C·(22.0233). Consequently, the annuity payment C = $5,000/22.0233 = **$227.03**.

4. Suppose that you believe that you can pay $9,000 per year ($750 per month) for 25 years to purchase a house. If the mortgage interest rate is 8%, what is the most expensive house you can afford?

Answer: Mortgage problems are best calculated using monthly payments. This generally necessitates a financial calculator. However, using annual data and Table 5, we can find PVAN = $9,000·PVIFA(8%, 25) = $9,000·(10.6748) = **$96,073.20**. The mortgage company will probably require a down payment.

Appendix B

Tables

This appendix briefly discusses the 6 tables that appear in the Appendix of the textbook. It provides simple examples of how to use each table.

Table 1 — Value of the Standard Normal Distribution Function

1. Table 1 gives the probability of a value that is less than Z standard deviations from the mean.

2. To use the Table 1, a random variable must be "standardized". Standardization entails subtracting the mean from the variable, and then dividing that remainder by the standard error.

3. The formula is: $Z = (X - \mu)/\sigma$, where X is the random variable, μ is the mean, and σ is the standard error. Z is a normal variable. A standardized variable is normally distributed with a mean of zero and a standard deviation of one.

4. EXAMPLE: The mean height of adult women is 63.5 inches, with a standard deviation of 6.5 inches. What is the probability of randomly selecting a woman who is five feet, ten inches tall? (That is, 70 inches).

   Answer: To find out the number of standard deviations 70 is away from the mean, we find the standardized value: $Z = (X - \mu)/\sigma = (70 - 63.5)/6.5 = 6.5/6.5 = 1$. Accordingly, we look down the first column of Z values to find Z = 1.00, which is .8413. This says that 84.13% of all adult women are less than or equal to 70 inches. This means that (1 - .8413) = .1587, or 15.87% of all adult women are taller than 70 inches. Note that the numbers across the top of the table are the second decimal point of the Z values.

Table 2 — Table of "Student's" Distribution: Value of t

1. The standard normal distribution in Table 1 assumed that σ was known. In Table 2, σ is unknown so it must come from a sample.

2. Along the top of the table are the probabilities for two-tailed tests. For example, a probability of .05 allows for .025 in the one tail of the distribution and .025 in the other, which is a .05 significance level.

3. The left-hand vertical column gives the **degrees of freedom**. Degrees of freedom vary depending on the size of the sample and the nature of the issue. For hypothesis testing of regression coefficients, the degrees of freedom, d.f. = number of observations minus the number of independent variables minus one.

4. Table 2 provides *critical* t-statistics. For example, if there are 13 degrees of freedom, then the critical t-statistic at the .05 significance level is 2.16.

5. The *estimated* t-statistic depends on the nature of the hypothesis to be tested. In regression analysis, we are typically testing if a regression coefficient, ß, is different from zero. In that case the estimated t-statistic is: $\mathbf{t = (ß - 0)/\sigma_ß}$.

6. The rule in hypothesis testing is: if the absolute value of the *estimated* t-statistic is greater than the *critical* t-statistic, then we **reject** the null hypothesis.

7. EXAMPLE: A regression of $Q = a + b \cdot P + c \cdot I$ is run using 16 monthly observations. The coefficient on P is found to be b= -.89, with a standard deviation of .44. Using a .05 significance level, test the null hypothesis H_0: b = 0, against the alternative hypothesis H_a: b≠ 0.

Answer: The estimated t = -.89/.44 = -2.03. There are 13 degrees of freedom, so the critical t-statistic is 2.16. We cannot reject the null hypothesis because the absolute value of the estimated t-statistic (2.03) is NOT greater than the critical t-statistic (2.16). In common parlance, we say that the coefficient is not statistically significant.

Table 3 — <u>The F Distribution: Upper 5% Points and Upper 1% Points</u>

1. The F distribution is useful in *analysis of variance* and *regression analysis*. In this textbook, the F distribution is used to test the hypothesis that all of the regression coefficients equal zero.

2. In the regression equation: $Y = ß_0 + ß_1 \cdot X_1 + ß_2 \cdot X_2 + \varepsilon$, we form the null hypothesis H_0: $ß_1 = ß_2 = 0$. The alternative is, H_a: not all of the betas equal zero.

3. The *estimated* F is reported in regression outputs. If the estimated F is greater than the *critical* F given in Table 3, then we reject the null hypothesis.

4. The critical F in Table 3 has the number of the independent variables along the horizontal line as δ_1. The number of *degrees of freedom* is given along the vertical as δ_2. The significance level is 5% in the first of the two Table 5s, and 1% in the second.

5. EXAMPLE: A regression with two independent variables and a constant is estimated. The estimated F statistic is given as 6.33. The sample size is 20. Test the hypothesis that both of the coefficients equal zero.

   Answer: The number of degrees of freedom is 20 - 3 = 17. With two independent variables, we look down the column headed by a 2, and look across the row headed by 17. The critical F is 3.59 at the 5% significance level. We can reject the null hypothesis at that level. In addition, the critical F in the 1% significance level Table is 6.11. Again, the estimated F value is greater than the critical F value, so we reject the view that both of the coefficients equal zero. In common usage, the coefficients are significant.

Table 4 — <u>Present Value of $1 (PVIF)</u>

1. The present value interest factor, $PVIF = 1/(1 + r)^n$, for interest rate r and for **n** periods into the future. Table 4 lists different interest rates and different number of periods into the future.

2. The present value is readily calculated using the PVIF table. The simple formula is given as $PV = FV \cdot PVIF(r, n)$, where FV is a future value we receive in time **n**.

3. EXAMPLE: What is the value today of a zero coupon bond which will pay $10,000 in 6 years, if the relevant interest rate used for discounting similar assets is 7%?

   Answer: The present value of the zero coupon bond is $PV = FV \cdot PVIF(7\%, 6)$ = $10,000 \cdot (.66634) = $6,663.40. A zero coupon bond pays out its par value at maturity and does not pay any cash interest payments in the interim.

Table 5 — <u>Present Value of an Annuity of $1 (PVIFA)</u>

1. The present value of an annuity interest factor, PVIFA, is used to calculate the value today of a stream of equal cash flows, $C. The $PVIFA = (1/r)[1 - 1/(1+r)^n]$, and lists the outcome for different interest rates, r, and periods, **n**.

2. The present value of a annuity (PVAN) is found using a simple formula: $PVAN = C \cdot PVIFA(r, n)$. As **n** rises, the value of the annuity rises. As r rises, the present value of the annuity declines.

3. EXAMPLE: Diane has borrowed money for her first automobile from her parents. She has four annual payments left of $2,000 each. Because of her position in the mergers & acquisitions department of brokerage business, she was rewarded with a $6,500 bonus. If the relevant interest rate is 5%, does she have enough money in this bonus to pay off her indebtedness to her parents fairly?

> *Answer:* The four payments are an annuity. Diane can find the present value of this payment at a 5% rate. This amount of money would fairly pay off the debt, as her parents would likely prefer the money sooner rather than later. The PVAN = C·PVIFA(r, n) = $2,000·PVIF(5%, 4) = $2,000·3.5459 = $7,091.80. Diane does not quite have enough with this bonus check to cancel her entire indebtedness.

Table 6 — <u>Durbin-Watson Statistics, 2.5% One-Tail, and 5% Two-Tail Significance</u>

1. The Durbin-Watson Statistics test for first order autocorrelation in the error terms. The number of independent variables is designated by **m** along the top. The number of observations is given along the vertical column on the left. The estimated Durbin-Watson statistic is designated as d.

2. The Durbin-Watson statistics are designed to test the null hypothesis that there is NO autocorrelation. Three possible outcomes occur: (1) we can reject the null; (2) we can accept the null, and (3) the information is inconclusive. Table 6 gives us both a lower and an upper critical d-statistic to determine which of these three is appropriate.

3. Two-Tailed Tests:

   a. We can reject the null if $d < d_L$ or $d > (4 - d_L)$.

   b. We can accept the null if $d_U < d < (4 - d_U)$.

   c. It is inconclusive if $d_L \leq d \leq d_U$ or $(4 - d_U) \leq d \leq (4 - d_L)$.

4. One-Tailed Tests:

   a. We can reject no *positive* autocorrelation if $d < d_L$.

   b. We can accept no *positive* autocorrelation if $d > d_U$.

   c. We can reject no *negative* autocorrelation if $d > (4 - d_L)$.

d. We can accept no *negative* autocorrelation if $d < (4 - d_U)$.

5. EXAMPLE: The estimated Durbin-Watson statistic is 2.43. There were two independent variables and the sample size was 22 observations in the regression. Do we have significant autocorrelation

> *Answer:* The critical lower and upper d-values are $d_L = 1.04$ and $d_U = 1.42$. Under the null hypothesis that there is no autocorrelation, we see if we can reject it in a two-tailed test. Looking at rule 3a above, and knowing that $d = 2.43$, we see that d is **not** lower than 1.04, nor is d larger than 2.58, or $(4 - 1.42)$. Therefore we cannot reject the null hypothesis. Looking next at rule 3b, we find that $1.42 < 2.43 < (4 - 1.42) = 2.56$. We must ACCEPT the null, and claim that the autocorrelation is insignificant at the 5% level for a two-tailed test. Similarly, for a one-tailed test, we can ACCEPT the null hypothesis that there is no *negative* autocorrelation.

Table 7 — Critical Values for the Dickey-Fuller Test

1. Economic data are often nonstationary. This affects the types and accuracy of statistical tests. The Dickey-Fuller (DF) Test and the augmented Dickey-Fuller (ADF) Test are a quick ways to examine whether or not a time series is stationary. Some statistical packages, such as SHAZAM and Micro TSP will do these tests, but we can run simple regressions to find whether or not the series is stationary.

2. If a times series (Y) with 25 observations is estimated as: $Y_t = \rho \cdot Y_{t-1}$, then if $\rho = 1$, the series is nonstationary. In that case, the series has a *unit root*. If the t-value (known as tau, or τ) is less than the critical τ give in Table 7, then we accept that the series is nonstationary. The critical τ is 2.16 [given as AR(1) model on the table] for 25 observations and declines slightly with sample size.

3. If we included a constant, the regression with 25 observations is: $Y_t = \beta_1 + \rho \cdot Y_{t-1}$, then if $\rho = 1$, again the series is nonstationary. The critical τ is given as the row AR(1) with constant. For example if $\tau = 1.2$ and the critical τ is .072, we would reject the hypothesis that $\rho = 1$. The series does not have a unit root and is stationary.

4. If we included a constant and a time trend, we have the augmented Dickey-Fuller test. The regression is $Y_t = \beta_1 + \beta_2 \cdot t + \rho \cdot Y_{t-1}$, then if $\rho = 1$, the series is nonstationary. The critical τ is given on the last row of Table 7.

5. Generally, if a time series has a unit root and is therefore nonstationary, it is easy to transform the data into a stationary series by taking the *first differences*: $\Delta Y_t = Y_t - Y_{t-1}$.